Confessions of Faith in the Anabaptist Tradition 1527–1660

Classics of the Radical Reformation

Classics of the Radical Reformation is an English-language series of Anabaptist and Free Church documents translated and annotated under the direction of the Institute of Mennonite Studies, which is the research agency of the Anabaptist Mennonite Biblical Seminaries, and published by Plough Publishing House.

1. *The Legacy of Michael Sattler.* Trans., ed. John Howard Yoder.

2. *The Writings of Pilgram Marpeck.* Trans., ed. William Klassen and Walter Klaassen.

3. *Anabaptism in Outline: Selected Primary Sources.* Trans., ed. Walter Klaassen.

4. *The Sources of Swiss Anabaptism: The Grebel Letters and Related Documents.* Ed. Leland Harder.

5. *Balthasar Hubmaier: Theologian of Anabaptism.* Ed. H. Wayne Pipkin and John Howard Yoder.

6. *The Writings of Dirk Philips.* Ed. Cornelius J. Dyck, William E. Keeney, and Alvin J. Beachy.

7. *The Anabaptist Writings of David Joris: 1535–1543.* Ed. Gary K. Waite.

8. *The Essential Carlstadt: Fifteen Tracts by Andreas Bodenstein.* Trans., ed. E. J. Furcha.

9. *Peter Riedemann's Hutterite Confession of Faith.* Ed. John J. Friesen.

10. Sources of South German/Austrian Anabaptism. Ed. C. Arnold Snyder, trans. Walter Klaassen, Frank Friesen, and Werner O. Packull.

11. *Confessions of Faith in the Anabaptist Tradition: 1527–1660.* Ed. Karl Koop.

12. *Jörg Maler's Kunstbuch: Writings of the Pilgram Marpeck Circle.* Ed. John D. Rempel.

13. *Later Writings of the Swiss Anabaptists: 1529–1592.* Ed. C. Arnold Snyder.

Confessions of Faith in the Anabaptist Tradition 1527–1660

Translated by
Cornelius J. Dyck, James Jakob Fehr,
Irvin B. Horst, Walter Klaassen, Karl Koop, Werner
O. Packull, John D. Rempel, Vic Thiessen, Gary
K. Waite, and John Howard Yoder

Edited with an Introduction by
Karl Koop

PLOUGH PUBLISHING HOUSE

Published by Plough Publishing House
Walden, New York
Robertsbridge, England
Elsmore, Australia
www.plough.com

Plough produces books, a quarterly magazine, and Plough.com to encourage people and help them put their faith into action. We believe Jesus can transform the world and that his teachings and example apply to all aspects of life. At the same time, we seek common ground with all people regardless of their creed.

Plough is the publishing house of the Bruderhof, an international community of families and singles seeking to follow Jesus together. Members of the Bruderhof are committed to a way of radical discipleship in the spirit of the Sermon on the Mount. Inspired by the first church in Jerusalem (Acts 2 and 4), they renounce private property and share everything in common in a life of nonviolence, justice, and service to neighbors near and far. To learn more about the Bruderhof's faith, history, and daily life, see Bruderhof.com. (Views expressed by Plough authors are their own and do not necessarily reflect the position of the Bruderhof.)

ISBN: 978-0-874-86277-5

Library of Congress Cataloging-in-Publication Data

Names: Koop, Karl, 1959- editor.
Title: Confessions of faith in the Anabaptist tradition, 1527 - 1660 / translated by Karl Koop, Cornelius J. Dyck, James Jacob Fehr, Ivrin B. Horst, Walter Klaassen, Karl Koop, Werner O. Packull, John D. Rempel, Vic Thiessen, Gary K. Waite, John Howard Yoder ; edited with an introduction by Karl Koop.
Description: Walden, New York : Plough Publishing House, 2019. | Series: Classics of the radical Reformation ; 11 | Includes bibliographical references and index. | Summary: "The volume brings together early statements of belief from across the Radical Reformation"-- Provided by publisher.
Identifiers: LCCN 2019044929 (print) | LCCN 2019044930 (ebook) | ISBN 9780874862775 (paperback) | ISBN 9780874862782 (ebook)
Subjects: LCSH: Anabaptists--Creeds--Early works to 1800. | Anabaptists--Doctrines--Early works to 1800.
Classification: LCC BX4931.3 .C66 2019 (print) | LCC BX4931.3 (ebook) | DDC 238/.43--dc23
LC record available at https://lccn.loc.gov/2019044929
LC ebook record available at https://lccn.loc.gov/2019044930

"For now we see in a mirror, dimly,
but then we will see face to face.
Now I know only in part;
then I will know fully,
even as I have been fully known."
(1 Cor. 13:12, NRSV)

Dedicated with affection to students
at AMBS and CMU,
who have taught me much
about my Christian convictions
and commitments.

—Karl Koop

Table of Contents

Classics of the Radical Reformation

General Editor's Preface

We are now solidly into the third phase of the modern publication of sixteenth century Anabaptist source documents. Since the 1920s scholars working with German language texts, both treatises and court records, have issued meticulously annotated editions of seminal texts from the Radical Reformation. Early in the twentieth century and again more recently the similarly impressive publication of Dutch language sources has gained momentum.

Classics of the Radical Reformation (CRR) was inaugurated to make major selections from this literature available in translation with interpretive introductions for a broad English language readership.

Karl Koop's *Confessions of Faith in the Anabaptist Tradition* is the eleventh volume in the CRR series. It breaks new ground both in its subject matter and its span of time. Perplexingly little attention has been paid by twentieth century academics or church leaders to the Mennonite confessional tradition. Koop's masterful study documents this communal form of theologizing at an opportune time, when interest is rising in the development of Anabaptist thought beyond its first, formative generations. The publication of *Confessions of Faith in the Anabaptist Tradition* bodes well for the future of CRR.

It is an honor for me to write this general editor's preface as a successor to Cornelius J. Dyck, long time director of the Institute of Mennonite Studies, and formative editor of the *Classics of the Radical Reformation*. His visionary and self-effacing scholarship was crucial to the publication of most of the previous volumes.

Arnold Snyder of Pandora Press, the publisher of the last two CRR volumes, has joined IMS in carrying forward this series in Dyck's spirit. For this publishing partnership the staff of the Institute are deeply grateful.

John D. Rempel, Editor, CRR
Institute of Mennonite Studies
Elkhart, Indiana

Editor's Acknowledgements

This volume is a collaborative effort involving several persons and institutions. I want to thank, first of all, the translators who worked diligently in producing excellent texts in translation. They are: Vic Thiessen, Werner O. Packull, Cornelius J. Dyck, James Jakob Fehr, Gary K. Waite, Walter Klaassen, Irvin B. Horst and John Rempel. Translation work by the late John Howard Yoder is also included in this volume. The translations were reviewed and revised as needed, but the final outcome in this volume is essentially the work of the translators.

Special thanks goes to Adriaan Plak, Curator of Church History Collections at the University of Amsterdam, and to Joe Springer, Curator at the Mennonite Historical Library at Goshen College, for helping to locate early print editions of the 1660 Prussian confession of faith. Victor Kliewer was also very helpful in transcribing an early manuscript of this same confessional statement.

This volume was accepted for publication in the *Classics of the Radical Reformation* series. I wish to express my appreciation to the Institute of Mennonite Studies at Associated Mennonite Biblical Seminary for its continuing interest and support of making radical reformation texts available in the English language. I am grateful for the encouragement that I have received from John Rempel, editor of the series. AMBS was accommodating in granting me a course release that allowed me to carry on with my own translation work, and also enabled me to give more attention to the managing of this project. Canadian Mennonite University was generous in providing a faculty research grant that made it possible to rework some of the formatting of the translated texts. Finally, I wish to thank Arnold Snyder of Pandora Press, who was willing to publish this achievement, and who provided helpful editorial assistance throughout.

I wish to acknowledge the following publishers for allowing me to reprint significant selections from copyrighted material:

The "Brotherly Union" and the "Congregational Order" reprinted by permission, Herald Press, Scottdale, PA, from *The Legacy of Michael Sattler* by John Howard Yoder. All rights reserved.

The "Dordrecht Confession of Faith" is used by permission, Lancaster Mennonite Historical Society, 2215 Millstream Road, Lancaster PA, from *Mennonite Confession of Faith* by Irvin B. Horst. All rights reserved.

"The First Waterlandian Confession of Faith" translated by Cornelius J. Dyck, *Mennonite Quarterly Review* (January 1962), 8-13, used by permission.

"A Short Confession of Faith by Hans de Ries," translated by Cornelius J. Dyck, *Mennonite Quarterly Review* (January 1964), 11-19, used by permission.

"The Nicene Creed" and "The Apostles' Creed" are reprinted by permission of the Office of the General Assembly, Presbyterian Church (U.S.A.) from *Book of Confessions* (Louisville KY, 1996).

Introduction[1]

Confessions of faith have been an integral dimension of Anabaptist expression. Anabaptists affirmed ancient creedal formulas, especially the Apostles' Creed, and produced their own confessional statements summarizing the essentials of the faith. The first adult baptisms took place in January 1525 in Zürich, and already by 1527 Swiss Anabaptists adopted a seven-article statement of faith entitled the "Brotherly Union," sometimes referred to as the "Schleitheim Confession" that included articles on baptism, church discipline, the Lord's Supper, separation from the world, church leadership, the use of force, and oath swearing.[2] Almost two decades later another group of Anabaptists in the Lower Rhine region produced a summary statement referred to as the "Kempen Confession." Created in 1545, this document included articles on the incarnation, baptism, the Lord's Supper, church leadership, the secular authorities, and the use of force.[3]

Between 1577 and 1632, Mennonite communities in the Netherlands produced an unusually high number of confessional statements, and several of them were brought together in two separate collections published in 1665 and 1666.[4] In subsequent years single confessional statements or collections were reprinted "so that altogether over 100 printings were in circulation by the end of the eighteenth century."[5] These documents were produced during an era following the Reformation that historians have identified as "the confessional age," an era of identity formation when most churches in Europe were seeking to make explicit the central tenets of the faith. Anabaptist groups, especially in northern Europe, were drawn into the spirit of this "confessional age" and many communities in the region formulated doctrinal statements to reinforce internal doctrinal cohesion, to facilitate discussions between groups seeking to unite, and to foster ecumenical

1

witness. For the Dutch Mennonites, the confessional age came to an end after the 1660s due to the influences of the early enlightenment, the rise of early pietism, and in reaction to a strict confessionalism that threatened the unity of the church. Yet, Anabaptist communities especially in the regions of Prussia, Poland and southern Russia, continued to produce an abundance of confessional statements.[6] It is possible that adherents of Anabaptism produced more confessions of faith than any other Protestant stream.[7]

This volume contains a collection of representative confessions of faith in translation that Anabaptist and Mennonite communities produced from 1527 to 1660, representing an early phase in Anabaptist-Mennonite doctrinal development. While not exhaustive, the present compilation includes some of the most significant confessional statements of Swiss/South German and North German/Dutch Anabaptism. Many of these confessions have shaped and molded the Anabaptist theological tradition far beyond the sixteenth and seventeenth centuries.

Also incorporated at the back of this volume are the Apostles' and the Nicene creeds. Anabaptists often affirmed these statements, especially the Apostles' Creed, in conversation with others when they were asked to explain the content of their faith. They are included as a point of reference for readers wishing to draw comparisons between the Anabaptist confessions and this classical creedal tradition.

Confessions of Faith and Anabaptist Scholarship

It has sometimes been assumed that Anabaptists were non-creedal and non-confessional, that they emphasized ethics rather than doctrine, that their theology was implicit rather than explicit. Given these assumptions, it is not surprising that scholars have often failed to recognize the significance of the confessional tradition. Beyond the introductory encyclopaedic summary of Christian Neff in the *Mennonitisches Lexikon*,[8] the only study on confessions to materialize in the first half of the twentieth century was Emil Händiges' short monograph, *Die Lehre der Mennoniten in Geschichte und Gegenwart*, in which Mennonite doctrines were examined on the basis of several

Anabaptist and Mennonite confessions.[9] In the decades that followed, translations and editions of individual confessions of faith were forthcoming, and brief theological commentaries on some of these statements emerged, but generally speaking scholarly energies in Europe and in North America were focussed elsewhere, or reflected a level of ambivalence toward the study of confessions. For instance, the Dutch historian, Nanne van der Zijpp, upon acceptance of the position of lecturer at the Mennonite seminary in Amsterdam in 1954, found little positive to say about Mennonite confessional statements. While recognizing that Mennonites went through a confessional period, van der Zijpp—along with other Mennonite historians like Wilhelmus J. Kühler and Hendrick W. Meihuizen, who believed that the true Anabaptist-Mennonite legacy was one that emphasized the inner, spiritual, and individual Christian life—claimed that Mennonite confessional statements were intended merely to bring about unity and were applicable only for a particular era.[10] As to contents, the confessions did not present a complete Christian teaching of faith, but reflected mainly the questions that preoccupied the groups that were seeking to unite. Van der Zijpp also believed that the confessions were poorly formulated because "their originators hardly ever were trained theologians."[11] For him, paying significant attention to Mennonite confessional statements did not seem to be a worthwhile endeavour. Van der Zijpp and others recognized that Mennonites wrote confessions of faith but held that the exercise of writing such statements was not consonant with the genuine spirit of Anabaptism and Mennonitism.

In North American an explicitly negative assessment of the Anabaptist-Mennonite confessional tradition was mainly absent. The *Mennonite Encyclopedia*, published in the 1950s contained a substantial article on Mennonite confessions of faith by Christian Neff, J. C. Wenger and Harold S. Bender.[12] Cornelius J. Dyck contributed to the field of study through his translation work of several confessions of faith produced by the Waterlander Mennonites.[13] Other scholars contributed studies on the Schleitheim articles of the Swiss Brethren. Still, the notion that Anabaptists were "noncreedal," "anticreedal" or had an "anti-confessional bias," also persisted among North American scholars.[14]

The Dutch historian and theologian, Sjouke Voolstra, has attributed the anti-confessional attitude among Dutch Mennonites in previous years to a number of historical factors such as a mixture of early pietism and Enlightenment rationalism in the seventeenth and eighteenth-centuries, as well as liberalism in the nineteenth and twentieth centuries.[15] Similar influences affected North American Mennonites, but anti-confessional attitudes in the middle of the twentieth century may be best explained by examining Anabaptist historiography following World War II.

It is widely recognized that Harold S. Bender's "Anabaptist Vision" influenced historical writing and theological reflection during this period. Bender, a professor of history at Goshen College in Indiana, set out to rehabilitate the Anabaptists in a vigorous and public fashion, and he achieved this principally through his now well-known essay entitled "The Anabaptist Vision," published in 1944.[16] Instead of viewing Anabaptism as a heretical movement—which is how it had been seen by most non-Mennonite historians since the sixteenth century—Bender argued that Anabaptism was the culmination of sixteenth-century reform. The Anabaptists fulfilled the original visions of Luther and Zwingli, and sought "to recreate without compromise the original New Testament church, the vision of Christ and the Apostles."[17] "Anabaptism proper" had its genesis and locus in Switzerland, and from there it expanded to other regions of Europe.[18] The central features of the movement were, first, "a new conception of the essence of Christianity as discipleship; second, a new conception of the church as a brotherhood; and third, a new ethic of love and nonresistance."[19]

Bender's "Vision" was compelling particularly for Mennonite historians and leaders of Mennonite churches. Not only was it a description of sixteenth century Anabaptism but also a treatise that re-defined contemporary Mennonite identity in new, attractive ways. In trying to stay clear of what seemed to be the prevailing options for North American Mennonites—fundamentalism, revivalism, and liberalism—Bender provided an alternative: a return to Anabaptism with attention to the concept of discipleship and a focus on values such as community and peace.

It was perhaps the liberation from fundamentalism that was most appealing in Bender's "Vision." In the first decades of the twentieth-century, in both Canada and the United States, Mennonites were influenced by a fundamentalist mood that was alienating especially for those who were becoming part of the North American mainstream. Bender's thesis allowed Mennonites to break free from what was perceived to be an oppressive dogmatism, while still remaining true to their own heritage.

As A. James Reimer has pointed out, Bender's "Anabaptist Vision" was couched in ethical terms.[20] Accordingly, "the early Anabaptists emphasized not primarily intellectual understanding, doctrinal belief, or subjective experience, but rather a regenerate life best described by the term 'Nachfolge Christi'".[21] This description reflected the position of a generation of scholars, who saw the Anabaptist tradition making a contribution in ethics rather than doctrine. The Anabaptists were hailed for their willingness to challenge Constantinian Christianity, their willingness to form egalitarian communities, and their willingness to obey Jesus Christ and follow him in life. They were studied and admired for their orthopraxis—their concern to live rightly—not their orthodoxy.

Not surprisingly, scholars affected by this climate of opinion viewed Anabaptist confessional developments with little interest. They considered confessions to be a part of a genre that seemed to contradict the early Anabaptist emphasis on practical living. In addition, it was recognized that the confessions had emerged primarily at the end of the sixteenth and at the beginning of the seventeenth centuries in the Netherlands—an era and even a geographical location perceived to be exhibiting characteristics of spiritual decline, judged to be far removed from the golden age of Anabaptist origins. Hence, for North American scholars, fed by the presuppositions of the "Anabaptist Vision," studies in Mennonite confessional developments from the Netherlands were not very relevant or interesting.

Since the 1970s and 1980s, Anabaptist research, reflecting larger trends in Reformation historiography, shifted somewhat away from denominational interests and moved in the direction of understanding Anabaptism in social-historical terms. Historians, appropriating tools of scientific research, developed what came to be known as a "polygenesis" paradigm that described Anabaptism as a heterogeneous movement with distinctive origins: the Swiss, the south German-Austrian, and the north German-Dutch.[22] Anabaptism was understood not only or even primarily in ecclesiastical-religious terms, but in social-political ones, linked closely to the aspirations of the commoner. The polygenesis paradigm served to correct earlier assumptions dominating the Bender era, for example, that Anabaptism was primarily a monolithic reforming movement begun in Zurich Switzerland, or that Anabaptism was the culmination of the Reformation, fulfilling the original vision of Luther and Zwingli. The new approach was a fruitful corrective, in that studies were directed to more specific geographical areas, resulting in more nuanced and differentiated conclusions. No longer could historians describe Anabaptism credibly, without first making careful distinctions concerning which branch and specific period was under consideration. Neither could historians ascribe primacy or normativity to any one tradition. During the Bender era, the Swiss tradition was often viewed as the most pristine or genuine form of Anabaptism. With the passing of the "Anabaptist Vision" paradigm the north German and Dutch heritage could stand in its own right.[23]

As helpful as the polygenesis paradigm was in terms of describing Anabaptist origins and diversity, however, it did not encourage scholars to reflect on Anabaptist-Mennonite confessional developments.[24] Students of the paradigm were more inclined to address the social and historical causes lying *behind* Anabaptist theological suppositions, than the theological suppositions themselves. In addition, polygenesis research focused mainly on examining Anabaptist origins but did not contribute significant insight beyond the developments of the beginning years. While fascinating and crucial for an understanding of radical reform in the sixteenth century, this kind of concentrated investigation was not useful in understanding change and development among the various Anabaptist reforming movements over time. In fairness to the historians of this era, it must be pointed out that the polygenesis paradigm was never meant to be a comprehensive approach. Yet, it sometimes functioned like one, with the result that the Anabaptist field as a whole continued to be weak in producing scholarly material beyond the first decades of the movement.

In recent years, leading exponents of the polygenesis paradigm have moved beyond the study of origins, and have given more attention to developments among second generation Anabaptists. There has also been a renewed interest in theological questions with some studies considering the Anabaptist and Mennonite confessional legacy. In the mid 1980s, Howard John Loewen produced a compendium of North America Mennonite confessions in a volume entitled *One Lord, One Church, One Hope, and One God: Mennonite Confessions of Faith*. In his work, Loewen sought to move beyond polygenesis scholarship and suggested that there was a consistent theological centre in the confessions that contributed "to a truly integrative pluralism in the Mennonite family of faith."[25] Karl Koop came to similar conclusions in his historical and systematic investigations of early seventeenth century confessions entitled *Anabaptist-Mennonite Confessions of Faith: The Development of a Tradition*, emphasizing that, while diverse and evolving, early seventeenth century Mennonite confessions of faith represented an identifiable and coherent theological trajectory that was in continuity with sixteenth century Anabaptism.[26]

Motivated by these earlier studies, the present volume seeks to bring together for the first time a representative collection of confessions produced by Anabaptist groups from 1527 to 1660. Included are confessions from the Swiss Brethren, the Marpeck circle, the Rhinelanders, and various Mennonite communities in the north referred to as Waterlanders, Frisians, Flemish, and High Germans. Unlike Loewen's compendium that focused on confessional statements used principally by North American communities in the nineteenth and twentieth centuries, the present collection attends to the earliest phase of Anabaptist and Mennonite confessional writing in Europe, laying bare the foundations that set the stage for later confessional developments. The volume also includes introductions to each of the confessions, bringing into view the specific context out of which each doctrinal statement emerged.

Function

Some general observations about how confessions of faith in general have functioned is worth noting. In the first centuries of the church's existence, Christian communities used confessional documents in the context of worship, confession of sin, catechetical preparation and baptism. As theological controversies intensified, confessions were also used to define right doctrine. The church felt compelled to define the parameters of orthodox belief especially for the clergy. It was no longer sufficient simply to confess that one believed in Jesus Christ; it became necessary to confess in a more specific manner, what it was that one believed about this Christ. This concern for doctrinal orthodoxy was further heightened in the Middle Ages when ecclesiastical authorities became more centralized, and when Church and Empire moved closer together. In this context statements of faith took on not only an ecclesial but also a political function with universal authority, while the liturgical uses of the confessions became less important.

In the sixteenth century, Protestants likewise used their confessions to define right doctrine and in some cases their church statements became legal documents sanctioned by the state, to serve as instruments of political and ecclesial unity. Historians have used terms such as "confessionalism" and "confessionalization" to describe the incisive development that penetrated virtually every aspect of European society and propelled Europeans forward into the modern age. While some historians have identified this period as occurring between 1560 and 1650, it is evident that the beginnings of the confessional age were observable as early as the 1520s and that its development extended well beyond the seventeenth century.[27]

The confessional age shaped the churches above all. Heinz Schilling has noted that where the Reformation succeeded, the confessional era "witnessed institutional reconstruction of doctrine and liturgy in a great burst of church ordinances, confessional statements and confessional alliances."[28] These developments were apparent especially in central Europe in Protestant territorial states and free cities where the boundaries between Lutheranism and Calvinism were yet to be clarified. The confessional age saw changes in church structures and practices, and influenced the way in which doctrine functioned within the churches. After years of creativity and change, the churches felt driven to consolidate, to explicate and elaborate the essentials of the faith. Not only by means confessions of faith and catechisms, but also through the spoken word, the production of martyrologies, hymn writing and devotional materials, Christians of the various Reformation traditions sought to define who they were vis-à-vis one another. This approach to communications fit well during the Renaissance and early modern period when symbolic and visual approaches of communication were often put aside in favour of more word-oriented modes, supported by the invention of the Gutenburg printing press and the rise of literacy among Europeans. The drive for consolidation during the confessional age was conserving in character, and the outcome was not always constructive in that the strategies employed by the churches often drove a wedge between Christian communities. Yet, confessional writing could also lead to a process of creative theologizing that could help communities face the challenges of their time.

In this larger milieu Anabaptists drafted and adopted confessional statements as a way of bolstering internal cohesion and preserving theological distinctives. Sometimes confessional statements were also used as instruments of unity between groups that were seeking to overcome differences. At the end of the sixteenth and the beginning of the seventeenth century, the Dutch, more than any other Anabaptist group, felt the need to write confessional documents (hence the relatively long list of Dutch confessions included in this volume). The churches had split into numerous factions and the need for reconciliation and reunion was urgent. In addition, Dutch Anabaptists were no longer persecuted, unlike their forebears or their Anabaptist relatives in other parts of Europe. While this growing acceptance of Anabaptism was preferable to an earlier age of intolerance, the new world with its pluralisms and competing worldviews was fraught with difficulties. In response, the Anabaptist communities in the north saw the need to summarize the essentials of the faith beyond the summary statements of Apostles' and Nicene Creeds. Definable communities of discourse had emerged, led by leaders who had the skills to reflect systematically about the faith. The writing of confessions was thus a natural unfolding of a movement that was fast becoming established, requiring instruments of support necessary for survival in a changing social, political, and religious context.

Authority

Historians have variously assessed the extent to which Anabaptist confessions of faith were authoritative in the sixteenth and seventeenth century period. With reference to the confessions in northern Europe, Nanne van der Zijpp maintained that Mennonite confessional statements were merely instruments of unity, while Cornelius J. Dyck gave the confessional statements broader significance, noting that even among the liberal Waterlanders, confessions of faith were given serious consideration.[29] Arnold Snyder observed that the doctrines of the Schleitheim Confession played a formative role in the development of Swiss Anabaptism.[30]

That Anabaptists took their doctrinal statements of faith seriously, however, is not to suggest that the statements carried the same authoritative weight in their churches as the confessions of faith did in the Catholic or Protestant churches. In Reformation times the confessions adopted by the mainstream churches were eventually sanctioned and enforced by political authorities. In contrast, the Anabaptist and Mennonite confessions of faith never had this kind of political or ecclesial status. Without centralized ecclesial authority and without political approval, confessional statements depended on congregation assent. As historian Piet Visser has noted, the confessions of one particular Anabaptist group, the Waterlanders, had representative, rather than constitutive authority. They were authoritative only in so far as they were consonant with Scripture and reflected agreement in the congregations, often requiring widespread approval.[31] The Waterlanders appear to have recognized the potentially abusive power of their confessional statements. They did not want to take their statements lightly but were adamant in some of their writings that confessions of faith should be placed under the authority of Scripture and subordinate to the unity of the Christian community.[32]

This positioning of the confessional statements in relation to Scripture and Christian unity was not always maintained in northern Europe, and less moderate voices gained prominence, which led to an unfortunate conflict that some observers labelled "the War of the Lambs." This conflict erupted at a time when questions concerning identity were at the forefront of the Dutch Mennonites. Fearing cultural assimilation and growing secularization, some leaders saw the need for greater discipline within the churches and called for greater accountability and loyalty to the confessions of the church. In 1649 a major faction of the Flemish leadership met several times to discuss issues of leadership and authority. While maintaining that ultimate authority resides in the Word of God, they came to the conclusion that unity with groups such as the Waterlanders could only proceed on the basis of the confessions of faith that had been adopted in previous years.

Yet, not everyone was comfortable with the exclusion of the Waterlanders, and not everyone wanted to define the church in such narrow terms. In 1657, two leaders in the Flemish Mennonite church in Amsterdam, Galenus Abrahamsz. and David Spruyt, presented a nineteen-article manuscript which denied that any church could be the one true church. They argued that church leaders should conform solely to New Testament principles and not demand absolute conformity in doctrinal and other church matters.

An attempt to resolve the dispute was made in 1660 under the chairmanship of Thieleman Jansz. van Braght whereupon the Flemish determined that a single, new and authoritative confession of faith based on the older confessions should be formulated, and that Galenus Abrahmsz. and David Spruyt should be asked to conform to the teachings of the church or give up their ministry. The two Amsterdam preachers, however, refused these alternatives, arguing that only their local congregation, not a meeting of congregations, had the authority to make such decisions. An attempt to influence the Amsterdam congregation failed since many members did not share the views of the larger body. The acrimony reached new heights when David Spruyt proclaimed from the pulpit that "synods and the like were the work of the Antichrist."[33]

The confessionalists held their ground and soon took further action. Thieleman Janz. van Braght released his martyr book, the *Bloedigh Tooneel* (the *Bloody Theater*) known in the English-speaking world as the *Martyrs Mirror*.[34] He had been working on his martyr-project for some time, which was essentially a work building on the martyr tradition a century earlier, begun by Jan Hendricks van Schoorewoerd and substantially revised by Hans de Ries.[35] Van Braght's edition was intended to call the church back to the faithfulness of the early church and the sixteenth-century Anabaptist martyrs at a time when, in his view, Mennonites were succumbing to worldly pleasures and distractions. But in issuing his martyrology, van Braght was also advancing the confessionalist cause. His introduction in the *Martyrs Mirror* included the Apostles' Creed as well as three Anabaptist-Mennonite confessions of faith. By placing the creed and the confessions together in this way, van Braght was making the point that Mennonite confessional statements were in continuity with the first Christians and with all the faithful throughout the centuries, including the Anabaptist saints who had died for their steadfast faith. The confessions, van Braght argued, "might seem in superficial ways to be different, but, as was the case with the whole tradition of Christianity since the time of the first persecutions, all orthodox confessions elaborated on the same unchanging beliefs."[36]

This use of the martyr tradition did not impress van Braght's opponents, and the dispute and the theological debate widened. Eventually the conflict spread throughout much of Holland and into other Dutch provinces. When in the spring of 1664 the differences of opinion could not be resolved the two factions moved apart; the confessionalists came to be known as Zonists, the anti-confessionalists came to be known as Lamists. The Zonists worked toward church unity on the basis of the confessional tradition, a new constitution, and a five-article document requiring preachers and deacons to conform to the principles of the confessions; the Lamists sought unity through common adherence to the Bible. Over time the tension between the two factions diminished, although the Zonists and the Lamists remained divided until the early nineteenth century. Evidently, while confessions could sometimes be quite helpful in facilitating unity between groups that wanted to unite, the unfolding story of the Mennonite confessions suggests that they could also become instruments of division.

Theological Orientation

Like most other confessional statements of the Reformation period, the Anabaptist confessions include an abundance of Scripture references as a way of validating doctrinal views. An investigation into the way in which Scripture is used in the confessions of faith indicates that Anabaptist communities of this time period had a profound knowledge of biblical literature. It is also the case that they often appropriated biblical references as "proof texts" in ways that might seem highly questionable in our time.

Most of the confessions in this volume include the whole range of Christian doctrine and reflect views generally held by other Christians. Nevertheless, in the common loci of Christian belief and in specific areas of Christian conduct, Anabaptists often appropriated their own particular language and produced their own distinct theological accent. For instance, while acknowledging the sovereignty of God, the confessions generally emphasize that human beings have a free will and therefore have the capacity to choose between good and evil. The experience of salvation includes personal regeneration and a new birth which is expressed concretely in daily discipleship. Discipleship, in turn, is based not only on the teachings but also the life of Christ; it is not an option for a select few but an essential characteristic of all Christians.

The church is understood to be the body of Christ, called into being by God. It is a voluntary gathering of spiritually regenerated Christians, who follow Christ's teaching and example. Entry into this body takes place through baptism, based on personal faith in Christ; it is a rite that symbolizes the new birth that the individual experiences inwardly through faith. The Supper, which takes place in the presence of Christ, is a memorial of Christ's death and sacrifice, and symbolizes the unity and fellowship of the Christian community. Accountability within the Christian community is maintained through church discipline, which is intended primarily to bring the sinner to repentance and renewed fellowship with other believers. Christians are to relate to the world in a peaceable manner; violence and warfare is reject, as well as the swearing of oaths.

That the Anabaptist confessions reflect these theological accents is not to suggest, however, that they are uniform. The confessions diverge on topics such as revelation, the incarnation, the inner and outer dimensions of the sacraments, the visibility and invisibility of the church, and the practice of church discipline. In addition, changes in language and doctrinal perspective over time, even within particular communities, indicate that the confessions represent not a fixed, but rather a dynamic and developing theological tradition. Later editions do not always mirror the contents of earlier editions. Evidently, Anabaptist communities have not hesitated to change or "improve" earlier formulations. While many of the essential commitments of the Anabaptist community have not changed, the contexts in which the confessions were used were in constant flux and clearly led to certain revisions.[37] This calls attention to the provisional quality of Christian theology, even as one may choose to acknowledge its divine revelatory character or the universal nature of its truth. Christian theology is always context-dependent, shaped by historical developments and beset by human limitation.

A central question that has divided scholars has to do with the nature of Anabaptist theology as it relates to the wider Christian tradition. In his study of early sixteenth century Anabaptism, Harold Bender placed the Anabaptists primarily in Protestant company. He argued that Anabaptism was a radical break with Catholic history and culture, and that it was in fact "the culmination of the Reformation, the fulfillment of the original vision of Luther and Zwingli"[38] and thus represented a consistent evangelical Protestantism that sought to faithfully recreate the original New Testament church. Bender's argument was in part directed against interpretations of the past that proposed that the Anabaptists represented a continuation of late-medieval mystical or ascetic traditions, or that they perpetuated humanist sentiments.

The connection between the wider Christian tradition and Anabaptism has been revisited by historians such as Kenneth Davis and Arnold Snyder, who have argued that there was a close connection between Anabaptism and medieval asceticism. Davis has maintained that Christian Erasmianism mediated the ascetic principles of the *Devotio Moderna* to Anabaptism. To a lesser degree, a more "practical, activist, ascetic tradition was also mediated to Anabaptism through the influence of the *Theologia Germanica* and indirectly (perhaps even directly in Anabaptism's initial urban thrust) through the Franciscan Tertiary movement."[39] In a similar vein, Arnold Snyder, in an essay on Anabaptist spirituality, has observed that Anabaptism was "*fundamentally* ascetic and Catholic, and only *superficially* Protestant."[40] More recently, Snyder has noted that while the Anabaptists did not feel at home in either Roman Catholicism or Protestantism, spiritual ideals common in monasticism and late medieval piety as well as Protestant reforming ideas shaped Anabaptist views.[41]

An examination of the confessions of faith in this volume should call attention to the fact that it is impossible to unhinge Anabaptism from the broader Christian world—both Catholic *and* Protestant. Anabaptists communities were never able to jump back 1,500 years of history and reject the mediation of tradition, nor were they able develop their theology in isolation from the surrounding religious milieu, which was both Catholic and Protestant in character. And, of course, no confessional statements were produced by Anabaptist groups without the influence of wider historical, social and cultural factors. The confessions were products of their time, fashioned by multiple issues and specific concerns.

When reading these statements that reflect the views of several different Anabaptist communities we would do well not to overestimate their importance. Confessional statements may tell us something about the ideal convictions of a community or its leadership, but doctrinal statements, by themselves, do not tell us how people actually lived. We ought to recognize, moreover, that Anabaptist communities, like most communities of the Reformation era, produced other kinds of literature besides confessions of faith, such as catechisms, martyrologies, hymns, liturgies, devotional writings, and various other theological treatises, from which much insight can be gained from the past. Nevertheless, confessions of faith should not be underestimated either. They are a significant genre of literature with many of the confessions representing core convictions that Anabaptist communities have held for centuries. Collectively, the confessions of faith in this volume bring into view the Anabaptist theological tradition in its early phase, and have the potential to shed light on the character of contemporary Anabaptism.

I

Confessions of Swiss/
South German Anabaptism

1

Congregational Order (1527?)

Introduction

Congregational orders in Anabaptism usually reflected patterns of practical living and church discipline. Probably the oldest Anabaptist congregational order, this Swiss document may well have predated the Schleitheim Articles. Details, such as frequent gatherings, a common meal, and celebration of the Lord's Supper, point to a congregational life that was relatively public, which would have been possible only briefly, at the very beginning of the Anabaptist movement, before persecution drove Anabaptists underground or into exile.

No authorship is given, nor is it possible to identify in certain terms which congregations might have adopted this document, although conditions for practicing the faith in accordance with this Swiss Congregational Order may have been suitable for a time in towns such as Zollikon, and in territories such as St. Gall and Appenzell.

While John Howard Yoder has suggested an historic linkage to the Schleitheim Articles, it is likely that it circulated as an independent document. Unlike Schleitheim, the Order does not include any details about baptism, the ban, or about separation, and it appears to advocate a different leadership structure. Further, the document appears to promote a different set of economic practices with its emphasis on community of goods based on a reading of Acts 2 and 4. In this connection, James Stayer believes that Swiss Anabaptists who followed the practices of the Order not only pioneered the practice of community of goods, but also inspired other groups to follow similar economic practices.

Werner O. Packull, in his study of various congregational orders, has shown that this Order became the basis of *The Church Discipline* (1529?) used among Hutterites in Moravia, and the *Common Order* (1540?) used among Anabaptists associated with Pilgram Marpeck. Both of these documents appear to have been adapted and modified in their respective contexts, but originally influenced by this Swiss Congregational Order. That it was adapted in this manner underscores the fact that the Swiss influenced Anabaptists in the regions of Upper Germany, Austria and Moravia.

The Congregational Order is a practical document emerging from a young community that appears to be strongly democratic, open to the Spirit's leading, and optimistic about the reformation of church and society.

This translation, by John Howard Yoder, is based on unpublished materials received from Heinold Fast.

Bibliographical Sources

Werner O. Packull, *Hutterite Beginnings: Communitarian Experiments during the Reformation* (Baltimore and London: The Johns Hopkins University Press, 1995); C. Arnold Snyder, *Anabaptist History and Theology: Student Edition* (Kitchener: Pandora Press, 1997); James M. Stayer, *The German Peasants' War and Anabaptist Community of Goods* (Montreal and Kingston: McGill-Queen's University Press, 1991); John Howard Yoder, ed., *The Legacy of Michael Sattler* (Scottdale, PA: Herald Press, 1973).

[Congregational Order][1]

Translated by John Howard Yoder

Since the almighty eternal and merciful God has made His wonderful light break forth in this world and [in this] most dangerous time, we recognize the mystery of the divine will, that the Word is preached to us according to the proper ordering of the Lord, whereby we have been called into His fellowship. Therefore, according to the command of the Lord and the teachings of His apostles, in Christian order, we should observe the new commandment in love one toward another, so that love and unity may be maintained, which all brothers and sisters of the entire congregation should agree to hold to as follows:

1. The brothers and sisters should meet at least three or four time a week, to exercise themselves in the teaching of Christ and His apostles and heartily to exhort one another to remain faithful to the Lord as they have pledged.

2. When the brothers and sisters are together, they shall take up something to read together. The one to whom God has given the best understanding shall explain it, the others should be still and listen, so that there are not two or three carrying on a private conversation, bothering the others. The Psalter shall be read daily at home.

3. Let none be frivolous in the church of God, neither in words nor in actions. Good conduct shall be maintained by them all also before the heathen.

4. When a brother sees his brother erring, he shall warn him according to the command of Christ, and shall admonish him in a Christian and brotherly way, as everyone is bound and obliged to do out of love.

5. Of all the brothers and sisters of this congregation none shall have anything of his own, but rather, as the Christians in the time of the apostles held all in common, and especially stored up a common fund, from which aid can be given to the poor, according as each will have need, and as in the apostles' time permit no brother to be in need.

6. All gluttony shall be avoided among the brothers who are gathered in the congregation; serve a soup or a minimum of vegetable and meat, for eating and drinking are not the kingdom of heaven.

7. The Lord's Supper shall be held, as often as the brothers are together, thereby proclaiming the death of the Lord, and thereby warning each one to commemorate, how Christ gave His life for us, and shed His blood for us, that we might also be willing to give our body and life for Christ's sake, which means for the sake of all the brothers.

2

Schleitheim Articles/Brotherly Union (1527)

Introduction

Swiss Anabaptists adopted the Brotherly Union on February 24, 1527. Often referred to as the Schleitheim Articles or the Schleitheim Confession, the document played a formative role in the Swiss tradition, although it was never universally adopted or accepted even in the Swiss regions.

Michael Sattler probably drafted the Articles together with the prefatory letter and concluding postscript. Sattler had been a Benedictine monk and prior at St. Peter's of the Black Forest near the city of Freiburg, and may have joined the Anabaptist movement in the summer of 1526. His Anabaptist activities took him to the regions of Zürich and Strasbourg, and then to the Schaffhausen area to the town of Schleitheim, where the seven articles were adopted. Within days of the Anabaptist conference at Schleitheim, Sattler was arrested by Austrian authorities in the Württemberg town of Horb on the Neckar. He was tried, tortured, and then executed on May 21, 1527.

The Articles are polemical in tone and represent the views of a community under hostile political repression, awaiting the imminent return of Christ. While John Howard Yoder has suggested that the confession was directed against mainline reformers, such as Martin Bucer and Wolfgang Capito, most scholars have concluded that the confession points to an internal dispute among diverging Anabaptist groups.

Scholarly debate has especially focussed on the theological influences that might have shaped the confession's theological orientation. In the mid-twentieth century it was assumed that the confession represented theological views in continuity with Zürich Anabaptist beginnings. More recently, scholars have argued that the confession represents a later development in Anabaptist thought, and that it also embodies the language of peasant aspirations, late medieval asceticism, Benedictine communalism, or some combination of these influences. Whatever the influences may have been, the confession served to demarcate Swiss Anabaptist thought and practice from Catholics, mainline reformers, spiritualists, and revolutionaries.

The confession takes for granted the beliefs of the wider Christian church, but seeks to highlight Anabaptist ecclesiological distinctives. The theme of unity among true Christians is emphasized throughout the confession; at the same time true Christians are instructed to reject all worldly associations and false expressions of Christianity, thereby underscoring the Anabaptist resolve to uphold a sectarian ecclesiology. Also characteristic of the confession is its strong Christological emphasis. The nature of the voluntary, disciplined community, which has chosen to view itself as an alternative society, is based on being one with Christ, including his life and teachings.

This translation by John H. Yoder is based on a text prepared by Heinold Fast for the *Quellen zur Geschichte der Täufer in der Schweiz* series.

Bibliographical Sources

Heinold Fast, ed. *Quellen zur Geschichte der Täufer in der Schweiz*. Vol. 2 (Zürich, Switzerland: Theologischer Verlag, 1973); Hans-Jürgen Goertz, *The Anabaptists*. Translated by Trevor Johnson (London and New York: Routledge, 1996); C. Arnold Snyder, *The Life and Thought of Michael Sattler* (Scottdale, PA: Herald Press, 1984); C. Arnold Snyder, "The Influence of the Schleitheim Articles on the Anabaptist Movement: An Historical Evaluation." *Mennonite Quarterly Review* 63.4 (October 1989): 323-344; John H. Yoder, ed. *The Legacy of Michael Sattler* (Scottdale, PA: Herald Press, 1973).

[Schleitheim Articles/Brotherly Union (1527)]

Translated by John Howard Yoder

Brotherly Union of a Number of Children of God Concerning Seven Articles

The Cover Letter

May joy, peace, mercy from our Father, through the atonement of the blood of Christ Jesus, together with the gifts of the Spirit — who is sent by the Father to all believers to [give] strength and consolation and constance in all tribulation until the end, Amen, be with all who love God and all children of light, who are scattered everywhere, wherever they might have been placed by God our Father, wherever they might be gathered in unity of spirit in one God and Father of us all; grace and peace of heart be with you all. Amen.

Beloved brothers and sisters in the Lord; first and primordially we are always concerned for your consolation and the assurance of your conscience (which was sometime confused), so that you might not always be separated from us as aliens and by right almost completely excluded, but that you might turn to the true implanted members of Christ, who have been armed through patience and the knowledge of self, and thus be again united with us in the power of a godly Christian spirit and zeal for God.

It is manifest with what manifold cunning the devil has turned us aside, so that he might destroy and cast down the work of God, which in us mercifully and graciously has been partially begun. But the true Shepherd of our souls, Christ, who has begun such in us, will direct and teach the same unto the end, to His glory and our salvation, Amen.

Dear brothers and sisters, we who have been assembled in the Lord at Schleitheim on the Randen make known, in points and articles, unto all that love God, that as far as we are concerned, we have been united to stand fast in the Lord as obedient children of God, sons and daughters, who have been and shall be separated from the world in all that we do and leave undone, and (the praise and glory be to God alone) uncontradicted by all the brothers, completely at peace. Herein we have sensed the unity of the Father and of our common Christ as present with us in their Spirit. For the Lord is a Lord of peace and not of quarreling, as Paul indicates. So that you understand at what points this occurred, you should observe and understand [what follows]:

A very great offense has been introduced by some false brothers among us, whereby several have turned away from the faith, thinking to practice and observe the freedom of the Spirit and of Christ. But such have fallen short of the truth and (to their own condemnation) are given over to the lasciviousness and license of the flesh. They have esteemed that faith and love may do and permit everything and that nothing can harm nor condemn them, since they are "believers."

Note well, you members of God in Christ Jesus, that faith in the heavenly Father through Jesus Christ is not thus formed; it produces and brings forth no such things as these false brothers and sisters practice and teach. Guard yourselves and be warned of such people, for they do not serve our Father, but their father, the devil.

But for you it is not so; for they who are Christ's have crucified their flesh with all its lusts and desires. You understand me well, and [know] the brothers whom we mean. Separate yourselves from them, for they are perverted. Pray the Lord that they may have knowledge unto repentance, and for us that we may have constance to persevere along the path we have entered upon, unto the glory of God and of Christ His Son. Amen.

[The Seven Articles]

The articles we have dealt with, and in which we have been united, are these: baptism, ban, the breaking of bread, separation from abomination, shepherds in the congregation, the sword, the oath.

[I. Baptism]

Notice concerning baptism. Baptism shall be given to all those who have been taught repentance and the amendment of life and [who] believe truly that their sins are taken away through Christ, and to all those who desire to walk in the resurrection of Jesus Christ and be buried with Him in death, so that they might rise with Him; to all those who with such an understanding themselves desire and request it from us; hereby is excluded all infant baptism, the greatest and first abomination of the Pope. For this you have the reasons and the testimony of the writings and the practice of the apostles. We wish simply yet resolutely and with assurance to hold to the same.

[II. Ban]

We have been united as follows concerning the ban. The ban shall be employed with all those who have given themselves over to the Lord, to walk after [Him] in His commandments; those who have been baptized into the one body of Christ, and let themselves be called brothers or sisters, and still somehow slip and fall into error and sin, being inadvertently overtaken. The same [shall] be warned twice privately and the third time be publicly admonished before the entire congregation according to the command of Christ (Matt. 18). But this shall be done according to the ordering of the Spirit of God before the breaking of bread, so that we may all in one spirit and in one love break and eat from one bread and drink from one cup.

[III. Breaking Bread]

Concerning the breaking of bread, we have become one and agree thus: all those who desire to break the one bread in remembrance of the broken body of Christ and all those who wish to drink of one drink in remembrance of the shed blood of Christ, they must beforehand be united in the one body of Christ, that is the congregation of God, whose head is Christ, and that by baptism. For as Paul indicates, we cannot be partakers at the same time of the table of the Lord and the table of devils. Nor can we at the same time partake and drink of the cup of the Lord and the cup of devils. That is: all those who have fellowship with the dead works of darkness have no part in the light. Thus all who follow the devil and the world, have no part with those who have been called out of the world unto God. All those who lie in evil have no part in the good.

So it shall and must be, that whoever does not share the calling of the one God to one faith, to one baptism, to one spirit, to one body together with all the children of God, may not be made one loaf together with them, as must be true if one wishes truly to break bread according to the command of Christ.

[IV. Separation]

We have been united concerning the separation that shall take place from the evil and the wickedness which the devil has planted in the world, simply in this; that we have no fellowship with them, and do not run with them in the confusion of their abominations. So it is; since all who have not entered into the obedience of faith and have not united themselves with God so that they will to do His will, are a great abomination before God, therefore nothing else can or really will grow or spring forth from them than abominable things. Now there is nothing else in the world and all creation than good or evil, believing and unbelieving, darkness and light, the world and those who are [come] out of the world, God's temple and idols, Christ and Belial, and none will have part with the other.

To us, then, the commandment of the Lord is also obvious, whereby He orders us to be and to become separated from the evil one, and thus He will be our God and we shall be His sons and daughters.

Further, He admonishes us therefore to go out from Babylon and from the earthly Egypt, that we may not be partakers in their torment and suffering, which the Lord will bring upon them.

From all this we should learn that everything which has not been united with our God in Christ is nothing but an abomination which we should shun. By this are meant all popish and repopish works and idolatry, gatherings, church attendance, winehouses, guarantees and commitments of unbelief, and other things of the kind, which the world regards highly, and yet which are carnal or flatly counter to the command of God, after the pattern of all the iniquity which is in the world. From all this we shall be separated and have no part with such, for they are nothing but abominations, which cause us to be hated before our Christ Jesus, who has freed us from the servitude of the flesh and fitted us for the service of God and the Spirit whom He has given us.

Thereby shall also fall away from us the diabolical weapons of violence such as sword, armor, and the like, and all of their use to protect friends or against enemies by virtue of the word of Christ: "you shall not resist evil."

[V. Shepherds]

We have been united as follows concerning shepherds in the church of God. The shepherd in the church shall be a person according to the rule of Paul, fully and completely, who has a good report of those who are outside the faith. The office of such a person shall be to read and exhort and teach, warn, admonish, or ban in the congregation, and properly to preside among the sisters and brothers in prayer, and in the breaking of bread, and in all things to take care of the body of Christ, that it may be built up and developed, so that the name of God might be praised and honored through us, and the mouth of the mocker be stopped.

He shall be supported, wherein he has need, by the congregation which has chosen him, so that he who serves the gospel can also live therefrom, as the Lord has ordered. But should a shepherd do something worthy of reprimand, nothing shall be done with him without the voice of two or three witnesses. If they sin they shall be publicly reprimanded, so that others might fear.

But if the shepherd should be driven away or led to the Lord by the cross, at the same hour another shall be ordained to his place, so that the little folk and the little flock of God may not be destroyed, but be preserved by warning and be consoled.

[VI. Sword]

We have been united as follows concerning the sword. The sword is an ordering of God outside the perfection of Christ. It punishes and kills the wicked, and guards and protects the good. In the law the sword is established over the wicked for punishment and for death, and the secular rulers are established to wield the same.

But within the perfection of Christ only the ban is used for the admonition and exclusion of the one who has sinned, without the death of the flesh, simply the warning and the command to sin no more.

Now many, who do not understand Christ's will for us, will ask: whether a Christian may or should use the sword against the wicked for the protection and defense of the good, or for the sake of love.

The answer is unanimously revealed: Christ teaches and commands us to learn from Him, for He is meek and lowly of heart and thus we shall find rest for our souls. Now Christ says to the woman who was taken in adultery, not that she should be stoned according to the law of His Father (and yet He says, "what the Father commanded me, that I do") but with mercy and forgiveness and the warning to sin no more, says: "Go, sin no more." Exactly thus should we also proceed, according to the rule of the ban.

Second, is asked concerning the sword: whether a Christian shall pass sentence in disputes and strife about worldly matters, such as the unbelievers have with one another. The answer: Christ did not wish to decide or pass judgment between brother and brother concerning inheritance, but refused to do so. So should we also do.

Third, is asked concerning the sword: whether the Christian should be a magistrate if he is chosen thereto. This is answered thus: Christ was to be made king, but He fled and did not discern the ordinance of His Father. Thus we should also do as His did and follow after Him, and we shall not walk in darkness. For He Himself says: "Whoever would come after me, let him deny himself and take up his cross and follow me." He Himself further forbids the violence of the sword when He says; "The princes of this world lord it over them etc., but among you it shall not be so." Further Paul says, "Whom God has foreknown, the same he has also predestined to be conformed to the image of his Son," etc. Peter also says: "Christ has suffered (not ruled) and has left us an example, that you should follow after in his steps."

Lastly one can see in the following points that it does not befit a Christian to be a magistrate: the rule of the government is according to the flesh, that of the Christians according to the spirit. Their houses and dwelling remain in this world, that of the Christians is in heaven. Their citizenship is in this world, that of the Christians is in heaven. The weapons of their battle and warfare are carnal and only against the flesh, but the weapons of Christians are spiritual, against the fortification of the devil. The worldly are armed with steel and iron, but Christians are armed with the armor of God, with truth, righteousness, peace, faith, salvation, and with the Word of God. In sum: as Christ our Head is minded, so also must be minded the members of the body of Christ through Him, so that there be no division in the body, through which it would be destroyed. Since then Christ is as is written of Him, so must His members also be the same, so that His body may remain whole and unified for its own advancement and upbuilding. For any kingdom which is divided within itself will be destroyed.

[VII. Oath]

We have been united as follows concerning the oath. The oath is a confirmation among those who are quarreling or making promises. In the law it is commanded that it should be done only in the name of God, truthfully and not falsely. Christ, who teaches the perfection of the law, forbids His [followers] all swearing, whether true nor false; neither by heaven nor by earth, neither by Jerusalem nor by our head; and that for the reason which He goes on to give: "For you cannot make one hair white or black." You see, thereby all swearing is forbidden. We cannot perform what is promised in swearing, for we are not able to change the smallest part of ourselves.

Now there are some who do not believe the simple commandment of God and who say, "But God swore by Himself to Abraham, because He was God (as He promised him that He would do good to him and would be his God if he kept His commandments). Why then should I not swear if I promise something to someone?" The answer: hear what Scripture says: "God, since he wished to prove overabundantly to the heirs of His promise that His will did not change, inserted an oath so that by two immutable things we might have a stronger consolation (for it is impossible that God should lie)." Notice the meaning of the passage: God has the power to do what He forbids you, for everything is possible to Him. God swore an oath to Abraham, Scripture says, in order to prove that His counsel is immutable. That means: no one can withstand and thwart His will; thus He can keep His oath. But we cannot, as Christ said above, hold or perform our oath, therefore we should not swear.

Others say that swearing cannot be forbidden by God in the New Testament when it was commanded in the Old, but that it is forbidden only to swear by heaven, earth, Jerusalem, and our head. Answer: hear the Scripture. He who swears by heaven, swears by God's throne and by Him who sits thereon. Observe: swearing by heaven is forbidden, which is only God's throne; how much more is it forbidden to swear by God Himself. You blind fools, what is greater, the throne or He who sits upon it?

Others say, if it is then wrong to use God for truth, then the apostles Peter and Paul also swore. Answer: Peter and Paul only testify to that which God promised Abraham, whom we long after have received. But when one testifies, one testifies concerning that which is present, whether it be good or evil. Thus Simeon spoke of Christ to Mary and testified: "Behold: this one is ordained for the falling and rising of many in Israel and to be a sign which will be spoken against."

Christ taught us similarly when He says: Your speech shall be yea, yea; and nay, nay; for what is more than that comes of evil. He says, your speech or your word shall be yes and no, so that no one might understand that He had permitted it. Christ is simply yea and nay, and all those who seek Him simply will understand His Word. Amen.

The Cover Letter

Dear Brothers and Sisters in the Lord; these are the articles which some brothers previously had understood wrongly and in a way not conformed to the true meaning. Thereby many weak consciences were confused, whereby the name of God has been grossly slandered, for which reason it was needful that we should be brought to agreement in the Lord, which has come to pass. To God be praise and glory!

Now that you have abundantly understood the will of God as revealed through us at this time, you must fulfill this will, now known, persistently and unswervingly. For you know well what is the reward of the servant who knowingly sins.

Everything which you have done unknowingly and now confess to have done wrongly, is forgiven you, through that believing prayer, which is offered among us in our meeting for all our shortcomings and guilt, through the gracious forgiveness of God and through the blood of Jesus Christ. Amen.

Watch out for all who do not walk in simplicity of divine truth, which has been stated by us in this letter in our meeting, so that everyone might be governed among us by the rule of the ban, and that henceforth the entry of false brothers and sisters among us might be prevented.

Put away from you that which is evil, and the Lord will be your God, and you will be His sons and daughters.

Dear brothers, keep in mind what Paul admonished Titus. He says: "The saving grace of God has appeared to all, and disciplines us, that we should deny ungodliness and worldly lusts, and live circumspect righteous and godly lives in this world; awaiting the same hope and the appearing of the glory of the great God and of our Saviour Jesus Christ, who gave himself for us, to redeem us from all unrighteousness and to purify unto himself a people of his own, that would be zealous of good works." Think on this, and exercise yourselves therein, and the Lord of peace will be with you.

May the name of God be forever blessed and greatly praised, Amen. May the Lord give you His peace, Amen.

Done at Schleitheim, St. Matthew's Day, Anno MDXXVII.

3

A Confession of Faith by Jörg Maler (1554)

According to the Treasures of the Holy Scriptures

Introduction

Jörg Probst Rotenfelder was a south German Anabaptist leader, who compiled the *Kunstbuch* in 1561, a collection of significant Anabaptist writings that stemmed from the community associated with Pilgram Marpeck. Scholars at one time assumed that Marpeck's brand of Anabaptism died out in South Germany, but recent evidence suggests that Marpeckite ideas appeared in later Swiss Anabaptist writings, a point that future scholars studying later Swiss materials will need to take into consideration.

Jörg came from the city of Augsburg, and in 1513 began an apprenticeship in painting. Eventually he came to be known in association with his profession—hence, the name Jörg Maler (in German: Jörg, the Painter).

Maler's relationship to his home city was often tenuous. In 1526, after a drinking episode with his companions, he was caught up in an altercation that involved assaulting a young woman. He was briefly imprisoned, and although repentant, officials banished him from the city until he had paid restitution. Later he had difficulty remaining in Augsburg because of his associations with Anabaptism.

Maler joined the Anabaptist cause in 1532, having been baptized by the goldsmith Sebolt Feuchter from Nürnberg. Anabaptism in Augsburg had reached a high point in 1527 and 1528, with numerous Anabaptists from Switzerland, Strasbourg, central Germany and Austria flocking to this relatively tolerant city. Leaders such as Hans Hut, Lienhard Schiemer and Hans Schlaffer were in Augsburg in 1527, and their writings would eventually find their way into Maler's *Kunstbuch*. By the time Maler was baptized, however, the authorities had managed to suppress the Anabaptist movement in Augsburg. They had arrested many Anabaptists in 1533, and after imprisonment and interrogation, most recanted, including Maler. Maler was set free, but because of further associations with Anabaptists, he was again exiled from the city. He would return to Augsburg several more times—he was imprisoned there in 1550—but he also managed to carry out his Anabaptist activities in places like St. Gallen and Appenzell. Heinold Fast has noted that Maler's leadership style was remarkably democratic in that he believed, following the example of the Pauline community in 1 Corinthians 14, that the interpretation of the biblical text was primarily the responsibility of the gathered community, not the preacher.

Maler was a respected leader, but his views were sometimes also in contradiction with his co-religionists. Unlike the Swiss Anabaptists, for instance, he believed that under certain circumstances oath swearing was permissible, that carrying a sword was not against the will of God, and that it was not improper for a believer to marry someone of a different faith. As the *Kunstbuch* collection demonstrates, Maler was willing to borrow theological material from non-Anabaptist sources, such as from the Spiritualist Sebastian Franck and the Lutheran Hartmut von Cronberg. Hartmut's military activities, his services to those in government, and his personal relationship to Martin Luther would probably not have impressed Maler's Anabaptist readers. The willingness of Maler to appropriate a Lutheran document for his own purposes raises the question about the open interaction and continuities between the various reformation streams.

Confidence in the importance of the Apostles' Creed appears to have been widely present in most Anabaptist circles, and producing commentaries on the basis of the Creed was not uncommon. Maler was often asked about his faith and questioners would have been interested in specifics. Maler's interpretation of the Creed, produced sometime in 1554, demonstrates his orthodox faith and includes an emphasis on personal regeneration, spiritual rebirth, and trust in God for one's salvation.

This translation by Victor Thiessen is based on the work of Heinold Fast and Martin Rothkegel and the recent publication of *Das Kunstbuch*.

Bibliographical Sources

Heinold Fast, "Vom Amt des 'Lesers' zum Kompilator des sogenannten Kunstbuches. Auf den Spuren Jörg Malers" in *Aussenseiter Zwischen Mittelalter und Neuzeit: Festschrift für Hans-Jürgen Goertz zum 60. Geburtstag*, ed. Norbert Fischer and Marion Kobelt-Groch (Leiden, New York, Köln: Brill, 1997), 187-217; Heinold Fast, "Zur Überlieferung des Leser-Amtes bei den oberdeutschen Täufern," *Mennonitische Geschichtsblätter* 54 (1997): 61-68; Heinold Fast and Martin Rothkegel, eds., *Das Kunstbuch: Briefe und Schriften Oberdeutscher Täufer 1527-1561. Gesammelt von Jörg Probst Rotenfelder Genannt Maler*. Quellen zur Geschichte der Täufer XVII. Band (Gütersloh: Gütersloher Verlagshaus Gerd Mohn, 2005); William Klassen, "The Legacy of the Marpeck Community in Anabaptist Scholarship," *Mennonite Quarterly Review* 78.1 (January 2004): 7-28; Russel Snyder-Penner, "The Ten Commandments, the Lord's Prayer and the Apostles' Creed as early Anabaptist Texts," *Mennonite Quarterly Review* 68.3 (July 1994): 318-335. Victor Thiessen, "Flugschriften eines Ritters im Kunstbuch des Marpeck-Kreises," *Mennonitische Geschichtsblätter* 60 (2003): 65-79.

A Confession of Faith by Jörg Maler (1554)

Translated by Victor Thiessen

A confession of faith based on the Holy Scriptures, put together as follows:

[I. Father]

The Father: I believe in God, Father, almighty creator of heaven and earth. In him alone I place all my comfort, hope and confidence; and in his grace and mercy, that alone (and no creature, be it as holy as it may be) can help me in all my fear and need and whatever might confront me, for the sake of his truth (Hos. 13 [:4]). And since he has become my father through Jesus Christ, I believe firmly that he will gladly help me with all his heart (Ps. 50 [:15]) according to his promise, and will stand beside me in all danger and will never forsake me (as long as I do not forsake him) neither here nor there. And since he is the almighty Lord, thus I believe that he can protect and sustain me against all things that oppose me, and wish to turn me away from him. For he alone is and will always be strong enough to oppose my enemies (be they visible or invisible), because of his omnipotence. And since he is also the creator of heaven and earth, I believe that he has all creatures in his hand and in his power (Rom. 8 [:38f.]), [so] that none of these can inflict a single wound upon me against his fatherly will. Thus I am made worthy of all good things and eternal life by this almighty Lord, God, Father, and creator. For from him alone all things come and whatever we require (out of necessity) will be given by him. For he will give himself wholly and completely to me (if I offer myself to him) with all that he is and has in heaven and earth, together with all creatures

(Rom. 8 [:28]) that serve me, are useful for me, and further me to eternal life, which God has prepared for all those who love him and obey his commands. He also offers godly power and strength in faith.

[II. Son]

The Son: I believe in Jesus Christ, his only begotten son, our Lord, who was conceived of the Holy Spirit, born of the virgin Mary, suffered under Pontius Pilate, was crucified, died, and was buried, descended to hell, rose again from death on the third day, ascended to heaven, sitting at the right hand of the just God, almighty Father, from where he will judge the living and the dead.

I believe from the heart that Jesus Christ, the Father's only son from eternity, took upon himself human form for my sake; was conceived by means of the Holy Spirit (Rom. 9 [:5]) (without human involvement), and was born of the pure virgin Mary (as from a proper, natural mother). And that this man was also truly God, as an eternal, inseparable person, both God and man (2 Cor. 5 [:15, 19]). And that this son of God and son of Mary, our Lord Jesus Christ, has suffered for me, a poor sinner, was crucified for me and died (according to the flesh), so that he could redeem me, a poor sinner, with his innocent blood from sin, death and the eternal wrath of God (Heb. 2 [:18]; Rev. 1 [:5]). Who himself suffered fear and death and experienced and overcame eternal hell, so that I was reconciled to God (through him), and in him became Lord over all my enemies through my faith in him.

I believe that without the death of this son, our Lord Jesus Christ (Gal. 3 [:5]), I could not have come to God's grace nor salvation, either through works or merits. I believe that Jesus Christ (Heb. 2 [:11]), my brother (1 Cor. 15 [:4]), is risen from the dead for the sake of my righteousness through him, and (Eph. 4 [:8]) has taken death and hell captive, that they can do no harm ever again.

For I confess that I would have had to die eternal death, if Christ had not come to my assistance (2 Cor. 5 [:21]), and took upon himself my sins and well-earned guilt, damnation and eternal death and paid for it through his suffering (Gal. 3 [:13]) (like an innocent lamb) (Isa. 53 [:5]); [he] also became condemned for my sake. I believe (John

1:[1]; Rom. 8 [:27]) that he still stands in my place and represents me daily before the Father as a true, merciful mediator, Saviour and sole, eternal high priest (1 Pet. 2 [:25]; 1 Tim. 2 [:5]) and bishop of my soul.

(Eph. 1 [:20-22]; Matt. 28 [:18]) I believe that Christ rules all things and fulfils all things together with God, also has power over all things in heaven and earth, a lord above all lords, (1 Tim. 6 [:15]) a king above all kings, and over all creatures in heaven, earth and under the earth, over death and life, over sin and righteousness. This same king and lord will go before me in my suffering (in the world) and death, will fight and do battle for me, so that I can be lord together with him over all my enemies (of the faith) for ever and always.

I believe also that the crucified Christ (the son of man) will come in the future (Luke 22 [:69]; Matt. 12 [:36, 41f.]) at the last day and judge and condemn all those (according to the words which he speaks) who did not believe in him (Rom. 2 [:6]; Rev. 2 [:23]), giving each according to his works, but will preserve me, together with all the faithful (and obedient) (whoever does not believe will be damned, (Mark 16 [:16]; Heb. 3 [:19]) from the severe judgment of eternal damnation, and will say to us, "Come here, you blessed of my Father, inherit the kingdom that has been prepared for you since the beginning of the world," Matthew 25 [:34].

[III. Holy Spirit]

(John 20 [:22f.]; Acts 2 [:3f.]; John 16 [:7]) I believe also in the Holy Spirit, who together with the Father and the Son is truly one God, and comes from and goes to the Father and the Son eternally, but in godly being and nature is a different person.

I believe in faith that I will be crowned by the same (who is a living, eternal, godly gift and offering), freed from sin, raised from the dead, happy and comforted, made free and secure in conscience. For this is my comfort (but not in the flesh) against all attacks of the enemies, which I sense and carry in my conscience and heart (Rom. 8

[:14]; Gal. 3 [:26]), that God wants to be my Father, forgive my sins through Christ and offer me eternal life through this Holy Spirit.

(Rom. 8 [:26]) I believe that this Holy Spirit helps me bear my weakness and represents me with unspeakable yearnings and sighs, strengthens me and enlightens my heart to acknowledge (Eph. 2: [7f.]) the unfathomable riches of fatherly mercy; that he has given and presented to me through pure grace, without any merits and works of my own effort, solely for the sake of Christ his beloved son, through which such things of the Father are and will be offered to me.

The Holy Spirit alone has enabled me to know all this, who ignites my heart (with love) and enlightens me with the understanding and wisdom that such gifts come from above, as Christ promised me when he said (John 7 [:38f]), "'Whoever believes in me, as the Scriptures say, from his body will flow streams of living water.' This he said of the Spirit, who all shall receive who believe in him." From this faith the fruits of the Holy Spirit arise and flow, as Paul proclaims (Gal. 5 [:22]): "Love, peace, joy, patience, kindness, goodness, faithfulness, gentleness, power are of him."

[IV. Church]

I believe in one holy Christian church, which is the community of saints, gathered through the Holy Spirit. I believe that the Christian church is on earth (and will be, Matt. 24 [:14]; 1 Thess. 4 [:16f.]), until he comes again at the end to proclaim judgment).[1] That is the community and number or assembly of all Christians, in which there is one God, one Lord, one Spirit, one faith, one baptism, Eph. 4 [:4-6]; of which Jesus Christ is the one partner and bridegroom of the church. I believe that this church is the spiritual body and Christ is its only head.

I believe that Christ is the Saviour of this, his body and church (Eph. 5 [:25-27]; Titus 3 [:5]), "and gave himself for it (out of love), by which means he has made her holy and has purified her through baptism in the word. Thus he has fashioned for himself a glorious community that has neither spot nor wrinkle nor anything of the sort" (that is, punishes evil according to the word, at least as much as has been revealed); "they are, rather, holy and without blemish"[2] (foremost before the judgment seat), "a pillar and foundation of truth" and without argument ([1] Tim. 3 [:15].

[V. Forgiveness]

I believe that forgiveness of sins [takes place] in this Christian community (Matt. 18 [:15-18]) (where it is gathered in the Lord), for it is a kingdom of grace (in Christ), of true indulgences [*Ablass*] for sin (not from Rome) (Matt. 16 [:19]). And outside of such Christendom [*christenheit*] there is no salvation nor forgiveness of sins (1 Pet. 3 [:21]; Rom. 6 [:3f.]; Rom. 8 [:4]). I believe that no one can be saved unless they are planted (that is, through baptism) with good water (according to the order of the Spirit of Christ) in this community and church as a living member in its body through personal faith. I believe, that in this kingdom, sins will be forgiven not just once (1 John 2 [:1]; Heb. 5 [:1]), but as often as one seeks and desires it from the heart.[3] For Christ is the true doctor, who cares for the sick and waits upon them, helps them, strengthens them and makes them healthy, as Isaiah says, "A bruised reed he will not break, and [will] not extinguish a glowing wick" Isaiah 42:3.

[VI. Resurrection]

I believe in the resurrection of the flesh, that my body—which the worms eat, or will be taken away in another way as God ordains it (1 Cor. 15 [:42])—will rise again incorruptible (Phil. 3 [:21]; 2 Cor. 3 [:10f.]) in clarity according to the pleas of Christ to the Father (John 17 [:9f.]); for Christ will raise him up on the last day according to his promise, when he says, [John 6 [:40, 54] "This is the will of him who has sent me, that whoever sees the son (meaning, with spiritual eyes) and believes in him, has eternal life. And I will raise him up on the last day." "And whoever eats of my flesh and drinks of my blood, he has eternal life, and I will raise him up on the last day."[4]

[VII. Eternal Life]

I believe that after this life there will be an eternal life, that I shall live forever and eternally with Christ (and all those who belong to him and confess him alone), according to the words of his promise, where he says (John 5 [:24]), "Truly, truly, I say to you, whoever hears my words (meaning: with the inner ear) and believes in him who sent me, has eternal life and will not face judgment, but he has already passed from death to life." And (John 8 [:51]) "Truly, truly, I say to you, if one obeys my word, he will not see eternal death" (John 6 [:51]). "I am the living bread come from heaven" (says Christ), "whoever eats from this bread will have eternal life."[5]

[Summary and Conclusion]

In summary and conclusion, here is my advice (out of love), that every God-fearing Christian who is devoted to the truth should build on this most holy faith of Christ (Jude 1 [:20]) through the Holy Spirit (Wis. 1 [:5]) (who alone will live in them who are not subject to sin) and fight nobly (2 Tim. 2 [:5]) (for no one will be crowned who does not fight well). And in all patience (Phil. 2 [:15]) be manly as a holy Christian through all trials and temptations, like a light in the world in the midst of this adulterous and perverted race. There is no other way about it: (2 Tim. 3 [:12]) whoever will live a sanctified life in Christ must suffer persecution and (Acts 14 [:22]) can only enter into the kingdom of God through much tribulation (Isa. 59 [:15]). Truly, whoever refrains from evil is allowed the spoils. Therefore hold fast to the comforting assurance of Christ, your Saviour (who also took this path). Believe firmly in his word, when he says (John 11: [25f.]), "I am the resurrection and the life; whoever believes in me, will live, even though he die. And whoever lives in this way, and believes in me, he will not die eternally."

Christ your Saviour will not forsake you. Be comforted by his words, when he says (John 16 [:33]), "In me you have joy, in the world fear; but be comforted, I have overcome the world." And this (2 Tim. 2 [:19]): "The solid ground of God is firm and has this seal: The Lord knows his own" (Rom. 8 [:9, 16]). He who has the Spirit of Christ is his, and the same Spirit assures our spirit, that we are God's children, as Christ also says (John 10 [:27-30]), "My sheep hear my voice and I know them and they follow me, and I give them eternal life, and no one will take them out of my hand. The Father, who has given them to me, is greater than all, and nothing can tear them from my Father's hand. I and my Father are one."

In a final summation, dear Christian, commend your soul, indeed all your ways (Ps. 31 [:6]; 37 [:5]) and things to your true God and Father, to whom you have entrusted and given yourself through faith and baptism (in Christ) according to his holy command, and speak with your heart as did your trustworthy brother Christ on the cross [Ps. 31 [:6]]: "Father, into your hands I commend my spirit for all time." May the eternal Father help us (in grace) to true rest, and lead us through his good angels, that we may achieve a happy resurrection (with Christ) at the last judgment. Amen. He wishes that we not be separated from his grace. Amen. But may his holy union (in Christ) be borne in mind at all times by us, the poor and needy, from now to eternity. Amen. Protect holiness and look upon that which is upright in all that you do (Ps. 37 [:11]), for in the end you will have peace with God in eternity.

In Christ the Lord,
Jörg Probst Rotenfelder, whom they
call Maler [painter]
1554

4

Swiss Brethren Confession of Hesse [(1578)]

Introduction

Beginning in the late 1520s, a rich variety of Anabaptists were active in the German territory of Hesse, partially due to the tolerant policies of Landgrave Philip of Hesse and his heirs. The first Anabaptists in the region were sympathetic to peasant anticlericalism, no doubt influenced by their leader, Melchior Rinck, erstwhile associate of Thomas Müntzer. In the 1530s, a number of Melchiorites came to the territory under the leadership of Peter Tasch and Georg Schnabel. After a number of these joined the state church in 1539, Swiss Brethren and a remnant of Hutterites emerged as primary representatives of Hessian Anabaptism.

In January, 1577, administrators informed Landgrave Ludwig of Upper Hesse that Anabaptists were in his territory. One of the Anabaptist leaders, Hans Pauly Kuchenbecker, was summoned for questioning in Marburg. Kuchenbecker faced a number of Lutheran theologians, who were concerned about defining and preserving orthodoxy, and would publish their own standard in 1580, the *Book of Concord*. In response to this questioning Kuchenbecker produced a 38-article confession of faith, which did not simply reflect his own views, but was a representative document shaped and informed by several years of debate between Swiss Brethren and magisterial reformers.

The Hessian confession begins by following the outline of the Apostles' Creed, and then addresses other central loci of Christian theology. It also includes topics related to economics and family matters including the proper upbringing of children, which suggests that the Swiss were becoming concerned about practical matters of daily living and were facing questions related to how one passes on the faith to the next generation. Other emphases in the confession include the importance of conversion, rebirth, and living a morally upright life. In continuity with the Schleitheim Articles of 1527, the confession also stresses the conviction that Christians are to be separate from the world.

Unusual is the fact that the Hessian confession does not include any articles relating to the sword or the oath. It is unlikely that the Swiss had changed their views on these matters. Above all, the Swiss were interested in producing an irenic document that would find acceptance among Lutheran authorities.

Interesting to note is that the supporting Scripture passages for the articles are written out in full. The Swiss Brethren were attempting to be biblically transparent with their theological arguments. The Swiss, furthermore, employ supporting biblical texts beginning systematically with Old Testament passages and then moving to the New Testament.

This translation by Werner O. Packull is based on Günther Franz's edition of the confession in his volume *Urkundliche Quellen zur hessischen Reformationsgeschichte*, IV.

Bibliographical Sources

Günther Franz, *Urkundliche Quellen zur hessischen Reformationsgeschichte*, IV: *Wiedertäuferakten 1527-1626* (Marburg: N. G. Elwert'sche Verlagsbuchhandlung, 1951); Werner, O. Packull, "The Confession of Swiss Brethren in Hesse, 1578: Introduction" (Waterloo: Unpublished manuscript, 2001); C. Arnold Snyder, "The Confession of the Swiss Brethren in Hesse, 1578," in *Anabaptism Revisited: Essays on Anabaptist/Mennonite studies in honor of C. J. Dyck*, edited by Walter Klaassen (Waterloo: Herald Press, 1992), 29-49.

Swiss Brethren Confession of Hesse [(1578)]

Translated by Werner O. Packull

The Confession of Christian faith and brotherly union in the faith by some new born Christians and chosen children of God who are presently scattered here and there.[1]

> *He who is pious and upright will live in his faith and trust.* Hab. 2 [:4], Rom. 1 [:17], Heb. 10 [:38].
>
> *For if one believes with the heart, one becomes righteous, and if one confesses with the mouth, one becomes blessed [selig].* Rom. 10 [:10].
>
> *Without faith it is impossible to please God. For whoever wants to come to God must believe that he exists and that he rewards those who seek him.* Heb. 11 [:6].
>
> *Whoever is wise, will understand these things; whoever understands will recognize them; for the ways of the Lord are true, and the upright will walk in them, but the godless will stumble in them.* Hos. 14 [:9].

Since true faith in Christ justifies,[2]

it should be thoughtfully meditated on, which is not every person's gift.

For this reason we should not consider it lightly.

For if a person does not have love and does not bear good fruit, as James tells us, that person is dead.

For this reason we need to examine and test ourselves, whether we stand in the true faith, grounded in the holy Scriptures; in a faith not invented by humans,

but based on Jesus Christ, the true corner stone.

Such a faith will endure like gold and silver which has been tried and purified seven times in fire.

So it is with a true Christian who is tried and purified.

He will be given an inheritance,

an imperishable crown, eternal life.

Amen. Amen. Amen.

Preface

Our Lord Jesus Christ teaches us in the Gospel that if we believe in him and remain in his Word, we will be his true disciples and recognize the truth,[3] and through such faith we will inherit eternal life; as he promises: *whoever believes in me has eternal life*. Item: *All who believe in me will not be lost, but have eternal life*. Item: *Whoever believes in him will live, even though he die and the person who lives and believes in me, will never die eternally*. John. 3 [:15, 16, 36]; 6 [:40, 47]; 8 [:51]; 11 [:25, 26]; 20 [:31]. Item: *Who hears my word and believes the one who has sent me, has eternal life and does not come into the judgment, but has prevailed from death to life*. John 5 [:24] Of this there is much testimony in the Gospel.

The holy apostles teach us also that there is no other salvation and *no other name given to humankind through which they will be saved [than the name of Christ Jesus]*. And there is manifold witness: *the one who believes and is baptized will be saved [selig]*, but *the one who does not believe is condemned*, Mark 16 [:16]. For *you are all children of God through Christ Jesus; for as many as are baptized they have put on Christ, for in Christ neither circumcision nor foreskin counts, but faith active in love.* Gal. 3 [:26-27]; 5 [:6].

Because of your faith *you will rejoice with unspeakable and exalted joy, and you will attain the purpose of your faith, namely the salvation of your soul.* 1 Pet. 1 [:9].

And in addition Christ faithfully warned his disciples and followers when he spoke to them concerning the end of the world, Matt. 24 [:5], that they should be on guard, not to be misled, for many will come in His name and mislead many. People will rise against people, and one kingdom against the other, and false Christians and false prophets will arise and do many signs and wonders in order to mislead the elect. And the elect will be hated by all and persecuted, and the abomination will stand in the holy place. And because unrighteousness will take over, love will grow cold in many, in the same measure as was the case at the time of Moses and Lot.

Thus the apostles also faithfully warn us in regard to the falling away; as Paul states in 2 Thess. 2 [:1-4, 11-12]: *that the day of the Lord will come only after the falling away, so that the son of perdition who places himself in the temple and claims to be god may be revealed.* Item: *God will send them a strong delusion, and will thus judge them because they did not believe the truth but took pleasure in unrighteousness.*

Item: *in the last days there will come a horrible time, because humans will care only about themselves; love money, be proud and arrogant, blaspheme, be disobedient to their parents, ungrateful, unspiritual, unfriendly, contrary, abusive, unchaste, without love for the good, from whom we must turn away; who always learn but never arrive at the knowledge of truth.* 2 Tim. 3 [:1-5, 7].

Item: *in the last days some will depart from the faith and join the erring, deceiving spirits who have seared consciences, who forbid marriage and insist on abstinence from foods which God created.* 1 Tim. 4 [:1-3].

For this reason the Apostle Paul teaches and admonishes us to *practice what he taught by word of mouth and in his Epistles, so that we should separate ourselves from every brother who does not walk according to the instructions we have received from Paul.* 2 Thess. 2 [:15]; 3 [:6].

For there is no other Gospel than that of our Lord Jesus Christ, which some want to pervert. But Paul states: *that even if we or an angel from heaven should preach a gospel contrary to that which we preached to you, let him be accursed,* Gal. 1 [:8], a statement Paul repeated a second time.

Since then in these last days, we see and hear of such errors, abominations, divisions, open sins and unrighteousness, we have, in the fear of God, taken this to heart and humbled ourselves before God with a repentant life, and prayed to God the highest for understanding and for the power of his holy Spirit. We have diligently examined the holy Scriptures, of the prophets, of Christ and of his apostles, and have taken cognizance of their teaching, life and behaviour, their order [*Ordnung*], practice and commandments. We have united in a union of brotherly love and brought together in writing the confession of faith which follows, as we have understood it, and we are prepared to confess this faith and also to support it with holy Scriptures.

It is our desire to exercise Christian virtue in confessing our faith in humility, patience and brotherly love, and to demonstrate this faith in common love so that we may with all the believers rejoice eternally for the sake of the Christian faith, with unspeakable glorious joy, and inherit the end of our faith, that is the salvation of our soul. And this we wish all our enemies and friends and all who desire it in their heart, through Jesus Christ, our Lord and Saviour. Amen.

[I.] Concerning the Holy Scriptures

We believe, acknowledge and confess that the holy Scriptures, both Old and New Testaments, were ordered by God to be written, and that they were written by holy men driven [*getrieben*] by the Spirit of God. The believing new-born Christians and children of God should therefore use the Scriptures for teaching, admonition, for discipline and improvement, and to demonstrate that the foundation of their faith is in harmony with the Scriptures.

Witness of the Holy Scriptures

And the Lord said to Moses, "Write these words; for in accordance with these words I have made a covenant with you and with Israel." Exod. 34 [:27].

Send into me the Holy Spirit, and I will write everything, which has happened from the beginning of the world, so that the people who will live in the last days may find a way and live. 4. Esdra 14 [Abs. 4].

Go, therefore, and write it on their tablet, and inscribe it in a book, that it may be a law, so that it may remain with their descendants as a continuing witness. Isa. 30 [:8].

And thus did the Lord speak to Jeremiah: *Record diligently all the words that I have spoken to you in a book.* [Jer. 36:2].

One will record it in writing so that the descendants read it and that future generations praise the Lord. Ps. 102 [:18].

Search the Scriptures of the Lord and read them: nothing will remain unfulfilled; none shall be wanting, not even a companion, for what the mouth of the Lord has commanded his Spirit carries out. Isa. 34 [:16].

The Jews at Berea were more noble and better behaved than those in Thessalonica, for they accepted the Word and examined the Scriptures daily to see if these things were so. Acts 17 [:11].

But what was written before our time was written for our instruction, so that by steadfastness and by encouragement of the Scriptures we might have hope. Rom. 15 [:4].

And since you know the Scriptures from childhood on, they can make you wise unto salvation through faith in Christ Jesus; because all Scripture is inspired by God and profitable for teaching, for discipline, in righteousness that a man of God may be complete, equipped for every good work. 2 Tim. 3 [:15-17].

For no prophecy ever came by the mere impulse of man, but holy men spoke, moved by the Holy Spirit. 2 Pet. 1 [:21].

But they were written down for our instruction, upon whom the end of the ages has come. 1 Cor. 10 [:11].

[II.] Concerning God

We believe, acknowledge and confess one united, eternal and almighty God, who has neither beginning nor end, who fills all in heaven and earth and sustains all being [wesen], who is invisible and incomprehensible, to whom nothing is hidden, who knows the heart, desires and thoughts of all humans, who hears, knows and sees all things in heaven and earth, in the sea and under the earth.

Witness of the Holy Scriptures

Hear , O Israel: The Lord our God is one Lord; and you shall love the Lord your God with all your heart, and with all your soul, and with all your might. Deut. 6 [:4-5].

I am the God Schadai,[4] that is the Almighty sufficient one who overflows with goodness. Gen. 17 [:1].

For who is a God like the Lord? And who is a rock like our God? Ps. 18 [:31].

But the Lord is a true God; he is a living God and an everlasting King. When he is angry the earth quakes. Jer. 10 [:10].

But ask the beasts, and they will inform you; the birds of the air, and they will tell you; or ask the plants of the earth, and they will tell you; and the fish of the sea they will reveal it to you; namely that the hand of the Lord has done all this. In his hand is the soul of every living thing and the breath of all humankind. Job 12 [:7-10].

Then Job answered the Lord and said: "I know that you can do all things, and that nothing is hidden from you. Job 42 [:1-2].

Whatever the Lord pleases he does, in heaven and on earth, in the sea and in the deep. Ps. 134 [:135:6].

The seven eyes signify that the Lord's eyes range through the whole earth. Zech. 4 [:10].

The word of the Lord came to Jeremiah: Behold, I am the Lord, the God of all flesh; is anything too hard for me? Jer. 32 [:27].

I am the one who is; I am the first and the last. My hand laid the foundation of the earth, and my right hand spread out the heavens; Isa. 48 [12-13].

But Jesus looked at them and said to them, "With men this is impossible, but with God all things are possible". Matt. 19 [:26]; Mark 10 [:27]; Luke 18 [:27].

I am the A [Alpha] and the O [Omega], that is, the beginning and the end, says the Lord, who is and who was and who comes, the Almighty. Rev. 1 [:8].

And before him no creature is invisible, but all are open and laid bare to his eyes; about him we have to speak. Heb. 4 [:13].

[III.] Concerning God

We believe, acknowledge and confess God as Lord and Creator of heaven and earth and of all that is in it, visible or invisible, also the sea and all flowing water, all living creatures in heaven and on earth, in the sea and under the earth.

Witness of the Holy Scriptures

In the beginning God created heaven and earth, the sea and everything that is therein, all beasts and worms, everything that is on the earth, all the birds under the heavens, and also humankind. Gen.1.

Behold, the heaven and the heaven of heavens is the Lord's and the earth with all that is in it. Deut.10 [:14].

Happy is he whose strength is the God of Jacob, whose hope is in God his Lord, who made heaven and earth, the sea, and all that is in them. Ps. 145 [146: 5-6].

O Lord God of hosts, you alone are God, over all the kingdoms of the earth; you alone created the heaven and earth. Isa. 37 [:16].

It is I who by my great power and my outstretched arm have made the earth, with the humans and the beasts that are on the earth. Jer. 27 [:5].

And the apostles lifted their voices united to God and said: Lord, you are the God who made the heaven, the earth and the sea and everything that is in them. Acts 4 [:24].

Paul and Barnas said: we preach to you the Gospel, to convert you from these useless things to the living God, who made heaven and earth and the sea and all that is in it. Acts 14 [:15].

God who made the world and everything in it, since he is a Lord over heaven and earth, and has given everyone and everything life and breath, does not live in a temple made by human hands and does not need to be nurtured by human hands as if he needed someone's help. Acts 17 [:24-25].

And you Lord have from the beginning founded the earth, and the heavens are the work of your hands. They will pass away, but you will remain. Heb. 1 [:10-11].

For every dwelling is created by someone, but God is the one who created all things. Heb. 3 [:4].

[IV.] Concerning God

We believe, acknowledge and confess God, the Father of Jesus Christ and of all believers, of the new-born Christians, who through his Word and the power of the Holy Spirit are born again, who in their life time believed God's Word, repented, turned from sin and to God.

Witness of the Holy Scriptures

You are our Father, though Abraham does not know us and Israel does not acknowledge us; you, O Lord, are our Father and our Redeemer; this is your name from eternity. Isa. 63 [:16].

Praised are you, Lord God of Israel, our father from eternity to eternity. 1 Chron. 29 [:10].

For as a father loves and forgives his children, so the Lord is to those who keep him before their eyes. Ps. 103 [:13].

I will tell of the decree of the Lord: He said to me: You are my son, today I have begotten you. Ps. 2 [:7].

Thus we have only one God, the Father, from whom all things exist and we in him. 1 Cor. 8 [:6].

Jesus said: I praise you, Father, Lord of heaven and earth. Matt. 11 [:25].

You shall call no man your father on earth, for one is your father, the one who is in heaven. Matt. 23 [:9].

For this reason I bow my knees before the Father of our Lord Jesus Christ who is the true father over everything that is called father in heaven and on earth. Eph. 3 [:14-15].

For through faith in Christ Jesus you are all God's children; for as many of you as are baptized have put on Christ. Gal. 3 [:26-27].

And because we are his children, God has sent the Spirit of his Son into our hearts, crying, Abba! Father! Gal. 4 [:6].

One Lord, one faith, one baptism, one God and Father of us all, who is above all and through all and in us all. Eph. 4 [:5-6].

See what great love the Father has given us, that we should be called children of God. For this reason the world does not know us, because it does not know him either. 1 John 3 [:1].

I will be to him a father, and he shall be to me a son. Heb. 1 [:5].

[V.] Concerning God

We believe, acknowledge and confess that God is not a father of the unbelievers, of the unrepentant or of the godless of the world who remain hardened in their sins and in unbelief, and who remain in their evil and unrepentant ways to the end, who do not accept Christ and who do not want to turn to God.

Witness of the Holy Scriptures

The wrong and perverted ways have corrupted him and they are no longer his children because of their blemish. Deut. 32 [:5].

A son honours his father, and a servant his master. If then I am a father, where is my honor? And if I am a master, where is the fear of me? Mal. 1 [:6].

Jesus said to them, if God were your Father, you would love me, for I proceeded and came from God.

You are of your father the devil, and your will is to do your father's desires. He was a murderer from the beginning, and has nothing to do with the truth, because there is no truth in him, for he is a liar and the father of lies. John 8 [:42, 44].

These are not the children of God but of the flesh. Only the children of God, of the promise, are reckoned as the seed. Rom 9 [:8].

Whoever is born of God does not sin; for God's seed abides in him, and because he is born of God he cannot sin. By this the children of God are manifest as well as the children of the devil; for whoever does not act righteously is not of God, neither is the one who does not love his brother. 1 John 3 [:9-10].

Anyone who transgresses and does not abide in the teachings of Christ does not have God; he who abides in the teaching of Christ has both the Father and the Son. 2 John 1 [:9].

We know that anyone born of God does not sin, but keeps himself, and the evil one does not touch him. We know that we are of God, but the whole world is in the power of the evil one. 1 John 5 [:18-19].

For whatever is born of God overcomes the world; and our faith is the victory that has overcome the world. 1 John 5 [:4].

[VI.] Concerning Christ

We believe, acknowledge and confess Jesus Christ, a Son of God, our Lord, born of the Father, God of God, of divine being, like God in might, power, glory; the eternal Word of the Father through whom all things were created, the first born of all creatures, the image of the invisible God and the splendour of his glory.

Witness of the Holy Scriptures

The Lord said to me: You are my son, today I have given birth to you. Ps. 2 [:7].

You love righteousness and hate wickedness [unbill]. Therefore God, your God, has anointed you with the oil of gladness above your fellows. Ps. 44 [45:7].

And his name will be called wonderful counselor, mighty God, eternal father, the prince of peace. Isa. 9 [:6].

In the beginning was the Word, and the Word was with God, and God was the Word. The same Word was in the beginning with God; all things were made through it, and without it nothing was made. John 1 [:1-3].

I and the Father are one. John 10 [:30].

Philip, he who has seen me has seen the Father. Do you not believe that I am in the Father and the Father in me? John 14 [:9-10].

He is the image of the invisible God, the first-born of all creatures; for through him all things were created in heaven and on earth, the visible and invisible. Col. 1 [:15-16].

For in him dwells the whole fullness of deity bodily, and you are full of the same who is the head of all principalities and authority. Col. 2 [:9-10].

And we are in him who is true, in his Son Jesus Christ, who is the true God and eternal life. 1 John 5 [:20].

For to what angel did God ever say, You are my Son, today I have given birth to you? Or again, I will be a father to him and he will be a son to me? Heb. 1 [:5].

And this is his commandment, that we should believe in the name of his Son Jesus Christ.

Whoever confesses that Jesus is God's Son, in him God abides and he in God. 1 John 3 [:23]; 4 [:15].

[VII.] Concerning Christ

We believe, acknowledge and confess that Jesus Christ, God's Son, our Lord and Saviour, is the true Messiah and champion [*silo*], prophet and king, who was to come into the world, whom God had promised from the beginning in the Scriptures to the patriarchs.

Witness of the Holy Scriptures

I will put enmity between you and the woman, between your seed and her seed; and it shall bruise your head and you will bruise his head. Gen. 3 [:15].

The scepter shall be taken from Judah,... until the champion comes and to him all peoples will pay homage. Gen. 49 [:10].

A star shall come forth out of Jacob, and a scepter shall rise out of Israel. Num. 24 [:17].

The Lord your God will raise up for you a prophet like me from among you, from your brethren -- him you shall heed. Deut. 18 [:15].

I will raise up for myself a faithful priest, who shall do according to what is in my heart and in my mind [gemuet]. 1 Kings 2 [1 Sam. 2:35].

Nevertheless, I will install my king over holy Mount Zion. I will tell of the law; the Lord has said to me: You are my son, today I have given birth to you. Ps. 2 [:6-7].

Behold, a young woman shall conceive and bear a son, and shall call his name Immanuel, God with us. Isa. 7 [:14].

Behold your God! Behold, the Lord God the Almighty will come with might and rule with his arm. Isa. 40 [:10].

Behold, the days are coming, says the Lord, when I will raise up for David a righteous branch,[5] *and he shall reign and administer wisely, and shall execute justice and restore righteousness in the land.* Jer. 23 [:5-6].

And you, Bethlehem Ephratah, you are too little to be numbered among the glorious princely cities of Judah; nevertheless, from you shall come forth one who is to be a ruler and sovereign in Israel. Mic. 5 [:2].

Rejoice, O daughter of Zion! Take notice; your king comes to you; the righteous one, humbly[6] *and riding on a donkey, on a young foal of a she-donkey.* Zech 9 [:9].

[VIII.] Concerning Christ

We believe, acknowledge, and confess that Jesus Christ, God's Son, our Lord and Saviour, the promised Messiah, the Word of the Father, was sent by God the Father from Heaven for our salvation.

Witness of the Holy Scriptures

Behold, I am laying a stone, a tested stone, a precious cornerstone, for a sure foundation in Zion, so that the one who trusts in him will be well founded. Isa. 28 [:16].

For the glory of the Lord shall appear, and all flesh shall see it, for the mouth of the Lord has spoken it. Isa. 40 [:5].

O you heavens, shower from above, and let the clouds rain down righteousness; let the earth open up and bring salvation so that righteousness may bloom forth; I the Lord shall bring it about. Isa. 45 [:8].

The Lord shall bare his holy arm before the eyes of all the gentiles; and all the ends of the earth shall see the salvation of our God. Isa. 52 [:10].

And in the days of these kings the God of heaven will set up an eternal kingdom, which will never be destroyed. It will be like a stone torn from a mountain without the use of human hand. Dan. 2 [:44-45].

Joseph, you son of David, do not fear to take Mary as your wife, for that which is conceived in her is of the Holy Spirit. Matt. 1 [:20]; Luke 1.

No one ascends into heaven except the one who descended from heaven, namely the Son of man, who is in heaven. John 3 [:13].

I am the living bread which came down from heaven; the one who eats of this bread will live in eternity. John 6 [:51].

And he said to them: You are from below, I am come from above; you are of this world, I am not of this world. John 8 [:23].

I proceeded from the Father and have come into the world; I am leaving the world again and going to the Father. John 16 [:28].

The first Adam was made into the natural being; the last Adam into the spiritual one. The first man was from the earth and earthly; the second man is the Lord from heaven. 1 Cor. 15 [:45, 47].

Sacrifices and offerings you did not desire, but a body you have prepared for me. Heb. 10 [:5].

[IX.] Concerning Christ

We believe, acknowledge and confess that Jesus Christ, God's Son, our Lord and Saviour, the Word of the Father, came into the flesh, was conceived by the Holy Spirit; took on the seed of Abraham according to the promise; became flesh in the virgin Mary through the power and work of the Holy Spirit.

Witness of the Holy Scriptures

And God said to Abraham, in you shall all generations be blessed. Gen. 12 [:3].

There shall come forth a shoot from the stump of Jesse, and a branch shall grow out of his roots. And the Spirit of the Lord will rest upon him. Isa. 11 [:1-2].

I have found David, the son of Jesse, a man after my own heart, who will do all my will. Out of his seed God has, according to his promise, raised a Saviour for the people of Israel. Acts 13 [:22-23]

Now the promises were made to Abraham and to his offspring. He does not speak of the offspring in the plural, but as of one, and "in your seed," which is Christ. Gal. 3 [:16].

That is why the promise was made through faith, in order that the promise may rest on grace and be guaranteed to all his descendants. Rom. 4 [:16].

To them belong also the patriarchs from whom Christ has come according to the flesh. God who is over all be blessed forever. Rom. 9 [:5].

God sent his Son in the form of sinful flesh. Rom. 8 [:3].

Since therefore children share in flesh and blood, he himself likewise partook of the same nature. For he nowhere takes on the nature of angels, but the seed of Abraham. He had to become like his brethren in every respect. Heb. 2 [:14, 16].

By this you recognize the Spirit of God: every spirit which does not confess that Jesus Christ has come in the flesh is not of God. And this is the spirit of antichrist, of whom you have heard that he comes and is already in the world. 1 John 4 [:2-3].

[X.] Concerning Christ

We believe, acknowledge and confess that Christ Jesus, God's Son, our Lord and Saviour, the promised Messiah, the Word of the Father, who became human, was born out of Mary, the pure virgin. He is true God and man.

Witness of the Holy Scriptures

Behold, a young woman shall conceive and bear a son, and give him the name Immanuel, that is, *God with us.* Isa. 7 [:14].

For to us a child is born and a son is given; and the empire will rest on his shoulders. Isa. 9 [:6].

Which God has promised through his prophets in the Holy Scriptures, concerning his Son, who was to be born of the seed of David, according to the flesh and proven a Son of God according to the Spirit. Rom. 1 [:2-4].

But when the time was fulfilled, God sent his Son, who was born of a woman under the law, so that he might redeem those who were under the law. Gal. 4 [:4-5].

She will bear a son, and you shall call his name Jesus, for he will save his people from their sins. Matt. 1 [:21].

When Jesus was born in Bethlehem in the Jewish land during the days of King Herod, behold wise men came from the East, etc. Matt. 2 [:1].

And while they were there, the time came for her to be delivered, and she gave birth to her first-born son and wrapped him in diapers. Luke 2 [:6-7].

And the angel said to the shepherds: Be not afraid; for behold, I bring you great joy which will come to all the people; for to you is born this day in the city of David a Saviour, Christ the Lord. Luke 2 [:10-11].

And the shepherds went and found both Mary and Joseph, and the babe lying in the manger. And when they had seen it, they spread the word which had been told them concerning this child; and all who heard it wondered at what the shepherds told them. Luke 2 [:16-18].

[XI.] Concerning Christ

We believe, acknowledge and confess that Jesus Christ, God's Son, our Lord and Saviour, suffered in the flesh at Jerusalem under Pontius Pilate,[7] was crucified, died and was buried.

Witness of the Holy Scriptures

He is led like a sheep to the slaughter, and like a little lamb before its shearers opened not his mouth. He was taken away without justification and without delay, and they made his grave with the godless and with the rich in his death. Isa. 53 [:7-9].

Behold, we are going up to Jerusalem; and the Son of man will be delivered to the chief priests and scribes, and they will condemn him to death, and deliver him to the Gentiles to be mocked and scourged and crucified. Matt. 20 [:18-19].

Pilate released Barabbas, but Jesus he ordered to be flogged and turned him over to be crucified. Matt. 27 [:26]; Mark 15 [:15]; Luke 23 [:25]; John 19 [:16].

And he said to them: O you foolish ones and slow of heart to believe all that the prophets have spoken! Did not Christ have to suffer these things? Luke 24 [:25-26].

Let all the house of Israel therefore know assuredly that God has made this Jesus whom you crucified both Lord and Christ. Acts 2 [:36].

For to this you have been called, because Christ also suffered for us, leaving us an example, that we should follow in his steps. 1 Pet. 2 [:21].

Since therefore Christ suffered in the flesh for us, arm yourselves with the same thought. 1 Pet. 4 [:1].

Through suffering and death Jesus was crowned with glory and honour, because he, by God's grace, was the first to taste death. Because he suffered and has been tempted, he is able to help those who are tempted. Heb. 2 [:9, 18].

He humbled himself and became obedient unto death, yes, even to death on a cross. Phil. 2 [:8].

[XII.] Concerning Christ

We believe, acknowledge and confess that Jesus Christ, God's Son, our Lord and Saviour, through divine power descended into hell and redeemed the souls of the believing Old Testament patriarchs.

Witness of the Holy Scriptures

The Lord kills and brings to life; he leads into hell and out again. 1 Sam. 2 [:6].

For this reason I will make you a light to the gentiles, to open the eyes that are blind, to ransom the prisoners and those who sit in the darkness of dungeons. Isa. 42 [:6-7].

I will redeem them from hell, save them from death. I will be your death, O death; I will be your destruction, O hell. Hos. 14 [:14].

For you will not forsake my soul in hell, and you will not permit your beloved to see decay. Ps. 16 [:10].

But God will redeem my soul from hell's power, for he has accepted me. Ps. 49 [:16].

For his soul has not been abandoned in hell, and his flesh has not seen corruption. Acts 2 [:27].

He ascended on high and led captivity captive. He gave gifts to humankind. To say he ascended implies that he had first descended into the lower parts of the earth. Eph. 4 [:8-9].

Death is swallowed up in victory. Death, where is your sting? Hell, where is your victory? 1 Cor. 15 [:55].

He went and preached to the spirits in prison, who formerly did not believe. 1 Pet. 3 [:19-20].

For this is why the gospel is also preached to the dead, so that they too may be judged in the flesh like other humans, but that in spirit they may live unto God. 1 Pet. 4 [:6].

I have the keys of death and hell. Rev 1 [:18].

I saw an angel coming down from heaven, holding in his hand the key of the bottomless pit and a great chain, and he seized the dragon, that ancient serpent. Rev. 20 [:1-2].

[XIII.] Concerning Christ

We believe, acknowledge and confess that Jesus Christ, God's Son, our Lord and Saviour, rose from the dead on the third day.

Witness of the Holy Scriptures

For as Jonah was three days and three nights in the belly of the whale, so the Son of man will be three days and three nights in the heart of the earth. Matt. 12 [:40].

It is written, that Christ should suffer and on the third day rise from the dead, and that repentance and forgiveness of sins should be preached in his name to all nations. Luke 24 [:46-47].

But the angel said to the women: He is not here; for he has risen, as he said. Matt. 28 [:6].

Why do you seek the living among the dead? He is not here, but risen. Luke 24 [:5].

For as yet they did not know the Scripture, that he must rise from the dead. John 20 [:9].

And with great power the apostles gave their testimony to the resurrection of the Lord Jesus. Acts 4 [:33].

We believe in him who raised our Lord Jesus from the dead, who was put to death for reasons of our sins, and who was raised for the sake of righteousness. Rom. 4 [:24-25].

If now the spirit of him who raised Jesus from the dead dwells in you, then he who raised Christ Jesus from the dead will also bring alive your mortal bodies. Rom. 8 [:11].

For to this end Christ died and rose again, that he might be Lord both of the dead and of the living. Rom. 14 [:9].

But Christ has been raised from the dead, and has become the first among those who have fallen asleep. 1 Cor. 15 [:20].

When therefore he was raised from the dead, his disciples remembered that he had said this. John 2 [:22].

But if you confess with your mouth that Jesus is the Lord, and believe in your heart that God raised him from the dead, you will be saved [selig]. Rom. 10 [:9].

[XIV.] Concerning Christ

We believe, acknowledge and confess that Jesus Christ, God's Son, our Lord and Saviour, ascended into heaven and is seated at the right hand of God, the almighty Father.

Witness of the Holy Scriptures

The Lord says to my lord: Sit at my right hand, till I make your enemies your footstool. Ps. 110 [:1].

And after he had spoken to them, the Lord was taken up into heaven, and seated himself at the right hand of God. Mark 16 [:19].

And it happened that while he blessed them, he parted from them and ascended into heaven; and they worshiped him. Luke 24 [:51-52].

I am ascending to my Father and your Father, to my God and your God. John 20 [:17].

No one ascends into heaven but he who descended from heaven, namely the Son of man who is in heaven. John 3 [:13].

When he had said this and as they were looking on, he was lifted up, and a cloud took him out of their sight. Acts 1 [:9].

But when Stephen, full of the Holy Spirit, gazed into heaven, he saw the glory of God, and Jesus standing at the right hand of God; and he said: Behold, I see the heavens open, and the Son of man standing at the right hand of God. Acts 7 [:55].

And he made him sit at his right hand in heaven and placed him above all principalities and powers and dominions, and above every name that is named, not only in this world but also in the one to come. Eph. 1 [:20-21].

For this reason God has exalted him and bestowed on him the name which is above every name, that at the name of Jesus every knee should bow, in heaven and on earth and under the earth. Phil. 2 [:9-10].

Who has gone into heaven and is at the right hand of God, and to him are subject all angels, authorities, and powers. 1 Pet. 3 [:22].

[XV.] Concerning Christ

We believe, acknowledge and confess that Jesus Christ, God's Son, our Lord and Saviour, will come again on the last day to judge the living and the dead.

Witness of the Holy Scriptures

For the Son of man will come with his holy angels in the glory of his Father and he will repay every one according to their works. Matt. 16 [:27].

Before him will be gathered all the nations, and he will separate them one from another like a shepherd separates the sheep from the rams. Matt. 25 [:32].

The Father has given the son all power to hold the judgment. John 5 [:22].

Jesus said: All authority in heaven and on earth has been given to me. Matt 28 [:18].

This Jesus, who was taken up from you into heaven, will come in the same way as you saw him go into heaven. Acts 1 [:11].

And he commanded us to preach to the people, and to testify that he is the one ordained by God to be judge of the living and the dead. Acts 10 [:42].

Now he commands all humans everywhere to repent, because he has set a day on which he will judge the whole world in righteousness by a man whom he has appointed. Acts 17 [:30-31].

For we must all appear before the judgment seat of Christ, so that each one may receive good or evil, according to what he has done in the body. 2 Cor. 5 [:10].

When the Lord Jesus is revealed from heaven with his mighty angels in flaming fire, inflicting vengeance upon those who do not know God and upon those who do not obey the gospel. 2 Thess. 1 [:7-8].

And those who curse you will have to give account to him who is ready to judge the living and the dead. 1 Pet. 4 [:4-5].

Behold, he is coming with the clouds, and every eye will see him and every one who pierced him. Rev 1 [:7].

[XVI.] Concerning the Holy Spirit

We believe, acknowledge and confess one Holy Spirit who proceeds from the Father and the Son, the same God, divine might, power and glory, so that God the Father, Son and Holy Spirit in the Holy Trinity are one divinity.

Witness of the Holy Scriptures

There are three that give witness in heaven, the Father, the Word and the Holy Spirit; and these three are one. 1 John 5 [:7-8].

In the beginning God created the heavens and the earth... and darkness was upon the face of the deep; and the Spirit of God was moving over the waters. Gen. 1 [:1-2].

By the word of the Lord the heavens were made, and all their host by the Spirit of his mouth. Ps. 33 [:6].

The Spirit of God has made me, and the breath of the Almighty has given me life. Job 33 [:4].

The Spirit of the Lord fills the whole earth, considers what is high to be good, preserves all things, and knows all that is said. Wisdom 1 [:7].

What his mouth commands, his Spirit completes. Isa. 34 [:16].

After that I will pour out my Spirit on all flesh and as a result your sons and daughters will prophecy. Joel 2 [:28].

And John saw the Spirit of God descending like a dove, and come over him. Matt. 3 [:16].

I will pray to the Father, and he will give you another comforter, to be with you for ever, namely the Spirit of truth, whom the world cannot receive. John 14 [:16-17].

And they were all filled with the Holy Spirit and began to speak in other tongues, as the Spirit gave them to speak. Acts 2 [:4].

All who are led[8] by the Spirit of God are children of God. The same Spirit bears witness to our spirit that we are children of God. Rom. 8 [:14, 16].

The Spirit of God's glory and goodness rests upon you; by others he is blasphemed, but by you he is honoured. 1 Pet. 4 [:14].

The natural person perceives nothing of the Spirit of God, for it is folly to him, and he is not able to recognize it. 1 Cor. 3 [2:14].

[XVII.] Concerning the Christian Church

We believe, acknowledge and confess one holy Christian church, one fellowship of saints, that is, of all believing new-born Christians and children of God, who through God's Word and the Holy Spirit are born again from above.

Witness of the Holy Scriptures

If then you will obey my voice and keep my covenant, you shall be my own possession among all peoples; for all the earth is mine. Exod. 19 [:5].

That which is perfect and most pure will overflow in righteousness, for the Lord God of hosts will create a perfect and cleansed church [gemein] in the midst of all the land. Isa. 10.

He has cleansed her through the Word and water bath, so that he might present a glorious church to himself, without spot or wrinkle or any flaw. Eph. 5 [:26-27].

I am in the fellowship of all who fear you and keep your commandments. Ps. 119

God is faithful in his promise through which you were called into the fellowship of his Son, Jesus Christ our Lord. 1 Cor. 1: [:9].

But you have come to Mount Zion, the city of the living God, to the heavenly Jerusalem, and to the many thousands of angels, and to the assembly of the first-born, who are enrolled in heaven. Heb. 12 [:22-23].

What we have seen and heard that we proclaim to you, so that you may have fellowship with us; and our fellowship is with the Father and with his Son Jesus Christ. If we say we have fellowship with him while we walk in darkness, we lie and do not live according to the truth. But if we walk in the light, as he is in the light, we have fellowship with one another, and the blood of Jesus his Son cleanses us from all sin. 1 John 1 [:3-7].

[XVIII.] Concerning the Forgiveness of Sin

We believe, acknowledge and confess the forgiveness of sin through the death and blood of our Lord Jesus Christ; [we believe, acknowledge and confess] the Christian church and community of the saints, [being those] who turn from their sins.

Witness of the Holy Scriptures

Is it not the case that if you do what is right, your sins will be forgiven; but if you do not what is right, sin waits before the door. Gen. 4 [:7].

Blessed is the person to whose deeds the Lord does not take into account, in whom there is no deceit. Ps. 18 [32:12].

As far as the sunrise is from the sunset, so far does he remove our transgressions from us. Ps. 103 [:2].

I will forgive their iniquity, and I will remember their sin no more. Jer. 31 [:34].

I have no pleasure in the death of the sinner, says the Lord God, but rather that he should turn from his way and live. Ezek. 18 [:23].

Who is a God like you, who pardons iniquity and passes over transgression? Mic. 7 [:18].

He who tries to conceal his transgressions will not prosper, but he who confesses and forsakes them will obtain mercy. Prov. 28 [:13].

Therefore I tell you, every sin and blasphemy will be forgiven, except the blasphemy against the Holy Spirit. Matt. 12 [:31].

If we confess our sin, he is faithful and just, and forgives our sin. 1 John 2 [1:9].

Of him all the prophets bear witness that every one who believes in him receives forgiveness of sins through his name. Acts 10 [:43].

[Paul was sent to the Gentiles] so that they might convert from darkness to light and from the power of the devil to God, so that they might receive the forgiveness of sins. Acts 26 [:18].

I am writing to you, little children, that your sins are forgiven and remitted through his name. 1 John 2 [:12].

[XIX.] Concerning the Resurrection of the Flesh

We believe, acknowledge and confess the resurrection of the flesh on the judgment day of both, the righteous and unrighteous. Every soul will take its body again and those who have done good will rise to eternal life, but those who have done evil will go to eternal damnation and pain.

Witness of the Holy Scriptures

For I know that my redeemer and protector lives, and that in the latter days he will stand upon the earth; and even though my flesh and skin be destroyed, I shall see God in my flesh. Job 19 [:25-26].

But your dead, like my dead body will rise again. Awake you who lie in the earth. Isa. 26 [:19].

And many of those who sleep in the dust of the earth shall awake, some to everlasting life, and some to eternal shame and contempt. Dan. 12 [:2].

And I will awaken the dead from their places and lead them out of their graves. 4. Esdra 2

But God is not a God of the dead, but of the living; because all live for him. Luke 20 [:38].

Do not marvel at this; for the hour is coming when all who are in the graves will hear his voice and come forth, those who have done good, to the resurrection of life, and those who have done evil, to the resurrection of judgment. John 5 [:28-29].

I have hope in God that there will be a future resurrection of the dead for which these also wait, namely both the just and the unjust. Acts 24 [:15].

The dead in Christ will rise first; after that we who are left alive. 1 Thess. 4 [:16-17].

And I saw the dead, great and small, standing before God, and the books were opened; and the dead were judged according to their works. And if one's name was not found written in the book of life, that person was thrown into the lake of fire. Rev. 20 [:12, 15].

[XX.] Concerning Eternal Life

We believe, acknowledge and confess an eternal life, which God wants to give to all believers and chosen ones who during their time on earth believed God's Word and in Christ, and turned from their sins [*bekert haben*].

Witness of the Holy Scriptures

What no eye has seen, nor ear has heard nor human heart conceived, that God has prepared for them who love him. Isa. 64 [:4]; 1 Cor. 2 [:9].

They shall have everlasting joy; joy and gladness will be with them and all sorrow and sadness will disappear. Isa. 35 [:10].

The Lord God will wipe away all tears and take away the reproach of his people from all the earth. Isa. 25 [:8].

And the meek shall praise the Lord, and their souls will live forever. Ps. 22.

And those who turn many to righteousness shall shine like the stars forever and ever. Dan. 12 [:3].

And every one who leaves houses or brother or sister or father or mother or wife or child or land for my name's sake will receive a hundredfold, and inherit eternal life. Mat. 19 [:29].

He who believes in the Son has eternal life; he who does not believe the Son will not see life, but the wrath of God remains upon him. John 3 [:36].

Truly, truly, I say to you, he who hears my word and believes him who has sent me has eternal life. John 6 [:47].

And the throne of God and of the Lamb shall be in it, and his servants shall serve him and they shall see his face, and his name will be on their foreheads. And night shall be no more; and they need neither lamp nor light of the sun, for the Lord God will illumine them, and they shall reign for ever and ever. Rev. 21 [22:3-5].

Amen. Amen. Amen.

[XXI.] Concerning Repentance[9]

We believe, acknowledge and confess that whoever wants to come to God and become a partaker of his heavenly kingdom, of his grace and Holy Spirit, must recognize and confess his sin and die to the same; turn to God with a repentant life, believe in Christ and be renewed through the Gospel.

Witness of the Holy Scriptures

You children of Israel, return to the Lord, the God of Abraham, and of Isaac, and of Israel; and he will again turn to you. 2 Chron. 30 [:6]

I will open and reveal my ways to him; for it is he who helps me and makes me whole. Before him the godless cannot survive. Job 13 [:15-16].

As soon as I said: I will confess my transgressions to the Lord, from that hour on you forgave my mischievous sin. Ps. 31 [32:5].

Seek the Lord while he may be found, call upon him while he is near; let the godless forsake his ways, and the unrighteous his plans; let him return to the Lord, that he may have mercy on him. Isa. 55 [:6-7].

Yet even now, says the Lord, return to me with all your heart, with fasting, with weeping, and with mourning. Joel 2 [:12].

Turn to the Lord and do not delay it from one day to the next, for his anger will come quickly and on the day of vengeance you will perish. Sir. 5 [:7].

Humble yourself while you can and indicate in time that you want to desist from evil. Let nothing hinder you from praying in time, and do not save your improvement until death. Sir. 18 [:20-21].

Behold, do proper fruits of repentance. The axe is already laid to the root of the tree. Every tree that does not bear good fruit will be cut down and thrown into the fire. Matt. 3 [:8, 10].

I came to call sinners to repentance and not the righteous. Matt. 9 [:13].

But if we confess our sins, he is faithful and just, and will forgive our sins and cleanse us from all unrighteousness. 1 John 2 [1:9].

And while God has overlooked the time of past ignorance, he now commands all humans everywhere to repent. Acts 17 [:30].

[XXII.] Concerning Baptism

We believe, acknowledge and confess a Christian baptism, which has to happen internally and externally; internally with the Holy Spirit and fire, outwardly with water, in the name of the Father, the Son and the Holy Spirit, to those who have repented, believed the Gospel, confessed their faith and desired to be baptized.

Witness of the Holy Scriptures

I baptize you with water for repentance, but he who comes after me will baptize you with the Holy Spirit and with fire. Matt. 3 [:11]; Mark 1 [:8]; John 1 [:26].

For John baptized you with water, but you will be baptized with the Holy Spirit not many days from now. Acts 1 [:5]

Therefore go into all the world, teach all nations and baptize them in the name of the Father and the Son and the Holy Spirit, teaching them to observe all that I have commanded you. Matt. 28 [:19-20]; Mark 16 [:15-16].

Peter said: Repent, and be baptized every one of you in the name of Jesus Christ for the forgiveness of your sins; and you shall receive the gift of the Holy Spirit. Those who received his word gladly were baptized, and there were added that day about three thousand souls. Acts 2 [:38, 41].

But when they believed Philip's preaching concerning the kingdom of God and in the name of Jesus Christ, they were baptized, both men and women. Acts 8 [:12].

And the official [eunuch] said: See, here is water! What is to prevent my being baptized? Philip said: If you believe with all your heart, you may be baptized. And he replied: I believe that Jesus Christ is the Son of God, and they both went down into the water, and Philip baptized him. Acts 8 [:36-38].

Peter said: Can any one forbid these people to be baptized with water, who have received the Holy Spirit just as we have? And he ordered their baptism in the name of Jesus Christ. Acts 10 [:47-48].

And they told [the jailor] the word of the Lord and to all who were in his house. And he and all his family were baptized at once. Acts 16 [:32, 33].

And many of the Corinthians who listened to Paul believed and were baptized. Acts 18 [:8].

On hearing this, they were baptized in the name of the Lord Jesus. And when Paul laid his hands on them, the Holy Spirit came upon them. There were twelve men in all. Acts 19 [:5-7].

[XXIII.] Concerning the Lord's Supper [*nachtmahl*]

We believe, acknowledge and confess that the Lord's Supper is an ordinance [*insatzung*] and commanded by our Lord Jesus Christ, and a strong bonding of the blessed fellowship of all believers with their Lord Jesus Christ. Just as the bread and wine are received with the mouth, so also the heavenly body, the flesh and blood of Jesus Christ, are received by the believing soul spiritually in faith.

Witness of the Holy Scriptures

For the Lord Jesus on the night when he was betrayed took the bread and gave thanks, broke it and gave it to his disciples and said: Take and eat, this is my body given for you. Do this in my remembrance. In the same way he also took the cup after the meal and said: Take and drink out of it, all of you. This cup is the new covenant in my blood shed for you. Do this as often as you drink in remembrance of me. Matt. 26 [:26-28]; Mark 14 [:22-24]; Luke 22 [:19-20]; 1 Cor. 11 [:23-25].

For as often as you eat of this bread and drink of this drink, you shall proclaim the Lord's death until he comes. 1 Cor. 11 [:26].

I speak to you as to wise ones; judge for yourselves what I say. The cup of thanksgiving with which we give thanks, is it not the fellowship of the blood of Christ? The bread which we break, is it not a fellowship of the body of Christ? For we, the many, are one bread and one body; because we are all partakers of one bread. 1 Cor. 10 [:15-17].

He who eats my flesh and drinks my blood has eternal life, and I will raise him up at the last day. For my flesh is food indeed, and my blood is drink indeed. He who eats my flesh and drinks my blood abides in me, and I in him. But when Jesus noted that his disciples murmured about it, he said to them: Does this offend you? What if you were to see the Son of man ascending to where he was before? It is the spirit that gives life, the flesh is of no avail; the words that I speak are spirit and life. But there are some among you who do not believe. John 6 [54-56]; [:61-64].

And they broke the bread in their houses. They partook of the food with joyful and generous hearts, praising God. Acts 3 [2:46-47].

[XXIV.] Concerning Authority

We believe, acknowledge and confess that the office and the authority to govern is ordained [*ingesatzt*] by God for the good of humankind. It is divinely ordained to rule and preserve. Servants of God should do nothing else except advance justice, protect the righteous and punish the evil doer.

Witness of the Holy Scriptures

Whoever sheds human blood that person's blood shall be shed by human hands. Gen. 9 [:6].

Search among the people for honest, god-fearing, trustworthy persons who hate profiteering and place them as rulers over the people. Exod. 18 [:21].

And Samuel said to all the people: There you see the Lord has chosen none is like him. And all the people said: Good fortune to the king! 1 Sam. 10 [:24].

He removes and installs kings; he gives wisdom to the wise and knowledge to those who have understanding; he reveals deep mysteries. Dan. 2 [:21-22].

You shall be wet with the dew of heaven, and the same needs to occur seven years in succession until you become aware that the Most High rules the human kingdoms, and gives them to whom he will. Dan. 4: [25].

God has placed himself in the community of the powerful, in the midst of the judges, in order to give judgment: How long will you judge unjustly and show partiality to the wicked? Speak justice for the poor and the orphans, maintain the right of the afflicted and the destitute. Rescue the weak and the needy; protect them from the oppression of the godless. Ps. 81 [82:1-4].

By me kings reign, and rulers make the right decrees. By me princes rule, and the lords govern the earth. Prov. 8 [:15-16].

The king's heart is like a stream of water in the hand of the Lord; he turns it wherever he will. Prov. 21 [:1].

For this reason I speak to you: Oh you kings and regents, learn wisdom that you do not fall, for those who keep justice will also be judged rightly. Wis. 6 [:10-11]

Jesus answered him and said: You would have no power over me had it not been given to you from above. John 29 [19:11].

The authority that exists is ordained by God, for the magistrate is God's servant to execute God's wrath on the evil doers. Rom. 13 [1, 4].

[XXV.] Concerning the Subjects

We believe, acknowledge and confess that subjects owe obedience to the authority [*obrigkeit*] and are to give them their dues, customs, rents, tribute as well as respect in everything that is not against God; to be subject to them, to serve them and to pray for them.

Witness of the Holy Scriptures

Now I will give all these lands to the Babylonian king Nebucadnezer, my servant, into his control. I will also place the animals of the forest into his service. And all people shall serve him and his son and his children's children, until the time of his territory has come. And the people who serve Nebucadnezer, and who do not want to bend their neck to the yoke of the Babylonian king, I bring them home. Jer. 2 [:6-8].

And pray ye for the well being of Nebucadnezer, the king of Babylon, and for his son, Balthasar, that we may serve them and live under their protection. Bar. 1 [:11-12].

The king is to be feared like a growling lion; he who despises him forfeits his life. Prov. 20 [:2].

Even in your thoughts you should not curse the king. Ecc. 10 [:20].

Give unto Caesar what is Caesar's, and to God what is God's. Matt. 22 [:21].

Let every person be subject to the governing authorities. For there is no authority except from God. Therefore one must be subject, not only to avoid God's wrath but also for the sake of conscience. For the same reason you should also pay taxes, for the authorities are servants of God intended for your protection. Rom. 13 [:1, 5-6].

Thus I admonish above all things that supplications, earnest prayers, intercessions, and thanksgivings be made for all humans, for kings and for all who are in positions of authority, so that we may lead a quiet and peaceable life. 1 Tim. 2 [:1-2].

Remind them to be submissive to rulers and authorities, to be obedient, to be prepared for any good work. Titus 3 [:1].

Be subject for the Lord's sake to every human institution, whether it be to the king as supreme, or to governors as sent by him to punish the evil doers, to the praise of those who do right. 1 Pet. 2 [:13-14].

[XXVI.] Concerning the State of Matrimony

We believe, acknowledge and confess that marriage is a good, God-given ordinance [*insatzung*]; that there should be one husband and one wife living in matrimonial love and faithfulness with each other. The husband as the head should with good common sense be the leader; and the wife should be subordinate and obedient to the husband and the two should be one flesh.

Witness of the Holy Scripture

And God the Lord said: It is not good that man should be alone; I will make him a helper who will be closest to him. He created husband and wife. Gen. 1 [2:18].

For this reason a man leaves his father and his mother and cleaves to his wife, and they shall be one flesh. Gen 2 [:24].

The one who finds a good, pious wife has found something far more precious than precious jewels brought from afar; for her husband can confidently trust in her, and he will have no lack of gain. She does him good, and no harm all the days of her life. Prov. 31 [:10-12].

Jesus said: Have you not read that He who made the human being at the beginning made them man and wife, and the two shall be one flesh. Matt. 19 [:4-5].

But because of the temptation to immorality, each man should have his own wife and each woman her own husband. But if you marry, you do not sin, and if a young woman marries, she does not sin, but they will have sorrows in the flesh. The further meaning is that those who have wives should live as though they have none. 1 Cor. 7 [:2, 28, 29].

However, let each of you love his wife as himself, and let the wife fear her husband. Eph. 5 [:33].

The servants of the fellowship should be the husband of one wife and good managers of their children and their household. 1 Tim. 3 [:12]

Let all honour marriage, and let the marriage bed remain undefiled; for God will judge the immoral and the adulterous. Heb. 13 [:4].

[XXVII.] Concerning Divorce

We believe, acknowledge and confess that husband and wife, who through a providential bringing together in holy matrimony have become one flesh, cannot be separated by anything, neither by ban, belief or unbelief, anger, quarrels or hardness of heart, with the exception of adultery.

Witness of the Holy Scriptures

So take heed in your spirit, and let none be faithless to the wife of his youth. Mal. 2 [:15].

They are no longer two but one flesh. What therefore God has joined together, that no one should separate. Matt. 19 [:6].

It was also said; Whoever divorces his wife, let him give her a certificate of divorce. But I say to you, that every one who divorces his wife, except on the ground of unchastity, makes her an adulteress; and whoever marries a divorced woman commits adultery. Matt. 5 [:31-32].

Do not withdraw one from another except perhaps by common agreement for a time. 1 Cor. 7 [:5].

If a brother has an unbelieving wife and she consents to live with him, he should not divorce her. And if a wife has an unbelieving husband and he consents to live with her, she should not divorce him. For the unbelieving husband is consecrated through his wife, and the unbelieving wife is consecrated through her husband, otherwise your children would be unclean, but as it is they are holy. A wife is bound to the law as long as her husband lives, but if her husband dies, she is free to be married to whom she wishes, as long as it is done in the Lord. 1 Cor. 7 [:12-14, 39].

For no one has ever hated his own flesh, but nourishes and cherishes it, just as the Lord does the church. Eph. 5 [:29].

Not I but the Lord charges those married that the wife should not separate from her husband. 1 Cor. 7 [:10].

[XXVIII.] Concerning the Raising of Children

We believe, acknowledge and confess that the parents, father and mother, husband and wife, are ordained by God and responsible to raise their children in the fear of God and to teach them to keep his commandments.

Witness of the Holy Scriptures

And these words which I command you this day shall be upon your heart; and you shall teach them diligently to your children, inoculating them and you shall talk of them when you sit in your house, when you travel, when you lie down, and when you rise. Deut. 6 [:6-7].

For I know that Abraham will charge his children and his household after him to keep the way of the Lord and to do what is right and just; so that the Lord may bring upon Abraham what he has promised him. Gen. 18 [:19].

For he has established a testimony in Jacob, and given Israel a law, which he commanded our fathers to teach their children; that they should set their hope in God, not forget his works and keep his commandments. Ps. 77 [78:5-7].

Do not withhold discipline from the child; if you discipline it with a rod, it will not die, but you will save it from hell. Prov. 23 [:13-14].

If you have sons, raise them in discipline and teach them, and bend their stubbornness from youth on. If you have daughters, protect their bodies and show yourself stern towards them. Sir. 7 [:23-24].

He who loves his son uses strict discipline, so that he may rejoice in the end, for the one who teaches his son and disciplines him does well. For even though the father dies, he is as if he has not died for he leaves behind one who is like him. Sir. 30 [:4].

And Tobias had a son, whom he called after his own name. And from his infancy he taught him to fear God, and to abstain from all sin. Tob. 1 [:9-10].

Fathers, do not provoke your children to anger, but bring them up in the discipline and instruction of the Lord. Eph. 6 [:4].

A bishop must be above reproach, the husband of one wife, and manage his own household well, keeping his children obedient and respectful in every way. 1 Tim. 3 [:2, 4].

[XXIX.] Concerning the Obedience of Children

We believe, acknowledge and confess that children are responsible to follow their biological parents, father and mother, to listen to them, to be obedient and subject to them and to hold them in honour.

Witness of the Holy Scriptures

Honour your father and your mother, that things may go well with you and you may live long on the earth. Exod. 20 [:12]; Deut. 5 [:16].

You shall be holy; for I the Lord your God am holy. Every one of you shall fear your mother and father. Lev. 19 [:2-3].

You, son, diminish the aging of your father; do not add sorrow to his life, and when his understanding decreases, be patient with him. Sir. 3 [:13].

Accept, my son, your father's discipline, and leave not the law of your mother; for it will bring wonderful honour upon your head, and a golden necklace for your neck. Prov. 1 [:8-9].

When I was a son with my father and the only beloved child of my mother, he taught me, saying: Let your heart hold fast to my words; keep my commandments, and you will live blessed. Prov. 4 [:3-4].

Why do you transgress the commandment of God for the sake of your tradition? For God commanded: Honour your father and your mother, but he who speaks evil of father or his mother shall die. But when you tell your father or mother that what they hoped to gain from you has been given to God, it implies that no one needs to honour his father or mother. Matt. 15 [:3-6].

Children, obey your parents in the Lord, for that is right. Honour your father and mother so that it may be well with you and that you may live long on the earth. Eph. 6 [:1-3].

Children, obey your parents in everything, for this pleases the Lord. Col 3 [:20].

For what son is there whom his father does not discipline? If you are left without discipline, which all have received, then you are an illegitimate child and not an heir. If we have had earthly fathers to discipline us, should we not much more be subject to the Father of spirits and live? Heb. 12 [:7-9].

I rejoice greatly to find some of your children following the truth. 2 John 1 [:4].

[XXX.] Concerning Disobedient Children

We believe, acknowledge and confess that disobedient, unbelieving, contrary children who do not obey father and mother and who do not follow the Word of God are an abomination and cursed by God. The parents must therefore be all the more persistent, diligent and earnest in their discipline, in order to resist their children's unrighteousness.

Witness of the Holy Scriptures

If someone has a self-willed, disobedient son who does not listen to his father and his mother, and, though they discipline him, will not give heed to them, then his father and his mother shall take hold of him and bring him out to the elders of his city and they shall say to them: This our son is self-willed and disobedient, he will not listen or obey us; he is a glutton and a drunkard. Then all the people of the city shall stone him, and thus evil shall be purged from your midst. Deut. 21 [:18-21].

Whoever curses his father and mother shall be put to death. Exod. 20 [21:17].[10]

Cursed is he who dishonours his father and mother. And all the people shall say, Amen. Deut. 27 [:16].

He who robs his father or his mother and thinks he does no wrong is a companion of destruction. Prov. 28 [:24].

And I have told him that I have placed judgment on the house of Eli forever; because he knew the iniquitous behavior of his children but did nothing to restrain them. 1 Sam. 3 [:13].

A daughter who does not obey, keep under a watchful eye, lest she misuse your laxity. Sir. 26 [:10].

A disobedient daughter place under watch, lest you give your enemies a cause to rejoice and you become an object of derision in the city. Sir. 42 [:11].

The one who mocks his father and scorns his mother's warning will have his eyes picked out by the ravens of the valley. Prov. 30 [:17].

The one who curses his father and mother, his light will be put out in the midst of darkness. Prov. 20 [:20].

Do not desire children who are good for nothing, and do not delight in the godless sons, even if there are many. Do not expect them to make anything of their lives, unless they are godfearing. Do not count on them or trust their work. It is better to die without children than to have godless ones. Sir. 16 [:1-3].

[XXXI.] Concerning Young Children

We believe, acknowledge and confess that children are blessed [or saved] because of the promise as long as they remain innocent and cannot yet distinguish between good and evil. As for Adam's or inherited sin, it is not accounted to them, even though they are of a sinful disposition, because through the death of Christ and through Christ's shed blood they are reconciled.

Witness of the Holy Scriptures

And your little children about whom you said they would become a prey, and your sons, who presently have no knowledge of good or evil, they shall go in. Deut. 1 [:39].

The fathers shall not die for the children, nor shall the children be put to death because of the fathers; every person shall die for his own sin. Deut. 24 [:16].

In those days they shall no longer say: The fathers have eaten sour grapes, and the children's teeth are awful. But every one shall die for his own sin. Jer. 31 [:29-30].

For the soul that sins must die. The son shall not suffer for the iniquity of the father, and the father shall not suffer for the iniquity of the son. Ezek. 18 [:20].

They also brought some young children to him that he might touch them, but when the disciples saw it, they rebuked them; but Jesus called them to him and said: Let the children come to me, and do not hinder them; for to such belongs the kingdom of heaven. Truly, I say to you, whoever does not receive the kingdom of God like a child shall not enter it. Matt. 19 [:13-14]; Luke 18 [:15-17].

And there arose among them the thought which one among them might be the greatest. But when Jesus perceived the thoughts of their hearts, he took a child and put him by his side, and said to them: Whoever receives this child in my name receives me, and whoever receives me receives the one who sent me. Luke 9 [:46-48].

For it had been the Father's pleasure that in him all the fullness of God should dwell, and that through him all things should be reconciled unto the Father, whether on earth or in heaven; so that he might make peace through the blood of his cross. Col. 1 [:19-20].

And he is the reconciliation for our sins, and not for ours only but also for the sins of the whole world. 1 John 2 [:2].

[XXXII.] Concerning private Property

We believe, acknowledge and confess that the new-born Christians and children of God may purchase their own properties, own them and use them if the opportunity presents itself. Transfers into their possession should happen within the proper legalities, and they should aid the poor with accommodation and in other ways, paying taxes.

Witness of the Holy Scriptures

Thus the field of Ephron, which was to the east of Mamre, and had the two-storied cave [zweifach höl] in it, was declared Abraham's possession. Gen. 23 [:17-18].

And Jacob bought the piece of land from the children of Hamor for a hundred pieces of money. Gen 33 [:19].

Yet thou, O Lord God, hast said to me: Buy the field for money and get witnesses. Jer. 32 [:25].

It is better to have little with justice than much unjustly. Prov. 16 [:8].

Is not this the kind of fast that I like, that you share your bread with the hungry, and bring the homeless poor into your house? Isa. 58 [:6-7].

I was a guest and you accommodated me. Truly, I say to you, what you did to one of the least of these my brethren, you have done to me. Matt. 25 [:35, 40].

Further, [because the time is short], let those who have wives live as though they have none, and let those who buy do it as though they would not keep it, and let those who use the world do it as though they did not need it. For this world is passing away. 1 Cor. 7 [:29-31].

Thus also, whoever among you does not renounce all that he has cannot be my disciple. Luke 14 [:33]

Therefore let your abundance during this present time of scarcity supply their need, and do it out what you have. 2 Cor. 8 [:14, 11].

But if we have food and clothing, so let us be content, because those who desire to be rich fall into temptation, into a snare, into many senseless and hurtful lusts that plunge men into ruin and damnation. As for the rich in this world, charge them not to be haughty, nor to set their hopes on uncertain riches but on the living God. 1 Tim. 6 [:8-9, 17].

If any one comes to you and does not hold to this teaching, do not receive him into the house nor give him any greetings. 2 John 1 [:10].

[XXXIII.] Regarding the Poor

We believe, acknowledge and confess that the believing, new-born Christians and children of God are responsible to look after the poor members among their fellow believers: the old, the sick, the widows, the orphans; to feed and provide for them and in addition to show common love to others in need.

Witness of the Holy Scriptures

If your brother becomes poor, and cannot maintain himself, you shall take him in as a house mate and maintain him. Lev. 25 [:35].

If there is among you a poor brother, you shall not harden your heart nor close your hand against him, but you shall open your hand to him, and lend him sufficient for his need. Deut. 15 [:7-8].

Lend your money to your brother and to your neighbour and do not bury it under a stone, lest it rust or rot. Sir. 29 [:10].

Give according to your ability. If you have much, give abundantly; if you have little, take care to share even some of it willingly. Thus you will store up a treasure and a good reward. For alms deliver from death, and will not suffer the soul to go into darkness. Tob. 4 [:8-10].

Share your bread with the hungry, and bring the homeless poor into your house. If you see one naked, cover him, and do not hide yourself from your own flesh. Isa. 58 [:7].

If your enemy is hungry, feed him; if he is thirsty, give him drink; for by so doing you will heap burning coals upon his head. Rom. 12 [:20].

I tell you, make yourselves friends by means of unrighteous mammon, so that when you are in need, they may receive you into the eternal habitations. Luke 16 [:9].

So let your abundance in these dire days of scarcity supply their need, so that afterwards their abundance may supply your need, and even things out. 2 Cor. 8 [:14].

But if any one has the world's goods and sees his brother in need, yet closes his heart against him, how does God's love abide in him? 1 John 3 [:17].

If a brother or sister were naked and in lack of daily food, and one of you says to them: Go in peace, be warmed and filled, without giving them the things they need for the body's survival, what does it help? James 2 [:15-16].

[XXXIV.] Concerning Work

We believe, acknowledge and confess that the believing, newborn Christians and children of God should seek and win their daily nourishment with honest manual labour, that they should seek to share with those in need. But they shall not engage in lazy, dishonest and useless merchant enterprises.

Witness of the Holy Scriptures

Because of the abundance of your merchant trade and big business, your heart has been filled with sacrilege and you have sinned. Ezek. 28 [:16].

It is rare that a merchant or retailer does not transgress or an innkeeper does not fail and sin. Like a post driven between two stones, so transgression and wrong is lost between selling and buying. Sir. 27 [:1-2].

Despise not the enterprise of hard work or the tilling of the soil which was ordained by the Most High. Sir. 7 [:15].

I coveted no one's silver, gold or apparel. You yourselves know that these hands ministered to my necessities, and to those who were with me. In all things I have shown you that by so toiling one must help the weak. Acts 20 [:33-35].

Let the thief no longer steal, but rather let him labour, doing honest work with his hands, so that he may be able to give to those in need. Eph. 4 [:28].

But aspire to live quietly, to mind your own affairs, and to work with your own hands, so that you may relate honourably to outsiders, and that you are without need. 1 Thess. 4 [:11-12].

We hear that some of you are living in idleness, mere busybodies, not doing any work. Now such persons we command to do their work in quietness and to earn their own bread. 2 Thess 3 [:11-12].

For you know that you should imitate us; we were not idle or unruly when we were among you; we did not eat anyone's bread without paying, but we toiled and laboured night and day, that we might not be a burden to any of you. 2 Thess. 3 [:7-8].

And the merchants of the Babylonian wares, who gained wealth from it, will fear for their gain, weep and suffer sorrow. Rev 18 [:15].

[XXXV.] Concerning Usury

We believe, acknowledge and confess that the newborn Christians and chosen children of God should not engage in usury [*wucher*] with their money but that they should help the poor and the needy without expecting repayment with interest, that is, to lend them money and await their reward from God.[11]

Witness of the Holy Scriptures

If your brother becomes impoverished and cannot maintain himself, you shall accept him as a member of your household that he live with you. Take no interest from him nor take more than you have given him, but fear your God; so that your brother may live beside you. You shall not lend him your money at interest, nor profit from the food you give him. Lev. 25 [:35-37]; Deut. 23 [:19].

Then Nehemiah said to them: Do you want to exact interest from your brothers? What you are doing is not good. Let us leave this burden of interest off. Then they said: We will do so. Then I shook out what was in my lap and said: So also may God shake out every man from his house who does not keep this promise; and all the assembly said, Amen. Neh. 5 [:7-13].

O Lord, who shall sojourn in thy tent? Who shall dwell on your holy hill? He who walks blamelessly, lives righteously, does justice and faithfully practices the truth from his heart; he who does not put out money at interest, and does not take a bribe against the innocent. Ps. 15 [:1-2, 5].

Even though I have not lent money for interest to anyone, yet they curse me. Jer. 15 [:10].

He insults the poor and needy and does not restore what had been pawned. He commits abominations, lends at interest, and takes more than needed. If he has done all these abominable things, he will not live but shall surely die. His blood shall be upon himself. Ezek. 18 [:12-13].

He who augments his wealth by charging interest in order to increase his riches, will gather for one who will kindly and freely give it to the poor. Prov. 28 [:8].

Love your enemies, do good, and lend, expecting nothing in return; and your reward will be great, and you will be the sons of the Most High. Luke 6 [:35].

[XXXVI.] Concerning Food

We believe, acknowledge and confess that all creatures which God created in order to nourish humankind are good and not to be disdained by the believers, in as much as they are received and enjoyed without annoyance, with thanksgiving to God.

Witness of the Holy Scriptures

Everything that lives and moves shall be food for you. I have also given you the green plants. Gen. 9 [:3].

Not what goes into the mouth defiles a person, but what comes out of the mouth. Matt. 15 [:11].

And remain in the same house, eating and drinking what they give you. Luke 10 [:7].

And there came a voice to him, "Rise, Peter; kill and eat." And the voice came to him again a second time, "What God has cleansed, you must not call unclean." Acts 10 [:13, 15].

Therefore let no one pass judgment on you in questions of food and drink or with regard to special days. Col. 2 [:16].

But I know and am persuaded in the Lord Jesus that nothing is unclean in itself; unless someone considers it unclean, for that person it is unclean. But if your brother is saddened by what you eat, you are no longer walking in love. Rom. 14 [:14-15].

Therefore, if a food offends or injures my brother, I would not eat meat eternally lest I irritate or anger my brother. 1 Cor. 8 [:13].

The Spirit says expressly that in later times some will depart from the faith and attach themselves to deceitful spirits who forbid marriage and enjoin abstinence from foods which God created to be taken with thanksgiving. For everything created by God is good, and nothing is to be rejected if it is received with thanksgiving; for then it is consecrated by the word of God and prayer. 1 Tim. 4 [:1, 3-5].

To the pure all things are pure, but to the impure and unbelieving nothing is pure; both their very mind [gemuet] and consciences are impure. Titus 1 [:15].

[XXXVII.] Concerning Pride

We believe, acknowledge and confess that all the arrogance, pride and pomp of this world are an abomination and hated by God. For this reason the believing, newborn Christians and chosen children of God should avoid arrogance in words, works, dress and in manners.

Witness of the Holy Scriptures

Arrogant pomp and pride are hated by God and all humans, and out of both arises much injustice. Why are you presumptuous, earth and ashes, arrogance and pride? I have rejected your inner being. Arrogance and pride of humans originates in their rejection of God who made them. Sir. 10 [:7, 9, 12].

Tobias admonishes his son and said: Never let pride or arrogance rule your mind or words; for all perdition began in pride. Tob. 4 [:14].

O Lord, you were never pleased with the proud, but the prayer of the meek has always pleased you. Jdt. 9 [13].

The Lord hates the arrogant and the proud-hearted; be assured, he will not let them go unpunished. Prov. 16 [:5].

In that day the Lord will take away their finery, their anklets, necklaces, headbands, crescents, pendants, bracelets, and the scarfs; their headdresses, the armlets, the sashes, the perfume boxes, and the amulets; the signet rings, their nose and earrings; their festive robes, their mantles, the cloaks, and their handbags; their garments of gauze, their linen garments, their turbans and their veils. Isa. 3 [:18-23].

Your pomp and the sound of your harp have descended into hell; maggots will be your bed and worms your covering. Isa. 14 [:11].

For all that is in the world, the lust of the flesh and the lust of the eyes and the pride of life, is not of the Father but is of the world. 1 John 2 [:16].

In the last days there will come abominable times; for men will be lovers of self, lovers of money and proud, arrogant blasphemers. 2 Tim. 3 [:1-2].

But you demonstrate your humility by being subject to each other, for God opposes the proud, but to the lowly he gives grace. 1 Pet. 5 [:5].

[XXXVIII.] Concerning the Ban

We believe, acknowledge and confess that the believing, newborn Christians and chosen children of God have to use the ban on those who teach error, who live and walk contrary to the Gospel of Christ.

Witness of the Holy Scriptures

I will be no longer with you unless you ban the idolatrous things from among you.[12] Josh. 7 [:12].

If your brother sins against you, go and tell him his fault, between you and him alone. If he listens to you, you have gained a brother. But if he does not listen, take one or two others along with you. If he refuses to listen to them, tell it to the church community [gemein]; and if he refuses to listen even to the church community, consider him a Gentile and a tax collector. Truly, I say to you, whatever you bind on earth shall be bound in heaven, and whatever you loose on earth shall be loosed in heaven. Matt. 18 [:15-18].

And you are arrogant, and have not cared very much to remove from among you the one who has done this evil deed. 1 Cor. 5 [:2].

Do not associate with any one who claims to be a brother, but is guilty of immorality, greed, or is an idolater, reviler, drunkard or robber. With such a one you should not even eat. For what business of mine are outsiders that I should judge them. Judge those who are inside. God will judge those on the outside. Put out the evil person from among you. 1 Cor. 5 [:11-13].

But we command you, brethren, in the name of our Lord Jesus Christ, that you withdraw from any brother who is not living in accordance with the instructions received from us. If any one is disobedient, indicate it or note it in a letter. Have nothing to do with such a person, so that he may be ashamed. 2 Thess. 3 [:6, 14].

After a factious person has been admonished once or twice, avoid him, have nothing more to do with that person, knowing that such a person is perverted and sins; he has condemned himself. Titus 3 [:10-11].

Conclusion

Let us hear the summary and conclusion of these matters. Keep your eyes on God and keep his commandments; because this concerns everyone. God will judge every deed, all intentions and all machinations and hidden, secret things, whether good or evil. Eccles. 12 [:13-14].

Thus says the Lord: Go on the roads, investigate and search for the ancient path, and if it is the good way, walk in it, that you may find rest for your soul. Jer. 6 [:16].

But to God, the King of eternity, the immortal, the invisible, the only God, be honour and glory, praise and thanks for ever and ever. Amen. 1 Tim. 1 [:17].

II

Confessions of North German/
Dutch Anabaptism

Confessions of the Lower Rhine and at Wismar

5

Kempen Confession (1545)

Introduction

By the middle of the sixteenth century, Swiss and South German Anabaptists were moving northward into the Lower Rhine regions where they met Anabaptists from north Germany and the Netherlands. Anabaptism was first introduced to the Low Countries through the activities of Melchior Hoffman in 1530. The soil was well prepared in the north for change through late-medieval mystical reforming currents such as the Devotio Moderna and the Sacramentarian movement. Reforming ideas also were fed by increasing social unrest, anticlerical sentiments, and eschatological expectation. Hoffman's initial Anabaptist activities took place in the province of East Frisia in the city of Emden where he was able to baptize some 300 persons. From Emden, Melchiorite missionaries quickly carried their understanding of the Christian message to other places, and their ideas soon found acceptance in cities like Amsterdam, Leeuwarden and Münster, as well as surrounding environs. In 1531, Anabaptists were present in the city of Cologne, and a year later, in München-Gladbach. Soon congregations could also be found in towns like Kempen, Krefeld and Rheydt. The Anabaptist communities were not large, but they were able to survive partially due to the sympathetic views of the authorities, who were promoting a moderate reformation of their own.

By the early 1540s, the Anabaptists in the region came under the influence of Dutch Anabaptists like Menno Simons and Dirk Philips, who had contact with local leaders Theunis van Jüchen of Sasserath and Michiel Oistwart. When, in the spring of 1545, the authorities of Electoral Cologne asked Anabaptists in Kempen about their beliefs, the congregation submitted a six-article confession, which Theunis had formulated, as an account of their faith. The congregation consisting of about twelve young families who earlier had joined the Protestant cause and had only recently converted to Anabaptism.

The confession follows the spirit of Menno Simons at a number of points. It emphasizes Christ's heavenly origins and maintains that only true reborn believers may participate in baptism and the Holy Supper. Rejecting the brand of revolutionary Anabaptism that emerged in the city of Münster, the confession speaks positively of governmental authorities, yet also emphasizes that the weapons of a Christian cannot be material, but must only be spiritual. The fourth article, which is the longest, reflects strong anticlerical sentiment and indicates why the Anabaptists could not join the broader reforming movement. They are not critical of leadership *per se*, but are concerned about the current leadership. In their view, true reform is only possible when genuine, reborn pastors, who have a direct call from God, are placed in leadership positions.

This translation by Karl Koop is based on J. F. G. Goeters' transcription in *A Legacy of Faith*.

Bibliographical Sources

Peter Dykema and Heiko Oberman, eds., *Anticlericalism in Late Medieval and Early Modern Europe* (Leiden: E. J. Brill, 1994); J. F. G. Goeters, "Das älteste rheinische Täuferbekenntnis," in *A Legacy of Faith: A Sixtieth Anniversary Tribute to Cornelius Krahn*, ed. Cornelius J. Dyck (Newton, KS: Faith and Life Press, 1962), 197-212; Christian Hege, "Lower Rhine," *Mennonite Encyclopedia III*, 407-08; Jacobus ten Doornkaat Koolman, *Dirk Philips: Friend and Colleague of Menno Simons, 1504-1568*, trans. William E. Keeney and ed. C. Arnold Snyder (Kitchener: Pandora Press, 1998); Karl Koop, "Worldly preachers and true shepherds: Anabaptist anticlericalism in the Lower Rhine," in *The Heart of the Matter: Pastoral Ministry in Anabaptist Perspective*, ed. Erick Sawatzky (Telford PA: Cascadia Publishing House, 2004), 24-38. A version of this essay was also published as "Worldly Preachers and True Shepherds: Anticlericalism and Pastoral Identity among Anabaptists of the Lower Rhine," *Mennonite Quarterly Review* 76.4 (October 2002): 399-411. Cornelius Krahn, *Dutch Anabaptism: Origin, Spread, Life, and Thought* (Scottdale: Herald Press, 1981).

Kempen Confession (1545)

Translated by Karl Koop

Honourable and gracious young nobleman and Lord Rennenburch: We poor, well-meaning subjects give an account to E.L.[1] so that he may understand our faith in Jesus Christ, which has been revealed to us through the merciful God. We confess before God and E.L. the same saving faith in Jesus Christ with good intentions (1 Pet. 3 [:15]), and also before all people who wish to hear from us, so that E.L. will take notice and come to recognize that we wish nothing but to seek alone the salvation of our souls and, like Christ, seek the well-being of the souls and lives of all people (Matt. 5 [:11], 10 [:17-22], 19 [:27-30]). Today we wish to follow Christ in all righteousness until death, and be prepared, as he has shown us, to suffer oppression and scorn from all people. As he has taught and commanded us today, according to the witness of the Holy Scripture, we are to do good to our enemies (Matt. 5 [:44]; Luke 6 [:27-28]; Rom. 12 [:14]).

[I.] Confession Concerning Christ and His Holy Incarnation

We confess and testify with Saint Paul that the man Jesus Christ is the Lord of heaven and of all heavens, as Paul has sufficiently made clear in 1 Cor. 15 [:47]. As Saint Peter also has testified concerning him in Matt. 16 [:16] and Luke 9 [:20] where he states, "You are the Christ, the living Son of God." Therefore, we also confess as Saint Peter has proclaimed that he is the living Son of God. We confess also that this only Son of God is the first born of God from eternity (Col. 1 [:15]); that this only Son of God has also been the powerful word of the Father in that he has also made everything—indeed, heaven and earth

97

and everything that there is, as it is written in John 1 [:1-3], Col. 1 [:16], and Heb.1 [:2]. According to Scripture we confess that he became flesh, as John 1 [:14] has stated and given witness saying, "The Word became flesh." In the same way Paul with Peter above confesses that he has been recognized and perceived as a man of heaven, and also Lord from heaven, as the living Son of God, conceived from the Holy Spirit (Matt. 1 [:18, 20]) and, according to Holy Scripture, was born out of Mary (Luke 1 [:35]).

As Christ himself speaks and testifies (John 6 [:48, 51, 53-58]), so also do we confess that he is that bread from heaven, yes also that true heavenly bread that he himself claims to be. This same heavenly bread is flesh that was given for the life of the world. We are therefore here to testify concerning Christ and his incarnation, and are truly united with Christ and his apostles. In brief words, this is what we understand. With God's help we will remain faithful, and neither the learned nor the gates of hell will lead us astray (Matt. 16 [:18]). May the Lord keep and protect his sheep on the right path, Amen.

[II.] Our Confession Concerning the Holy Baptism of Jesus Christ

Further, we confess and testify that Christ Jesus, in his holy words and ordinances, will stand and remain forever. Heaven and earth will pass away before the faithful will lose sight of his words or find them to be untruthful (Matt. 5 [:18]).

Since his holy word is eternal and cannot be changed we must, therefore, also always confess with Christ and his holy apostles that there cannot be any usage or practice of water baptism other than the baptism of faith that is based on faith in Christ, which is according to all righteousness and according to the will and the pleasure of his heavenly father as Matt. 3 [:6, 11], 28 [:18-20] and Mark 16 [:16] clearly testify of Jesus Christ.

In the same way the holy apostles have shown in all of their writings that they have practiced and taught only believers' baptism. As has already been made clear, they baptised believers according to the commandments and ordinances of their master Jesus Christ. Therefore we are united and at one with Christ and his holy apostles in our practice of baptising believers, as is written in Acts 2 [:38], 8 [:35-38], 10 [:44-49], 16 [:31-33], 19 [:2-6], Rom. 6 [:3-11], 1 Cor. 12 [:13], Titus 3 [:3-7], 1 Pet. 3 [:21].

And just as Christ our master, along with his holy apostles neither taught, wrote nor exercised the false practice of child-baptism, so also must we, to avoid damnation of our souls, neither teach, write about, nor practice the same. For all will be cursed who reject Christ's law as it is written in Deut. 4 [:2]; Acts 22 [:18-19] and Matt. 15 [:13]. Accordingly, all plants that are not from God must be pulled out. The almighty God help us to remain in the true faith through Jesus Christ, Amen.

[III.] Confession concerning the Holy Supper of Jesus Christ and to whom it is rightly given and commanded

We believe and confess that Christ Jesus has given and instituted a holy Supper for his beloved, holy disciples, using bread and wine for the purpose of remembering and proclaiming his death until he comes, as it is written and explained in Matt. 26 [:26-28]; Luke 22: [:19-20], and 1 Cor. 5 [:7], 10 [:16-17], 11 [:23-26].

Christ has neither given nor commanded anyone to practice this holy Supper except his holy and dear disciples alone, who have been born of the Holy Spirit, have forsaken all, and have followed after him the way of the cross in all oppression, scorn and suffering, as he also commanded in Matt. 10 [:16-25], 16 [:21], 19 [:27-30]; Mark 8 [:34-38], 10 [:28-31]; Luke 14 [:26-27], etc.

We must also confess that this holy Supper of Christ is nowhere given to unrepentant, unbelievers, sinners, idolaters, plunderers, murderers, the greedy, the haughty, prostitutes, adulterers, liars and drunkards. For in this way your righteousness cannot be practiced without condemnation and loss of righteousness as experienced by Judas.

False Christians and hypocrites should never practice nor prepare the Christian Supper since they are not true, obedient disciples of Jesus Christ. They are not born of Christ (1 Pet. 1), nor do they possess his Holy Spirit. They do not exhibit a recognizable exemplary life (John

13:35) since they are not born of the Holy Spirit from above (John 3:3-6), nor guided by the Spirit of Christ (Rom. 8:14). They have not yet become the new creation (Gal. 6:15) that is spoken of according to the peace of God and his mercy, because they are not spiritual. Rather, they are oriented towards flesh, greed and hardness of heart [*ertz gesinnet synt*]. Their hearts are not pure, but impure. They have neither come nor journeyed with patience to the foot of the cross of Christ. Rather, they are persecutors of Christians and enemies of the cross; for rubbish is their god and condemnation is their end, as it is written in Phil. 3 [:18-19].

This is our reasoning and testimony that the Supper should not be given to such false Christians who have such a confused faith. Christ has neither ordered nor commanded the Supper to be practiced in this way. Their hearts can never be cleansed from sin [solely] through bread and wine (Luke 24 [:31-32]; Acts 2 [:39-40], 4 [:32], 10 [:38], 13 [:38]). They will die and come to ruin in their sin since they do not seek the true faith of Christ. They do not cleanse their hearts and souls, nor become righteous and separated from false Christians (1 Cor. 5 [:9-13]; 2 Cor. 6 [:14-18]). Hence, they are not in possession of a Christian congregation. They neither want to believe nor be obedient to Christ. For this reason they should not practice the aforementioned holy Supper, which Christ gave and commanded his believing, true disciples, according to the Holy Scripture.

This is our motive and testimony concerning why we cannot participate in the Supper with confused Christians (why we cannot participate in such hypocrisy and sin) for they do not partake nor participate in the true, holy Supper of Jesus Christ according to the Holy Scripture (1 Cor. 5 [:8], 10 [:20-21], 11 [:27-32]).

[IV.] Why we cannot listen to these worldly preachers nor be present with their followers

We understand and thoroughly teach that there is no one who belongs to Christ unless he is born of him (1 Pet. 1 [:23]), possesses his Spirit, and is guided by it, as Paul testifies in Romans, the eighth chapter [v. 14]. Those born of Christ reject all that is visible, customary and transitory in the world, and follow him to the cross where there is oppression, scorn and suffering, as Christ himself speaks and testifies (Matt. 5 [:11], 10 [:16-25, 16 [:24-25]; Mark 8 [:34-35], 10 [:21], 13 [:9-13], etc.

All Christians in Christ must become new creatures in such a way that the old life of sin has passed away and everything has been made new, as is thoroughly explained in 2 Cor. 5 [:17] and Gal. 6 [:15]. In truth none can be identified as Christians unless they are new born spiritual persons, who at all times are tested and known by their fruits, as it is written in Matt, the seventh chapter [:15-19].

It is for this very reason, before God and all people, that we do not want to listen to the worldly preachers, nor associate with their adherents; for they have not been born of God from above (John 3 [:3-5]) and neither have they been sent by him. They do not recognize his divine power nor the characteristics of his divine nature (John 10 [:3-5]). They are fleshly, greedily and earthly minded and sell their word and teaching for a temporal and earthly salary, as if Christ gave of himself for no reason (Matt. 10 [:8]).

Having confused the order of Christ they are, therefore, not true shepherds, but hirelings (John 10 [:12]). Through participation in this false and disgraceful baptism, Supper and ban, etc., they have depended on human law and practice. In the process they have also blasphemed and disgraced the true righteous children of God, and betrayed and persecuted those who, in view of the truth, do not wish to fail in their doctrine and life. Since not all are guilty of these things and some still have a goodly nature they must nevertheless do their best and come to realise that they are not walking in the true, apostolic teaching, practice and order of Jesus Christ. Some of these believe to be serving God as they work together with a greedy unbeliever who, contrary to what is right, is awarded with an earthly salary. O dear friend, how far and distant are these things from God and his true disciples, etc.

Since they do not live up to the holy words of God, neither inwardly nor outwardly, and are not united with the Holy Spirit, it is evident that they are sent neither from God nor from his Holy Spirit.

How are they to preach when they have not been sent etc. (Rom. 10 [:15])?

Since they go about their work without being sent and without consequence do not adhere to the word of the Lord both in doctrine and in life, therefore we are admonished by God and his Holy Spirit to flee from such preachers, and avoid being with them or having them in our homes (Matt. 7 [:15-23]; John 10 [:5]; Rom. 16 [:17-18]; 2 Thess. 3 [:6]; 2 Tim. 3 [:13-14]; 2 John 1 [:10]).

We must, therefore, come to recognize the true teachers according to the witness and instruction of Holy Scripture (1 Tim. 3 [:1-7]; Titus 2 [:6-9]). These teachers are sent by God and remain in the written word, teaching and order of Christ. They reject all [human] reason and godlessness. With clean hearts and great clarity they freely speak words of penance and grace. Regardless of person they punish lords and princes, the high and the low, the educated and uneducated, male, female; for they know that the powerful, penetrating word of God has been given to all flesh (John 17 [:6-8]; 1 Cor. 1 [:17-29]; Heb. 4 [:12]). For all who do not submit to the word of God nor receive it in faith, must be judged and punished (John 12 [:48]; Deut. 10 [:17]; Rom. 2 [:11]; Acts 10 [:34]; 1 Pet. 1 [:17]; Acts 20 [:12]) whether emperor, king, doctor or teacher; for God does not distinguish between persons. In life and in death, these preachers practice baptism and the Supper according to the divine order as it has been given and commanded according to God's holy word. They live a life that is innocent, clean and which bears fruit. Each day they die with Saint Paul for the sake of all, and because of their godly witness they are held as sheep before the slaughter (Rom. 8 [:36]).

These teachers are sent from Christ and his beloved father throughout all time and commissioned to work in his vineyard, as he says, "See I sent you like sheep among wolves" (Matt. 10 [:16]; John 17 [:18]). [In times past] such true servants and godly lovers of truth, who had a genuine, clean heart of faith in Jesus Christ, were named, affirmed and taken up in the congregations by Paul, Timothy and Titus (1 Tim. 3 [:2-7]; Titus 1 [:5-9]). They taught sound doctrine and led the people, their flock, in a blessed, loving walk of the holy righteous life in Jesus Christ. Christ names all such teachers (John 10

[:2-4]), who convert the sheep by their true penitent life, true shepherds (Acts 2 [:38-40]; 1 Pet. 1 [:23]; Col. 2 [:10-13]). With the word of God in their hearts they clean and cut away the sin from the ungodly. In faith they remove from the unclean membership the false antichrists, all false practices, sin and human customs, and so are cleansed through the recognized faith in Jesus Christ. It is in Christ through whom the true teachers lead the sheep to eternal life. The true sheep also follow with joy the way to eternal life. This is the true meaning and teaching of Jesus Christ (John 10: [4]). It is thus by their fruits that the true teachers shall be known (Matt. 7 [:16-17]).

We should therefore not acknowledge any teachers of God who stand outside of what the Holy Scriptures teach and indicate to us; for everything must be run, recognized and held according to the witness of Scripture, as Christ testified with his holy apostles and all true prophets. All the teachers which holy Scripture does not uphold are, according to Christ's word, thieves and murderers, (John 10 [:1]), blind tempters, godless (Matt. 23 [:13-16]) and false prophets (Matt. 7 [15-16]), whom one should be able to recognize by their fruits. So then, in Romans 16 [:18], Paul refers to those who one should run away from and avoid as "servants of the belly" [*bouckdiener*]. In 2 Cor. 11 [:13] Paul calls them false apostles and dangerous workers. In Phillipians 3 [:2, 18-19] he calls them dogs and evil workers who are enemies of the cross; their glory is their shame and their end is damnation. In 1 Timothy 4 [:1] he also calls some teachers the devil. In 2 Timothy 3 [:8] he names the leaders in Egypt the same; for they seem to live a righteous life and neverthless have lost the power of God. Peter, in 2 Peter 2 [:17], calls them wells of water that are overcome with eternal darkness. The Holy Spirit in Revelation 9 [:3-5] calls them locusts, which torment and torture the conscience but never cleanse it of sin or make it whole. Of what use is it to them if they do not honour God? They have sought value and esteem but have not found it. According to the Holy Scripture they must all be rejected by God and his locked door (Matt. 25 [:11-12]). Similarly the useless servant will be bound and condemned to the eternal fire just as Christ himself spoke and testified in the same chapter [:30].

Therefore all the teachers and preachers of this world do not have the order of Jesus Christ and his Holy Spirit as noted above. Further they have walked outside of the witness of Paul (1 Tim. 3 [:2-7]; Titus 1 [:5-9]). The sovereigns and princes of this world, gifted with large salaries, send them. They are not sent from Christ and his holy, loving father and gifted with spiritual gifts. Rather, they seek the disgraceful prize of Baal and go their own way, away from God as explained above. They do not seek to bring sheep to pasture; rather, they waste all their time and always want to be served, but do not serve anyone themselves. They misguide and do not teach; they kill and do not bring life (Matt. 12 [:30]); scatter rather than gather; they concern themselves at all times with themselves and not the concerns of Jesus Christ and those next to them, etc. (Friendship with the world is enmity against God (James 4 [:4]).

Christ and his beloved disciples have therefore been disgraced, blasphemed and disowned from these preachers who have willingly wanted their own honour to be recognized by the world. These preachers call those of the world Christian, and Christians they call heretics. In a shameful fashion they hold at a distance the pure holy salvific [selickmakende] word of God in their teaching and life. That is why the holy Scriptures also call us (1 Cor. 10 [:14]; 2 Cor. 6 [:14-17]; Acts 18 [:4]) to give way, avoid, shun and flee, as the Scriptures have adequately indicated above.

Thus we poor children stand between God and the authorities in fear because of the judgment of the Pharisees, who have constantly called, driven and pressured the authorities so that innocent blood should flow (Acts 6 [:9-11]) as it is also written in Matt. 23 [:29-35] and Acts 18 [:24].

O you dear Lords and sovereigns, who pursue and pressure us like the Pharisees and false prophets. Now that the Holy Scripture has awakened us and has told us to flee and avoid as has been explained above, who should we obey—the eternal God or you mortal humans? I always notice that E.G. will judge for himself that God above deserves all the praise, as he wants our praise, for he is able to perish in this life and eternally in hell (Matt. 10 [:28]). But he cannot take the life of humans. This is thus our testimony and reason why we do not listen to these preachers, nor can we be seen with your disciples, as we have already explained with the Holy Scripture.

If we are now obedient to God and his holy word, we fall into the hands and punishment of E.G. If we are obedient to E.L.[2] we fall under God's anger and his punishment. Concerning this, in Hebrews 10 [:31] it is written: "It is terrible to fall into the hands of the living God." May the eternal God strengthen us in the faith, that we will experience none of this dread, Amen.

[V.] Confession of our Faith Concerning the Dear Authorities

We believe, confess and bear witness before God and all people that the authorities have been instituted and ordained of God, according to the witness of the Holy Scripture (Rom. 13 [:1-7]; 1 Pet. 2 [:13-17]). Christ himself also testified to this and commanded the same (Matt. 17 [:24-27], 22 [:15-22]), "Give to Caesar what belongs to him, and give to God the good that belongs to him," just as Christ with Peter gave Caesar the tax. In the same way we also believe and confess according to what has been commanded, that believers are obligated to give to all authorities protection, duty and taxes so that they can serve the office which God has given them.

This office is given to protect and defend the good and the righteous, for evil rules the world with force, and takes or deprives life and goodness with force. Murderers, robbers, arsonists, and such evildoers and villains, will also fall many times into the hands of the authorities and will experience judgment, sentencing and punishment, as the Holy Scripture bears witness to this, and as mentioned above, as in Rom. 13 [:1-7], etc.

Therefore we also confess that it is our duty before God to please such authority, so that we may have a godly life and in every way experience peace, as Saint Paul has written in 1 Tim. 2: [1-2]. This is God's will, who wishes that all people would come to such divine recognition, through which they might experience life and become righteous. God wants to grant and give this to those who with a pure heart desire to believe in this way, Amen.

Further, we believe and confess with pure hearts that no one should rise up or oppose with one's own power or with outward weapons, nor fight against the authorities in this way. Such a person will fall to the wrath and punishment of God, and also to the punishment of the authorities. May the mighty God give us wisdom in all things, that we rightly honour him, and that we may also rightly honour and give obedience to the dear government and conform to it in every way. This we do in order that we may be found righteous and blameless before the strict judgment of God. May everyone be paid according to his works as Christ clearly spoke about this in Matthew 25 [:14-46].

Moreover it is our belief and confession concerning power and authority that has been instituted, that the sword is given from God for the sake of evil to punish all evildoers. The eternal, almighty God wants to give the authorities wisdom and understanding, for them to understand their office in this manner, and to administer their responsibilities before God in a proper way. They should not dirty themselves at the expense of the innocent blood of the righteous through the advice of the academics who always harm the righteous, just as they did before and after all time with Christ and all the true prophets and apostles. God wants to treat the authorities with grace and forgiveness, who unwisely misappropriated innocent blood, and who long for the grace of God, and who wish to better themselves, so that no innocent blood will be forgotten nor before God upon someone's conscience.

We also do not desire to bring into action any violent, false and devilish spirits, who want to fight and dispute with the sword against the authorities or against some other people. For we believe and confess that such evil ones will fall many times together into the judgment and punishment of the authorities and also God, even if they have been baptized a hundred times. For, whoever is not given the sword, should also not take it up. Rather, the one who has been given the sword, that person alone should use it, as we above have sufficiently explained and given witness to with the Holy Scriptures.

[VI.] Concerning the Weapons of the True Faith in Christ

The weapon of the faithful, with which we should arm ourselves in times of conflict, is alone the powerful, holy, saving word of God. We take this on in faith and with a clean heart and fight with it against the enemy of our souls, which are all the devilish spirits, who with false teaching and human wisdom want to direct us away from Christ and his holy word of life. Indeed, before all devilish spirits and godlessness, we want to protect ourselves with the holy word of life, which can hold us and make us righteous.

We also confess that no other outward weapon is given or commanded except alone this spiritual sword, which is the word of God. And all insincere people or enemies, which we, with this holy word of God and weapon of the faithful in the Holy Spirit, cannot and are not able to quiet—because of these people we must suffer, and also carry all disgrace to our deaths in the same way as our master, Jesus Christ, has gone before us in all suffering. He has also called us to follow in disgrace, oppression and suffering. We also have the example of all the saints who have also had to suffer unto death, and had to carry all the insult of the world for the sake of the truth, which they have seen in Christ. Since Christ himself with his life has become an example of the cross and suffering, so also does the almighty, living God want to strengthen us in faith, that we may carry our cross and suffering with patience, through Jesus Christ, Amen.

For Christ speaks: Whoever acknowledges me before others, that person will I also acknowledge before my father in heaven (Matt. 10 [:32]). In this way we have also given our confession concerning the truth of Jesus Christ, so that it is recognizable that we seek nothing but alone the honour and praise of God, and we also want to show our obedience to the dear authorities, according to what Christ and his apostles have taught (Rom. 13 [:1]). We also wish all people, their lives and their souls goodwill, so that we may also become righteous and inherit an eternal kingdom, which is in heaven as Christ gave witness to, and who said that his kingdom was not of this world.

Therefore we do not desire to protect ourselves with weapons of outer steel [*ousserlichen ertzen wapen*] nor do we want to cause uproar. All who have done this or have planned to do such, these we note, as we made known above, that they have all fallen to the judgment of the authorities.

O you dear judges and lords; would that you let the innocent remain blameless and that you would preside over a just court, so that you will also not be judged from God, as Christ has taught (Matthew 7 [:1-2]). May the almighty God help us through his goodness to remain in the true faith through Jesus Christ, Amen.

6

Wismar Articles (1554)

Introduction

The issue of church discipline was central for Dutch Anabaptists and would occupy much of their theological discussion throughout the sixteenth and seventeenth centuries. A major challenge for the Anabaptists was to find agreement concerning the appropriate reasons for enforcing the ban, and to agree on the extent to which the practice of avoidance or shunning should be carried out.

The resolutions at a conference at Wismar, in Mecklenburg, Germany, represent an attempt by seven Dutch Anabaptist leaders to find consensus in these matters. According to Karel Vos, the following leaders were present at Wismar: Menno Simons, Dirk Philips, Leenaert Bouwens, Gillis van Aken, Herman van Tielt, Hans Busschaert, and Hoyte Riencx. Of the nine resolutions agreed to at Wismar, seven dealt with marriage, church discipline or polity issues.

While the resolutions were intended to resolve differences, they actually heightened the conflict between those who were advocating a more tolerant approach on church discipline, and those who were promoting a relatively strict position.

The eighth article that deals with whether Christians should be allowed to carry weapons corresponds with Menno Simons' and Dirk Philips' absolute rejection of warfare. However, that permission to carry a weapon is granted raises the question of whether the Dutch intended to support a strategy of avoiding detection, since failing to carry customary weapons might automatically identify one as an Anabaptist; or whether they were suggesting that limited self-defence, or defence of one's family, was permissible.

This translation by Cornelius J. Dyck is based primarily on the edition located in *Bibliotheca Reformatoria Neerlandica VII*, but also includes some comparisons of the editions listed below prepared by S. Blaupot ten Cate and Karel Vos.

Bibliographical Sources

S. Blaupot ten Cate, *Geschiedenis der Doopsgezinden in Groningen, Overijssel en Oost-Friesland, I* (Leeuwarden, 1842); S. Cramer and F. Pijper, *Bibliotheca Reformatoria Neerlandica VII* ('S-Gravenhage: Martinus Nijhoff, 1910); C. Arnold Snyder, *Anabaptist History and Theology: An Introduction* (Kitchener: Pandora Press, 1995); James M. Stayer, *Anabaptists and the Sword*, second edition (Lawrence: Coronado Press, 1976); Karel Vos, *Menno Simons, 1496-1561* (1914); Nanne van der Zijpp, "Wismar Resolutions," *Mennonite Encyclopedia IV*, 966.

[The Wismar Articles, 1554]

Translated by Cornelius J. Dyck

[I.]

First, we confess that persons who marry [someone] from outside of the congregation shall be put outside of the congregation and avoided until they show a proper Christian life before God and the brethren. Then the congregation is at liberty to receive them again, whether brother or sister, still observing their life and conduct for a time.

[II.]

Second, we confess and understand concerning the ban that buying and selling is wrong, unless the erring [banned] member is in need.

[III.]

Third, concerning relations between a husband and wife, we understand that the erring spouse, whether husband or wife, must be avoided and shunned, but if it is a case of a sick conscience which cannot understand the issue, the Scriptures militate against it. Therefore, a careful investigation should be undertaken to determine whether it is a sick conscience or simply the flesh. This can be clearly seen. And, if anyone wishes to join the congregation, but whose spouse is apostate, these rules shall apply.[1]

[IV.]

Fourth, if a believer and an unbeliever are married to each other and the unbeliever commits adultery, the marriage bond is broken. If it is one who confesses that he has fallen into sin, and desires to mend his ways, then the believers permit the believing mate to go to the unfaithful one to admonish him, if her conscience allows it in view of the circumstances. But if he is a deliberate adulterer, then the innocent party is free, provided that she confers with the congregation and remarries, according to opportunity, and concludes the matter with understanding.

[V.]

Fifth, concerning a believer and an unbeliever, if the unbeliever desires to separate from his spouse for reasons of faith, then the believer shall conduct herself honestly without marrying [another] for as long as the unbeliever is not remarried. But if the unbeliever marries, or commits adultery, then the believer may also marry, in accordance with the counsel of the elders and the congregation.

[VI.]

Sixth, if believing children, who have believing parents, [wish to be married] the congregation agrees not to consent to their marriage without the approval of the parents, if they are supported by their parents. But if the children have then honoured their parents in this matter, but the parents refuse to consent, they cannot deny the right of the children.

Yet if children have unbelieving parents the children should still honour them and seek their counsel. But if unbelieving parents refuse to give their consent the children shall submit themselves to the counsel of the congregation. We say that secret marriages are not desirable.

[VII.]

Seventh, we agree that it is in order to demand just payment for debts owed, provided that no ungodliness results from it.

[VIII.]

Eighth, concerning weapons, the elders are unable to consider it impure if a believer, traveling on a road according to the conditions of the land, carries an honest staff or a dagger over his shoulder as is the custom of the land. But to carry attack weapons, and to present them [for inspection] or use them, according to a command of the magistracy, the elders do not permit—except in a citizens army for national defense.

[IX.]

Ninth, no one is to undertake to preach or teach in the congregations of his own accord, but only if he is ordained or commissioned for this task by a congregation or the elders.

7

Concept of Cologne (1591)

Introduction

As Anabaptists from the southern regions of Germany continued to have contact with Anabaptists in the north, it became increasingly evident that the groups differed in matters of doctrine and church practice. For instance, many Dutch Anabaptists were shaped by Melchior Hoffman's doctrine of the incarnation that recognized that Christ had become human, but assumed that his flesh was "heavenly" and did not come from Mary. Most Dutch Anabaptist leaders, such as Menno Simons and Dirk Philips, held some version of this Melchiorite doctrine, while South German Anabaptists, often referred to as High Germans or Upper Germans, generally followed the understanding of the wider church, maintaining that Christ was fully divine and fully human, "born of the Virgin Mary."

On the matter of church discipline, differences between Anabaptists in the north and south also existed. Many of the northerners promoted a strict view of the ban, advocating even spousal separation in cases where one of the partners in a marriage had been banned. While acknowledging the importance of church discipline, the High Germans held more moderate views, rejecting the practice of spousal separation, and maintaining that the institution of marriage must be respected at all times.

From the 1550s onward, several conferences on these matters of difference were held in Strasbourg and Cologne. At a conference in Cologne, in 1559, the debate over church discipline was particularly long and furious resulting in the northerners excommunicating their coreligionists to the south. The division had far reaching consequences, dividing congregations throughout the Netherlands and Germany.

The Concept of Cologne was intended to heal this division, and it was also designed to address the problem of disunity among Anabaptist churches more generally. High German and Frisan representatives met in May 1, 1591. The meeting might have been held in secret, for the civil authorities did not have any knowledge of the gathering. A few days earlier, authorities in Cologne had ordered that Anabaptists and other undesirables be eliminated from the region, and perhaps for this reason the Anabaptists did not wish to draw attention to themselves.

Leenaerdt Clock, a Mennonite originally from South Germany, who later moved to the Netherlands, took a leading role in writing up the document. The confession is concise, yet addresses most of main themes in Christian theology. The Frisians and High Germans approved the document and agreed to a merger. Some time later another Anabaptist group, the Waterlanders, also agreed to the document and an expanded union emerged that came to be known as the Conciliated Brotherhood (*Bevredigde Broederschap*). Attempts to extend the union to the Flemish Mennonites failed in 1604. In subsequent years Leenaert Clock began to question the level of tolerance of the Conciliated Brotherhood. Concerned that church discipline was becoming too lax, especially among the Waterlanders, Clock led the majority of the High Germans and Frisians out of the union to form a separate group in 1613.

While lasting unity was not achieved, the Concept of Cologne is an irenic document that seeks to represent a *via media* between opposing factions. Regarding the incarnation, the confession tries to find middle ground, without any explicit language about Christ's heavenly flesh, or that Christ's flesh did not come from Mary. On church discipline, the confession advocates separating erring members from the believing community, but the practice of separation should not to be applied between marriage partners. Above all, the love of God should govern the way in which members treat one another.

This translation by James Jakob Fehr is based on the edition printed in *Handelinge Der Ver-eeinigde Vlaemse, en Duytse Doops-gesinde Gemeynten.*

Bibliographical Sources

James R. Coggins, *John Smyth's Congregation: English Separatism, Mennonite Influence, and the Elect Nation* (Scottdale: Herald Press, 1991); *Handelinge Der Ver-eenigde Vlaemse, en Duytse Doops-gesinde Gemeynten, Gehounden Tot Haerlem, Anno 1649 in Junio Met De Dry Confessien aldaer geapprobeert of aengenomen* (Vlissighe, Gelyen Jansz., 1666); Christian Hege, "Concept of Cologne," *Mennonite Encyclopedia I*, 663-64; Jacobus ten Doornkaat Koolman, *Dirk Philips: Friend and Colleague of Menno Simons, 1504-1568*, trans. William E. Keeney and ed. C. Arnold Snyder (Kitchener: Pandora Press, 1997); Cornelius Krahn, "Incarnation of Christ," *Mennonite Encyclopedia III*, 18-20; John S. Oyder, "The Strasbourg Conferences of the Anabaptists, 1554-1607," *Mennonite Quarterly Review* 58.3 (July 1984): 218-229; Hans H. Th. Stiasny, *Die Strafrechtliche Verfolgung der Täufer in der Freien Reichsttadt Köln 1529 bis 1618* (Münster: Aschendorffsche Verlagsbuchhandlung), 1962.

Concept of Cologne (1591)

Translated by James Jakob Fehr

We, the servants, elders and brothers of both sides, who until now have been distinguished by two names, namely, on the one hand the *Netherlandish* or *Frisians*, on the other hand the *Uplanders*[1] or *High Germans*, commend and wish all righteous [*vrome*] children of God and lovers of eternal truth and divine peace, much grace, peace and mercy from God, our heavenly Father, through Jesus Christ his beloved Son, our Lord and Saviour, in the power and mediation of the Holy Spirit. Amen.

Having expressed these good wishes in the Lord, we are unable to express to those of you who may read this, the vast, inexpressible grace that our merciful God and loving Father has shown to us. Nor do we know the full measure of gratitude we should convey to him for the fact that he has shown mercy to his inheritance that has lain scattered. And now while many in these times have fallen into quarrels and disunity, the Lord has looked down upon us with grace for His name's sake, and has given those of us on both sides a desire and love for complete peace and unity in our hearts; and not only that, but also the living power of his Holy Spirit, to establish the long-aspired peace with hearts desirous of unity. For this cause we have come from many regions and towns and assembled together on this day, the 1st of May 1591, in Cologne, and have begun by praying to the Lord for wisdom and understanding on bended knees and with kindred hearts, in renewed love for one another, and have deliberated the articles of faith and Christian ordinances in our congregations. Since then, we have found no difference or Godly reason to hinder our peace,[2] for the hearts on both sides are entirely committed to and inclined toward the contemplation of the honour of God and the advancement of the Gospel, as a light unto the world and for the edification of the congregations.

Then, after once again praying earnestly, we approached each other again and accepted each other as our dearly beloved brothers with their acknowledged tasks and offices, in accordance with the first Concept. And to confirm the issues and as signs of love, peace and unity, fully intending, believing and hoping to commune regularly and gently with God and with each other, we have given each other a handshake and brotherly kiss,[3] and thereafter we again bowed down together with joy in our hearts, thanked the Lord with tears in our eyes and prayed as follows: that he might give us strength through his peaceable Holy Spirit, in order that this newly begun work might be sustained and completed for the sake of his divine praise. And so we have agreed to compose the following statements and articles in the form or manner in which we stand in agreement with each other, so that every God-fearing and peace-loving person who is an enemy of conflict might measure this text with the Spirit of God and the teachings of the Gospel, and thereby seek the truth in it, be freed from all old and new quarrels, join our good-hearted and peaceful community, and in concord with her thank and praise God, forever and ever, Amen.

We now present the following statements and articles that we have set down together through God's help in the rebirth and having received the anointing of the Holy Spirit, punishing any critics through a holy and sanctified life and through good works after the example and character of Jesus Christ, and not through quarrels and disputes.

The following are the Articles of Faith:

First of all, [we believe] in the divine Trinity, Father, Son and Holy Spirit, that there is one single, eternal, omnipotent God.

And [we believe] in Jesus Christ, who from eternity is the only Son of the Father, who in the fullness of time through the power of the Almighty and the participation of the Holy Spirit was born of Mary, and that this eternal Word of the Father was made flesh.

We also confess that the Holy Spirit is a power of God, sent forth from the Father through the Son, promised by Christ and sent as a consolation to the believers.

Thus, whoever now believes in this Son of God, that he is the Saviour, Liberator and Redeemer [*Heylandt, Salighmacker ende Verlosser*] promised and sent from God, is free from all sin.

A person who confesses his sinfulness, carries out and demonstrates the true fruit of repentance, gladly takes on the Word of Christ and expresses a personal desire to be baptized—that person is to be baptized with water by a faultless appointed servant in the name of the Father, the Son, and the Holy Spirit: And anyone who has been thus experienced this and has been baptized—that person should not be rebaptized.

Therefore, all who have been baptized by one Spirit into one body should celebrate communion with each other, remembering thereby his great love and his bitter death, and this with common bread and wine.

This community of the saints has the power to bind and to loose by means of the keys of the Kingdom of Heaven, and it should therefore use the rule of Matt. 18 against the lapse into sin between brother and brother.

However, manifest works of the flesh are to be reproved after thoughtful consideration of God's Word, in accordance with the teaching of Paul in 1 Corinthians 5, not having anything to do with these persons or eating with them. Yet not by means of harsh mistreatment, as it has sadly often been practised, through which the abuse of the practice of shunning marital partners and further disorder has followed, but rather by the anointing of the Holy Spirit demonstrating love toward those who are being punished, in order that they may improve and be corrected. And if this teaching from Paul is understood by some in a more elaborate and by others in a simpler sense, nevertheless the God-fearing on both sides should always abide in love toward one another until we receive further grace from God,[4] and each person should use his knowledge in a loving manner, without quarrels or arguments. Likewise, an heretical person should be shunned [only] after having been censured once or twice.

We confess further from the Holy Scriptures of the Old and New Testaments that believers have not been given the freedom to marry anyone other than a person who through faith has become a member of Christ and a brother or sister. They should be two free persons in accord with the first decree that began with Adam and Eve. And those who disobey this decree have made themselves punishable before the congregation, and one should not have any brotherly unity with them, unless one senses the true fruit of remorse and repentance. They are to be admonished to be faithful to their previous marriage vows, and neither to abandon their spouses nor to marry another person. All of this should be performed in accordance with the anointing.

And also the maintenance of the footwashing of the holy, when asked by our fellow believers, is to be received in love and their feet to be washed with heartfelt humility.

A bishop or teacher should be without blame, and after he has been well-tried one should let him serve. And he is to be commended into service through the laying on of hands of the elders and appointed by the congregation in harmony and in accordance with the example of the Apostolic congregations. Deacons are also to be appointed to care for the destitute, dispensing the voluntary donations into the hands of the poor for their relief, so that the gifts be given in secret, in accordance with the teaching of Christ.

No oaths are to be sworn, in accordance with the teaching of Christ and of James. For all words and actions should be confirmed by a solemn Yes or No, without anything further, and this speaking with the truth is to be esteemed as a sworn oath.

And since usury is an outrage before God and is held to be disgraceful by society, anything that can be shown by means of the Holy Scriptures to be usury is not to be permitted in any way.

No revenge is permitted; forbidden is not only the use of material weapons, but also replying to insults with insults.

We also confess the bodily resurrection of the dead, both of the just and the unjust, and that at the Last Judgment everyone will be judged in accordance with their deeds.

Furthermore, we have discussed our apprehensions concerning the growing inclination of the merchant class toward temporal greed and the vanity of ostentatious clothing, which imitate the world rather than displaying the humility of Christ. And because these are insidious, creeping sins, and it is to be feared that they will lead many to destruction, although one can hardly prescribe for anyone how much business he should do or what he should wear, yet we desire that each of us would restrict his business activities and dress modestly, indeed that he might enlighten the world in all he does, and not attire himself like the world, after the manner of the discontented and the insatiable. For this reason we have agreed that all who keep watch over the House of God should censure the members in all faithfulness and in the power of the Scriptures, and thereby keep them pure from the perdition of the disobedient, and in this way each brother [admonish] the other, but with a fatherly heart, so that the admonition will be the more tolerable. This has been signed by many persons, including the following:

I, Leonhard Klock, confess for myself and for my fellow servants that this text has met with the approval and agreement of the servants and elders of the congregations in the regions of Elsace, Breisgau, Strasbourg, Weissenburg, Landau, Neustadt, Landesheim[5], Worms and Kreuznach. L.K.

[Further signatories include:]
Ameldonck Leeuw, Cologne
David Rutgers
Claes van Landerschrift, Landesheim
Jan Koch, Hauffen
Casper van Dollendort
Diderich Verwer, Millen and van der Mase
Goossen Schrotten
Frans van Rijnbach, Flamerse
Wolter van Wetschewel, Odekercke
Teunis Comes, Gladbeck
Aernolt Boeckholst, Bergslandt
Hendrick Frinch-winckel, Liebers
Lucas de Grand and Jan Gerrits van Solingh, Cologne
Louijs Boudewijns, Rees

B

Waterlander Confessions

8

Waterlander Confession (1577)

Introduction

In the 1550s Dutch Anabaptists became known for their practice of strict church discipline. The practice was based on the assumption that Christians were a part of the community of saints who lived in obedience to the commands of Christ. In order to maintain the ethical purity of the community, those who committed serious moral transgressions were disciplined or removed from the fellowship until they had repented of their ways. Anabaptist leaders such as Dirk Philips and Leenaert Bouwens were especially strong advocates of the ban and the practice of avoidance.

Not all Anabaptist groups, however, accepted rigourous forms of church discipline. Besides the South Germans, who questioned the strict discipline of their northern counterparts, a number of churches in the Netherlands also voiced their concerns. In the fall of 1556 Mennonites living in the Waterland district of northern Holland could no longer go along with the strict practices of some of the leadership, and as a result separated themselves from the Anabaptist mainstream. Other groups soon followed a more moderate path, often resulting in negative consequences. In 1555 or 1556, Jacob Jansz. Scheedemaker, a Dutch Mennonite leader and preacher at Emden in East Friesland was excommunicated by Leenaert Bouwens for not being strict enough in matters related to church discipline. Around the same time two church leaders from the town of Franeker in Friesland, Hendrick Naeldeman and Jorianen Heynsz, were excommunicated for similar reasons. These two groups, sometimes referred to as "Scheedemakers" and

"Franekeraars," along with a group living in the Waterland district, came to be generally known as the Waterlanders.

After his excommunication in Emden, Jacob Jansz Scheedemaker moved to the Waterland district, and soon took on significant leadership responsibilities. In 1577, probably at the request of a ministers' conference held in the same year, Scheedemaker, along with several other colleagues, drew up a doctrinal statement that proved to be the first comprehensive Anabaptist confession of faith outlining all the major themes of Christian theology. With this confession the Waterlanders sought to strengthen the unity of their community, to recruit more independent congregations into their fellowship, and to facilitate conversations with other Anabaptist groups.

It is noteworthy that the Melchiorite doctrine of the incarnation does not appear in the confession, suggesting that the Waterlanders were at odds with this doctrine. Articles dealing with God's foreknowledge and the Fall suggest that the Waterlanders were likely faced with questions related to predestination and original sin, which would likely have arisen in conversations with their Calvinist neighbours who were becoming the dominant Protestant force in the region. Concerning church discipline, the Waterlanders clearly supported the practices of the ban and avoidance, but also stressed the limitations to such practices.

The confession includes an article on footwashing, a practice first taken up by Anabaptists in the Netherlands and only later practiced among Swiss and South German Anabaptists. Somewhat unusual is the absence of an article on the sword. Also unusual in the confession is the absence of numerous supporting Scripture references. Perhaps because the confession was principally intended as an internal document, limited to Anabaptist communities, the Waterlanders did not feel the need to supply these references.

This translation by Cornelius J. Dyck is based on the original manuscript (Archief I, #471) and on ten Cate's edition in the *Doopsgezinde Bijdragen*. The confession of faith was first published in the English language in the *Mennonite Quarterly Review* in 1962. This translation is the same with minor changes.

Bibliographical Sources

E. M. ten Cate, "De eerste waterlansche belijdenis," *Doopsgezinde Bijdragen* (1904); Cornelius J. Dyck, "The First Waterlandian Confession of Faith," *Mennonite Quarterly Review* 36.1 (January 1962): 5-13; George Hunston Williams, *The Radical Reformation*, third edition (Kirksville: Sixteenth Century Journal Publishers, 1992); Nanne van der Zijpp, "Jacob Jansz Scheedemaker," *Mennonite Encyclopedia III*, 61; Nanne van der Zijpp, "Waterlanders," *Mennonite Encyclopedia IV*, 895-96.

[The First Waterlander Confession of Faith. Alkmaar, September 22, 1577]

Translated by Cornelius J. Dyck

The following articles, having been written and signed by us, are grounded in the Word of God. We the undersigned are of one faith, one heart and mind, one feeling concerning these articles, united to the praise and glory of God. Furthermore, we confess before God and all people, that the following is the pure, eternal, and everlasting truth.

[I. Concerning the one God, Threefold in Being, Creator and Sustainer of the World]

We confess, believe, and acknowledge with Holy Scripture, that there is but one God, almighty, holy, righteous, and merciful, having neither beginning nor end, an eternal, divine, incomprehensible and spiritual Being; yes, Father, Son, and Holy Spirit. Besides him there is no other. From eternity he brought forth his Son in an incomprehensible, and inexpressible manner; through whom also, when it seemed good to him, God created and ordered the world, sustaining and ruling it according to his pleasure.

[II. Concerning Jesus Christ, Human and Divine]

We confess, believe, and acknowledge with Holy Scripture that Jesus Christ, together with his human nature is truly God, the Son of God from eternity, begotten of the Father, born out of him not in a manner which placed him outside of the Father as a separate Being, but being born from the Father in an inexpressible and incomprehensible manner he nevertheless remained in the Father. Because of this eternal birth out of the Father, he is the only begotten, first-born Son of God, of one Being with the Father and the Holy Spirit, one substance, truly God. Father, Son, and Holy Spirit are one, divine, incomprehensible, eternal, spiritual Being. We say that Father, Son, and Holy Spirit are of one will, one mind, one essence, one Being, and therefore the only true, living, almighty, and eternal God.

[III. Concerning the Holy Spirit]

We believe, acknowledge, and confess with Holy Scripture that the Holy Spirit is of one essence [*wesens*] with the Father and the Son, of one substance. Therefore we confess him to be God with the Father and the Son. We confess also that though this Spirit is of one essence with the Father and the Son, undivided, he nevertheless proceeds from the Father and the Son.

[IV. Concerning the Incarnation of Christ]

We believe, acknowledge, and confess with Holy Scripture that in the fullness of time God sent his only begotten, first-born Son to be born of the blessed Virgin Mary, whom the heavenly Father had chosen, prepared, sanctified, and blessed. Thus there was born in her through the power of the Almighty, the Saviour of the world, God having promised that he would be of the seed of woman (Genesis 3), the seed of Abraham, Isaac, and Jacob. In the fullness of time God fulfilled his promise, as also the Apostle teaches, saying that Christ is in the lineage of the fathers according to the flesh, blessed of God in all eternity. Therefore we confess Christ Jesus to be true God and Son of God from all eternity; that in the fullness of time he became completely human, and that he thus has both a divine and a human nature.

[V. Concerning the Attributes of God]

We believe with Holy Scripture that in his Being, God cannot be laid hold of nor touched. He is a Spirit, a spiritual Being, having neither beginning nor end. He is invisible, immeasurable, incomprehensible, above all, immutable, and eternal; always perfect in love, longsuffering, gentle, kind, merciful, righteous and almighty, a fountain of life, from whom all good gifts flow. Without preferring one before the other, it is his desire that no one should be lost, and that all might be converted and become righteous.

[VI. Concerning the Foreknowledge of God]

We believe with Holy Scripture that God has known from all eternity all things that happen, have happened, and will happen, both good and bad. Nevertheless this foreknowledge compels no one to sin. We confess also that, though he foreknows all things, that which happens is not all his will nor work. Even as he is a fountain of life, a Father of light, and in himself the only true good, so also everything that proceeds and flows from him, being willed, foreordained, and worked by him, is good, holy, righteous and light, for the eternal God cannot will, ordain, or bring forth anything contrary to his own character or nature. Therefore we confess that God so governs the world that whatever is virtuous, good, and righteous upon earth comes through his providence and eternal will. We confess further that whatever appears before God as presumptuous, as a departure from his commandment—all disobedience, all sin, all malice and evil brought forth among people— is neither contrary nor in accordance with his will, work or order, though he patiently sees and allows it. In summary, we confess that God at times punishes people because of his righteousness. This punishment, though it seems evil to human eyes, is righteous before God. Therefore he also orders, and brings to a good end, the evil works of the godless.

[VII. Concerning the Fall, Damnation, and Salvation]

We believe that in Adam God created all people for salvation and eternal life, but because of their fall, and departure from eternal good and life, God foreordained his Son from the beginning as the mercy seat, sending him in the form of a servant when the time was fulfilled. Through him life and salvation was proclaimed to all people, as many as accepted his word, repented, and believed in him. (We speak of the old ones), therefore, we confess that God saw and knew, before the foundation of the world, who would hear the Word of his Son, accept his teaching, and receive him by faith.[1] By this foreknowledge he promised, in his grace, to reveal his glory through his Son, by the granting of eternal life. Therefore, even as he has seen the obedience of those who believe, so also he has foreknown the unbelief, deliberate disobedience, the perversity, the hardening of the heart, the ungratefulness [against] God, the voluntary submission of the will to the flesh, of some people, that is, the unbelievers. Therefore, because of their own guilt and perversity, because they have put themselves outside of the will of God, and because they persist, without conversion, in running to the abyss of hell, he has promised [them] eternal punishment.

[VIII. Concerning the Body and Soul]

We believe that God created humans as two-fold beings, consisting of body and soul, of soul and body. The soul is not the essence of the body, nor is the body the essence of the soul. The body is the house, temple, or tabernacle in which the soul lives, but the soul is the spirit dwelling in the body, the natural life and ruler, which the Scriptures in various places call spirit, breath, or life. Even as every person has only one body, so also every person has one soul, the two together united, body and soul, making the person complete.

[IX. Concerning the Immortality of the Soul]

We believe thus that humans, consisting of body and soul, are destined once to die, which death is a departure of the soul from the body. Though the body loses its natural life when the soul departs, the body being under [the judgment of] death, the soul, nevertheless, retains the power of life, being imperishable and immortal.

[X. Concerning Eternal Life]

We believe that the souls of believers, after being separated from the body in death, are carried by angels to places where they taste and feel joy and happiness, which places we do not conveniently know how to name except as Holy Scripture itself instructs, namely Abraham's bosom, Paradise. And we confess, contrariwise, that the souls of unbelievers, after being separated from the body in death, are carried [to places] where they suffer pain and fear. With this simple confession about these places we must be content.

[XI. Concerning Original Sin]

We believe that through transgression Adam seriously impaired his life, bringing upon himself and his posterity temporal and eternal death; yes, humanity has lost the image of God in him, and through the gifts of evil, God himself. Yet we confess that this same human being has not been robbed completely of the image and light of God, else he would have become complete darkness even as the devils are. We confess, however, that in his mercy, God left a trace of light in fallen humanity and its descendants. Through this it is still able to achieve some virtues and avoid some sins, and can, through trust and the grace of God, come to a closer walk [with God].

[XII. Concerning Redemption through Christ]

We believe and confess that Christ has freed the entire human race from the power of original sin, which is death. Therefore, we know of no children who are to be damned because of it, before the time when persons deliberately will to live by and pursue their inner failures. Therefore, we confess a person's rehabilitation to be equal to the fall.

[XIII. Concerning the Church of God]

We confess concerning the church [*kerk*] of God, that it consists of all people upon the face of the earth who, through the power of God, have come to a renewal of their inner being by grace, in whom the true likeness and mind of Christ dwells, and who are truly obedient to God. All these we confess, believe, and hold to be true members of the church [*gemeynde*] of Jesus Christ.

[XIV. Concerning the Ministers and Servants of the Church]

We confess concerning the mission and call of ministers [*predicanten*] and servants of the church that in times of need[2] the congregation [*ghemeynt*] shall prepare itself before God with fasting and prayer, calling upon him for help—for he alone can send the right servants into his harvest—that our heavenly Father may prepare the right messengers among the congregations to the glory of his name. [That they] be servants who will proclaim his holy word truthfully, and in true Christian love, according to his pleasure, to hungry souls, [as well as] administering the sacraments and the ban. In the choice of these servants the congregation shall deal according to the custom of the Apostles, as we read in Acts 6.

[XV. Concerning the Law]

We confess concerning the Law that it is the word of command that was given to Moses at Mount Sinai, declaring to us the will of the most high.

[XVI. Concerning the Gospel]

We confess concerning the gospel, that it is the good news of the grace of God. [It is] made manifest in Christ, proclaiming the blessing of eternal salvation and life to the entire human race through the shed blood of Christ, upon the condition of faith in what follows:[3]

[XVII. Concerning Baptism]

We confess concerning baptism that those who accept the word of the ministers, who repent and believe the gospel, shall be baptized with water in the congregation, by a true messenger of God, in the name of the Father, the Son, and the Holy Spirit, as was taught by Christ, and practiced by the apostles.

[XVIII. Concerning the Lord's Supper]

We confess concerning the Supper of the Lord [*Aventmael des Heeren*], that it is a sign of divine grace, a seal of the eternal covenant of God, a visible ordinance or ceremony, instituted by Jesus Christ in the congregation of God. It was instituted with bread and wine, the bread broken in remembrance of the death of Christ, the wine received in remembrance of the pouring out of his blood. In receiving it, believing Christian members search themselves to find the true essence to which the Lord's Supper does point. Whatever the Scriptures further teach of the Lord's Supper and its meaning, we believe.

[XIX. Concerning the Ban]

We confess concerning the ban or Christian chastisement that one must admonish the brother of the faith according to the teaching of Christ in Matthew 18, who through transgression or otherwise has fallen or remained in sin, not excluding the works of the flesh. [This we do] in order that he may be restored and won again, that his soul may be won, and that those who hear and institute the admonition may in brotherly love, forget and cover his transgression. On the other hand, we confess that the stubborn and deliberate sinner or transgressor, after sufficient admonition by the congregation shall be separated and cut off from the body of Christ to God's honor; that his church may remain pure and an instrument for the conversion of the fallen.

[XX. Concerning Confession of Guilt]

We confess that if a brother did fall into sin as we have mentioned above, and this occurred with, or became known to, the common people, such person shall be punished with a public confession of guilt before the congregation, provided two or three witnesses have verified his transgression.

[XXI. Concerning Avoidance]

Concerning the avoidance [*mijdinghe*] of a fallen brother, we confess that one should avoid all deliberate sinners who have been cut off from the congregation, and who persist in carnal living. [One should] neither eat nor drink with them that they may be shamed and corrected. Nevertheless, since the ban should lead to healing, we do not wish to be so hard that fellowship should be denied him in time of need, or when the one who has fallen, through such eating and drinking, might be converted and won again.

[XXII. Concerning Footwashing]

Concerning footwashing among the saints, we confess that [this practice be applied] to all scattered, poor, and despised brethren; [that is], to those who suffer need, oppression, and through persecution have come to us; yes, all the brethren who come to be received into our houses in love. Also [we confess] that all [will receive] proper Christian love, yes, as a sign of love, fellowship, of lowliness and meekness according to the example of the saints of the Old Testament, and the example of Christ and his teaching; that they be received with footwashing, as was also practiced among the believers of the New Testament, Timothy 8.[4]

[XXIII. Concerning Marriage]

We confess that marriage is an arrangement of God. When a man and woman have, in chastity, been united in the state of marriage, this marriage is so binding that it may not be separated or broken for any reason except adultery, according to the words of Christ, Matthew 18.

[XXIV. Concerning the Oath]

We confess that all light-hearted oaths are forbidden to the Christian; also all false oaths, as well as all oaths in the name of God and the saints. However, when need and Christian love require it, to the praise of God, we permit that one call upon God as witness to the truth of a statement made, even as Paul did, saying "I take God as my witness that the testimony I have given is true."

[XXV. Concerning the Resurrection of the Dead]

We confess, believe, and expect a resurrection of the righteous and the unrighteous. In the last days all people who have been, now are, and will be, shall arise from the dead and be resurrected; that is, their body shall be united with the departed soul, the body being the same and no other, but the accidents shall be changed. Thus all people shall appear before the judgment seat of God, the good to eternal life, the evil to eternal punishment.

Jacop Jans S.
[Simon Michelssoon]
[Simon Jacobssoon]
[Albert Verspeck]
[Hans de Ries]

9

Short Confession of Faith and the Essential Elements of Christian Doctrine (1610)

Introduction

The Short Confession of Faith served as a basis of union between the Waterlanders and English Separatists. In opposition to the Church of England, Separatists advocated, among other things, Bible-based preaching in place of elaborate liturgical worship, presbyterian or congregational church polity, and church practices that called for high ethical standards. Several separatist groups came to the Netherlands in search of religious freedom under the direction of leaders such as Francis Johnson and John Smyth. Over time, a bloc within Smyth's congregation desired "believers" baptism, and after having baptized themselves, a number in the congregation expressed an interest in joining the Waterlander church in Amsterdam. Several conversations took place after which time members of John Smyth's congregation were accepted into the Waterlander church on the basis of the Short Confession of Faith.

For the Waterlanders, union with the English Separatists was not a simple matter as their ecumenical negotiations threatened to put a strain on inter-Mennonite relationships. The Amsterdam congregation was allied with Waterlander, Frisian and High German congregations throughout the Netherlands that belonged to an alliance known as the Conciliated Brotherhood. Because the relationship in this coalition was already tenuous—with the Waterlanders frequently being viewed as too lax in their practices of church discipline—it was important for the Waterlanders to proceed with caution. A conference on May 23,

1610, was proposed with the view that the Conciliated Brotherhood could be present and union with the English Separatists could take place. For a number of Frisian pastors, however, such a conference was premature, and they preferred to first consult with other Frisian leaders throughout Germany and Prussia before moving forward toward union on the basis of the Short Confession. The historical records are silent as to what happened next, but it is quite possible that the conference took place as scheduled, and that the Short Confession of Faith served as a unity statement. Records indicate that some forty-three members of the Smyth congregation eventually agreed to its tenets. The Waterlander leader, Hans de Ries, who had also been involved in formulating the first Waterlander confession in 1577, initially prepared a draft of the Short Confession with 38 articles likely with the help of another leader, Lubbert Gerrits. By the time of its publication in June, the confession contained 40 articles that included additional material on Christology, soteriology, and eschatology. Changes in the draft may have taken place as a result of further discussions with the wider Waterlander community.

The Waterlander-English Separatist union was successful, but the already fragile alliance with the Frisian congregations could not be maintained. When the Frisians asked the Waterlanders to delay the adoption of the Short Confession to no avail, they responded by leaving the Conciliated Brotherhood to form their own conference.

The confession represents a comprehensive and highly systematic treatment of the chief articles of Christian doctrine. Significant attention is given to issues related to predestination and free will suggesting that this might have been a central concern for the English separatists. Certainly it was a burning issue in the Reformed church where Calvinists and Arminians sparred over this issue. The confession also gives extensive attention to Christology, the doctrine of rebirth, and relates teachings about peace to the atonement. In typical Waterlandian fashion, the confession stresses the importance of love in the context of church discipline, and underscores the significance of the marriage institution, which can only be breached in cases where adultery has taken place. The article on marriage also speaks against the practice of separating spouses when one of partners has been placed under the ban.

A strong mystical/spiritualist impulse permeates the confession of faith in regards to knowledge about Christ and the sacraments. Christ cannot simply be known according to the flesh, but must also be apprehended according to the Spirit; baptism and the Supper are not merely external ceremonies, but also point to profound inner experiences of the faithful. Unclear is whether the spiritualist influence was mediated through spiritualists such as Caspar Schwenckfeld, Sebastian Franck, and Dirk Volckertsz Coornhert, or whether the spiritualism among the Waterlanders can be traced directly to the ongoing influence of Anabaptists such as Melchior Hoffman and David Joris, or even to the south German Anabaptist, Hans Denck.

This translation by Cornelius J. Dyck is based on the 1618 edition in *Het boeck der Gesangen* with comparative references to the 1686 edition. The confession of faith was first published in the English language in the *Mennonite Quarterly Review* in 1964. This translation is the same with minor changes.

Bibliographical Sources

James R. Coggins, *John Smyth's Congregation: English Separatism, Mennonite Influence, and the Elect Nation* (Scottdale and Waterloo: Herald Press, 1991); "Corte Belijdenisse des Geloofs," in *Het boeck der Gesangen* (Hoorn: Jan Jochimsz. Byvanck, 1618); Cornelius J. Dyck, "A Short Confession of Faith by Hans de Ries," *Mennonite Quarterly Review* 38.1 (January 1964): 5-19; Karl Koop, *Anabaptist-Mennonite Confessions of Faith: The Development of a Tradition.* (Kitchener: Pandora Press, 2004).

Short Confession of Faith and the Essential Elements of Christian Doctrine (1610)

Translated by Cornelius J. Dyck

2 Corinthians 4:13

But just as we have the same spirit of faith that is in accordance with Scripture—"I believed, and so I spoke"—we also believe, and so we speak.

Matthew 10:32

Everyone therefore who acknowledges me before others, I also will acknowledge before my Father in heaven; but whoever denies me before others, I also will deny before my Father in heaven.

1 Peter 3:15

Always be ready to make your defense to anyone who demands from you an accounting for the hope that is in you; yet do it with gentleness and reverence.

At Hoorn

Printed by Jan Jochimsz. Byvanck
Haerlem, Anno 1618

I. That there is only one God, and who He is

We believe and confess, by the power and instruction of Holy Scripture, that there is (Deut. 6:4, 32:39) one God alone (John 4:24), a Spirit or spiritual Being (Rom. 1:20), eternal (Gen. 21:33; Rom. 16:26), incomprehensible (Ps. 129:6; Rom. 11:33), everlasting (1 Kings 8:27;

Matt. 5:34; Acts 7:48), invisible (Col. 1:15), immutable (James 1:17), almighty (Gen. 17:1; 2 Cor. 6:18), merciful (Exod. 34:6-7; Luke 6:36), righteous (Ps. 11:7; Col. 3:21, 26), perfect (Lev. 19:2; Matt. 5:48), wise (1 Tim. 1:17), alone good (Ps. 103:8; Matt. 19:17), a fountain of life (Jer. 2:13), the source of all good (James 1:17), a Creator (Gen. 1:1; Exod. 20:11; Acts 4:24) and Sustainer (1 John 5:7) of heaven and earth, of things visible and invisible.

II. How this only God is to be distinguished in Holy Scripture

This one only God is revealed and distinguished in the Holy Scriptures as Father, Son, and Holy Spirit (Matt. 3:16-17, 28:19), being three (1 John 5:7) yet, nevertheless, one God.

III. How Father, Son, and Holy Spirit, according to this distinction, are three and one

The Father is the origin and beginning of all things (Rom. 11:36; 1 Cor. 8:6), having brought forth his Son from eternity (Micah 5:2) before all creation (Col. 1:15) in an incomprehensible manner (Heb. 7:3; Psalm 2:7). The Son is the eternal Word and wisdom of the Father (John 1:1), in whom all things consist (1 Cor. 1:22; Col. 2:3). The Holy Spirit (John 14:26) is God's power and might (Luke 1:31), proceeding from the Father and the Son (John 15:26, 16:7). The three are neither divided nor different in nature, essence, or essential attributes (Rev. 22:1; 1 John 5:7). They are eternal, omnipotent, invisible, immortal, glorious, and the like.

IV. Concerning Creation, the Fall, and Restoration of Humanity

This only God created humans good (Gen. 1:31) in his own image and likeness (Gen. 1:27), for happiness and salvation, and in him all people [were created] to a blessed end (Rom. 5:18). These first humans fell into sin and disgrace (Gen. 3:9; Rom. 5:19). Nevertheless, they have been restored by God and given eternal life (Gen. 3:15, 21), together with all those who had fallen in them (Gen. 12:3, 22:13, 26:4; Rom. 5:18), according to the comforting promises of God. Consequently, none of their descendants, being included in this redemption, are born with sin or guilt.

V. Concerning the Ability of Humanity before and after the Fall

Because humans were created good (Gen. 1:31), they had in themselves the ability to hear, accept, or reject the wrong with which they were tempted by the spirit of evil (Gen. 3:1, 4:6). Thus when they fell they still had the ability, though standing in this evil, to hear, accept, or reject the good which the Lord himself placed before them (Gen. 3:8, 10, 11, 12). Even as they were able to hear and accept the evil before the fall (Gen. 3:6), so also they are able to hear and accept the good that is before them after the fall. This ability to accept or reject the grace of God has remained with the posterity of the first humans as a gift of grace (Gen. 3, 8, 9, 10, 15; Gen. 4: 6-7, 6:2, 3,12; Deut. 11:26, 30:19; Ps. 81:14; Isa. 1:19-20, 42:18-21; Jer. 8:7, 25:4, Matt. 11:16, 22:23, 36; Luke 13:32; John 5:34, 40)

VI. Concerning the Foreknowledge of God

God has foreseen and foreknown all things that have occurred, occur, and will occur, both good and bad, from all eternity (Job 28:24-27; Isa. 41:14; 15:16, 48:3; Jer. 1:5). Since he is the only good and perfect fountain of life, we confess him to be the only author, source and creator of the things that are good, holy, clean, pure, and conformable to his nature (Ps. 103:8; Matt. 19:17; Ps. 36:9; Jer. 2:13). In no sense, however, is he the origin of sin or evil that leads to damnation. God commands the good, desires obedience to the good (Deut. 5:29, 32:29; Luke 19:42), counsels and admonishes to do the good, giving great promises to those who obey (Rev. 3:18). On the other hand he forbids evil, warns evildoers and pleads with them, announcing to them eternal punishment and sometimes punishing them in this life (Deut. 28; Matt. 24:13). In this he testifies that he is the enemy of the sinner, that all unrighteousness is contrary to his holy nature. Thus, not the

God who is good, but humans who are evil, through their free choice of sin, together with the spirit of evil within them, are the authors, source, and workers of sin and evil, being thereby guilty and punishable (Gen. 2:17, 4, 6; Deut. 27:15, 28:15; Ps. 7:12; Gen. 8:19, 24; Matt. 3:12, 25:47; Hosea 13:9; Micah 6:2; Eph. 2: 1-3).

VII. Concerning God's Predestination, Election, and Rejection

The cause or reason of humanity's calamity and damnation is their own free choice of darkness (John 3:19; James 1:15), their affirming of sins and their willingness to live in them. Destruction comes from humans, not from the good Creator. God, being perfectly good and love itself (according to the nature of perfect love and goodness) (Matt. 19:17; 1 John 4:8), desired the best for his creatures, namely, healing and salvation. Therefore he neither predestined, determined, nor created anyone for damnation, neither willing nor ordaining their sinful life in order to bring them to destruction. Rather (since as a good God he had no desire, as surely as he lives, that any one should perish but that all might be saved) (Ezek. 33:11; 2 Peter 3:9), he created all humans for salvation (1 Tim. 2:4; Gen. 1:27). When they fell he restored them, with infinite love, through Christ who has become for all humans a medicine of life (Gen. 12:3, 22:18; Rom. 5:10; Sophia 1:19-20; 1 John 2:2; Heb. 2:9; John 3:16, 4:14). [This Christ] was given over to be sacrificed, and to die for the reconciliation of all humanity (Eph. 5:2), affirming his desire that all creatures and nations should hear, and have offered to them through evangelical preaching, universal love and compassion (Matt. 28:19; Mark 16:15; Eph. 1:9). All those who now receive or accept this gracious benefit of God in Christ (who came for the salvation of the world) with penitent and believing hearts and remain in him are and remain the elect whom God has ordained before the foundation of the world that they should share his glory (1 John 2:2; Mark 16, Mark 15:16; John 1:12; Matt. 24:13; Rev. 2:10; Matt. 22:14; Eph. 1:4; Matt. 25:34, 22:5). Those, however, who despise or reject this grace of God, who love darkness more than light, who remain unrepentant and unbelieving, make themselves unworthy of salvation through their own perversity, and are therefore justly rejected by God because of their own evil (John 3:19; Acts 13:46; 2 Chron. 15:2; 1 Kings 15, 22:30; 2 Thess. 2:10-11; 1 Pet. 2:8; Matt. 22:3; Luke 14:16, 17:24). These will not reach the end for which they were created and for which they were ordained in Christ, neither shall they taste the Supper of the Lord, to which they had been invited and called, in all eternity.

VIII. Concerning the Incarnation of the Son of God

The esteemed intention of God, before the foundation of the world, to reconcile the world which he saw falling into wrath and disgrace has been accomplished in the fullness of time through the sending of his Son, the eternal Word from heaven, as the fulfillment of the promise to the Fathers (Gal. 4:4; Gen. 3:15, 22:18, 26:4; Deut. 18:15; Isa. 7:14, 9:5, 11:1; Jer. 23:5). Sent from heaven, born of the holy Virgin Mary, he became flesh through the miraculous work of the Holy Spirit (John 13:3, 16:28, 17:18; Luke 1:27; John 1:14; Luke 1:31; Matt. 1:20). This, however, not in a manner by which a part of the eternal essence of the eternal Word was changed into visible, mortal flesh or humanness, thereby ceasing to be Spirit, Deity, or God; rather, the eternal Son of God, remaining what he had been before, namely, God and Spirit, became that which he had formerly not been, namely, flesh or human (Heb. 1:10-12; Rom. 9:5; 2 Cor. 3:17; John 1:14). Thus Jesus Christ, our Emmanuel, is at the same time in one Person both true God and human, born of Mary, visible and invisible, external and internal, very Son of the Living God (Matt. 1:23; 1 John 5:20; John 8:40; 1 Tim. 2:5; Matt. 16:16; John 6:69, 9:35-37).

IX. Why Christ came into the World, and his threefold Office

Being then both God and human, Son of the Living God, Christ came into the world to make sinners righteous, to reconcile the sinful world to God the Father (1 John 5:20; John 8:40; Matt. 16:16, 9:15; 1 Tim. 1:15; 2 Cor. 5:19). Therefore we confess him to be our only Mediator, prophet, priest, and king, a lawgiver and teacher whom God had promised to send into the world (1 John 2:2; 1 Tim. 2:5; Deut. 18:15;

Ps. 110:4; Heb. 3:1; Jer. 33:15; Matt. 21:5, 17:5, 28:20; Gal. 6:4; Deut. 18:15; Matt. 17:5; John 3:36, 8:12). Him we hear, believe, and must follow.

X. Concerning the Abolition of the Law and things of the Law

Christ has brought to an end and removed from among his people the unbearable burden of the law of Moses (Acts 15:10; 2 Cor. 3:11, 14; Col. 2:16-17; Heb. 8:4-5, 10:1) with its shadows and figures, the priestly office of the temple, altar, sacrifice and all else that was a part of the figurative priestly office—the kingly office and all that belonged to it: the kingdom, sword, law of revenge, war, and whatever prefigured his person and office (Luke 1:28-29; John 18:33; Matt. 20:25-27; Mark 10:43-45; Isa. 2:4, Mic. 4:3; Matt. 5:38; Zach. 9:10). These were the image, the shadow of him who was to come.

XI. Concerning the Prophetic Office of Christ

As the true prophet of the promise Christ has revealed and proclaimed to us the will of God, that which God requires of the people of the New Testament (John 17:8; Heb. 1:2; Deut. 18:16, 18). Even as God spoke to the people of the Old Testament through Moses and the prophets, declaring his will to them, so in the last days he has spoken to us through this prophet (his Son), proclaiming that which had been hidden during all time (Heb. 1:2; Matt. 13:35; Heb. 3:5). Thus he preached to us the good news, instituted and ordered the sacraments, offices and services provided by God (Mark 1:14; Matt. 26:25-26). With his life and teaching he pointed out the law of Christians, the rule of life, and the path to eternal life (Matt. 5; John 10:27-28; 1 Pet. 2:21; 1 John 2:6, Gal. 6:4; John 8:12).

XII. Concerning the Priestly office of Christ

Beyond this, as the only High Priest and Mediator of the New Testament (Heb. 5:10, 6:20; 2 Tim. 2:5) he interceded with his heavenly Father for all believers as well as for all those who crucified and killed him (John 17, 9:11, 15, 20; Luke 23:33). Finally he himself obediently entered into the extremity of suffering, offering himself to the Father through his death upon the cross, a universal offering and gift of sweet savour and eternal worth (Phil. 2:8; Matt. 27:49; Mark 15:39; Eph. 5:2; Heb. 10:12).

XIII. Concerning the Power and Merit of the Obedience and Unique Sacrifice of Jesus Christ

We confess that the obedience of the Son of God, his bitter suffering, death, shed blood and unique sacrifice upon the cross is the reconciliation and satisfaction for all our sins and the sins of the world (Ps. 2:8; 1 Pet. 3:18; Rom. 4:25; Heb. 9:13, 24, 28). Therefore we have been reconciled with God and are at peace, having a certain high hope and assurance of entry into eternal life (2 Cor. 5:19; 1 John 2:2; Col. 1:14; Eph. 1:13; Heb. 10:13).

XIV. Concerning the Office of Christ as King

Jesus Christ, our prophet and priest, as the promised one has also established a spiritual kingdom of the New Testament (Deut. 18:15; Heb. 3:1; Jer. 23:6; Zach. 9:9; Matt. 18:1, 3, 23), having instituted and gathered a multitude of believing and spiritual people whom he has provided with spiritual laws and weapons in the manner of his heavenly kingdom (Jer. 33:15; 2 Cor. 10:4; Eph. 6:12; Jer. 23:5; 1 Cor. 12:28). In this kingdom he has ordained righteousness and those who dwell therein as servants of righteousness. He himself is the preserver, protector, fortress, castle and rock, and shall remain king of this kingdom forever (Ps. 121:4, 5, 18:31, 91:2; Acts 4:11; Luke 1:29).

XV. Concerning the Burial and Resurrection of Christ and its Profitableness

After he had completed his work here upon earth through his death upon the cross he was buried as a sure sign of his death (Matt. 27:58,

59; 1 Cor. 15:4; Matt. 28:6; Acts 10:40). On the third day he arose again from the dead, showing himself thereby as Lord and conqueror over death, one who could no longer be held by the grave (Acts 2:24; 1 Cor. 15: 12, 13, 21). In this he became to all believers a comforting assurance of their redemption and final resurrection from the dead.

XVI. Concerning the Ascension and Glorification of Christ after his Resurrection

Following this he walked among his disciples forty days, showing himself to them in order that no doubt should remain concerning his resurrection (Acts 1:3; Mark 16:19; Acts 1:9; Luke 24:25). Then, received by a cloud, he ascended to heaven and entered into his glory (Eph. 4:8; Col. 2:15). Thus he led captivity captive, establishing a glorious triumph over his enemies. Seated at the right hand of the majesty of God (Mark 16:19; Heb. 8:1; Acts 2:36; John 17:5; Phil. 3:21, 2:9) he has been made both Lord and Christ, glorified in his body, exalted, crowned with praise and honor, remaining priest and king over Mount Zion in all eternity (Heb. 2:6; Ps. 2:6; Ps. 110: 2-4; Heb. 7:2-3).

XVII. What Christ has now Accomplished in Glory according to his Priestly Office

The holy office of this glorified priest, king, lord, and Christ in his heavenly Being (Heb. 8:1; Rev. 1:5; Acts 2:36, 2:33) consists in serving, guiding, and ruling his holy church amidst the storms of this world by the strength of his Spirit (Heb. 8:2; Rom. 8:34; 1 John 2:2; 1 Cor. 2:5). According to his priestly office, as servant of the sacred things, the true tabernacle, he is our intercessor, spokesman, and mediator with the Father (John 14:26, 16:13, 1:33; Matt. 3:11). He teaches, comforts, strengthens, and baptizes us with the Holy Spirit and with fire, bringing us heavenly gifts (Rev. 3:20; John 6:32-34). He celebrates his spiritual Supper with believing souls, making them partakers of the living food and drink of the soul. In these holy sacraments alone is appropriated the fruit, power, and worth of his work upon the cross (Ps. 2:9; Rom. 8:11,14).

XVIII. What Christ has now Accomplished in Glory according to his Royal Office

According to his royal office in that heavenly state, Christ rules over the hearts of the believers through his Word and Holy Spirit (Ps. 2:9; Rom. 8:11,14). He takes them into his care, covers them with the shadow of his wings, arms them with spiritual weapons for a spiritual warfare against all their enemies, the spirits of evil under heaven with their associates upon earth (John 10:28; Matt. 23:36; 2 Cor. 10:4; Eph. 6: 17,13). This glorious, almighty, and heavenly king stands by the faithful believers in every need, delivering and freeing them from the hands of their enemies, conquering the enemy and winning the field of battle, thus preparing for his own a crown of righteousness in heaven (Matt. 28:18; Luke 1:69; 2 Cor. 2:16, 4:8; Rev. 2:10). These are the redeemed of the Lord, living in the house of the Lord and on holy Mount Zion (Heb. 12:23; Isa. 2:4; Mic. 4:2, 3; 2 Cor. 10:4). They have changed their carnal weapons, their swords, into ploughshares and their spears into sickles. They neither lift a sword, nor teach, nor participate in carnal warfare.

XIX. Concerning knowing Christ According to the Spirit, and its Importance

From what has thus far been said concerning the ascension, glorification, office, and service of Christ in glory, we believe and confess that he must not only be known according to the flesh, or confessed literally according to historical knowledge, or only in his holy incarnation, birth, manifestation in the flesh, his life, miracles, suffering, death, cross and other events (2 Cor. 5:16). Rather we must rise higher, and know and confess Christ also according to the Spirit, in his exaltation and glory, according to his glorious office and, as the holy Scriptures teach, receive this knowledge with a believing heart (Phil. 3:20; Col.

3:11; Phil. 3:9; John 17:5; Heb. 8:1). We must continue in fervent prayer to God, so that his holy presence may take place within us according to the Spirit, and a knowledge of him be given to us, revealed through his infinite patience and love. All this must be sought to the end that his image and likeness may be born within us, that he himself may be revealed in us, living, walking, teaching, and preaching; that the miracles he performed in the flesh may be worked in us according to the Spirit, healing us of the sickness of the soul, deafness, blindness, leprosy, uncleanness, sin and death (Matt. 12:50; Gal. 4:19; James 1:18; John 14:11, 23; Eph. 3:17; 2 Cor. 6:16; Rev. 3:20; Matt. 9:2; Isa. 53:4-5). We must know Christ according to the Spirit that he may baptize us, and wash us with the Spirit and with fire, feed us with heavenly food and drink, and make us partakers of his divine nature (Matt. 3:11; Eph. 5:30; John 6:48-50; 1 Cor. 12:13, 2 Pet. 1:4). In this power we can crucify the old being in us, becoming like him in his suffering and death. We through him rise and are resurrected to a new life, to a different knowledge through the power of his resurrection, to the glory and honour of God our heavenly Father. This is what we call knowing Christ according to the Spirit, without which experience the knowledge of Christ according to the flesh is not sufficient for salvation (Rom. 6:5-6; Phil. 3:10; 2 Cor. 5:16-17).

XX. Concerning True, Saving Faith

All the spiritual gifts and mercies which Jesus Christ won for the salvation of sinners through his own merit, we enjoy by grace through a genuine living faith active in love (John 3:16, 36; Acts 15:9; Rom. 5:1-2; Gal. 5:6). This faith is a certain heartfelt knowledge or cognition of God, of Christ, and other heavenly things which, received by grace and the Word of God, are necessary for us to know and to believe for our salvation (Rom. 10:9; John 17:3). This knowledge, together with the love of God, a heartfelt trust in the one, only God as a gracious, heavenly Father who provides all that is necessary for the salvation of our body and soul, are given to us by him for the sake of Christ and his merit (Gal. 5:6; Heb. 11:1; Matt. 7:11; John 16:23).

XXI. Concerning Justification

Through this living faith we are truly justified, that is, we are pardoned of all past and present sins through the shed blood of Jesus Christ, receiving the true righteousness which he pours out richly upon us in co-operation with the Holy Spirit (Gal. 5:6; Rom. 5:1; Ps. 32:1; 1 John 1:7; 1 Cor. 6:11; Rom. 4:15; 1 John 3:7). Thus we are transformed from being evil to being good, from a carnal state to a spiritual state, from selfishness to mildness, from pride to humility, being changed from unrighteousness to righteousness (Titus 3: 5-6; 1 Cor. 6:12). This justification flows from the rebirth [*wedergeboorte*].

XXII. Concerning the Rebirth

The new birth is an act of God effected in the soul of the truly penitent, a restoring of the image of God in us, a renewing of mind and heart, a true enlightening of reason and a knowledge of the truth (Eph. 4:24; Col. 3:9-10; Rom. 12: 2; Eph. 4:23; John 8:32). This new birth brings with it a transformation of the will, of carnal desires and lust, a sincere putting to death of all evil within, of the old nature with its desires and life of sin and rebellion (Eph. 4:22-24; Col. 3:9-10). At the same time the new birth brings with it an awakening of new life in God, in true goodness, righteousness and holiness (Ezek. 36:26; Eph. 4:17-18). It is a taking away of a heart of stone with its pride, ignorance, blindness, lawlessness, sin and sinful lusts, and a gracious granting of the promised fleshly heart filled with the law of God, light, wisdom, understanding, virtue and holy desires. This new birth comes from God through Christ (Jer. 31:38; Heb. 8:10; John 8:47; 1 John 1:4, 2:6-7; 1 Pet. 1:3, 23). The means by which this is worked in us is the Holy Spirit with his fire and power, not by any creaturely means. Therefore the regenerate person also testifies to being born again, not by his own efforts but is born out of God (James 1:18; John 3:5-6). Hereby we become children of God, heavenly, spiritual-minded, righteous and holy. We believe and teach that this new birth is necessary for salvation according to the words of Christ: "Truly, truly, I say to you, unless one is born from above, he cannot see the kingdom of

God," and again, "unless one is born of water and the Spirit, he cannot enter the kingdom of God" (John 1:13; 1 John 3:9; John 1:12, John 3:3).

XXIII. Concerning Good Works

When humans have thus been born again and justified by God through Jesus Christ, they live in love (which the Holy Spirit has poured into their hearts), rejoicing in all good works, in the law, commandments, and morality given them by God through Christ (1 John 14: 21, 23; Gal. 5:6; Rom. 3:5; Ps. 103: 2, 10:2). Thus they thank and bless God from a pure heart through a holy life, for all his gifts, particularly the spiritual gifts to the soul. These souls are sacred plants of the Lord, trees of righteousness honouring God through good works, awaiting the blessed reward which God in his abundant goodness has promised to them (Ps. 103:1; Matt. 5:8; Isa. 61:3; Matt. 5:16; Luke 6:23; 1 Cor. 3:14; Eph. 2:7).

XXIV. Concerning the Church or Congregation

All who believe and are born again, though scattered to the ends of the earth, are the true church of God, or church of Jesus Christ upon earth. These he has loved and given himself for them that they may be sanctified through him (Matt. 8:11, 24:3). Yes, he has sanctified them through the baptism ['*tWaterbat in't woort*] of the Word of life (Rev. 6:9; Eph. 5:25). Of this church Jesus Christ is the foundation, the head, the shepherd, leader, Lord, King, Master (1 Cor. 3:11; Eph. 5:23; John 10:11; Luke 2:11; Matt. 21:5; John 13:13, 3:29). She alone is his beautiful bride, his holy body, clothing, and people who through the new birth have become part of his flesh and body (Rev. 21:2; Eph. 5:23; John 10:16; Eph. 5:30; Matt. 13:24-25, 47, 48, 25:1). While there are among these some hypocrites and pretenders, those who have been born again in Christ and sanctified are the true members of the body of Christ and will inherit his blessed promises. Of these great blessings the pretenders and hypocrites, through their own fault, will have no part (2 Cor. 5:17; Luke 14:24).

XXV. Concerning Offices that Belong in the Church

In this his holy church God has ordained the evangelical office of teaching the divine Word, administering the holy sacraments, and serving the poor (Matt. 28:19, 18:15; Acts 6:2-4). Likewise God intended the servants of these offices to admonish the brethren, to chastise and finally to separate the unrepentant from the brotherhood (Matt. 18:15; Luke 17:3). These holy ordinances are contained in, and must be administered according to, the Word of God (Matt. 17:5).

XXVI. Concerning Orders and Offices to be held in the Church

Even as a body consists of diverse members of which each has its own particular function since not every member is the hand, eye, or foot, so also in the church of God (Rom. 12:4). Though every believer is a member of the body of Christ, not every one is a teacher, elder, or deacon, but only those who have been designated to these offices (Heb. 3:7). Therefore the administration of these offices belongs only to those who have been ordained, not to every layman.

XXVII. How the Election to the Offices shall Occur

The calling or electing of servants to these offices takes place through the ministers of the church together with the congregation (Acts 1:21, 14:23). They call upon the name of the Lord, for he alone knows the human heart, he is in the midst of the believers gathered in his holy name, guiding them by his Holy Spirit (Matt. 18:19-20). Thus he knows the minds and hearts of his own, bringing into service those who will best serve his church.

XXVIII. Concerning the Installation of these Offices

Although the calling and election of these servants occurs as stated, the installation [*bevestinge*] into their office is the work of the elders of the church through the laying on of hands (Acts 6:6, 13:3; 1 Tim. 4:14; 2 Tim. 1:6).

XXIX. Concerning the Teaching and Doctrinal Books of these Servants

The doctrine taught by ordained servants of the people is the same as Jesus brought from heaven, which he taught by Word and deed (that is, with life and teaching) to the people (Heb. 2:3, 12:25; Acts 1:1), and which was preached by the apostles at the command of Christ and by his Spirit (Matt. 28:19; Mark 16:15). This doctrine we find described (as much as is necessary for our salvation) in the writings of the New Testament, to which we add all that is contained in the canonical books of the Old Testament which is in harmony with the teaching of Christ and his apostles, which is in harmony with and conforms to the rule of his spiritual kingdom (Deut. 4:1-2; 2 Tim. 3:16).

XXX. Concerning the Holy Sacraments

Jesus Christ has instituted two sacraments in his holy congregation, baptism and the Holy Supper, attaching their administration to the teaching office [*Leer-ampt*] (Matt. 28:19; Mark 16:15; Matt. 26:25; Luke 22:19). These are external, visible actions and undeserved divine grace given to us, though unworthy, by God (Titus 3:5; Eph. 5:29; Rev. 3:20). They are the inner, invisible and spiritual act of God through Christ (in co-operation with the Holy Spirit), bringing us justification, spiritual nourishment and sustenance to repentant and believing souls. Likewise we testify thereby [in partaking of the sacraments] to our religion, repentance, faith, and obedience, committing ourselves in good conscience to the service of God (Acts 2:38, 8:30; Matt. 3:15).

XXXI. Concerning Holy External Baptism

Holy baptism is an external, visible, evangelical act in which, for a holy purpose, the believer is baptized with water in the name of the Father, Son, and Holy Spirit according to the command of Christ and the practice of the apostles (1 Pet. 3:11; Matt. 28:19; Mark 16:15; Acts 2:38, 41, 8:11, 36-37, 19:15, 48, 10:15, 32-34, 18:8, 19:5). Those who hear, believe, and gladly receive the teaching of the holy gospel with penitent hearts are thus commanded by Jesus to be baptized. But this does not include minor children (Matt. 3:15; Acts 2:31; Rom. 6:3-4; Col. 2:12).

XXXII. Concerning the Inner Significance of Baptism

The whole external, visible act of baptism testifies and signifies that Jesus Christ himself baptizes the repentant believer inwardly with the bath of the new birth and renewal through the Holy Spirit, washing the soul from all filth and sin through the merit of his shed blood (Matt. 3:17; John 1:33; Eph. 5:26; Titus 3:5). Through the power and work of the Holy Spirit the heavenly, spiritual and living water washes the soul of all uncleanness, making it heavenly, spiritual and alive in goodness and righteousness (1 John 1:7; Isa. 44:3; Ezek. 39: 27; Joel 2:28; John 7:38; 1 Cor. 6:11; Titus 3:5-7; Phil. 3:20; Rom. 8:9; Eph. 2:4-5). Therefore water baptism points us to Christ and to his holy office in glory, brings this to our remembrance, and signifies and bears witness to his work to the hearts of the faithful. This external baptism admonishes us not to rely upon the external but in holy prayer to ascend to Christ and to seek the gifts he graciously bestows and multiplies in the hearts of those who receive the sacraments in true faith (John 7:38).

XXXIII. Concerning the Holy Supper

The holy Supper, even as holy baptism, is an external, visible, evangelical act in which, according to the command of Christ and the example of the apostles, bread and wine is received for a holy purpose (Luke 22:19; Acts 2:48, 20:11; 1 Cor. 11:22, 10:15, 11:28). The bread is broken, the wine poured out and given to those who have been baptized upon their faith according to the ordinance of Christ. In eating the bread and drinking the wine Christ's death, passion, and bitter suffering is thereby proclaimed (1 Cor. 11:24-25; Luke 22:19). All this is done in remembrance of him.

XXXIV. Concerning the Significance of the Holy Supper

The entire external, visible practice of the Supper testifies and signifies that Christ's holy body was broken upon the cross, his holy blood shed for the forgiveness of our sins, that in his glorified state he is the living bread, food and drink of our soul (Luke 22:19; 1 Cor. 12:23; Mark 14:24; John 6:51, 55). The external Supper brings to our mind the office and ministry of Christ in glory, his institution of the spiritual Supper with believing souls, feeding them with truly spiritual food (Rev. 3:20; Eph. 5:29). Likewise the external Supper teaches us to rise above the external with holy prayer in our hearts, truly longing for the reality of the gift of Christ. It also teaches us to be thankful to God and to live in love and unity with each other (Col. 3:1-2; 1 Cor. 10:16, 17).

XXXV. Concerning the Ban or Separation

Church discipline or the extreme penalty is an external act among believers by which the unrepentant sinner, after due Christian admonition and sufficient exhortation, is denied the communion of saints and eternal goodness. Due to sin, the wrath of God is announced to him unless he returns in repentance (Matt. 18:15-18; 1 Cor. 5:2, 12). Thus through external separation is shown to the church how God deals with the unrepentant. The initiative in judgment over the fallen sinner lies with God; the church's action follows (John 5:22, 12:48). Therefore it is important to note that no one should be judged by the church unless he has first been judged by the Word of God.

XXXVI. Concerning Avoidance or the Withdrawal of the Unfaithful

Those who are separated from the congregation are in no case allowed to partake of the holy Supper or other ordinances of the church as long as they continue in sin. Also withdrawn from them are all other activities which signify holy communion, fraternity, or spiritual fellowship. Thus their ungodly and misguided life, conversation and daily activity, which is detrimental to the faithful, at times irritating and a burden, is rejected for the preservation of holiness and the honour of the name of the Lord (1 Cor. 5:5; 2 Tim. 2:13, 16-18; Titus 3:10). The faithful withdraw from relationships with such a person and his slander, that the purity of their soul might be preserved. All this, however, must be done in keeping with the Word of God. Married persons may not be separated from each other nor hindered in their marital relationships. Also, nothing may be undertaken that is contrary to love and mercy, nor may their needs and other requirements of daily living be ignored.

XXXVII. Concerning the Office of Worldly Power or Government

Worldly power or government is a necessary ordinance of God, ordained and instituted for the maintenance of public life and orderly citizenship, for the protection of the good and punishment of evil (Rom. 13:1, 3, 4, 6). We confess our obligation, according to the Word of God, to fear, honour, and obey the secular powers in all things not contrary to the Word of the Lord. We are called upon to pray for these powers, to thank God for good and honest government, to give to her without complaint the taxes and assessments which are her due (Titus 3:1; 1 Pet. 2:13, 17; Acts 4:19; Jer. 22:7; 1 Tim. 2:1-2; Matt. 22:17; Rom. 13:7). This office of worldly power has not been given by the Lord Jesus in his spiritual kingdom to the congregation of the New Testament, nor has he added it to the offices of the church (1 Cor. 12:28; Eph. 4:11). He has also not called his disciples or followers to be worldly kings, princes, dukes, or authorities, nor instructed them to seek and assume such office, nor to rule the world in a worldly manner (Matt. 20:25-28; Luke 22:25-27). Much less has he given to the members of his church a law that would fit such an office and government. Rather, with a continuing voice from heaven, they are called to follow his nonresistant life and cross-bearing footsteps for which there is no evidence of worldly government, power, or sword (Matt. 17:5; John 8:12, 10:27; Heb. 12:2, 3; 1 Pet. 2:21-23). Nothing is further from this call than to rule this world with power and the sword. All this then, together with the many other things which are attached to worldly office—the waging of war, the destroying of life and property of the enemy, etc., which things do not harmonize with the new life in Christ—lead us to avoid these offices and services. With this, however, we in no way seek to despise or judge honest government nor give it a lesser place than that given by the Holy Spirit through the writings of the Apostle Paul (Rom. 13:1-3).

XXXVIII. Concerning Swearing of the Oath

Jesus Christ, king and lawgiver of the New Testament, has forbidden all swearing of oaths to Christians. Therefore the swearing of oaths is also not permitted by believers of the New Testament (Matt. 28:20; Gal. 6:4; Matt. 5:34; James 5:10).

XXXIX. Concerning the State of Marriage

We hold marriage to be an ordinance of God, as was the first marriage (Gen. 2:22; Matt. 19:9), instituted in such a manner that every husband shall have his own and only wife, and every wife her own and only husband (1 Cor. 7:2; Eph. 5:31). These may not separate except for reasons of adultery (Matt. 19:9). Neither do we believe that one of our church may marry an ungodly, unbelieving, carnal person outside of the church without being disciplined, as are other sins, by the Word of God, and, according to the circumstances (Deut. 7:2; 1 Cor. 7:30)

XL. Concerning the Return of Christ, the Resurrection of the Dead, and the last Judgment

Finally, we believe and teach that Jesus Christ, our glorified Lord and king (Acts 1:11; Matt. 24:30, 25:31; 2 Thess. 1:7, 1:10; Acts 10:42; 2 Tim. 4:1, 1:1; Matt. 25:32; John 5:28), will come again, visibly, in a manner like unto his ascension, in great power and glory and all the holy angels with him, to reveal himself in his holy ones and all who believe, to judge the living and the dead. Then all people who have lived upon the earth and have died, both good and bad, shall arise imperishable from the grave (1 Cor. 15:42). Their soul shall be united with the body in which they lived sinfully or virtuously. Those who have not died but remain alive upon earth shall be changed in a moment into an eternal state, and all humanity shall appear before the judgment seat of Christ to receive their reward according to their works, either good or evil (2 Cor. 5:10; 1 Cor. 15:51, 52; Matt. 25:32; 2 Cor. 5:10; Matt. 25:10, 32, 35-38, 47). Then Jesus shall separate the sheep from the goats as a shepherd divides his flock, putting the sheep to his right and the goats to his left, and pronounce his judgment upon them. The righteous, who led a holy life here on earth, who did works of love and mercy, he shall separate and take to himself as the bridegroom (John 5:29; Matt. 25:47; 1 Thess. 4:17). They shall enter with him into eternal life, into their heavenly joy and rest, remaining always in the presence of the Lord and inheriting the kingdom which God the Father prepared for them from the foundation of the world (Matt. 25:34; 1 Thess. 1:9). The unrighteous, however, who did not know God nor obeyed the gospel of our Lord Jesus Christ, shall be sent into the eternal fire prepared for the devil and his angels. These shall suffer torment, eternal damnation before the glory and majesty of the Lord (2 Thess. 1:8; Matt. 25:42; Isa. 2:10). May the almighty God, full of grace and mercy, save us from the judgment of the ungodly and grant us grace to live a holy life, to die blessedly, and to arise joyfully at the last day with all true believers. Amen.

10

[The Thirteen Articles (1626)]

Introduction

The relation between the inner word and the outer word of God was debated among many sixteenth century reformers. Mainstream theologians tended to emphasize the authority of the written word (*sola scriptura*), while mystics and spiritualists placed greater value on the illuminating inspiration of the Holy Spirit. Anabaptists reformers usually avoided the polar extremes; nevertheless, they could be found all along the word-spirit continuum.

The debate among theologians regarding the significance of the "inner" and the "outer" continued into the seventeenth century especially in the Netherlands, where early Pietism associated with the *Nadere Reformatie* (the Second Reformation) was making significant inroads in Protestant as well as Catholic circles. Among Anabaptists, the Waterlanders were the most receptive to the spiritualist impulse, and this characteristic often became a stumbling block in their relations with other Anabaptist groups that were more "word" oriented.

That the Waterlanders themselves were not united on the question of the relation between the inner and outer word can be seen in the controversy that took place in the 1620s. A Waterland preacher in Amsterdam, Nittert Obbes, along with his associates, stressed the sufficiency of the outer Word, while Pieter Andries Hesseling, Cornelis Claes Anslo, Reinier Wybrants Wybma, and Hans de Ries embraced the doctrine of the dual Word. In the words of a Remonstrant leader, Simon Episcopius, who sided with Nittert Obbes, the issue among the Waterlanders had to do with "whether the external Word of God, preached or written, is the means or instrument by which God wants to make clear to the people his whole will, perfect and ready, necessary and of service to their eternal salvation...or whether another inner, hidden Word or meaning...is necessary to understand God's will and to obey" (quoted in Voolstra, 110).

The conflict may have begun as early as 1610 when Nittert observed "Schwenckfeldian" characteristics in the Short Confession of Faith, such as the distinction that was made between the inner and outer dimensions of the Christian life. However, Nittert's concerns first became public in 1622 when he voiced his objections regarding the teaching on the dual Word to Hans de Ries. In 1625 Nittert's concerns were brought to a church council meeting in the form of 26 questions composed in his *Raeghbesem*. In Nittert's view, hearing, understanding, and improving one's life on the basis of Scripture and scriptural preaching was sufficient for regeneration.

In response to the growing conflict among the Waterlanders, preachers from the outside were called in to intervene. They drafted thirteen articles, to which Nittert Obbes and his associates finally agreed. In signing the document Nittert indicated that he concurred with the teaching of the dual word. Beyond the written word, he agreed that the Holy Spirit "actually enlightens us inwardly," enabling Christians "as newly awakened, born again people, to live in holiness" (article VIII).

This translation by Cornelius J. Dyck is based on the 1627 printed edition of the *Derthien Artyckelen*, which can be found in the volume by Gerardus Maatschoen. The confession of faith was first printed in the English language in Dyck's dissertation. This translation is the same with minor changes.

Bibliographical Sources

Cornelius J. Dyck, "Hans de Ries: Theologian and Churchman: A Study in Second Generation Dutch Anabaptism" (Ph.D Dissertation, Chicago Divinity School, 1962); Gerardus Maatschoen, *Aanhangsel, dienende tot een Vervolg of derde deel van de Geschiedenisse der Mennoniten* (Amsterdam: Kornelis de Wit, 1745); Sjouke Voolstra, "The Path to Conversion: the controversy between Hans de Ries and Nittert Obbes," in *Anabaptism Revisited: Essays in Anabaptist/Mennonite studies in honor of C. J. Dyck*, edited by Walter Klaassen (Scottdale: Herald Press, 1992) 98-114.

[The Thirteen Articles (1626)]

Translated by Cornelius J. Dyck

Thirteen articles, drafted by Rippert Eenkes and his helpers, besides him signed by Yeme de Ring, Hans Alenson, Engel Pietersz, Gerrit Jansz, and Jan de Plae. Laid before Nittert Obbes, and signed by him for the sake of peace, on September 8, 1626, at Amsterdam.

I.

We believe, confess, and teach that there is one, eternal, and almighty God, or Godly Being, consisting of Father, Son, and Holy Spirit, indistinguishable from one another yet distinguishable in the one Being. To these we ascribe the same eternal nature, being incomprehensible, almighty, everlasting, glorious, omniscient, concerning all things past and things to come, and other similar characteristics uniquely belonging alone to the supreme Godly being.

II.

Item, that there is a two-fold Word of God, the Father Almighty.[1] The one is Jesus Christ, the only begotten Son of God, who is the living, almighty, quickening Word from all eternity to all eternity; through whom God the Father created and made all creatures, the visible heavens and the earth, with all that is therein, besides all things invisible. The other is the written Word of God, contained in the canonical books of the Holy Scriptures, which began in time, was revealed and given to us, and which in time shall end.

III.

Item, that this two-fold Word has been given to us by God the Father for our salvation; that is, the Word of Holy Scripture is given to reveal to us what we are—sinners—what we must become—saints—and how to achieve this through Jesus Christ, the living Word of the Father. To this he himself points, bringing his Word of promise and comfort, and finally eternal salvation. Beyond this our help, reconciliation, deliverance from sin—putting it to death—as well as true enlightenment, the gift of new desires, and divine strength for holy living, lies in him.

IV.

Item, that we, therefore, cannot be saved except through Jesus Christ, the eternal Word of the Father, whom we confess in the following to be our Saviour. That is, he who from all eternity has been the true, almighty God, existing as one and the same Being with the Father and the Holy Spirit, is, and shall be in all eternity. He, we say, became a human being in the fullness of time, though remaining God, divine and a spiritual Being with the Father and the Holy Spirit, as he has been from all eternity. He became what he was not, truly human, like us in all things, except sin, that in his lowly state he might serve us as Saviour.

V.

In order to save us he (being truly human), in his human form lived holy and perfect before us, setting us a perfect example, teaching and confirming his teaching with divine miracles. Finally, after much suffering, he died a bitter death, his blood was shed. Through this blood and death he has become a sacrifice, ransom, and payment for the sins of the world, through his death thus winning reconciliation for the sins of the world before the Father.

VI.

Item, he arose from the dead, ascended into heaven, sitting at the right hand of the Father almighty, sending us from there his Holy Spirit for our renewal, new birth, justification and sanctification.

VII.

Since we cannot attain eternal salvation without this renewal, new birth, justification and sanctification, we confess herewith that we are called, admonished, and moved to this through the written Word of God. In this written Word of God are also revealed to us the saving works, which must come about in us through the power and working of the Holy Spirit. Therefore we confess with Paul that all Scripture is given by God, being profitable for doctrine, for reproof, for correction, for instruction in righteousness, that the children of God may be perfectly equipped for all good works (2 Timothy 3:16, 17).

VIII.

Nevertheless, it is he, Jesus Christ, the Word of the Father, who through the gift of his Holy Spirit actually enlightens us inwardly, teaching, moving, drawing us to all good works, also giving us strength and ability (which we lacked before), to do these good works. [Through him] we do them willingly, denying and putting to death sin, becoming alive and happy in true righteousness. Thus he enables us, as newly awakened, born again people, to live in holiness. This we say, cannot come to pass without this gift, but solely through the written Word.

IX.

Item, that our Lord Jesus Christ, as an expression of his benevolence and grace, as also for instruction and teaching, has commanded his believers that they be baptized with water externally in the name of the Father, etc. and that these baptized members, at a convenient time, should break and eat bread together, and similarly drinking an external wine. By these signs of holy baptism and communion they remind themselves that he permitted his blood to be shed, thereby washing away all sin, and baptizing them with the Holy Spirit. Thus in renouncing all sin they arise to new life, living in true communion with each other. To this end he also gave his body to be broken, that by faith this may become food for our souls, strengthening and helping us.

X.

Item, that this Jesus, our Lord, at the end of the world, shall reveal himself in the clouds of heaven, bringing to life and resurrecting from the dead all people, great and small, old and young, mature and immature, who have died from the beginning of the world to that time.

XI.

Item, that all these resurrected, together with those who will be found alive at his appearing, shall appear before his judgment throne to be judged by him, finally being divided into two groups.

XII.

Item, that the one group shall enter into eternal, unending blessedness, where they, in confessing the divine presence, shall rejoice eternally. Among those blessed shall be included all the innocent, or immature children who from the beginning of the world to that time shall have lived and died.

XIII.

Item, that the other group shall go into eternal fire and damnation, where they shall feel the pain of fire, where there shall be weeping and gnashing of teeth, likewise remaining there through all eternity, even as the blessed shall enjoy their happiness and salvation.

We, the undersigned ministers, confess these preceding articles to be our faith, conviction and teaching. Signed by our hand, September 5, 1626, in Amsterdam.

R. Eenkes
Tomas Piges
Yemen de Ring
Pieter Danielsz
Hans Alenson
Hans de Rees
Engel Pietersz
Reynier Wybrantsz
G. Jansz
Pieter Andriesz
Ian de Pla
Cornelis Claesz

I, Nettert Obbes, the undersigned, confess that all the above articles, drafted and signed by the ministers on September 5, 1626, have been clearly read to me and a copy of them given to me for consideration. [I confess further] that after sufficient consideration I declared and confessed, even as I still declare and confess with all my heart, that I believe in and agree in every substance and detail with the articles of these teachers, desiring further that my book, the *Raag-Bezem*, as well as all my other writings which may seem contrary [to these articles] shall be judged in the light of this, my confession. Witnessed by my hand and those of Rippert Eenkes and Yeme de Ring, at my request. Amsterdam, September 8, 1626.

Nettert Obbes
Rippert Eenkes
Yeme de Ringh

C

Frisian, Flemish, and High German Confessions

11

Thirty-Three Articles (1617)
Confession of Faith According to God's Word

Introduction

In the early seventeenth century the largest Anabaptist groups in the Netherlands were the Waterlanders, the Frisians, the Flemish and the High Germans. The Waterlanders came from the Waterland district in northern Holland; the High Germans, sometimes also referred to as Upper Germans, were a group of Anabaptists originally from South Germany that had migrated northward and had found refuge primarily in urban centres; the Frisians came from the Dutch province of Friesland, and the Flemish originated from the province of Flanders (a part of present-day Belgium).

In the 1560s, many Flemish sought refuge from persecution and settled in the province of Friesland where they came into close proximity with the Frisians. Conflicts soon erupted between these two groups having to do with cultural and theological differences, as well as church practices. The most contentious issue had to do with church discipline which led not only to divisions between the major groups, but also brought about divisions within each group. By the end of the sixteenth century, there were both conservative and liberal factions present in the Frisians and Flemish as well as other Anabaptist groups.

The "Confession of Faith according to God's Word," sometimes referred to as the Thirty-Three Articles, was the work of one of the most conservative Mennonite groups of the early seventeenth century, the so-called Old Frisians. It is the most extensive confessional statement in this genre of confessional writing of all confessions of faith that

Dutch Mennonites adopted in the sixteenth or seventeenth century. Syvaert Pieters likely drafted this major work with consent from the most important Old Frisian leader at the time, Pieter Jansz. Twisck. It was used in a dispute between the Old Frisians and the Waterlanders.

Ostensibly, the catalyst for the disagreement was Hans de Ries's revised martryology, published in 1615 entitled *History of the Martyrs or Genuine Witnesses of Jesus Christ (Historie der Martelaren ofte waerachtighe Getuygen Jesu Christi)*. The Anabaptist martyrology tradition in the Netherlands had begun in 1562 with Jan Hendricks van Schoonrewoerd's *The Sacrifice unto the Lord (Het offer des Heern)*. The first edition was a palm-sized collection of letters and songs that Anabaptist martyrs had written in times of severe persecution. From the 1560s onward the *Sacrifice unto the Lord* went through numerous editions and expansions, so that by the time Thieleman Janz. van Braght's edition appeared in 1660 under the now well-known title, *Martyrs Mirror*, it had become a huge folio. The most significant revisions, however, were not the work of van Braght but that of Hans de Ries. De Ries changed much of the poetic sections of the martyrology into prose, and expanded the martyr book so that it included Anabaptists from across Europe irrespective of their doctrine or behaviour. His criterion for inclusion appears to have been adult baptism. Earlier editors had consciously limited their material to the Dutch tradition, ignoring the martyrs of the Swiss, South German, or Hutterite traditions. According to Brad Gregory, including this wider circle "would have implied doctrinal agreement with these martyrs, an issue vexing enough among the Mennonites themselves" (Gregory, 239).

Hans de Ries boldly challenged this sectarianism within his own tradition and shrewdly cast the martyrological tradition in an inclusive mold. In the preface to his martyr book de Ries claimed that there were really no substantial differences between the various martyrs representing the different Anabaptist groups. On the matter of differences, de Ries, speaking on behalf of his colleagues, maintained, "[W]e do not find that they differ concerning any article of Christian faith about which anyone might rightly be considered or judged as unbelieving, damned, or not saved" (Gregory, 240).

Liberals welcomed such a pronouncement, but it soon raised the ire of the most conservative Mennonite group, the Old Frisians. Their leader, Pieter Jansz Twisck, responded with a martyrology of his own in 1617 entitled *History of the True Witnesses of Jesus Christ (Historie der Warachtighe getuygen Jesus Christi)*. A new preface and title accompanied the volume that was otherwise identical to what de Ries had published two years earlier. Twisck probably knew that the task of questioning the doctrinal integrity and moral character of each martyr in de Ries's huge tome would be impossible, but he and Syvaert Pieters were able to indirectly challenge the Waterlanders by drafting a new preface that included the "Confession of Faith According to God's Word." In the preface, Pieters and Twisck claimed that the martyrs were unanimous in their theology that was specified in their confessional statement. In short, they "contended that all the martyrs held views that harmonized with Old Frisian teachings as elaborated in [their] confession of faith" (Gregory, 241).

It is beyond the scope of this introduction to elaborate on the events that unfolded following the publication of the Frisian martyr book. In brief, it can be stated that de Ries's vision of the martyr tradition prevailed. Yet the confession of faith that challenged the ecumenism of the Waterlanders did not ultimately fade from view. The "Confession of Faith According to God's Word" did find its way into van Braght's *Martyrs Mirror*, and as a stand-alone document it has been reprinted several times and continues to be used by a number of conservative Mennonite groups up to the present day.

The Old Frisians were concerned about the marginalization of Menno Simons' and Dirk Philips' teachings in their day and they sought to recover the old faith and stand once again in the sixteenth century Dutch Anabaptist tradition. In the confession, Melchior Hoffman's doctrine of the incarnation is left intact and, in a number of places, explicit references are made to Menno Simons and Dirk Philips.

This translation by Gary K. Waite is based on the text found in *Historie der Warachtighe getuygen Jesus Christi*.

Bibliographical Sources

Brad Gregory, *Salvation at Stake: Christian Martyrdom in Early Modern Europe* (Cambridge and London: Harvard University Press, 1999); Christian Neff and Nanne van der Zijpp, "Frisian Mennonites," *Mennonite Encyclopedia II*, 413-14; Christian Neff and Nanne van der Zijpp, "Flemish Menonites," *Mennonite Encyclopedia II*, 337-340; Archie Penner, "Pieter Jansz. Twisck—Second Generation Anabaptist/Mennonite Churchman, Writer and Polemicist" (Ph.D Dissertation, University of Iowa, 1971); [Sijwert Pietersz en Pieter Janz. Twisck], "Bekentenisse des Gheloofs," in *Historie der Warachtighe getuygen Jesus Christi* (Hoorn: Zacharias Cornelisz., 1617).

Thirty-Three Articles (1617)

Translated by Gary K. Waite

Confession of Faith/ according to God's Word;
the same that has been believed, taught and experienced
in this way for many years and still today by those called
Mennonites.
And a great many of the same, through various torments, have
testified to
and established this by their death and blood, as
one can see and read in the Histories of the pious witnesses of
Jesus Christ.[1]

2 Cor. 4:13

Since we have the same Spirit of the faith (according to that
which is written: I have believed, therefore I have spoken) so we have
believed, therefore we also speak. Ps. 116:10.

Rom. 10:10

For if one believes from the heart, he is justified; and if one
confesses with the mouth,
then one is saved.

John 7:38

Who believes in me, just as the scriptures say, from his life will
flow floods of living water. So that you not believe and stand upon
human wisdom, but upon the power of God. 1 Cor. 2:5.

1 Pet. 1:8

On account of the faith, you shall rejoice, with unspeakable, glorious gladness, and thereby bring your faith to a conclusion, which is the soul's salvation.

At Hoorn

Published by Zacharias Cornelisz. Bookseller, living in the New Street, in the Liesveltschen Bybel. 1617

To the Reader:

One finds (dearest reader) that many people feel and express differences about these thoughts given here regarding the remembrance of those who confess Jesus Christ. Some do this out of ignorance, others through great bias and bitterness, incriminating them as if they had had no sincere faith (founded on God's word); as if they were driven only by their own conceived opinion, and thus, uncertain, were driven to all of these cruel torments. Also, one hears spoken from these above mentioned ones such evil opinions (some out of ill will, others through ignorance) that they judge as those who are blind and dull (1 Pet. 2:12; Jude 1:12). So we thought it good (for the benefit of well-meaning people) to place before the reader (in as few clear words as we can) the principal, foundational articles and doctrines in simple form and shape just as they have been taught, believed and confessed by these people and their followers, who are now called Mennonites, and who believe and follow after them. And [we have included] also the principal texts from which such [beliefs] are taken, so that all well intentioned investigators and examiners of these things will be able to find how those who confess Jesus Christ, have neither run nor fought with uncertainty (1 Cor. 9:26), but as wise builders (Matt. 7:24; 1 Cor. 1:10) have founded and built their house of faith upon Christ Jesus (Matt. 16:18) and his pure, incorruptible word of truth (John 17:20). For this reason their building has endured and stood against all of these fearful downpours and storm winds (by God's grace) (Matt. 7:25). We have had these aforementioned articles read and reread by diverse (and we trust) God-fearing persons instructed in the word of truth (Acts 18:25-26). For many years until now [these people] have declared the same as God's word and his church [*ghemeente Gods*], and now have come to significant agreement and unity. Also nothing else is composed here except that which is believed and taught by the blessed Menno Simons and Dirk Philips (who were the foremost teachers and elders in this bloody time) and with them, many significant teachers and ministers who have died. Nor could they find, in the reading of this book, that any of these martyrs had made a contrary confession in their chains. But they found the [martyrs] (from which the articles one sees this book has been made) to be of one voice. Read here about Michael Sattler in his confession, and especially the writings of Jaques Dauchy, Louwerens vander Leye, Harmen Timmerman, Jacob de Roer, and his fourth letter, and Jacob vander Weghe with many others who here and there make mention of these aforementioned articles. And we will finish this little [introduction] with a humble prayer: if the reader be pleased to examine these points with simple, impartial hearts (James 3:17; Matt. 11:29), we are confident that they will lead you not to any human commands or discretionary glosses, but only to Christ, and his pure, indisputable Word of the Truth (John 7:38 and 17:20; 2 Tim. 3:1). And we hope that anyone who at this present time agrees with these articles will see that the opponents respond contrary to reason as a clear and detailed treatment of these articles shows. Here also abides the great God of Heaven who commands his high, praiseworthy grace (Acts 20:32).

I. [One God]

Concerning the one God of heaven and earth, we believe with the heart (Num. 10:10) and confess with the mouth that there is only one (Gal. 3:21) eternal (Ps. 90:2), almighty (Gen. 17:1; Sir. 1:7), and true God (John 3:33; Gal. 3:4), who is creator of heaven and earth (Gen. 1:7; Heb. 11:3), together with all visible and invisible things; that all things have their origin and being from him alone (Rev. 4:11) and through his almighty Word all things are supported, ruled and maintained (Heb. 1:3). He is a sincere, perfect, holy, spiritual being

(John 4:24), existing out of or through himself; having no need of any help or assistance from anything, but is himself the origin and fountain of all good things. All perfect, good gifts spring and descend from his out-flowing goodness (James 1:17). This only wise and high God (Rom. 16:26) lives with his most praiseworthy, glorious nature, in heaven above (1 Kings 8:39; Matt. 6:9), in a light which no one has seen nor can see (1 Tim. 6:16). His spirit and power is over all today, filling heaven and earth (Jer. 33:24). Heaven is his throne, and the earth a footstool (Matt. 5:34; Isa. 66:1), from whose all seeing eyes nothing is concealed; for he is an all-knowing hearer and observer of all secrets of human hearts, senses and thoughts; everything is bare and uncovered before his eyes (Heb. 4:13; Sir. 23:18). He is an all-knowing God, full of grace and mercy, and a God of all comfort (2 Cor. 1:3), in whom alone is found the fountain of wisdom and all good gifts (James 1:17; Ps. 36:9). He will give his godly honour to no other (Isa. 42:8 and 48:11). All humans are responsible with ardent prayer to seek (in him and him alone) all pardon, grace, peace, and remittance of sins, and eternal life (with desirous hearts). This only powerful king of all kings and Lord of all lords (1 Tim. 6:15) —before whose most praiseworthy majesty the angels stand with trembling (2 Esd. 8:22; Dan. 7:10; Sir. 1:7; Rev. 5:11), whose word is certain and whose command is strong- -is a righteous judge over all (2 Tim. 4:8). Before him, finally, all knees must bend and bow and all tongues will confess that he alone is the Lord, to the praise of his glory (Isa. 45:23; Rom. 14:11; Phil. 2:10[:10-11]). This one eternal, true God of Abraham, Isaac and Jacob (Exod. 3:15), exists as true Father, Son, and Holy Spirit (1 Cor. 8:6; 1 John 5:7). Apart from this only God, there has never been, nor shall there be found any other eternally (Isa. 43:10 [:10-11]; Bar. 3:35; Isa. 44:6).

Concerning this one, eternal God. Read: "Hear Israel the Lord your God is one Lord." Deut. 6:4; Mark 12:29.

And he spoke through Isaiah: "For I am God and no other. One God who has no likeness anywhere." Isa. 46:8, and 44:6 and 41:4.

And through Paul also: "There is no god in the world and no other God than the only one." 1 Cor. 8:4 and 12:6; Eph. 4:6.

And one must necessarily believe in this one God (as a beginning and foundation of Christian faith) in order to be saved. Read: "For whoever will come to God, must believe that he is; and those who seek him, he will reward them." Heb. 11:6.

To believe in this God is also called a beginning of Christian doctrine. Read: Heb. 6:2; James 2: 19; John 17: 3 and 14:1; Wisdom 15:3; Gen. 15:6; Rom. 4:4.

II. [The Incarnation]

Concerning the eternal birth and divinity of the one, eternal Son of God, it is confessed that before all time in eternity the Son of God was born and proceeded (in an inexpressible manner) from the true God his Father (Mic. 5:2; John 16:28, 30); from the nature and substance of the Almighty God, as light from true light (John 1:6), true God from true God; being in a divine form (Phil. 2:6) an identical image of the invisible God, a glimmer of his glory (Heb. 1:3) and the true image of his nature. That is, he was born and proceeded from God his Father as a reflection of the eternal light (Wis. 7:26) and a mirror without blemish of the majesty of God and in an image of his divinity; having his Father's nature, form and quality—for example being eternal, almighty, holy and so on (Phil. 2:6); for it is inevitable that like produces like (John 5:18). It is, however, also a matter of faith and not of reason (Heb. 11:1). This must be understood only in a spiritual and godly fashion, not in a fleshly and human fashion (1 Cor. 2:13). In this way this only born Son must be confessed (John 5:32), honoured, worshipped and regarded (John 9:38, Heb. 1:6) as the true God (1 John 5:21 [John 5:21]) by all believers, and given the same worth as the Father.

Concerning this high, eternal birth and procession, read: "You are my Son, today have I given birth to you." Ps. 2:7; Acts 13:39; Heb. 1:5 and 5:8.

The prophet Micah, speaking about Bethlehem, said: "Out of you shall come one who will be a lord in Israel, whose origin is from the beginning and from eternity." Micah 5:1; John 16:28, 31.

And further through Paul: "That which is a true image of the invisible God, the first born before all creatures." Col. 1:15; Rev. 3:14.

By John: "no one has ever seen God. The only born Son who is in the bosom of the father has proclaimed him to us." John 1:18 and 14ff.

Read further: Prov. 6:8, 23; Dan. 2:34-45; Sir. 24:13; Rom. 8:29. Of the divinity of Christ, read: Ps. 45:8; Heb. 1:8; John 1:1 and 20:28; Rom. 9:5; John 5:20.

III. [Holy Spirit]

Concerning the Holy Spirit, it is believed and confessed: that there is a true, real [*wesentlijcke*] Holy Spirit (Matt. 3:16; John 1:32), whose being [must be] understood as one, eternal and divine in nature, who proceeds from the Father and the Son (John 15:26 and 14:26). He is the power of the Most High (Luke 1:35), through whom the Father and Son work (Ps. 33:6) and through whom heaven and earth, with all the heavenly hosts, have been created and made. To him is ascribed the divine qualities, such as eternal, almighty, holy, and all-knowing (Heb. 9:14), who examines the depths of the divinity (1 Cor. 2:12 [10-12]), who knows what is in God, and who penetrates and examines all spirits, regardless of how obvious or subtle they may be (Wis. 7:24; Isa. 40:13). For this reason he is confessed as true God (Acts 5:4 and 17:28) with the Father and Son. He is a subtle breath of the power of God (Wis. 7:25), who with his divine inspiration (John 20:21 and 3:8) enlightens the hearts of people and makes them fiery, and establishes and leads them in all truth. He is given by God to all who are obedient to him (Acts 5:32). All who are driven[2] by this Spirit are God's children (Rom. 8:9, 14). Whoever does not have this Spirit does not belong to God. [The Holy Spirit] is called the seal and pledge of the inheritance of all true children of God (Eph. 1:14 and 4:30). Whoever blasphemes this Spirit can expect no forgiveness for eternity (Matt. 12:31). It is commanded by Christ to baptize believers also in his name (Matt. 28:19).

Concerning this only Spirit of God, read: "In the beginning God created heaven and earth, and the earth was void and empty, it was dark in the abyss, and God's Spirit hovered over the water." Gen. 1:1.

Through Paul: "There are many gifts, but there is one Spirit." 1 Cor. 12:4. "It is the same Spirit who does all this work and gives according to his will; for we are baptized in one Spirit to one body [whether] we are Jews or Greeks, slaves or free; for we are all instructed by one Spirit." 1 Cor. 12:13. Read also: 2 Sam. 23:2; Eph. 4:4; Matt. 10:20; Luke 12:11; Matt. 3:16; John 1:32; Matt. 28:19; Mark 16:15.

IIII.[3] [Father, Son and Holy Spirit]

How the attributes of the Father, Son and Holy Spirit are to be distinguished, it is confessed that in the one eternal divine nature there are not three vain or empty names, but each name has its own true significance and qualities. There is a true, real Father (1 Cor. 8:6) from whom all things are, a true, real Son (1 Cor. 8:6), through whom all things are, and a true, real Holy Spirit (Gen. 1:1; Matt. 3:16; John 1:32), through whom the Father and Son work (Ps. 33:6). The Father is the true Father, who has given birth to the Son before all time and from whom the Son has proceeded and come (Ps. 2:7; Heb. 1:5), and through the same are all things created and made (John 16:28), and through whom the Son was sent as a Saviour of the world (John 1:3). The Son is the one who was born of the Father, and proceeded and came from him (John 1, 4:14). Through the Son the Father has created all things; he was sent from the Father and came into the world (John 8:42 and 10:36). Through the active power of the Most High, he was conceived by Mary and born as a human being (Luke 1:27); who suffered, was crucified (Matt. 27:49), died, and rose again from the dead (Luke 24:45), ascended into heaven (Mark 16:19) and sits at the right hand of his almighty Father in heaven. The Holy Spirit is the one who proceeds and is sent from the Father and the Son (John 15:26 and 14:26), and through whom the Father and Son work (Acts 16:13). He does not speak on his own accord, but proclaims to his own what he has heard from the Father and from Christ. Hence, there are three true witnesses (1 John 5:7) (in one, identical divine nature) in heaven: the Father, the Word, and the Holy Spirit, of whom the glory of the only born Son of God appeared really and distinctly in the form of a servant upon the earth (Phil. 2:7), as also John the Baptist was allowed to see at the Jordan (John 1:14). And the Holy Spirit allowed himself to be distinctly seen by this same John in the form of a dove, descending out of heaven from God and abiding in Christ (Matt. 3:16; John 1:32). And the voice of the Father (who is an invisible Spirit and who cannot be seen by any mortal human's eyes) (Exod. 33:20; John 1:18; 1 John 4:12) was heard from heaven saying: "this is my beloved Son in whom I am well pleased" ([Matt. 3:17]).

Of these three true witnesses, it is also distinctly spoken: "If I testify on my own accord, my testimony is not certain. It is another who testifies of me." John 5:31.

"I am not alone, but I am with the Father who sent me. Also it stands written in your law that the testimony of two people is true. I am the one who testifies of myself, and the Father who sent me also testifies of me." John 8:16, verses 29, 54; 1 John 5:20; John 16:32 and 15:24.

And further by Paul: "There is one God and also one mediator between God and humanity, namely the man Jesus Christ." 1 Tim. 2:5; 1 Cor. 6:8.

"Whoever transgresses and remains not in the teaching of Christ has no God. Whoever remains in the teaching of Christ has both the Father and the Son." 2 John 1:9.

Of the Holy Spirit Christ said: "I will pray to the Father and he will give you another comforter, that he will abide with you forever. [He is] the Spirit of truth, which the world cannot receive." John 14:16; Matt. 12:32.

"But if I go away from you, so I will send him to you, for he will not speak of himself, but what he hears, that shall he speak, and whatever is in the future, that shall he proclaim. This one shall honour me, for he shall take whatever is mine and proclaim it to you." John 16:7 and 13-14.

"Jesus being baptized, climbed out of the water. And see, the heavens opened above him and John saw the Spirit of God descending like a dove, and coming upon him. And see, there came a voice from heaven, saying, 'This is my beloved Son, in whom I am well pleased.'" Matt. 3:16; John 1:32. Read also Ps. 110:1; 2 Esd. 13:32; John 1:1; 1 Cor. 12:5; 1 John 5:7.

"For there are three witnesses in Heaven: the Father, the Word and the Holy Spirit." 1 John 5:7; 1 Cor. 12:4; Rev. 3:14.[4]

V. [The Unity of God]

And since these three true witnesses are but one single, true God, it is confessed that it must surely follow from this that the Son is born and proceeds from the single, eternal being and substance of the Father. The Holy Spirit proceeds truly from the Father and Son, and is understood to be one, eternal, divine being with the Father and Son. Beyond this, it is abundantly testified and established in the Holy Scriptures that the divine works and properties that are ascribed to the Father, Son and Holy Spirit are not ascribed to any of the angels in heaven (Rev. 19:10 and 21:9; Acts 10:26 and 14:14 [:14-15]), much less to any other creatures, but are the property of only the one God. [His works include] creating (Ps. 43:6 [?]; John 1:3; Heb. 1:2), ruling and sustaining heaven and earth, with all visible and invisible things; sending the gracious gospel from heaven (1 Pet. 1:12); the commissioning of the apostles to preach the same among all people; resurrecting people from the dead (John 5:21) and giving them eternal life (John 10:28); [deserving] all godly worship, honour and reverence (Heb. 1:6; John 9:38). [These three] are perfectly one, not only in will, words and works, but also in being. Hence, what the Father does, the Son does as well (John 5:19, 21; Acts 1:2). And just as the Father raises the dead, so also the Son makes living those whom he will. This they all do in the power and in cooperation with the Holy Spirit (Luke 4:14) Therefore, with reason and truth, they must [together] be called the one God of heaven and earth (Deut. 6:4). Apart from this, there is no other God (Isa. 41:10), nor shall any other be found eternally. Therefore, with the phrase 'one God' is meant Father, Son and Holy Spirit (Matt. 28:19).

Read here the prophet Jeremiah: "The gods who did not make the heaven and earth will be destroyed from the earth under heaven." Jer. 10:11 and Isa. 44:24; Ps. 96:5.

"The heaven was made through the Word of the Lord, and all its hosts by the Spirit of his mouth." Ps. 33:6; Heb. 3:4; Acts 4:24.

"All things were created by the same, and without the same was nothing made that is made." John 1:3, and 5:19.

Of this perfect unity, read: "The Father has given me this (spoke Christ) who is greater than all, and no one can take it out of my Father's hand. I and the Father are one." John 10:19.

To Philip Christ said: "Who has seen me has seen the Father. Do you not believe that I am in the Father and the Father is in me?" John 14:9, and 12:45 and 17:21.

How the Holy Spirit is also called God, read: Peter to Ananias: "Why has Satan filled your heart that you have lied to the Holy Spirit." And shortly thereafter: "You have not lied to humans but to God." Acts 5:3-4.

"Those who preached the gospel to you have been sent by the Holy Spirit from heaven." 1 Pet. 1:12.

"The grace of our Lord Jesus Christ and the love of God, and the fellowship of the Holy Spirit be with you all. Amen." 2 Cor. 13:13.

"For there are given three witnesses in Heaven: The Father, the Word and the Holy Spirit. And these three are one." 1 John 5:7; Deut. 6:4; Matt. 12:29; 1 Cor. 8:6; Gal. 3:20.

VI. [Creation]

Concerning the creation of heaven and earth and of humanity, it is confessed that the one eternal God in the beginning was pleased (in a wonderful way, above all human understanding) (Gen. 1:1) to create and make from nothing the heavens with all their glorious, adorned, shining lights (Bar. 3:35; Bar. 3:32 [:32-34]), and the earth with all its gushing fountains and running streams (Rev. 14:17; Acts 14:14), the trees and animals, and all that lives thereupon and touches it, and also the sea with the great whales and all that lives therein and touches it (Gen. 1:21). At the moment that he had merely spoken the words "heaven and earth," his Word became a perfect work (2 Esd. 6:38). And he founded the earth out of the water and established it in the water (2 Pet. 3:5; Job 26:8), through his almighty Word, which shall be maintained until the great day of judgment. After God the Lord had created everything very wisely and good (Gen. 1:31; Prov. 3:19), he created humanity from the matter of the earth on the sixth day (Gen. 1:26), and breathed into him a living breath, and from Adam's rib created and prepared a wife and helper (Gen. 2:21; Gen. 5:1). With grace he chose and considered them above all creatures, adorned with majesty; thereafter he clothed them with his own divine virtues (Sir. 17:2; Eph. 4:24), which are righteousness and holiness. In addition he gifted them with wisdom, speech and reason, so that they could know, fear, serve, love and be obedient to their Creator; being so regarded and chosen that they should always live for him (Wis. 2:23 and 1:14), governing and ruling over all creatures which God the Lord had made (Gen. 1:26).

Of this wonderful creation, read: "In the beginning God created heaven and earth." Gen. 1:1; John 1:3; Ps. 33:6.

"God has spoken the word heaven and earth and your Word has become a perfect work." 2 Esd. 6:38.

"For your almighty hand has created the earth out of nothing." Wis. 11:18 [11:17]

The Mother of the Maccabees: "Son, I pray that you look to heaven and earth and all that is in them, and understand that God has made all out of nothing, including the human race." 2 Mac. 7:28.

"By faith we observe that the world was made through the word of God, so that the visible things should come from the invisible." Heb. 11:3; Acts 17:24; Ps. 128, 146:6.

Of the creation of humanity, read: "Let us make humanity an image that is like us." Gen. 1:26.

"And God the Lord made humanity from the matter of the earth and blew a living breath into his nose, and then humanity became a living soul." Gen. 2:6; Acts 17:25; 1 Cor. 15:45.

How he has created, read: "I have found that God has created humans upright." Eccles. 7:30 and Gen. 1:26 and 5:1.

"For God created humanity immortal and he made him after the image of his likeness." Wis. 2:23; Sir. 17:1.

"And put on the new humanity which is created after God in righteousness and holiness." Eph. 4:24.

"And God looked at what he had made, and saw that it was all very good." Gen. 1:31; Deut. 32:4.

VII. [The Fall]

Concerning the fall of the human beings and their punishment, it is confessed that the first humans, Adam and Eve, were gloriously created for eternal life after the image of their Creator (Gen. 1:26 and 5:2). [Yet] they did not remain long in this divine state. [Although] they were created free their Creator gave them a command not to eat of the tree of the knowledge of good and evil; for in the day that they would eat of it, they would die (Gen. 2:17). Notwithstanding this, they were led astray, moved and deceived away from God by Satan's lofty words (Tob. 4:21[3:18?]; Gen. 5:5; Sir. 10:13) that they could become like their Creator in wisdom and knowledge (1 Tim. 2:13 [:13-14]; Gen. 3:6). They were thus disobedient and wilfully disobeyed their Creator's command. The woman, who was created last, was deceived first. Having turned her ears away from God, she turned to Satan, and then also deceived her husband. Thus, they fell through sin into the wrath and disfavour of God, and on the same day became subject to temporal and eternal death (Gen. 3:29; Sir. 15:13 [:13-14]; 1 Cor. 15:21) — they and their descendants. As a result, they were stripped of the divine virtues, which are righteousness and holiness, and they became sinful. Furthermore, God who is righteous (and who hates and punishes sin) became so enraged over this misdeed that Adam, along with all of his descendants (Gen. 3:23) experienced the same punishment and disfavour, so that they were all driven out of the glorious paradise and garden to experience temporal and eternal death (Rom. 5:18). On account of this sin the earth became cursed (Gen. 3:27) and would not produce without great difficulty. And they covered their bodies' shame (1 Tim. 2:12), the woman became subject to the man's authority (1 Tim. 1:9), and had to give birth to children in suffering and pain (Gen. 3:16). [This punishment continues] until they finally return to the earth (as a wage of sin) (Gen. 3:19; Rom. 6:23; Gen. 2:17) from which they came.

Read here about how Adam, with the whole human race, has through sin fallen into temporal and eternal death and accordingly has become sinful. "Therefore, similarly as sin through one person has come into the world and death through sin, so death has spread to all people. But death has lordship from Adam to Moses, even over those who had not sinned. Similarly, through the sin of one sinner all became depraved. For the judgment has come out of one sin [leading] to damnation. For on account of one person's sin, death has had dominion. Similarly, through one sin damnation has come over all humans. For just as through one person's disobedience, many have become sinners." Rom. 5:12 verses 14, 17, 18.

"For just as through one man comes death, so also through one man [comes] the resurrection from the dead. For just as they all die in Adam, so shall they all be made alive in Christ." 1 Cor. 15:21.

"I am born of sinful seed, and in sin my mother conceived me." Ps. 51:7.

"Who can find a pure thing among the things where nothing is pure?" Job 14:4.

"Sin originates from a woman, and on her account we must all die." Sir. 25:33 [:24]; Titus 2:14; Wis. 2:24.

"The prophet Esdra: "The first Adam, burdened with an evil heart, transgressed and was overcome, yes, and all those born from him. He transgressed and immediately you brought death to him and his race." 2 Esd. 3:7, 21.

"O Adam, what have you done? For when you sinned, your fall was not made alone, but also for us all—we who have sprung from you." 2 Esd. 7:48.

Read further: John 3:6; Rom. 8:5; Eph. 2:3; Sir. 17:13; Gen. 6:5; Wis. 12:10.

Read further on how God announced to Adam the punishment for his sin, and how it extends to all his descendants: "Because you have listened to the voice of your wife and have eaten of the tree that I have forbidden, saying you shall not eat of it; cursed be the earth on your account; with work shall you eat of it all of your life; it will produce thorns and thistles for you, and you shall eat the plants of the field; in the sweat of your face shall you eat your bread until you return again to the earth from whence you have come. For you are dust, and you shall return to dust." Gen. 3:17, 23 and 24 verses. For the punishment to the wife read: Gen. 3:16; 1 Cor. 14:34; 1 Tim. 2:12.

VIII. [Restoration of Humanity]

Concerning the restoration or justification of humans it is confessed that Adam and Eve had thus fallen in sin together with all their descendants (Rom. 5:14). All originate out of an identical, sinful seed (Ps. 51:7; Job 14:4), and for this reason everyone from their youth on are inclined toward sin and evil (Gen. 6:5 and 8:21). Therefore, everyone has been captured by the power and authority of Satan and [are subject to] temporal and eternal death (Col. 1:13). However, the Creator of all things, who is the almighty God, rich in grace and mercy (2 Cor.1:3), had mercy again on the fallen human race and gave to them a trustworthy promise, saying to them [that he would send them] a Saviour, whom he would set as an enmity between Satan and the woman and between both of their seed (Gen. 3:15; Col. 2:15). And this same one will tread on the head of the serpent and thus take away the power of Satan (Heb. 2:14; 2 Tim. 1:10; 1 Cor. 15:4), and thereby deliver the whole human race from the wrath of God and from eternal death. And just as God the Lord, through this promise inwardly clothed Adam and his seed with his grace and mercy as a true sign ork evil through the fall of Adam, and have fallen into eternal damnation (Rom. 5:18), in the same way all humans (without any distinction of persons) (Rom. 5:18), solely by pure grace and mercy (Titus 2:11 and 3:5; 2 Tim. 1:9; John 3:16; 1 Tim. 4:10; Rom. 8:32), through the promise of the redeemer, Jesus Christ, are delivered, freed and made righteous again, without their own good works, out of the eternal death and damnation into which they have fallen and lay submerged through Adam. But God, the Lord, who hates and punishes sin, let the sinful nature abide in Adam and all his descendants, who are inclined to do evil from their youth [onward] (Gen. 8:27; Rom. 7:18). [The consequence of their sin is that they are] deprived of the beautiful paradise (Gen. 3:23); they must cover their nakedness; the woman is [subject] to the man's authority (1 Tim. 2:12); and children are born in suffering and pain (Gen. 3:18); and finally, [they will experience] temporal death and return again to dust and earth (Gen. 3:19; Heb. 9:28.).

Of these glorious and trustworthy promises of salvation, read: "And I shall set enmity between you and the woman, and between your seed and her seed; the same shall tread on your head." Gen. 3:15; Eph. 2:14-15.

How these promises are renewed in the seed and race of Adam, read: "A prophet like me the Lord your God shall awaken from your members and out of your brothers, him shall you hear." Deut. 18:15; Acts 7:37. [How these promises apply] to Abraham: Gen. 12:3; 22:18; Acts 10:43.

That these promises do not pertain to any particular persons but without distinction to all humans, read: "Similarly, just as through one person's sin damnation has come over all humans, so also through one person's righteousness salvation of life has come over all humans. For just as through one person's disobedience many have become sinners, so will also through one person's obedience many be made righteous." Rom. 5:18-19.

"For just as through one person came death, so also through one person comes the resurrection of the dead. For just as they all shall die in Adam, so shall they all be made living again in Christ." 1 Cor. 15:21.

"It was a true light that enlightens all humanity, through his coming into the world." John 1:9, 29.

"And the same is the reconciliation for our sin. Not only for our sin, but also for the whole world." 1 John 2:2.

"For it has been the pleasure of the Father that in him all fullness shall dwell and that all through him be reconciled to himself, be it on the earth or in heaven, there also that he himself has made peace through the blood of his cross." Col. 1:19-20.

"For the saving grace of God has appeared to all humans." Titus 2:11. Read further: Rom. 3:14 and 11:32; 1 Tim. 4:10; 2 Cor. 5:19; 1 John 4:10; Isa. 53:7; 1 Pet. 2:24.

IX. [Free Will]

Concerning free will and abilities of human beings, before and after the fall, it is confessed that Adam and Eve, being created after the image of God, and standing in this state of grace, had knowledge and understanding above all creatures (Sir. 17:6; Gen. 1:26). They also had a free will and were able to accept or oppose and reject the sin offered by Satan, which they demonstrated in the beginning when they first sinned (Gen. 3:3). Since they were not created immovable [*onbeweechelijck*], they [could] allow themselves to be deceived and led astray by the deception of Satan (who showed himself to be deceitful) (Gen. 2:6; 2 Cor. 11:5; Wis. 2:24). Thus they fell willingly through their own guilt into sin and death. Having thus fallen, Adam and Eve were nevertheless noticed and given grace so that they maintained knowledge and understanding above all creatures, and (by grace) also a free will (Gen. 3:15; 2 Pet. 1:3: Rom. 8:32). They have actually shown this in their reception of God's gracious promises. Such free will and ability (by God's grace) has remained in all their descendants (Rom. 7:18) (having come to their understanding)[5] so that they are able to accept or reject the bountiful grace of God (Sir. 11:10; Matt. 14:7). For the good (Matt. 19:17), righteous and merciful God (2 Cor. 1:3) has not desired that his chosen creatures above all creations should lose their divine gifts, and become like a beast, block or stone, without movement, knowledge and ability of God's grace and goodness. Would he threaten to punish them with the eternal death and damnation if they could desire only those things they were forced to [accept]? Even more, that they should neither will nor desire God himself? All true believers regard such [possibilities] as unacceptable and completely reprehensible. [Contrary to this way of thinking] it is confessed that God, through his gracious promises in Christ, has granted again to the entire fallen human race everything that serves them toward eternal life and a divinely blessed walk (1 Pet. 1:3). Hence, they can will and desire the grace of God (2 Cor. 3:6; Phil. 4:13), and to this end he has proclaimed his commands with his word (Matt. 16:25) in order to invite all people in all the ends of the earth (Isa. 45:22) to repentance and amendment [of life] (Rom. 2:4), and to come to his well prepared banquet (Matt. 22:4; Isa. 25:6); hereby also proving that he does not wish that anyone become lost (1 Tim. 2:4; 2 Pet. 3:9) but that everyone [is capable] of improvement and becoming saved. [This being the case, God has] thus good reason to punish despisers and rejecters of his grace with eternal death (Acts 13:46; Rom. 2:5), and [he has good reason] to save believers who accept the same grace (Bar. 3:39 [3:19?]), and thereby give them eternal life. Thus the perishing and destruction of the unbelieving and godless comes only through themselves (Hos. 13:6). And the salvation of the believing comes only from the Lord, who gives at the beginning (Phil. 2:13) and who strengthens and protects to the end (1 Pet. 1:5). For just as human beings have outward eyes and ears so that they can see and hear, but in no way through themselves, but only from God who gives (James 1:17; 2 Cor. 3:5), so God has given the will and understanding to humans so that they, through his grace (2 Esd. 2:37), can accept or reject gifts offered to them (Gal. 2:21). In this way the goodness of God comes, which by his Spirit the hearts of humans have been opened and inflamed (Luke 24:44 [:44-45]) so that his word may bear fruits (to his honour) (Matt. 13:23).

Read here from the many frequent Scripture-places wherein human beings are given a will. And the Holy Spirit through the writing speaks not in vain. God the Lord spoke to Cain: "But if you are not righteous, then sin calls at the door; do not allow it [to control], but rule over it." Gen. 4:7. "He has created human beings from the beginning and given them the choice. Will you keep the commandments and do what pleases him in true faith? He has set before you fire and water; grasp which ever one you will; a person has before him life and death, whichever he wills, that shall be given to him." Sir. 15:20; Deut. 11:26 and 30:15; 2 Esd. 7:59.

"He indeed could do much evil but he nevertheless did not do it; he could do much harm and also did not do it." Sir. 31:10 and 18:25, Luther's text.

And further by Paul: "For according to all their ability (which I witness) and also above their ability were they willing. Now fulfil what you have begun to do, so that just as there is a spirit inclined to will it, then there must also be a spirit inclined to do it." 2 Cor. 8: 3 and 11; Philem. 1:14; Mark 14:7.

"For God is the one who works in you, both willing and completing according to the good intention of the heart." Phil. 2:13.

"You live among a disobedient people who have eyes that they can see, but they will not see. And ears, that they can hear and yet they will not hear." Ezek. 12:2.

"I indeed have the will, but to fulfill the good, that I find not." Rom. 7:18, 19, 21.

Read here all the Scriptures that testify uniformly that God does not will the death of the sinners, but that they turn to him and live. Ezek. 18:32, and 33:11; Wis. 1:13; Isa. 55:7; Matt. 11:28.

"For it is good and also acceptable before God our Saviour: who also wills that all people be saved and come to the knowledge of truth." 1 Tim. 2:4.

"He is long-suffering toward you and wills not that anyone remain lost, but that everyone give himself to improvement." 2 Pet. 3:9; Rom. 2:4; James 1:6; Acts 13:46. Read also Matt. 23:36; Luke 13:32; 2 Esd. 1:30.

X. [Foreknowledge]

Concerning the foreknowledge [*voorsienicheydt*] of God, the election of believers and the rejection of unbelievers, just as God is almighty (Gen. 17:1; Luke 1:33) and nothing is impossible for him, it is believed and confessed that he also foresees and knows all things (Act 17:26), so that nothing (in heaven and earth) is hidden from him. This also includes those things that shall occur at the end of time (Sir. 23:28 [26?]), and those things that have happened from eternity. Through immeasurably high providence, knowledge and wisdom, which is unfathomable (Isa. 40:28; Rom. 11:33), from the beginning of time until the completion of the world, God has clearly seen and known who would become true believing recipients of his grace and mercy (Bar. 3:39 [:19]), and who would not believe, despising and rejecting the same (Act 13:46; Bar. 3:39 [?]). Concerning this he has known, foreseen, chosen and ordained all true believers from the beginning

(Rom. 8:29) and has given them possession of the inheritance of eternal salvation through Christ Jesus (Eph. 1:5; 1 Pet. 1:4), while the unbelieving, who have despised this grace, he has cast into eternal damnation (Mark 16:16; 2 Esd. 9:12). The [unbelieving] have thus come to destruction by themselves (Hos. 13:9). Their salvation is only through the Lord their God, without whom they are able to do nothing good (John 15:6; James 1:17). But in no way [is it true] that the gracious, merciful, righteous God (Acts 17:31; Ps. 7:11; 1 John 2:29; Deut. 32:5) (consistent with his holy nature) has determined from eternity that the vast majority of the human race at the appropriate time should be created for eternal damnation. If this were the case, then as a result of the sin of the first man Adam, he should have let them lie without help in eternal death and damnation, into which they had come without their knowledge, as a result of their own evil works (Rom. 5:14), without even having seen and known any righteous reason for their expulsion (Isa. 47:8). Such [thinking] about the only good (Matt. 19:17) and righteous God (Isa. 11:4)[6] is far from all believers. On the contrary, all true followers of Christ believe and confess that God, who is good, initially created human beings good (Gen. 1:31) and upright (Eccl. 7:30 [:29]), and that he does not hate (Wis. 1:14) the things that he has made (Wis. 11:25). Through the deception of the devil, they have fallen into eternal death, yet the good God (whose mercy covers all flesh (Sir. 18:12; Ps. 145:9; Wis. 11:25) and who wills that no one remain lost) (2 Pet. 3:9) delivered again (Col. 1:13) the whole human race (without any regard for persons) out of love and mercy (1 John 3:16), choosing (Rev. 5:9) and freeing them from eternal damnation through the atonement of our Lord and Saviour Jesus Christ. Hence, no one, on account of Adam's sin (Rom. 5:18) (given Christ's death) shall be lost, but God the righteous judge shall justly consider and judge the whole earth (Acts 17:31) and reward those who maintain the faith, and will repay each one according to the works and deeds which they have done (Rev. 20:12; Ps. 62:12). Believers who persevere in good works and seek eternal life (Rom. 2:6-7) shall experience praise and honour and the imperishable nature. But unbelievers and the disobedient [will come to experience] anguish, mourning and the eternal wrath of God (Rom. 2:8-9; 2 Thess. 1:8).

Of the providence and foreknowledge of God, read: "And he has foreseen from eternity, how long and how far they shall live." Acts 17:26; Deut. 32:8.

The Wisdom [of Solomon]: "She knows signs and wonders before they happened." Wis. 8:8; Dan. 2:28, 5:17.

"Oh eternal God, who knows all hidden things, who knows all things before they happen." Dan. 13:42; Isa. 46:9; Job 42:2; Rom. 9:11; Acts 2:23, 31; 1 Pet. 1:20.

"My frame was not hidden from you, while I was secretly made. As I was being created under the earth your eyes saw me, even when I was still unfinished. All days were written in your book, when none as yet existed." Ps. 139:15.

"All things are known to him before they are created, indeed, as if they are created." Sir. 23:28; Acts 15:18.

Hereby supports, with qualifications, how God through his foreknowledge has chosen the believers from the beginning in Christ and has rejected the unbelievers, read: "I have said to you before and I have told you before it has happened. But I know indeed that you should despise it and therefore you have been named a transgressor from your mother's body." Isa. 48:5,8; Mal. 1:2; Rom. 9:13; Eph. 3:11; 2 Tim. 1:9.

"And before they were sealed, those who believed were gathered as a treasure, then I thought of it." 2 Esd. 6:6.

"For who is like me? Let him call and proclaim and try me, how I had ordained the people from the beginning of the world." Isa. 44:7.

"We know that for those who love God, all things serve to the best which are called according to his purpose. For those whom he has foreknown, he has also ordained that they should be like the image of his Son, so that they will be the first born among many brothers. For those whom he has foreordained, these he has also called, and whom he has called, these he has also justified." Rom. 8:28 [:28-30].

"Before I prepared you in the mother's body, I knew you, and I have blessed you before you were born from your mother." Jer. 1:4.

"Just as he has chosen us through the same, before the foundation of the world was laid." Eph. 1: 4; 2 Tim. 1:9; John 15:16; Acts 13:48.

XI. [The Written Word]

Concerning the written word of God, the law of Moses and the gospel of Christ, it is confessed that the old law of Moses was given and had been granted through the ministry of angels (John 1:17; Acts 7:53) as a perfect teaching and rule for the descendants of Abraham and Jacob (Gen. 17:2) with whom God the Lord had made and established his covenant. According to the teaching and pronouncement of this law, the people were to order and govern themselves without breaking any of the same (Deut. 4:2 and 12:32 and 17:15), nor were they to omit any of it nor follow their own inclinations (Deut.12:8)—otherwise they risked being exterminated (Num. 15:31) and cursed (Deut. 27:26 [:15-16]; Gal. 3:10). The hearers, believers and fulfillers of this law were promised life (Lev. 18:5; Rom. 10:6), with many glorious blessings (Deut. 28:2). The blessings and curses extended mostly to temporal and physical things. This law of God (which is the five books of Moses, under which are also included all kings, priests and prophets [John 10:34] who have prophesied and spoken by God's Spirit among the people of Israel, in accordance with the law of Moses), which is the Old Testament, has been displayed by God's grace in the Bible.

This law is also spiritual (Rom. 7:14) and is an introduction to a better hope (Heb. 7:18); it is an instructor [*leer-meester*] pointing to Christ (Gal. 3:24), with its many figures and shadows (Heb. 10:1), such as the Levitical priesthood, the sermons and sacrifices, the land of Canaan, kings (Luke 1:29), the city of Jerusalem and temple. Like a hand it leads to Christ Jesus (Gal. 3:24); [yet] the old law has been [also] an unbearable yoke (Acts 15:10) of servitude (Gal. 5:1; Rom. 8:2) cursing all those who do not live according to what is written in the book of the law and who do not fulfill everything (Deut. 27:29). Human beings, through the weakness of the flesh (Rom. 8:3), have not been able to keep all of it perfectly. They could not obtain the eternal, blessed life through the law, but had to abide under the wrath (Rom. 4:15) and anger of God (Gal. 3:19).

Hence, Christ Jesus has come, being the end (Rom. 10:4) and the perfecter of the old law (Matt. 5:17) and the author of the new law (Heb. 8:9, 14), of perfect freedom (James 1:25); [he is] the true, clear light (John 1:9) to which all the dark shadows point. He is the one sent by God with perfect power and authority (Matt. 28:18) in heaven and on earth, and has with the citizens of Israel and men of Judah, established a New Testament (Jer. 31:31), and hereto invited all heathens and peoples of the earth who were far-off strangers and enemies (Eph. 2:12), but are now all invited through the grace (Rom. 4:17) along a path to life that is open and well-trodden (2 Esd. 2:32; Zech. 13:1). They can now (through obedience) become fellow citizens with all the saints and fellow householders of God (by grace) (Eph. 2:18). In the New Testament, perfect grace and peace (Eph. 2:13, 16; Mark 1:15), remission of sins and eternal life are proclaimed with everything that serves us for the life and blessed walk (2 Pet. 1:3), and informs us of the counsel of God (Acts 10:27).

In keeping with this pronouncement (2 Thess. 1:8) all believing children of the New Testament necessarily must regulate and order themselves, according to all matters [*stucken*] of the faith, who finally shall be held in eternal judgment (John 12:48; 1 Pet. 4:17). It is so much more worthy and firmer than the Old Testament, since it was given through a higher and worthier ambassador (Matt. 28:18), and was established and sealed by his most precious blood (1 Pet. 1:18; 1 Cor. 6:20). It shall also not cease, but shall exist until the end of the world (1 Tim. 6:14). And just as people may neither change nor add to a human testament once it is established (Gal. 3:15), similarly people must not add to the new and eternal Testament (Heb. 13:20) that is established by the most precious death and blood of our Lord Jesus Christ (1 Pet. 1:18 [:18-19]). Even much less can they annul it, nor through human discretion submit themselves according to their own reason (Rev. 22:18; Deut. 12:32). But all Christians are to submit themselves (John 14:23, 21) with their whole heart, with all their senses, and with their mind to the obedience of Christ (2 Cor. 10:5), according to the Holy Spirit (as expressed in the Holy Scriptures) (John 7:38), and to regulate and measure their whole faith and walk according to it (2 Tim. 3:15-17; Ps. 119:9). The Old Testament must be interpreted and reconciled according to the New Testament (Matt. 5:17; Acts 21:28) and must be distinguished among the people of God: (1 Tim. 1:3) Moses, with his strong, threatening, punishing law [that stands] over all unconverted sinners who are still under the law; (1 Tim. 1:10; Gal. 5:23) and Christ, with his new, joyous message of the holy gospel (Luke 2:10; Rev. 14:6) [that stands] over all believing, converted sinners who are not under the law (Gal. 5:23; Rom. 6:15) but under grace. Before this new law of Jesus Christ (1 Cor. 9:21) all resolutions of councils and ordinances made by any humans in the world (Gal. 1:8-9) (contradicting here) must yield.[7] All Christians must only regulate and order themselves (with regard to faith) according to this worthy gospel of Christ (1 Thess. 1:8; Mark 1:25; 2 Pet. 4:17). And just like the outward person lives by the morsel of bread (Matt. 4:4; Deut. 8:3; Wis. 16:26; Jer. 15:16), so the inward person, the soul, lives by the words that come out of the mouth of the Lord.

From the law of Moses, how these were written by the finger of God in stone tablets, and made available by ministry of angels, read: Exod. 20:2; Deut. 5:6; John 1:17; Acts 7:53; Exod. 31:18 and 32:16.

Concerning the law's severity, read: "Cursed are you who do not abide in all the words of this law and who do not fulfil this. And all the people shall say, Amen." Deut. 27:27; Gal. 3:10.

"All that I have commanded you, that alone shall you hold, and thereafter do. You shall not add to it nor take away from it." Deut. 12:32 and verse 8 and 29:19; Prov. 30:6; Deut. 4:2.

Of the incompleteness of the law, read: "For the law has the shadow of the future good things, not the nature of the good things themselves." Heb. 10:1; Col. 2:17.

"For where the priesthood was changed, there it was necessary that the law also be changed. For there also occurred a taking away of the preceding law, due to their weakness and unprofitable will. For the law has made nothing perfect but it was an introduction to a better hope." Heb. 7:12, 17 [:19]; Gal. 2:16; Acts 13:38; Rom. 8:3.

How Christ is the end and fulfilment of the law, read: "For Christ is the end of the law, unto righteousness for everyone who believes in him." Rom. 10:4; Matt. 5:17; Rom. 7:4; Gal. 2:20.

Of the power and worthiness of the holy gospel, read: "For I am not ashamed of the gospel of Christ, for it is a power of God to salvation for everyone who believes in it." Rom. 1:16; Luke 16:16; Mark 1:15; 1 Pet. 1:12.

"Who has taken away the power of death, and he has brought the life and the imperishable nature into the light through the gospel." 2 Tim. 1:10; 1 Pet. 1:25.

Of the usefulness and power of the Holy Scripture, and how one still must follow it, read: "From your childhood onward, you have known the Holy Scripture, which can instruct you to salvation, through faith in Christ Jesus. For all Scriptures are inspired from God and are useful for teaching, for chastisement, for improvement, for instruction in righteousness, that a person of God may be prepared perfect for all good works." 2 Tim. 3:15; 2 Pet. 3:15.

"Examine the Scriptures, for in them you believe to have life. Who believes in me believes as the scriptures say." John 5:39 and 7:38; James 1:21; Matt. 4:4; Deut. 8:3; Wis. 16:26; Rev. 22:18; Deut. 4:2 and 12:32; Prov. 30:6.

"For what is written for us, is written for our learning so that we, through patience and comfort of the Scriptures, might have hope." Rom. 15:4.

How Christ Jesus shall proclaim the last judgment according to the gospel, read: "The word that I have spoken, it shall judge them in the last day." John 12:48.

"Now when the Lord Jesus shall appear from heaven with the angels of his power and with flames of fire, he shall exercise vengeance on those who have not confessed God and on those who have not been obedient to the gospel of our Lord Jesus Christ; these shall suffer pain, being cast out from the face of the Lord." 2 Thess. 1:7; Matt. 24:14; Heb. 4:12; Rev. 20:12.

XII. [Saving Faith]

Concerning saving faith, it is confessed that it is not an empty or hidden thing born within humans. Nor is it the case that a person obtains it from historical information or knowledge of the Holy Scriptures, even if he can speak with much excitement about it, yet without exhibiting true faith and understanding its significance (1 Cor. 13:1). For true, upright faith that comes from God is a sure knowledge of the heart and a certain trust (Heb. 11:1) that people have received from God through the hearing of his Word (Rom. 10:17; Col. 2:12) and through the inspiration of the Holy Spirit (2 Cor. 3:3), printed and inscribed in the heart (Jer. 31:33; Heb. 8:10). And it works so powerfully in a person (1 Thess. 2:13) that through it he is drawn away from all visible, perishable things to the invisible, living God (1 Pet. 1:8; 2 Esd. 1:37), receiving through it a new spiritual taste of what is heavenly, not what is earthly (Col. 3:2). For saving faith (accompanied by true hope and love) (1 Cor. 13:13) is of such nature and property that it prepares [a person] for things unseen (Heb. 11:1). Therefore all true believers are pleased to submit themselves in obedience to all commands of God (1 Cor. 7:19) (contained within the Holy Scriptures) and to testify and confess the same with their mouths before kings, princes, lords and all people (as necessary) and not let themselves stray from [God's commands] through any means (Matt. 10:18), even to the point of losing money, goods, body and life, and being delivered over to water and fire (Matt. 19:29; 2 Esd. 16:71). For the power of God (1 Pet. 1:5) (which preserves them in the faith) strengthens them so that they regard all suffering of this time as brief and easy (2 Cor. 4:17). They suffer, without any desire for revenge (but pray for their persecutors) (Luke 23:33), on account of the name of the Lord. [They accept] what is laid upon them because of their faith, hope and love which they have toward their creator and his heavenly goods (1 Pet. 4:14). Where authentic faith is received in the heart there the fruits of the Holy Spirit must follow and flow (as the same testifies) (John 7:38). Unbelief with its unfruitful works of darkness [on the other hand] must yield to this (Eph. 5:11), like the darkness in clear sunlight (2 Cor. 4:6). Through this faith (which is the beginning of Christian doctrine) (Heb. 6:2) people become children of God (Gal. 3:26); they [are able] to defeat the world (1 John 5:4), and are armed against all the cunning assaults of the Devil (Eph. 6:16). Through this they are sanctified (Acts 26:18), justified (Rom. 10:10), saved (Eph. 2:7 [2:8?]), [*gheherlicht, rechtveerdich, salich*] and participate in the benefits of God (demonstrated in Christ Jesus), without which it is impossible to please God (Heb. 11:6). In this authentic faith people must not stand still (Gal. 5:6), but must persevere in all godly virtues with humble fasts, prayers and supplications in the Spirit (2 Cor. 6:5; Luke 18:7) until the end (Matt. 24:13), so that God will strengthen and protect them to the end. When [these virtues] are neglected, people fall away from the faith (Luke 8:12), the good Spirit is taken away (1 Kings 16:14; Ps. 51:11), they are erased from the book of life (Exod. 32:32; Ps. 69:29; Rev. 3:5), and their names are again written in the earth (Jer. 17:10; Prov. 3:31). It is necessary to come to this authentic faith (which is a noble gift from God) (Eph. 2:7) to which all people are called through God's word (Acts 17:30) (without distinction of persons); to come to an understanding and knowledge so that they are able to hear and understand the word of God (Rom. 10:17). But all young children and those whom God allows to remain in their childhood (Deut. 1:39) are exempted and separated out. They stand under the grace (Matt.19:14) and pleasure of God, through the satisfaction [*voldoeninghe*] of Jesus Christ (Rom. 5:18) whereby he has purified and redeemed the entire human race (through his blood) (Rev. 5:10) since the fall of Adam, without requiring from the same any other actions except faith, hope, love, and maintaining certain commands of God. In this way, true faith exists in the hearing (John 8:47), believing and accepting (Bar. 3:39 [?]) of all the good things which God presents to us through his word (Luke 16:16). And again disbelief [exists] in despising and rejecting these same things. [Conversely], young children have neither knowledge, nor ability, inclination, nor persuasion of any such things (Deut. 1:39; 1 Cor. 13:11) (as all who understand, see and know). It must certainly follow, that one may not expect faith nor disbelief from young children, for they are simple and ignorant (1 Cor. 14:20), and please God completely in this condition, representing an example for us to follow them in their plain simplicity (Matt. 18:4).

How true faith is a gift from God and becomes active in the heart of people through the hearing of God's word, read: "For by grace are you saved through faith, and that not from yourself, it is God's gift." Eph. 2:7; Rom. 12:3; Col. 2:12.

"Therefore faith comes from hearing, and hearing through the Word of God." Rom. 10:17; Heb. 6:2.

How one shall believe in God through his word, read: "For I pray not only for them, but also for those who through their word will believe in me." John 17:20; Eph. 1:9; John 7:38 and 14:1; Heb. 11:6; 1 Pet. 1:21; 2 Tim. 3:15.

How true faith is not empty but demonstrates its working power and quality, read: "Through which we have received the grace and the apostolic ministry in order to establish the obedience of faith among all heathen." Rom. 1:5 and 16:25; Acts 6:7.

"You have received from us the word of divine preaching, so receive it not as a word of humans but (just as it truly is) as God's word. Which also works powerfully in you, you who believe it." 1 Thess. 2:13.

"In Christ Jesus is neither circumcision nor uncircumcision but faith that works through love." Gal. 5:6.

Whoever does not give evidence of his faith—the seven required virtues: "This one is blind and stumbles with his hands from the path." 2 Pet. 1:9; James 2:26.

"But the righteous shall live by faith." Habac. 2:4; Heb. 10:38; Rom. 1:17; Gal. 3:11.

Through faith are people justified and participate in all the good things of God. Acts 26:18; Rom. 10:10; Gen. 15:6; Rom. 4:3; Gal. 3:6; Mark 16:16.

One must pray to God, in order to be strengthened and protected in the faith. Luke 17:5; 1 Pet. 1:5.

Where the grace of God is neglected through disbelief and evil works, one can fall away again from the faith, and be erased from the book of life: "For the Spirit says openly that in the last times some will depart from the faith." 1 Tim. 4:1; 2 Pet. 2:4.

"For a time they believe, but in the time of temptation they shall fall away." Luke 8:13.

"Whoever falls away from the correct faith [and follows] incorrect faith, these God has given over to the sword." Sir. 27:2 [?]; Jer. 17:13; Prov. 3:31; Heb. 6:6.

"The Lord spoke to Moses: whoever has sinned against me, I will blot out of my book." Exod. 32:32 [:33] Rev. 3:5; Ps. 69:29; Isa. 1:2 and 30:1; Jer. 18:7.

How the young children are simple and ignorant, and following this, one must not expect from them neither faith nor disbelief. But they please God through his grace, without any other means. "And your children, which you agreed would become a prey, and your sons, who to this day understand neither good nor evil, they shall enter therein, which I shall give to them, and they shall possess it." Deut. 1:39; Matt. 19:14.

"When I was a child, I spoke as a child, and judged as a child and had a childish reason, but when I became a man, I removed all that was childish." 1 Cor. 13:11; Heb. 5:16.

"Dear brothers, do not be children in your understanding, but be children in what is evil." 1 Cor. 14:20; Eph. 4:14; Matt. 18:2, 19:13; Mark 10:13; Luke 18:15.

XIII. [The New Birth]

Concerning the rebirth and new creature, it is confessed that after our first parents Adam and Eve were separated from God through their sin (2 Esd. 7:48; Rom. 5:8), they fell into temporal and eternal death (Gen. 3:19) with all their descendants. Because they lost the image of God, their nature was corrupted; [hence] they were inclined [*genegen*] from their youth on to [commit] sin and evil (Gen. 8:21). For this reason, no one (among all of humanity) by the strength of their first birth (John 3:6) (which was conceived and has its origins out of sinful seed) can neither achieve nor obtain faith and the God-blessed walk. Seeing that what is born out of the flesh (John 3:6; Rom. 8:5) is flesh, it follows that the fleshly minded and natural human beings cannot taste the Spirit of God (1 Cor. 2:14). Hence, all humans (having come from the earth) (Gen. 3:19) shall return to dust and earth. They are like earth that is cursed, which brings forth no useful wheat by itself, but must be prepared anew (Jer. 4:4) with good seed sown in it (Matt. 13:37). This is the case for all human beings, whose youth has passed by and who have come to [an age of] understanding and [are able to] distinguish [between] good and evil (Heb. 5:17). One observes that their fleshly hearts and earthly members (Col. 3:5) (being received in sin) (Ps. 51:7) are inclined to sin (Gen. 8:21 and 6:5), and through their own desire (James 1:15) they manifest in themselves that which sin awakens and gives birth. Through this they again fall out of grace (wherein they were purchased through Christ's atonement), and sin leads them to death (Rom. 8:5,13). For this reason God the Lord demands and orders through his Word again in all knowing humans, true reform and renewal (John 3:1) [*een ware reformatie ende vernieuwinghe*] from their actual sins (Rom. 6:2); that is, through hearing God's Word (Rom.10:17) they receive the faith, become reborn anew from above by God (John 3:3) in the inward senses of the heart, and are recreated and circumcised (Col. 2:11). They change from the fleshly to the spiritual, from disbelief to faith, from earth and Adam to heaven. They follow Jesus Christ (Phil. 2:5) in crucifying and mortifying the earthly members, feeling, sampling, and tasting that which is heavenly and not earthly (Col. 3:2). Here again, life (Rom. 8:13) and peace (Gal. 6:18) are promised from God, including all heavenly riches. The mind is sanctified in the Spirit (Eph. 4:23), and all good things from Christ, who has promised eternal salvation (which were lost through actual sin) are appropriated (Matt. 19:28). And where this renewal and conversion in the senses of the heart is not found or is not present (John 3:3; 2 Cor. 15:17) (among all who, knowing the sin, have served it) there Christ and life does not exist. Without this renewal, no circumcision nor uncircumcision (Gal. 6:17), baptism nor Lord's Supper, nor any ceremonies avail, however gloriously they may shine. And just as humans initially are born out of the flesh in pain and suffering (Gen. 3:16), so this second spiritual birth (John 1:13) is also called a birth [*een baringhe ende gheboorte*] (Gal. 4:19; 1 Pet. 1:23), which takes place with godly sorrow over sin (2 Cor. 7:10; James 4:9) and where earthly members are crucified and put to death (Gal. 5:24). Through this, the inborn sinful nature, affections and inclination to sin are not taken away entirely, but remain until the reborn person has died. So [in life] flesh lusts against the spirit (Gal. 5:17) and the indwelling sin fights against the law of the new mind (Rom. 7:17). Those who are reborn, therefore, are continually involved in a battle (Heb. 7:1; 2 Tim. 4:7). They must continually crucify and kill the lusts of the flesh (Col. 3:5), tame and constrain their bodies (1 Cor. 9:27), and keep themselves from the fleshly lusts which battle against the soul (1 Pet. 2:11). Fighting in this way, they do not obtain victory (1 Cor. 15:54, 57) until death (Rev. 2:10; 2 Esd. 2:47 and 7:57 [57-60]).

Of the heavenly birth from God and how it occurs through God's Spirit and Word, read: "Purify your soul through the obedience to the truth in the Spirit to true unfeigned brotherly love and have heartfelt love for each other out of pure hearts, as are the reborn; not out of the perishable, but out of the imperishable seed, as out of the inward word of God that abides forever." 1 Pet. 1:22 and 2:2; James 1:18; 1 Cor. 4:16; Gal. 4:19; Philem. verse 10.

"Not on the basis of works of righteousness that we have done but according to his mercy he has saved us through the bath of the rebirth and the renewal of the Holy Spirit." Titus 3:5.

And that the rebirth is not an empty or hidden thing but requires a new walk and following after Christ, and that the promises of eternal salvation are based on this, read: "Verily I say to you, that you who follow after me in the rebirth, when the Son of Man shall sit on the throne of his glory, you will also sit upon the twelve thrones and judge the twelve tribes of Israel." Matt. 19:28.

"For in Christ there is neither circumcision nor uncircumcision, but a new creature. And all those who walk after this rule, upon them be peace and mercy and upon the Israel of God." Gal. 6:17 [:16].

"But for as many who receive him, he gave the power to become children of God, those who believe in his name; those who are born not of blood nor of the will of the flesh, nor of the will of humans, but from God." John 1:12.

And all who have served sin and are not reborn, these are cut off from God's kingdom: "Verily, verily I say to you, if anyone is not born anew, he may not see the kingdom of God." And further: "Unless someone is reborn out of water and out of the spirit, he may not come into the kingdom of God. For what is born of flesh is flesh, and what is born of spirit is spirit. And do not be amazed that I have said to you: you must be born anew. The wind blows where he wills, and you hear his voice indeed, but you know not where he comes from, and where he travels. It is the same with each one who is born out of the spirit." John 3: verses 3, 5, 6, 7, 8.

And that the reborn do not become perfect in this life, but must fight against their flesh, world and sin until their death, read: "Not that I have obtained it now, or am now perfect, but I hunt after it." Phil. 3:12 and 1:30; Col. 2:29; Job 7:1; Rev. 2:10; 1 Cor. 9:27; Gal. 5:17.

XIIII. [The Incarnation]

Concerning the incarnation [*mensch-werdinghe*] of the eternal and only born Son of God, it is confessed that God, who is exalted and trustworthy (Deut. 32:5), has faithfully maintained and fulfilled his greatest and most valuable promise (2 Pet. 1:4; Rom. 1:2), which he made in the beginning concerning his Son, who was foreseen before the foundation of the world (1 Pet. 1:20), and who was revealed in the last days on our account. This glorious and trustworthy promise was given initially to Adam and Eve, who had fallen (Gen. 3:15); thereafter it was renewed in their seed, as in Abraham (Gen. 12:3, 22:18; Gal. 3:9.), Isaac and Jacob, Moses (Deut. 18:15; Acts 7:47), and David (Ps. 132:11; Isa. 11:1). From this [promise], all prophets have prophesied and all righteous forefathers with firm confidence (as if they had actually seen him) (Acts 10:45) have a hope that the hero from Judah (Heb. 11:27), this beautiful morning star from Jacob would arise and come forth (Gen. 49:10). [What has been promised] has also truly and actually happened. When everything fell silent, and the kingly sceptre of Judah (Num. 24:17) was turned away and the seed of Jacob was under the tribute of heathens, God who is gracious was mindful of his holy covenant (Wis. 18:14 [:14-15?]; Luke 1:67), and sent his true, real Word or Son out of heaven from his royal throne (John 16:28, 10; Micah 5:1), having foreseen and elected the righteous Joseph (Matt. 1:16 and 1:20) from the house and lineage of David (Luke 1:24, 26), being betrothed to Mary, his wife, who was chosen, blessed above all women. To Joseph and Mary (Luke 3:23, Matt. 1:16) the Holy Spirit points—like a hand—from generation to generation, and also to the city of Bethlehem (Mic. 5:1), from which this long-ago promised light should arise and come forth; so that through them all, those waiting with expectation and hope of this salvation (Luke 2:25; 2 Esd. 2:34) would have a certain trust and knowledge of where they could expect this redeemer, and Saviour of the world [to be born] (Luke 2:11). Thus Mary received the message through the angel of God (Luke 1:24, 34) that came to light by the power of the Most High (Luke 1:31), and she believed it. And she received from the Holy Spirit (Matt. 1:20; Isa. 7:15; Luke 1:27, 31) the true, actual Word, which was in the beginning with God (John 1:2), through whom all things have been made. Through the working power of the almighty God (Luke 1:33), this same one has become flesh or human in her (John 1:14). Out of her was born the Son of the most high God (Luke 1:28), which she previously had received from the Holy Spirit (Matt.1:20). In this way, the eternal and only born Son of the living God has become a visible (John 1:14; Bar. 3:38, suffering human being (1 Pet. 4:1), like his brothers in everything (Heb. 2:17), except without sin. He was wrapped in swaddling clothes (Luke 2:7), laid in a crib, and raised under the care of his father and mother in Nazareth (Luke 4:16). He experienced hunger (Matt. 4:2), thirst (John 19:28), fatigue from travel (John 4:6); he sighed (Mark 8:12), and wept (Luke 19:41) and grew in wisdom, maturity and grace with God and humanity (Luke 2:51). Out of singular love, he humbled and subjected himself in the form of a servant (Phil. 2:7), the only Son of the almighty God, in order to heal the human race from the serpent's hostile bite, and from eternal torment (1 John 3:8 and 4, 9, 14).

Therefore all true witnesses of Jesus Christ (1 John 5:10; John 1:1), on the basis and power of the Holy Spirit, believe and confess that even this same Word (John 1:1)—that was in the beginning with God and was also God himself, through whom all things are created—has proceeded from God his Father (John 16:26, 33), and has come into the world, and has himself become human or flesh through the power of God (John 1:24). Thus people have touched (John 20:17; 1 John 1:1) and seen (John 1:14) the glory of the only born Son of the Father, full of grace and truth. The same, who previously was like God his Father in clarity (John 17:5) and glory (Phil. 2:6; 2 Cor. 4:4) (not as a given [thing] or stolen likeness of God, but such was his own nature), has abandoned his clarity and glory (John 17:5), and has lowered and diminished himself (Phil. 2:7) and has become like us in human form (Phil. 2:7). Previously he was greater than the angels, in an invisible, immortal form like God his Father (2 Cor. 4:4). [Now he] has become less than the angels (Heb. 2:7, 9; Ps. 8:6), and like his brothers has become visible and mortal (Heb. 2:17). He who before must have rejoiced greatly with his Father, and was in an eternal kingdom, on our account became poor (2 Cor. 8:9; Luke 9:58). He suffered on the cross (Heb. 12:2), he was despised and shamed, and, in the presence of the apostles, he ascended into heaven (Acts 1:9). Thus, this same one—who before had descended from God in heaven (Eph. 4:9, 10, Ps. 68:19) into the lowest place of the earth— rose again above all heavens. This is the great and blessed secret (1 Tim. 3:15; Bar. 3:38 [?]; John 1:14) that few people believe (due to their fleshly and flickering reason) [*vleeschelijck ende swebende vernuft*], that God has thus revealed the Son in the flesh, who has appeared (as a true redeemer and Saviour and an eternal light) (Matt. 4:16; Luke 2:32), on those who sat in the darkness and in the shadow of death.

Just like the food which the Israelites ate in the wilderness, which was named bread of heaven or heavenly bread (Exod. 16:16; John 6:31), and which substance of the bread was no plant of this earth but came from heaven (even though the same had been prepared in the world in the appearance of bread), so also Christ called his own flesh the true bread from heaven (John 6:32, 57), that the Son of Man should again ascend to where he first had been (John 6:62), since his flesh or body was not from Mary or any creaturely substance, but became flesh from the word of life alone (which had come from heaven) (1 John 1:1; John 1:14). This is the same one who spoke with Moses on the mountain and in the wilderness (Acts 7:38; Eph. 19:3 [Exod. 19:3]), and the one the fathers tempted in the wilderness, opposing his spirit (1 Cor. 10:9; Acts 7:51); the same who was from the beginning (1 John 1:1); the one the apostles touched with their hands and beheld with their eyes. His life was revealed to them, they have seen it and have proclaimed it to the people. He was with the Father and was revealed to them, and was even the same word that spoke with them (John 8:25).

It is also the case that the eternal Son of the living God has abandoned his godly glory (John 17:5) and for a short time became lower than the angels (Heb. 2:7, 9), and appeared visibly in the form of a servant (John 1:15; Phil. 2:7). Yet through this, he has not lost his eternal sonship and divinity. But when God introduced his first and only born Son to the world (Heb. 1:6; Ps. 97:7), he prepared for him a body (Heb. 10:5, 6) (not of any creaturely substance, but only of the word of life which has become flesh) (John 1:14), which was honoured and worshipped by all the angels of God (as the true God) (Heb. 1:6). Similarly, Christ glorified himself before his apostles upon Mount Tabor so that his face shone like the clear sun (Matt. 17:2; Rev. 1:14). Out of heaven his Father confessed him to be his beloved Son (Matt. 17:5 and 3:17; 2 Pet. 1:17). In this way the highly enlightened [*hooch verlichte*] apostles and all true believers have confessed and proclaimed, honoured and worshipped (John 9:38; Matt. 4:11; Luke 24:51; Acts 7:59; Luke 23:42; Ps. 96:9; Heb.1:6) this visible and tangible Christ Jesus as the true God (1 John 5:20; John 20:28; Rom. 9:5) and God's Son (Matt. 16:16). Therefore all true believers follow this testimony of the Holy Scriptures, together with the examples of all the saints of God, that they should follow, believe and confess as necessary for salvation, that the entire crucified Christ Jesus, visible and invisible, mortal and immortal, is the true God (1 John 5:20) and God's Son (John 20:18; Matt. 16:16), God and human in one undivided person. To him be praise eternally (Rev. 5:12). Amen.

Here are denied and rejected as contrary to the Word of God those who attempt to divide the only Son of God into two very different natures and properties in which case the one is the eternal Son of God, born of the only, eternal, holy nature of the almighty Father before all time, having abided like the Father (also in the incarnation) in an invisible, immortal spirit; and the other has a bodily nature and soul that has taken on the creaturely, sinful body, blood or seed of Mary, who alone was to have suffered and died for us; and in whom the eternal Son of God was supposed to dwell as an invisible, nonsuffering spirit, without mixture of these two dissimilar natures and qualities. [It follows] (from this) that the human race could not have been reconciled with God through the death of God's only born and own Son, but only through the death of this delivered second Son, in which case humanity would have been helped and saved by itself.

Similarly, it is also rejected as a blasphemy of God, those who profess that this above mentioned, received creaturely body and soul of Christ, through the joining together with the eternal Son of God was supposedly changed or transformed into the eternal Son of God. Or that (according to these views) the temporal and sinful creature supposedly is changed and transformed into the eternal holy Creator; and the only, eternal being of the almighty God, is supposedly (as imperfect) joined into a whole person, with body and soul; and that one must worship and serve this God with all godly honour.[8]

Also denied and rejected are those who confess the whole Christ Jesus, visible and invisible, as a created creature, which did not exist before Mary. These above mentioned points of view are regarded by all true witnesses of Jesus Christ as lies concerning the incarnation of the eternal and only born Son of God, being entirely contrary to the word of God and for this reason completely denied and rejected.

Of these promises of the Saviour, read how God the Lord originally [gave] the same promise to fallen Adam and Eve and their descendants, and the same promise concerning enmity between Satan and the women: "And I will set enmity between you and the woman and between your seed and her seed, the same shall you tread upon the head." Gen. 3:15; Col. 1:19, and 3:15; Eph. 2:15.

"A prophet like me shall the Lord your God awaken out of your people and out of your brothers, this one shall you hear." Deut. 18:15; Acts 7:37. Read further: Deut. 22:18 and 18:3. Acts 3:25; Gal. 3:8; Gen. 49:10; Num. 24:17; Matt. 2:2; Jer. 23:5, 33:14; Isa. 9: 5, 11:1; Acts 10:43.

And that this Saviour of the world was sent and came not originally from the fathers, nor Mary, or any creature, but only from God; and was conceived and born of the Virgin Mary. Read: "See a virgin shall conceive and bear a son." Matt. 1:23; Isa. 7:14; Luke 2:21; Gal. 4:4.

"When Mary his mother was betrothed to Joseph, before they came together, so was it discovered that she had conceived of the Holy Spirit." And further: "Joseph, David's son, fear not. Take Mary your wife to yourself, for what is conceived in her—that is from the Holy Spirit." Matt. 1:18, 20.

The angel of God spoke to Mary: "See, you shall conceive in your body, and you will give birth to a son, and you shall call his name Jesus. This one shall be great and he shall be called a Son of the Most High. And God the Lord shall give him the throne of his father David, and he shall be king over the house of Jacob into eternity, and his kingdom shall have no end. Mary said to the angel, 'how shall this happen, for I have known no man?' And the angel answered her and said: 'the Holy Spirit shall come from above into you and the power of the most high shall shine around you. Therefore the holy one that shall be born of you shall be called the Son of God.'" Luke 1:27.

Read here from St. John, who also thoroughly reported this, saying, "In the beginning was the Word, and the Word was with God and God was that Word. The same was in the beginning with God. And the Word became flesh and dwelt among us and we saw his glory, a glory of the only born Son of the Father, full of grace and truth." John 1:1, 14; Bar. 3:38; Zech. 2:10.

And further: "That which was from the beginning, that we have heard, that we have seen with our eyes, that we have beheld, and our hands have touched from the Word of life. And the life is revealed, and we have seen it, and testified and proclaimed to you that life is eternal, which was with the Father and is revealed to us." 1 John 1:1; John 8:25; Mic. 5:1; 2 Pet. 1:16; John 20:27; Wis. 18:14.

Of the lowering of the eternal and only Son of God, read: "Who, although he was in divine form, yet he regarded it no robbery to be like God, but lowered himself, and took on the form of a servant, and has become like another human being, and was found in the countenance of a human." Phil. 2:6.

"You have, for a little time, made him lower than the angels. But the one who has become for a little time lower than the angels, we see that he is Jesus, through suffering and death crowned with honour." Heb. 2:7, 9; Ps. 8:6.

"For you know the grace of our Lord Jesus Christ well, that he on our account has become poor when he was rich, so that you through his poverty should become rich." 2 Cor. 8:9; Eccl. 9:15.

"And look to the pioneer of the faith and to the one who perfects, Jesus, who for the joy that was laid out before him, suffered on the cross, with despising and shame." Heb. 12:2.

"I am the living bread which has come from heaven; whoever eats this bread shall live into eternity. And the bread that I shall give you, that is my flesh, which I shall give for the life of the world." John 6:51, read still further 58, 62.

How the saints of God, of this humbled Jesus, also in the time of his flesh have confessed and worshipped him as the true God and God's Son, read: "Who do the people say that I am, the Son of Man?" After little discussion, "Simon Peter answered and said: you are Christ the Son of the living God." Matt. 16:13 and 16. Understand that the true Son was born and proceeded from the being of the Father. He did not come, nor was conceived in time as believers are, who on account of the faith will also be called God's sons and daughters. 2 John 1:3; John 1:49 and 10:36 and 11:27; Acts 8:36; Matt. 27:53.

Jesus [said] to the blind one: "Do you believe in God's Son? He answered and said: 'Who is it lord, so that I may believe in him?' Jesus said: 'You have seen him and the one you have spoken with is him.' He said: 'Lord, I believe,' and he worshipped him." John 9:36.

"Thomas answered and said to him: 'My Lord and my God.' Jesus said to him, 'For you have seen me Thomas, thus you have believed.'" John 20:28.

"In his Son Jesus Christ. This one is the true God and the eternal life. Children, keep yourselves from idols. Amen." 1 John 5:20; Rom. 9:5.

XV. [Human and Divine]

Concerning the knowledge of Jesus Christ, God and man in one person, it is confessed that all Christians (necessarily) must believe in Christ (Wis. 15:3; 1 John 5:10, 12; John 17:3) and confess as the chief article and the only foundation of our salvation that Christ Jesus is not only human (1 Tim. 2:5) but that he is also true God with his Father (1 John 5:20; Rom.9:5). Having proceeded and come from God the Father (John 16:28, 30) he has for our redemption and salvation (Rom. 4:25) become a visible (1 John 1:2; John 1:14), suffering human being (1 Pet. 4:1). Not divided or mixed of two very different natures or substances, he has become human or flesh (John 1:14) solely from the one, eternal, holy, divine nature of the Father, that is from the Word of life, and is thus God and human in one person; so that he could show us, with his present visible humanity (which is not from this fabric (Heb. 9:11) or sinful substance but is in its nature to be distinguished from sinners) (Heb. 7:23, 25) a holy, blameless example in doctrine and walk (Acts 1:3; 2 Pet. 2:23), in order to rouse all people to imitate him (Eph. 5:1). And according to his divine power and ability (2 Pet. 1:3) he can redeem and eternally save us from the captivity of sin (2 Tim. 2:26), hell (1 Cor. 15:55), the devil and death. Take note: humanity is given no other means or name (Acts 4:12), in heaven and earth (for salvation). To this end Christ has come from God for us (1 Cor. 1:29), to bring us his wisdom, righteousness, sanctification, and redemption. Neither Moses with his severe and punishing law and commandments (Rom. 8:3; Acts 13:38), nor Aaron with the entire Levitical priesthood (Heb. 9:25) and all their sacrifices and offerings (Heb. 10:5, 8, and 11:14), which occurred for the remembrance of sins (Heb. 10:3), [could forgive]. As a result the sinful, rejected human race (Ezek. 16:6) has perished and is without help (Luke 10:31). Hence, neither a mortal human is able to redeem his brother and reconcile him to God (Ps. 49:8, 9); nor is sinful substance able to redeem the soul from eternal death. But [redemption] has been completed and delivered by the revealed slain lamb (1 Pet. 1:20) who was foreordained and was manifest in the last days (Rev. 5:12). He has paid for what he has not robbed (Ps. 69:5). This innocent one has taken all of our guilt upon himself (1 Pet. 1:19; Heb. 7:25). (In heaven and earth) he alone is found worthy to open the locked book and its seven seals (Rev. 5:5). Through his (unsurpassed) coming into this world (John 1:9; Col. 1:13), he has reopened the closed entry ([the entry that has become closed] through sin) of the kingdom of God, not through oxen and goats (Heb. 10:4, 11), nor any perishable human blood, nor through any perishable silver or gold (1 Pet. 1:18, 19). Christ has paid and established such alone, with his own valuable and precious blood and hereby accomplished eternal redemption (Heb. 9:12). And just as the sun in the heavens is endowed by God with glorious, illuminating splendour (Ps. 19:5)—that illuminates this world, making light from darkness and spreading out over all visible things—[a light, whose source] it has received from none of the same; so too, Christ Jesus is much more the true sun of righteousness (Mal. 4:2; Wis. 5:6), who as a creator and ruler of the sun and of all things (John 1:2; Col. 1:16) has received help from no creaturely substance to establish the work of our salvation. But with his (high praiseworthy) light from God, he has come from heaven (John 16:28, 30) and shines in this dark world wherever he is received and wherever he rises in the heart of many as a beautiful illuminating morning star (2 Pet. 1:19). He has thus been a giver, not a recipient,[9] to whom, the only God of heaven and earth (1 Tim. 2:5) must alone be ascribed praise and honour (Rev. 5:12), for this redemption, and not any creaturely human (Ps. 49:8; Isa. 42:8, and 48:11). Otherwise, one would rob the creator of his proper honour, and ascribe the same to our sinful, creaturely flesh, regarding also our flesh as our poor redeemer god and Saviour (Jer. 17:5; Ps. 49:8), and hereby in our hearts deviate from God our Saviour and fall into damnable idolatry (1 John 5:21; Rom. 11:15), seeking life among the dead where it is not to be found (1 Pet. 4:1). It is that Christ has suffered in the flesh for us, that he was crucified and that he died (Matt. 27:49). It is, therefore, impossible that he could be kept by death (Ps. 16:10) or that his glorious flesh [*herlich vleesch*] could taste perishableness (Acts 2:34 and 27:31). He himself has the keys to death and hell (Rev. 1:18, and 3:7) and the authority to open and to close, to give up his life (John 10:18; Rev. 1:17, 18), and the authority to take it back again to himself. And he is the living one who was dead; see, he lives from eternity to eternity. On account of this it is necessary for salvation for all true believers to believe in the true knowledge of Jesus Christ (John 17:25; Wis. 15:3), both his true divinity and his pure, unblemished humanity. It was promised by the Holy Spirit for this life and for eternal salvation (John 3:16, 36; 1 John 5:12), that Christ would establish and build his assembly [*vergaderinghe*] on this foundation (Matt. 16:18) and the gates of hell would not overpower it. To the contrary, all unbelievers who do not confess that Jesus Christ has come in the flesh (1 John 5:3; 2 John 1:7; 1 John 2:22) (that is, that the Son of God became human and thus appeared coming in the flesh) are not from God, but are from the spirit of the Antichrist which began in the time of the apostles (1 John 2:18) and will greatly increase in the last days. Herein must believers learn to know the righteousness of God and how much he hates sin; that through the sin of the first human all was corrupted (Rom. 5:16) and that such can be paid and atoned by no other means except through the death and blood of God's own and only born Son (Rom. 5:10; Rev. 5:5; John 3:16; Rom. 8:32). This must be proclaimed and adhered to. Herein must one also perceive the love of Christ, which surpasses all knowledge (Eph. 3:19; Col. 2:2; 1 John 4:9).

Of the necessity of this knowledge of Jesus Christ, read: "And this is the eternal life, that they know you, the only true God, and Jesus Christ whom you have sent." John 17:3; Hos. 13:4.

"If you had known me, so should you have also known my Father." John 14:7.

"And all tongues must confess that Jesus Christ is Lord, to the praise of God the Father." Phil. 2:11; Rom. 14:11; Col. 2:2; Phil. 3:8.

And Jesus to Peter, after he had confessed and proclaimed the human Jesus as the Christ, the living God's Son: "Blessed are you, son of Simon Jonas, for flesh and blood has not revealed that to you, but my Father in heaven. And I say to you further: you are Peter, and upon this rock shall I build my church and the gates of hell will not overpower it." Matt. 16:16-18.

And when the apostle Thomas had confessed the visible and physical human Jesus as his Lord and God, Christ did not rebuke him for such. But he accepted and received it as belief in the truth, saying: "For you have seen me Thomas, thus have you believed. Blessed are those who do not see me and nevertheless believe." John 20:29 and 17:20; 1 Pet. 1:8.

Read hereby, the multitude of Scripture passages, how the apostles, through the Holy Spirit, have worked with their whole might, in order that people might imagine not that the eternal Son of God was dwelling hidden in the human Jesus, but only that the visible human Jesus was Christ (that is) the anointed one, and sent from heaven, Redeemer and Saviour of the world. And hereupon was promised the life, read: "Jesus did many other signs for his disciples which were not written in this book, but these are written so that you should believe that Jesus is

Christ, the Son of God and so that through this faith you might have life in his name." John 20:30.

"Whoever now confesses that Jesus is God's Son, in this one abides God and he in God." 1 John 4:15; 1 John 5:5; 2 John 1:3; John 6:47.

"Whoever believes that Jesus is Christ, is born of God." 1 John 5:1, 5, 10; Acts 18:5, 28.

"Who is a liar, that he denies that Jesus is Christ, that is, Antichrist, who denies the Father and the Son." 1 John 2:22.

"By this you know the Spirit of God, every spirit that confesses that Jesus Christ has come in the flesh" – that is, that the eternal word has become flesh and is also being flesh, has come into his property – "this one is from God. And every spirit who does not confess that Jesus Christ has come in the flesh, this one is not [from] God. And that is the spirit of the Antichrist, from which you have heard that he has come and is now presently in the world." 1 John 4:2, 3; 2 John 1:7.

Read further how that through no other means except through the death of God's Son can we be atoned and purchased:

"God has so loved the world that he gave his only Son." John 3:16; Rom. 5:8.

"For we were reconciled to God through the death of his Son, when we were still his enemies." Rom. 5:10; Heb. 5:11.

"If God is for us, who may be against us? Who did not spare his own Son, but has delivered him for us all." Rom. 8:31; 1 John 3:16.

"And know that you are not redeemed with perishable silver or gold, from your vain ways of the fatherly inheritance, but with the valuable blood of Christ, as an innocent, unblemished lamb." 1 Pet. 1:18.

"Thereby is revealed the love of God toward us, that God has sent his only born Son into this world that we might live through him." 1 John 4:9.

XVI. [The Life, Suffering, Death, Resurrection, Ascension, and Glorification of Christ]

Concerning the life, suffering, death, burial, resurrection and ascension of Jesus Christ and the receiving again of his glory and splendour by his Father, it is confessed that when the Lord Jesus was humiliated in the flesh (Heb. 5:10) (enduring for about thirty-three years), not only with words, but also with works (Acts 1:1) and deeds, he set himself up as a holy, divine example for us; he has been looked up to by all believers (as the founder of the faith) (Heb. 12:2), who follow him through the rebirth (Matt. 19:18). For he proved himself to be submissive to his father and mother (Luke 2:50). And after his time was fulfilled (Mark 1:15), in perfect obedience to his heavenly Father (Phil. 1:8) he entered into his prepared office and service, proclaiming to humanity his Father's pleasure (John 17:8), making the deaf hear (Matt. 11:5; Mark 7:37), the dumb speak, the blind see; purifying the lepers, casting out demons, raising the dead from their graves (John 11:44), forgiving the sins of humans (Mark 2:10; Mark 9:6), and promising eternal life to those who believe in him (John 10:28). These things he has not done in the same fashion and form as his apostles and others, who have only done miracles through a received authority and gift, loaned and given to them from Christ. Christ himself had all authority in heaven and earth (Matt. 28:18). Thus he spoke to two blind men: "Do you indeed believe that I can do this (Matt. 9:18)?" And further: "So that you may know that the Son of Man has the authority to forgive sins upon the earth (Mark 2:10; Matt. 9:6)." And still: "I shall raise them up in the last day and give them eternal life (John 6:40)." Thus the Lord Jesus has perfectly completed and accomplished the works of his Father (John 10:28 and 5:36) and has shone like a clear heavenly light in this dark world (John 8:12 and 1:9) convincing and revealing to the same their evil works (John 7:7). As a result he incurred the hatred of the blinded Scribes and Pharisees (who had not perceived the light of truth) (1 Cor. 2:6), who through envy (Matt. 17:18) rebuked all godly deeds in him and ascribed them to the devil (Matt. 12:24 and 9:34). By this means they delivered this innocent one into the hands of unbelieving heathens [associated with] Pontius Pilate (Matt. 27:2; Acts 2:23 and 3:13). These interrogated the voiceless lamb (Isa. 53:10; Acts 8:32) with many kinds of torture, deriding him (Matt. 27:28; Mark 15:16; John 19:1), spitting in his face, beating him with fists, scourging him, wounding his head with a crown of thorns, and finally disrobing him, stretching him out on a cross, nailing his hands and feet upon it (Ps. 22:17), and hanging him up naked (as a prince and captain of malefactors) between two murderers (John 19:18). Here, in his bitter thirst he was given to drink a mix of vinegar and gall (Ps. 69:21); they then opened his side with a lance so that water and blood flowed out of it (John 19:34). Then with loud cries he gave up his spirit and commended himself into his Father's hands (Matt. 27:45; Heb. 5:10). Thus having died, heaven and earth became so moved by this most valuable death that the sun and moon lost their brilliance and a darkness came over the entire earth (Matt. 27:44). And the earth stood shuddering and trembling (Matt. 27:50); the curtain of the temple was split from top to bottom, and many bodies of the saints rose from their graves (Matt. 27:51) and came into the holy city, and appeared to many. And just as in the time of his flesh (Heb. 5:10) he proved that he had become a human by suffering and dying, by this he also proved that he was also true God with his Father; that he had the authority over the keys of death and hell (Rev. 1:18); that in three days he could raise up again the broken temple of his body (John 2:19); that he had the authority to give up his life (John 10:18) and also to take it back again to himself; that it was impossible that he could be kept by death (Acts 2:24), or that his holy flesh could see corruption (Acts 2:31; Ps. 16:11). For on the third day he was triumphantly raised up again and resurrected from the dead (through the glory of his Father) (Acts 10:40; Rom. 6:4). He was revealed to his apostles and others (Acts 10:40); he appeared miraculously among them (where they were gathered behind locked doors) (John 20:19); he ate and drank with them,[10] and for forty days spoke with many of them about the kingdom of God (Acts 1:3). Thereafter, in the presence of the apostles, he was taken up with a cloud into heaven (Acts 1:9), and set at the right hand of his almighty Father in heaven (Mark 16:19; Heb. 1:3). Thus has the only born Son of God suffered, was crucified (Acts 1:25), and died after the flesh (1 Pet. 3:18), but [also] through this he was glorified again and made alive in the spirit. He has perfectly received again his previous divine glory (John 17:5) and the likeness of his Father (Phil. 2:6.). And he shall no longer die, nor shall death have any sovereignty over him (Rom. 6:9). But he shall live and reign as a ruling (Luke 1:29; Ps.

45:7) king of all kings and lord of all lords over Mount Zion and the house of Jacob (Rev. 19:16). And he shall reign forever and ever.

Of the irreproachable life and walk of Christ, and how he was subject to his father and mother, read: Luke 2:40; John 8:46; Acts 1:1.

And at his fulfilled time, how he entered into his assigned service and did many glorious deeds in his Father's name, read: Mark 1:15; Matt. 8:16 and 9:35 and 11:5 and 12:15; John 10; Acts 10:38; Isa. 53:7; 1 Pet. 2:24.

And how, as a light in the world, he has testified of their dark evil works, and through this has fallen into the hands of sinners, read: "The world cannot hate you, but it hates me, for I testify about them that their works are evil." John 7:7 and 1:5 and 3:19; Matt. 27:18.

How Christ was obedient to his heavenly Father (in the time of his humbled flesh): "He has humbled himself and has become obedient to the death, yes, to the death of the cross." Phil. 2:8.

"And although he was God's Son, so he learned obedience through what he suffered." Heb. 5:11 [:9].

Of the suffering, death and burial of Christ, read: Ps. 22:17 and 60:9, 21; Isa. 53:7 and 63:3; Acts 8:31; all of: Matt.27; Mark 15; Luke 23; John 19. Acts 3:15; 1 Cor. 25:4; Matt. 27:57; Isa. 15:3, 12.

Of the rising up and resurrection of Christ, read: Matt. 28:7; Mark 16:6; Luke 24:7; 1 Cor. 15:4, 20; Acts 3:24 and 10:40.

How Christ received again his abandoned divine glory and likeness. And how he has travelled to heaven, read: "And Jesus came to them and spoke with them: 'To me is given all authority in heaven and earth.'" Matt. 28:18; Ps. 8:7.

"You have made him for a little time less than the angels, you have crowned him with praise and honour, and you have set him over the works of your hands. You have subjected all under his feet." Heb. 2:7, 9; John 17:5; Eph. 2:8.

"The God of our fathers raised Jesus whom you have killed and hung on the tree. This one God has exalted to his right hand as a prince and Saviour." Acts 5:31 [:30-31]; Phil. 2:9; Acts 2:33, 36.

"And when he had said this, he was lifted up as they watched and a cloud took him up before their eyes." And when they saw him he ascended to heaven. Acts 1:9; Mark 16:19; Luke 24:50.

XVII. [The Church]

Concerning the church [*ghemeente*] of God and the fellowship of believers, it is believed and confessed that since humans on account of the natural birth of the flesh (having attained understanding) follow sin and evil (Gen. 6:5 and 8:21; Ps. 5:5), and through this deviate from God their creator, so the high and holy God (before whom the sinners and godless cannot stand), from the foundation of the world, has called and chosen out of all unbelieving peoples of the earth his own special people (Deut. 7:7; 2 Esd. 5:27), separating them from all other peoples (2 Cor. 6:17; Rev. 18:4). These are all those who turn their ears to the voice of God that calls (Matt. 11:28; Isa. 1:10), and who have separated themselves from the world with all its sinful lusts (Eph. 5:11) and all false worship (which fights against God's word), and have united themselves again with Christ, bowing down as obedient members and sheep of Jesus Christ (John 10:27), under his head (Eph. 5:23) and commanding voice. They avoid all foreign things that fight against this. They are inwardly renewed, and are circumcised, changed and converted through the Spirit of God (Col. 2:11), and live according to the Spirit (Rom. 8:1). This church of God was first begun on the earth with Adam and Eve in Paradise (Gen. 1:27), and after that with Enoch (Gen. 5:22), Noah (Gen. 6:8), and all their descendants, who honoured and called upon the high name of God (Gen. 4:16). During this first period they were before the law. Thereafter, God the Lord established his covenant with Abraham and his seed (Gen. 17:2, 11), giving them [the rite of] circumcision as a sign of the covenant with many laws, ceremonies, rights and customs, which endured until the coming of Christ. This second period was under the law of Moses. In the last days God has sent his Son (Heb. 1:2; Matt. 21:37), who possesses omnipotence (Matt. 18:18), and in heaven and earth has established a new perfect Testament with the citizens of Israel (Jer. 31:33; Heb. 8:8), and has called all heathens and peoples of the earth (Eph. 2:12; Mark 16:15)—and all those who improve their sinful lives and who bow their body (in obedience)—to this Testament. With all of these, Christ has established his church and assembly [*ghemeente ende vergaderinghe*] (Ps. 50:5), this being the third and final age.[11]

Those who endure (without changing in faith, conduct and laws) shall hold their standing until the return of Christ from heaven. Thus the people of God in these three times have had diverse and special laws and ceremonies after which they have had to live and conduct themselves (1 Tim. 6:14). Such has been the will of God and indeed his pleasure to have inspired and led, through one Spirit (1 Pet. 1:11), a single people of God (Heb. 11:40 and 12:22). This church or gathering of believers has not always been visible; for many times it has eluded the eyes of the sinful and bloodthirsty world (which is unworthy of it). As in the case of Noah with his family in the ark wherein they were hidden from the whole world (Gen. 7:13); the people of Israel in the Red Sea; here and there in the forty-year desert (Exod. 14:22); the righteous ones in Judah from the bloody sword of Manasseh (2 Kings 21:16; Jer. 2:25 and 11:13); and all the god-fearing in Israel from the abominable threats of Jezebel (1 Kings 19:10, 18:4, 13).[12] Similarly, the bride of the Lamb, the church of Jesus Christ had to be hidden in the desert, three times and a half (Rev. 12:19, 11:13; Dan. 7:25, 12:17) from the gruesome beast of the Antichrist who, with his tyrannical sword and fire, exalted himself above all that which is named and honoured as God. And it [i.e., the church] has thereafter (through God's grace) come again into the light and has been rebuilt upon the old apostolic foundation. And as the temple of Solomon was destroyed and its second construction maintained its existence until the first coming of Christ in the flesh (Neh. 6:1; John 2:14), so we maintain that the church of Jesus Christ (being rebuilt on the basis of the apostles and prophets) (Eph. 2:19) shall likewise remain standing openly in the light until the second coming of Christ from heaven. This church of God (which includes all believing people) as members of one body (Eph. 5:30, 4:3) are joined together through the faith and bonds of love, being united to each other according to Christ Jesus (Rom. 15:5; 1 Cor. 1:9; Phil. 2:2). They live according to the one rule of the divine word (Phil. 3:16), and with mutual love are bound together to each other (Phil. 2:2), and thus have fellowship with each other. God has blessed them with spiritual gifts, which serve also the souls of their neighbours (out of love) (1 Pet. 4:10, 5:2). God has blessed them with temporal property that serve also their neighbours in physical necessities (1 Tim. 6:18; 2

Cor. 8:14), proving thus that they have spiritual and temporal goods in common (Acts 2:44, 2:43).[13] and suffer no lack in spiritual and temporal gifts. This church of God has been on the earth from the beginning of the world (be it few or many, secret or public) and shall also abide until the end, and they shall dwell with Christ and his Spirit forever (Matt. 28:20; John 14:18).

That the Christian church is where all believing, reborn people are gathered and purified by the Holy Spirit, read: "The Lord your God has chosen you as a people of his attributes out of all peoples of the earth." Deut. 7:7 and 14:2 and 26:18; 1 Pet. 2:9.

"And out of all the multitude of peoples you have obtained for yourself a people, and above all, you have given this people (which you have desired) an efficacious law." 2 Esd. 5:27.

How the church of God is built upon Christ and must maintain itself as members obedient to the head, read: "And upon this stone (understand Christ) I shall build my church and the gates of hell shall not prevail against it." Matt. 16:18 and 28:20.

"You men love your wives just as Christ loves the church and has given himself for her so that he should make her holy and purified her through the water bath in the word, so that he should prepare for himself a glorious church, which has no spot or wrinkle, or anything like it, but that she is holy and without blame." Eph. 5:24, 25, 29, 32.

"That you then know how that you should conduct yourselves in the house of God, which is the church of the living God, a pillar and firm ground of the truth." 1 Tim. 3:14; Eph. 2:15 and 4:16; Heb. 12:22.

Of the fellowship of the believers, read: "For if we walk in the light, just as he is in the light, so we have fellowship with each other and the blood of Jesus Christ, his Son, purifies up from all sin." 1 John 1:7.

"And they remained persistent in the apostles' teaching and in the fellowship." Acts 2:42 and 4:34; 1 Cor. 12:12; Gal. 3:28; John 17:21.

XVIII. [The Distinguishing Signs of the Church]

Concerning the distinguishing signs of the church [*ken-teeckenen der ghemeente*] of God that distinguishes it from all other people, it is confessed and observed, [in the first place] that [Christians are known] by their holy walk [*Godtsalighe wandelinge*] in the pure fear of the Lord (Acts 9:31; Matt. 19:28). They are worthy of and measure up to the Gospel of Christ (Phil. 1:27), [and from their life] springs forth sincere faith [that comes from] the truth. Moreover they are as a light on a candlestick (Matt. 5:15), a city on a high mountain, shining and towering above all peoples (with godly virtues), among whom they shine as light in a dark world (Phil. 2:15); for a tree is known and distinguished by its fruits (Matt. 7:15-20).

Second, such can be observed regarding the rebirth (1 John 3:8, 9): Just as a human being, on account of his first birth out of the flesh, brings forth his human affections and attributes as evidence that he comes from, and is born of humans (John 3:6, 31), so too must all members of the body of Christ be born from above, from God (John 3:3), through this high divine birth, and produce heavenly and spiritual fruits (John 15:16), and thus express and bear the divine quality and nature (which they participate in through faith) in all ways. Through this godly-mindedness, [true Christians] are known and distinguished as new creatures born of God (Gal. 6:17; 2 Cor. 5:17).

Third, the church of God is known by its sincere ministers, shepherds and teachers [*Dienaers Harders ende Leeraers*] (Eph. 4:11; 1 Tim. 3:2; Titus 1:6) who, as sent messengers from God (John 3:34) speak not on their own, but only according the word of the Lord (1 Pet. 4:11; 2 Tim. 2:25), correctly cutting and dividing it according to the truth and presenting it to the people, [so that they may] also bear fruit. In presenting the will of God and the way of the Lord (2 Cor. 5:20), the people will turn from their evil paths (Jer. 23:32) and be won over to God.

Fourth, one can recognize the church of God in her glorious appellations with which she is also honoured and named by God: [The church is] a city and temple of the living God (2 Cor. 6:16; Ps. 122:3; Rev. 21:2, 10), in which God will dwell and walk. Just as one knows that it is proper for all cities and kingdoms to observe and keep commands and laws, in a similar way the city and house of God is known by the true teaching of the holy gospel (John 8:31), in its confession of Christ Jesus as the only supreme head, and in its submission to him (Eph. 5:24). [Christians are known] by their unity of the Spirit, [living] according to one rule (Phil. 3:16; 2 Cor.12:18). [They walk] in the same footsteps of the faith, and maintain all the commandments of God (obediently) (John 14:21).

Fifth, the church of God is known by the descriptions by which she is named: the daughter of Zion (Matt. 21:5; Zech. 9:9), the bride of the Lamb (John 3:29; Rev. 19:7 and 21:2), a pure Maiden (2 Cor. 11:4), which was joined to Christ through the gospel, to which Christ, in faith and truth is married and bound (Hos. 2:21 [2:20]; Zech. 8:8). Just as a pure maiden leaves friends and maidens together with all strange things [*boelen*][14] (Ps. 45:11; Gen. 24:58) and keeps herself solely as an obedient bride and submissive housewife under the will of her bridegroom and husband (Eph. 5:24), so too must all blessed members of the body of Christ separate themselves from worship of all false gods (1 Cor. 10:14), close their ears to strange voices (John 12:5) and thus avoid the same with heart and body (1 Cor. 6:10). The members are to be under the obedient worship of their only bridegroom, Christ Jesus, and listen only to his voice (John 10:27); and proclaim and declare through his holy messengers, and maintain everything that Christ has commanded them (Matt. 28:20).

And lastly, the church of God is known by her character [*velt-teecken*], namely, sincere brotherly and common love (John 13:54; 2 Pet. 1:7), which is shown to God and all people in words and works, which has been established by Christ himself as a mark of recognition. Therefore, just as the soldiers abandon their own life's business (2 Tim. 2:4) and give themselves under their prince and captain, taking his banner and character upon themselves so that they might please the one who has accepted them for battle—as proof that they are truly bound to him unto the death—in the same way, members of the church of Christ should also abandon their own evil works (Rom. 13:12; Eph. 5:11), depart from the world and their own flesh (John 2:15 and 5:4) and give themselves again under Christ's banner, putting on the true character of the love of Christ (Eph. 13:19; John 13:34). They should learn from him how to be humble and meek of heart (Matt. 11:29) since he, as a humble lamb, did not open his mouth (to vengeance against his persecutors and killers) (Isa. 53:10; 1 Pet. 2:25) but prayed for the same out of love (Luke 23:33). And showing himself among his own, as a servant, he gave his life for the salvation of many (Matt. 20:28). In the same way the members of Christ must learn from him and serve one another out of love, with spiritual gifts for the soul (Eph. 4:13), so that they might improve. [They should serve one another] with temporal gifts for the body so that there will be no lack of physical necessities among any of the same members of the body (Acts 4:34), and that under this true Israel of God there will be no beggars (Deut. 15:4). They must, according to their ability, show common love toward all people (2 Pet. 1:7; Gal. 6:12), even toward their enemies who persecute and kill them (Matt. 5:44). Neither must they oppose the same in any way with physical sword and force, nor repay their slander and verbal abuse with similar invectives (Titus 3:2; 1 Pet. 3:9). [Rather they are called] to suffer from the same (in all patience until death), and in the name of the Lord and with humble hearts they are to pray for the same (1 Tim. 2:2; Jer.29:7; Matt. 5:44). In this way they proclaim and show the nature and love of Christ in every way. Where [men and women] believe and confess from the heart a sincere faith in the Father, Son and Holy Spirit (1 John 5:7; Matt. 28:19); of the incarnation of the only born Son of God (John 1:14) and his suffering (1 Pet. 4:1; Matt. 27:41; Rom. 5:10), death and ascension (Acts 1:9); of the justification and salvation of people (Rom. 5:1; Col. 1:13); of the resurrection of the dead and the eternal judgment (Heb. 6:3); and where all commandments and ordinances of Christ, such as baptism (Matt. 28:19), Lord's Supper (Matt. 16:25), separation (Matt. 1) and similar things are correctly maintained according to the Scripture's report (which in part are recorded here in these points); and where people follow Christ in the pure fear of the Lord in the rebirth (Matt. 19:28)—there is the church and city of the living God, a tabernacle of God among the people (Rev. 21:3), in which God with his Spirit will dwell and walk (2 Cor. 6:16). Such a body has Christ as a head, provider, and Saviour (Eph. 5:23). However, where these signs are not thought of, but are treated according to human discretionary commandments, there no church of God exists, but [only] vain boasting (Rev. 2:2, 9).

How one shall know the true members of Christ and their sincere faith (expressed through a godly walk) in the rebirth, read: "All trees that do not produce good fruits shall be cut down and cast into the fire. Therefore you shall know them by their fruit. Not all those who say to me, 'Lord, Lord,' shall come into the kingdom of heaven. But those who do the will of my Father in heaven." Matt. 7:19; Matt. 12:50; John 15:14; Sir. 19:24.

"Do all things without murmuring and questioning, so that you will be blameless and pure, and not subject to punishment, as God's children among the cunning and false generation, whereby you shine as lights in the world, by maintaining the word of life." Phil. 2:14.

How one shall know and distinguish the false prophets from the sincere ministers of Jesus Christ, read: "Guard yourselves from the false prophets who come to you in sheep's clothing, for inwardly they are grasping wolves; by their fruits shall you know them." Matt. 7:15; Deut. 13:1.

"Whoever speaks on his own accord seeks his own praise, but whoever seeks the praise of the one who sent him, he is true, and there is no unrighteousness in him." John 7:18.

"For those whom God has sent speak God's words." John 3:34 and 8:31; 1 Pet. 4:11.

"For if they had remained in my counsel and preached my word to my people, then they would have turned from their evil ways and from their evil life." Jer. 23:22; Isa. 55:11; Matt. 23, entirely; Col. 1:6. Read further Titus 1:6; 1 Tim. 3 entirely.

How one shall know the people of God in that they have separated themselves from all other peoples, and have joined themselves under Christ their head, listening only to his voice and keeping his commandments, read: "Therefore my most beloved, flee from the worship of idols. You cannot drink from both the Lord's cup and the devil's cup; you cannot participate both in the Lord's table and the devil's table." 1 Cor. 10: 14, 21.

"Do not put on a strange yoke with the unbelievers. For what fellowship does righteousness have with unrighteousness? Depart out of the midst of them and separate from them, says the Lord, and do not touch what is impure." 2 Cor. 6:14, 17; Rev. 18:4; Isa. 52:11; Jer. 15:19 and 51:6.

"As I have said to you, that my sheep hear my voice and I know them, and they follow me. For they do not follow a stranger but flee from him, for they do not know the stranger's voice." John 10:27, 5.

"Teaching them to keep all that I have commanded you." Matt. 28:20; 2 Thess. 2:15; John 8:31 and 14:21 and 15:10; Matt. 11:29; 1 John 5:3.

How that the Christian crowd shall be known by love, read: "A new commandment I give you, that you love each other as I have loved you. Thereby shall everyone know that you are my disciples, if you love each other." John 13:34; 1 John 3:23.

"By this will one know which are the children of God and the children of the devil. Whoever does not do right, nor loves his brother is not from God." 1 John 3:10; John 15:12; Matt. 22:38; Eph. 5:2; 1 Pet. 1:22; 2 Pet. 1:7.

XIX. [The Office of Christ]

Concerning the office of Christ and the actual reason of his coming into the world, it is confessed that Christ is the true, promised Prophet (Acts 7:37), High Priest (Heb. 10:21), and King (Luke 1:29; John 1:49), whom Moses and all the prophets had predicted and proclaimed (Acts 10:41); to whom the previous priests and kings pointed (as figures and shadows) (Heb. 10:1 and 8:5; Col. 2:17). The actual reason for his coming into the world has been in order to break the works of the Devil (1 John 3:8), to seek the lost (Luke 19:10), and to deliver the whole human race (Acts 26:18) out of the captivity of sin (Eph. 4:8) the power of the Devil (1 John 2:2), and to save sinners (1 Tim. 1:15).

Regarding his prophetic office, he has come from God (John 16:30) and has come into the world in order to proclaim to the people the perfect counsel and will of God (John 6:38) (which was concealed from the beginning of the world) (Eph. 3:9), through the Gospel; [he has come] to preach redemption to the captives (Luke 4:18; Isa. 61:1; Matt. 11:5), and the gospel to the poor, and the acceptable year of the

Lord [*aenghename jaer*]. After the pronouncement (and at the time of fulfilment) (Heb. 1:2) all children of the New Testament are bound and united to live and to walk with him (who is a perfect rule of faith) (Matt. 28:20). These shall maintain their standing until the world has come to an end (2 Tim. 6:14).

Regarding his high priestly office, he has fulfilled and transformed the Levitical Priesthood (Heb. 7:11, 12, 8:13) and through his unique sacrifice (Heb. 10:14) on the cross he has opened the closed entry to the holy of holies in heaven (Rev. 5:5; Heb. 10:10). Through his unique sacrifice, which is of eternal value, he has fulfilled and completed the sacrifice of the law and has found an eternal redemption (Heb. 9:12). Having thus reconciled the human race with the Father (1 John 2:2), he has set himself at the right hand of the all-mighty in heaven (Heb. 1:3), and has become in the presence of God his Father the only faithful, advocate, mediator, high priest and intercessor (1 Tim. 2:5; John 2:1). And he lives always to pray for the same (Heb. 7:24 [:24-25]).

Regarding his kingly office, he has come from heaven with the full authority of his almighty Father (Matt. 28:18; John 6:38) in order, as a powerful king of all kings (Zach. 9:9) and ruler of all the people (Isa. 55:4) to re-establish justice and righteousness upon the earth (Jer. 23:5 and 33:15), thus [representing] the end and perfection of all kings of Israel (Rom. 10:4; Luke 1:29). Even so, his kingdom is not of this world (John 18:36). He has been a spiritual, heavenly king; he has shunned all earthly kingdoms of this world (John 6:19), and has desired and has had only a spiritual, heavenly kingdom. Among the adherents of his kingdom he has given, reformed, improved and fulfilled the commandments, laws and customs of Moses. (Matt. 5:17) To his adherents (as a commander) he has taught against and forbidden all vengeance (whether by words or works) (Matt. 20:25; Rom. 12:19; 1 Pet. 3:9), and has ordered them to [follow] his own example to be armed only with the armour of God and the sword of the spirit (which is God's word) (Eph. 6:13; 2 Cor. 10:4), in order to fight against flesh and blood, world and sin (1 John 5:4), and the manifold attacks of the Devil (2 Tim. 4:7). Finally [he has allowed his followers] to receive from this eternal king by grace the crown of eternal life (2 Tim. 4:8; 2 Esd. 2:43-47) as pay and as a very great reward (Gen. 15:1).

How Christ, who is the promised prophet from God, is the one whom people (as the perfect will of God) must hear and follow, read: "A prophet like me, the Lord, shall awaken from among your members and out of your brothers, whom you must hear." Deut. 18:15; Acts 7:37 and 3:22; Matt. 17:5.

"We have a firm prophetic word and you would do well to pay attention to it, as upon a light that shines in a dark corner." 2 Pet. 1:19.

"Since God previously has spoken many times and in various ways to the fathers through the prophets, so in these days he has finally spoken to us through the Son." Heb. 1:1.

Of his prophecies, read: Matt. 24 completely, Luke 17:20, and 19:21.

Of his priestly office, read: "And we have a high priest over the house of God, so let us go there with certain hearts in perfect faith." Heb. 10:20.

"Since the priesthood has been changed, it is therefore necessary that the law also be changed." Heb. 7:13 and 8:7 and 10:9.

"But Christ has come as a high priest, coming with good things." Heb. 9:11.

Of his preaching, read: Matt. 9:35; Mark 1:14; Matt. 5:1 and 11:1; Luke 4:15.

Of his kingly office, read: "You daughter of Zion rejoice, and you daughter of Jerusalem, exult; see, your king comes to you." Zach. 9:9; Matt. 21:5.

"At the same time I will raise up a plant of righteousness; [for] the same David shall be a king who shall reign well. And he shall re-establish justice and righteousness upon the earth." Jer. 23:5 and 33:15; Isa. 32:1.

"Rabbi, you are God's Son, you are the king of Israel." John 1:49; Acts 10:36; 2 Cor. 4:5; Phil. 2:11.

Of his spiritual kingdom and rule, read: "And God the Lord shall give him his father David's throne. And he shall reign eternally over Jacob's house, and there shall be no end to his kingdom." Luke 1:29.

"For he is a lord of all lords and a king of all kings. And those who with him are called and chosen and believe." Rev. 17:14.

"But you are the elect race, the royal priesthood." 1 Pet. 2:9; Exod. 19:6; Rev. 5:10; John 18:37, 38; Ps. 22:29.

Of his commands, read: "See, I have given him to the people as a witness, as a prince and ruler of the people." Isa. 55:4.

"There is one law giver who can save and damn." James 4:12; 1 Cor. 9:22; Matt. 12:8 and 28:19; James 1:25.

XX. [The Election of Ministers]

Concerning the ordinances of the church of God and the sending or election of ministers it is confessed, that just as a house, city or land cannot be maintained without laws and ordinances by which it can be ruled, nor can a human body exist or be maintained if the members do not perform their service (ordained by God) on behalf of the body (1 Cor. 12:14), so the Lord God has likewise established diverse ordinances, laws and commandments in his church (2 Cor. 12:28; Rom.12:5; Eph. 4:11), through which it might be constructed, established and improved.

Just as eyes, mouth, hands and feet are necessary for a body (as the most important members) to see, speak and work (2 Cor. 12:21), so that through these it can proceed and be maintained, thus Christ the Lord has ordained in his church (as necessary) [the following]: First, through his own present, commanding voice, he has sent out his apostles (Mark 16:15; Matt. 28:19) to preach the gospel among all peoples, teaching them to maintain his commands (Matt. 28:19; Mark 16:15; Acts 14:3), and has confirmed such with signs and miracles.[15] Similarly, through the Holy Spirit, the apostles have commanded their followers to choose pastors [*harders*] (Titus 1:5; 2 Tim. 2:2; Acts 6:3), teachers [*leeraers*], helpers [*hulpers*] and leaders [*regeerders*] in the church (2 Cor. 12:28; Eph. 4:12), who are to be shining stars (Rev. 1:20) with their good conduct and sound teaching (Titus1:9), who shall edifyingly shine in the spiritual firmament through the gospel (as peaceable messengers) (Rom. 10:13; Isa. 52:7; Eph. 6:15). They shall proclaim the good new message everywhere, so that through them the people might turn from their evil ways (Jer. 23:32), join the church, and in this way the body of Christ may be improved and built up (Eph. 4:11).

One knows that lacking faithful ministers, good teaching (Judges 2:11), and through the people's [own] unworthiness (2 Pet. 15:4 [2 Pet. 2:1-5]; Hos. 3:4; Isa. 24:31), the sheep of Christ fall into error. For this reason the people of God (lacking this) must not turn themselves to those voices that have learned about human wisdom (1 Cor. 1:18; Isa. 33:18) in the schools of high learning [*hooghe schoole*] (1 Cor. 2:4), who are able to clap and dispute [*klaapen ende disputeren*] (Titus 1:10), and who seek to sell their purchased gift for temporal gain (Titus 1:11; 2 Tim. 4:4), and do not follow Christ correctly in the humility of the rebirth (Matt. 19:28), as is common with the world. But the true members of Christ will turn themselves (according to the counsel of God) with humble (Acts 13:2) fasts and prayers (Mark 9:28; Luke 10:9), to the Father of the harvest (who is the true sender), [and will pray] that he will awaken men through his divine wisdom (Acts 13:21; Jer. 1:9), whom he, as a faithful (Luke 12:42; 1 Cor. 4:2) and wise householder (Jer. 3:10; 1 Cor. 1:22), will place over the members of his house (Gal. 6:2; Eph. 2:18), so that they might give them proper food at the right time and kindle and enflame their hearts with his Spirit, and lead them in his harvest (Matt. 22:3). So that they might feed the sheep of Christ (not for the milk and wool [Ezek. 34:3], but out of a mind inclined thereto [1 Pet. 5:2]), with teaching and wisdom (Jer. 3:10; Isa. 50:4), and lead them onto the correct path according to the kingdom of God (Isa. 48:17). And thus they might perform their God-given ministry through the power granted them by God (1 Pet. 4:11).

For this reason, believers (when they have this lack [of ministers]), after they have sought the face of God with intense prayer (Acts 6:6) shall turn their eyes to a God-fearing brother (Acts 16:2; 1 Tim. 3:7) whose body is tame and constrained (1 Cor. 9:27), and in whom the fruits of the Holy Spirit are detectable and visible (Gal. 5:22). This one, chosen by common voice (2 Cor. 8:19), shall be examined in the faith by the elders and leaders [*sorch-draghers*] of the church (1 Tim. 3:10), to see if he is of one voice with the church in all articles (according to God's Word), so that he too can teach another the path of truth which he himself knows (Matt. 15:14; Isa. 9:15). And having been found fit (Titus 1:8) he may thus come forward in the name of the Lord to proclaim the will of God to the people. And if it is found that God has entrusted the gospel to him to preach (Gal. 2:7), and that he correctly cuts and divides the word of God (2 Tim. 2:16) and is fruitful with it (Isa. 55:21; Col. 1:6), then the church (requiring such and he, after examination by the church, is found unyielding in the faith according to God's word) may choose him with one voice (2 Cor. 8:19) as an elder [*outste*] and teacher in the full ministry. Through the laying on of hands (1 Tim. 4:14; 2 Tim. 1:6; Acts 13:3) let the elders confirm this, and let him labour and work in the Lord's field (1 Cor. 3:9). Let him administer Christian baptism and the Lord's Supper and carry out all things pertaining to [these ceremonies]. Similarly, the church shall choose by common voice deacons for the poor (Acts 6:3, 6, 1 Tim. 3:8), and let the elders confirm this with the laying on of hands (after they have been examined and found wholesome in the faith [1 Tim. 3: 10; Titus 1:9]) as helpers and leaders [*regeerders*] (1 Cor. 12:28). Then, those who are willing, can deliver their gifts to these [deacons], who with these [gifts] can fill the needs of the poor members of Christ (Acts 6:2) (those who are needy and who according to their ability work and labor with their hands and do not want to shame themselves) (2 Cor. 9:12), so that among the people of God no beggars will be found (Deut. 15:4) nor lack of temporal necessities (2 Cor. 8:14). [In this way] the [identity] of the giver of good gifts is hidden from the people (Matt. 6:4), but revealed before God according to the teaching of Christ. If any one of the aforementioned ministers deviates from the (accepted) path of truth in faith or conduct (Matt. 18:8; 1 Tim. 1:20; 2 Tim. 2:17), then the church, which has chosen him (remaining pious and wholesome), shall chastise the same again, according to the nature of his deeds.

Of the ordinance of the church of Christ, read: "I rejoice and see your ordinance and the firmness of your faith in Christ." Col. 2:5; 1 Cor. 11:33 and 14:40; 2 Cor. 8:19.

How one should pray to God (who is the true sender) for faithful laborers, read: "The harvest is great but the workers are few. Therefore pray to the Lord of the harvest that he will send workers into his harvest." Matt. 9:37; Luke 10:2; Matt. 23:33; Luke 11:49; John 13:20; Matt. 10:40; Luke 10:16; Matt. 25:14; Luke 19:12; John 20:21.

How necessary these ministers are and how they should be capable to teach God's word, read: "The Lord God is over the spirits of all flesh; he will set a man over the churches who shall go out and in before their members, and lead these out and in, so that the church of the Lord will not be as sheep without shepherds." Num. 27:16.

"I will give you shepherds according to my heart who will feed you with doctrine and wisdom." Jer. 3:10 [:15].

"Those whom God has sent speak God's word." John 3:34 and 7:18.

"If anyone speaks, let him speak as God's word. If anyone has a ministry, that he minister [serve] from the strength which God provides so that God will be praised in all things through Jesus Christ." 1 Pet. 4:11.

"For no prophecy was brought about by human will. But the holy men of God have spoken, being driven by the Holy Spirit." 2 Pet. 1:21.

"For this reason I called you to Crete, so that you would further complete what I have left, and put elders in all places, as I have directed you." Titus 1:5.

And concerning their fitness, and how after examination they can minister, read: 1 Tim.3 entirely; 1 Cor. 12:28; Rom. 12:7; Eph. 4:11.

The order and how they are to be chosen, read: "We have sent a brother with him, who praises the gospel throughout all churches. Not only that, but he is also ordained by the church as an associate in our pilgrimage in the grace which is preached among you." 2 Cor. 8:18 [:18-19]; Acts 1:23.

"When they worshipped the Lord and fasted so said the Holy Spirit: 'set apart for me Barnabus and Saul to the work that I have called them to.' When they had fasted and prayed and laid their hands upon them, they let them go." Acts 13:2 and 20:28.

"What you have heard from me through many witnesses, entrust to faithful men, who are prepared to teach others." 2 Tim. 2:2.

"Tend the flock of Christ that is among you and care for them not out of force but willingly, not out of an improper desire for profit, but out of an inclined heart; not as those who have lordship over the inheritance, but as an example to the flock." 1 Pet. 5:2 [:2-3].

Of the choosing and confirmation of the deacons, read: "It is not proper that we abandon the preaching of the word of God and serve tables. Therefore dear brothers, chose among you seven men who have a good reputation, who are full of the Holy Spirit and wisdom, whom we might place into this service. These they brought before the apostles and they prayed and laid their hands upon them." Acts 6:3, 6; 1 Tim. 3:8, 10.

XXI. [Baptism]

Concerning Christian baptism, it is confessed that the same is an evangelical matter, use and ordinance which began first with the man of God, John the Baptist (Mark 1:2, 4), through the counsel and will of God (Luke 7:30); it was received by the worthy Son of God, Christ Jesus (who had lowered himself) (Matt. 3:16), to whom the aforementioned John had led and pointed with his teaching and baptism, as being the true baptizer with the Holy Spirit and fire (Matt. 3:11). He has proceeded and come from God (John 16:30) with perfect authority in heaven and earth (Matt. 18:18). He has sent out his apostles and commanded them to preach the gospel to all people and to baptize all true hearers and believers among them in the name of the Father, of the Son and of the Holy Spirit (Matt. 28:19; Mark 16:14; Rom. 10:11, and has taught them (before and after the baptism) to maintain all that he has commanded (Matt. 28:20).

All apostles of Christ (as obedient ministers of God) (1 Cor. 4:1, 2) have done [this] faithfully, beginning in Jerusalem (Luke 24:47; Acts 1:4). They have then preached the gospel throughout the lands (Rom. 10:18). All those who heard, believed and happily received this heavenly teaching (Acts 2:41) have been made disciples and followers and were baptized with water in the name of the triune God [*drie eeingen Gods*], and in this way are bound with Christ to maintain what he has commanded (Matt. 28:20)

Note that the teaching and commandments of Christ were instituted not for a certain time but are to be maintained until Jesus

Christ appears [again] from heaven (1 Tim. 6:14). He will remain with his followers by his Spirit until the completion of the world (Matt. 28:20). For this reason all believers and disciples of Christ are responsible neither to change nor disregard such teaching and commandments in any manner through human discretion, for they come through the command of God (Deut. 12:8, 4:2). Instead, they are to experience and maintain them continually according to the form and institution of Christ and his highly enlightened apostles. [They are to] preach the gospel to the people (Acts 10:41, 2:38, 8:34), and to all those who believe and who demonstrate penitence and improvement from sins. Those who submit themselves to the will of God will be baptized one time with water in the name of the Father and of the Son and of the Holy Spirit, by an irreproachable minister [*dienaer*] who is ordained to do this (Matt. 28:19).

External baptism with water does not really [bring the one who is baptized] into the kingdom of God (Gal. 3:26), nor does the visible element of the water contain any power or holiness in itself (1 Pet. 3:21), nor is it able to give any grace and blessedness [*salicheyt*]. Just as the water of the Jordan (2 Kings 5:14) and Siloam (John 9:9 [:9-11]) did not really heal leprosy and blindness, but only the power of God, to which they were submissive and obedient (Luke 8:46; Luke 5:30), so also is it true with respect to the water of baptism; it has no power [by itself] to forgive our sins or to purify the impurity of our flesh (1 Pet. 3:21). It is merely a sign and proof [*teecken ende bewijs*] of the grace and blood of Christ, the washing away of sins (Acts 22:16), which the person, through faith and rebirth (by grace), has received in the heart before baptism (Gal. 3:26; John 1:12) through the removal of the sinful body of the flesh (which is proclaimed in baptism) (Col. 2:11). Without this inward baptism, with the Holy Spirit and fire (Matt. 3:11), the visible baptism of the water (like the seal of an empty letter) (Rom. 2:8) is vain and useless.

For this reason are rejected (as a falsification of the ordinance of Christ and a human planting for the adornment of the kingdom of the Antichrist) (Matt. 15:13) those who baptize unknowing, speechless children (Deut. 1:39). No Christian elder is burdened or commanded by God to do this; it should be despised and trampled upon through the true baptism of Christ (Matt. 15:3). But all Christian people are commanded and responsible to conduct themselves as a good example for their children and to raise them in the fear of the Lord (Eph. 6:4), without using any baptism, Lord's Supper, or any other ceremony on them. One knows that it is impossible for anyone to bind someone else (without his will and knowledge) to the Lord (Heb. 2:43; Rom. 1:17; Heb. 10:38). But one finds that as soon as these people have grown up, they live according to their inborn sinful nature (Eph. 2:3) according to the flesh (John 3:6; Rom. 8:1). And through this they fall out of grace wherein they were purchased with the blood of Christ (1 Cor. 6:20). For it is necessary for their soul to hear God's word (Rom. 10:17) from which comes faith and rebirth, and after this, Christian baptism, which is from Christ, to whom faith and rebirth adhere, and from whom they can never be separated (Matt. 28:19; Mark 16:16). [This Christian baptism] is compared to a grave wherein humans can bury their own removed, actual sins (Rom.6:4), and also rise up with Christ in a new life, walking according to the Spirit. And just as no bath can be used for the washing away of the impurity of the body of a new born infant before a born infant is brought forth into the world, so also can Christian baptism (which is compared to a bath of the new born) (Titus 3:5) be given to no one according to the will of God, except to the reborn believers (Acts 8:35) who have died to sin and self desire (Rom. 6:2), and who have risen up from this death to sin (Col. 2:12) and walk in the new life, maintaining all that they have been commanded by Christ (Matt. 28:20). For this reason no one can be recognized as a brother or sister by the church of Christ or use any Christian ordinance on them unless they have received the above mentioned Christian baptism, which is the first ordinance (Acts 2:41) and reception into the Christian fellowship (1 Cor. 12:13). One also submits and binds himself to maintain immediately all commandments and ordinances of God) according to God's word upon his faith. And just as there is but one faith and one God (Eph. 4:5), so is there but one Christian baptism. This baptism is received once, upon a true faith, according to the institution of Christ; one may not rebaptize a second time, nor can the same be renewed.

Of the baptism of John, and how he was sent as a forerunning messenger for Christ, who preached the baptism of repentance, and performed it on Christ, read: "John baptized in the desert, preaching the baptism of repentance for the forgiveness of sins." Mark 1:4; Matt. 3:6, 11.

"I baptize with water, but there comes one stronger than I, whose thong of his sandals I am not worthy to untie; he shall baptize you with the Holy Spirit and fire." Luke 3:16; John 1:31.

How Christ Jesus commanded his disciples to preach the gospel, and to baptize not the speechless, unknowing children, but only the hearers and believers of this [gospel], read: "To me is given all authority in heaven and earth; therefore go and teach all people, baptizing them in the name of the Father and of the Son and of the Holy Spirit. And teach them to maintain all that I have commanded you. And see, I am with you all days, unto the end of the world." Matt. 28:19.

"Preach the gospel to all creatures. Those who believe it and are baptized will be saved. But whoever does not believe, shall be damned." Mark 16:16.

How the apostles (according to this high burden) preached the gospel, and have baptized only the hearers, believers and self-desiring receivers, read: "They who heard this ignited their heart and spoke to Peter and to the other apostles: 'you men, dear brothers, what shall we do?' Peter said to them, 'repent, and let each one be baptized in the name of Jesus Christ, to the forgiveness of sins. Those who happily received his words were baptized." Acts 2:37 [:37-38], 41.

"And the eunuch said: 'see, there is water, what hinders me from being baptized?' Philip said: 'if you believe with your whole heart, then it may truly happen.' He answered: 'I believe that Jesus Christ is God's Son.' And he stopped the wagon, and they both climbed out into the water, Philip and the eunuch, and he baptized him." Acts 8:35 [:35-38].

How the apostles (according to this basis) have taught and baptized some family households, after they heard and believed the word of God, having been filled with the Holy Spirit, ordained to the ministry of the saints and being regarded as believers, read: Acts 10:47 and 16:15, 32; 1 Cor. 16:15; Acts 18:8.

How the apostles have described Christian baptism as a burial of sins in the death of Christ; and as a resurrection, and walking in a new life; a clinging to Christ; a bath of rebirth; baptized through one Spirit into one body; and an assurance of a good conscience with God, read: Rom. 6:3; Col. 2:12; Gal. 3:27; Titus 3:5; 1 Cor. 12:13; 1 Pet. 3:21.

XXII. [The Lord's Supper]

Concerning the Lord's Supper or the breaking of bread, it is believed and confessed, that just as baptism is an ordinance and institution of Christ, through which the believers are joined together through one Spirit with Christ (1 Cor. 12:13) in the fellowship (Acts 2:42), so also is the Lord's Supper a worthy ordinance and institution of Christ, whereby believers, according to the ordinance of Christ, are baptized, taught and admonished to live and walk in Christ (Col. 2:6), just as they have received him through faith in baptism (Gal. 3:26), with brotherly love toward their neighbour are to be joined (Col. 1:24), with whom they should live and walk in unity of the Spirit (Eph. 4:3; Phil. 2:2; Rom. 12:10), according to one rule of the divine word (Phil. 3:16). Hereby they will remember the Lord's bitter suffering and death (1 Cor. 11:25) (with wholehearted remembrance).

So that people might be made mindful of this, the Lord Jesus has willed the use of bread and wine, being well known things among people, so that through these might be planted, in the hearts of the believers, heavenly and hidden things; hereby teaching to remember, just as the one bread was prepared beginning with many broken grains, and the wine was pressed from many grapes into one drink as necessary, beneficial and fit as food for the human body (Matt. 4:4; Deut. 8:3; Wis. 16:26).

So Christ allowed himself (out of fiery love [*uyt vyerighe liefde*]) to be broken on the trunk of the cross, where he shed his blood, and alone has trod the winepress of suffering (Isa. 63:3), in order to serve the soul of humans with his flesh and blood (John 6:54) as a necessary food and drink. Through this, all who worthily receive and eat such bread and wine with their mouth (1 Cor. 11:26), hereby, through faith in the Spirit (John 6:35, 63), receive and participate in Christ with all his heavenly goods. In this way they are strengthened in the faith, nourished in the soul (John 6:55), and are joined with burning love to God and their neighbours (Eph. 4:3; Col. 3:15).

Believers, however, should in no way place their trust in these visible memorial signs [*sichtbare ghedenck-teeckenen*], as if these things in themselves should be more holy and worthy than other similar common food and drink, or that these things have the ability to give to people grace and forgiveness of sins. In doing such, one's heart is separated from the Creator (Jer. 17:5); [it is] seeking grace from creation where it is not to be found (Rom. 14:14 [:14-15]). Believers should receive these signs in no other way except as bread and wine. With firm hearts they should rely only on what is taught and signified by these things, and what these signs point to and regard, as the Holy Spirit is accustomed to in the Holy Scripture—to name the signs according to the things that they signify (John 10:9, 14:6, 15:1; 1 Cor. 10:4; Gal. 4:24). In this institution of the Lord's Supper of Christ, the cup is named the new testament in his blood (Matt. 26:27; 1 Cor. 11:24). It is understood hereby that just as a testament maker ascribes his goods to his heirs through a testament which they must receive and use after his death (Heb. 9:17), similarly, Christ, in his Last Supper has ascribed to his disciples his last and final will (after which he could no longer remain with them) (John 16:5) in the New Testament, with all his heavenly goods, so that all those who are specified and signed in this testament as children of God and heirs of Christ, will receive all his heavenly goods. In this way the ordinance of the Lord's Supper shall be maintained in his remembrance (Luke 22:19; 1 Cor. 11:22).

For this reason believers shall use all such worthy institutions of Christ among each other through an ordained minister—who is without blame—with great reverence, proclaiming the Lord's bitter suffering and death (1 Cor. 11:25). And after having said thanks to God for his limitless grace and mercy (with humble heart) (Col. 1:12), and invoking [God] with intense prayer [*vyerighe ghebeden*] (Eph. 6:18), the bread shall be broken by the minister, the wine poured, and received by all the believers who have been baptized according to the ordinance of Christ (and with heartfelt remembrance of the Lord Jesus' broken body and spilled blood) and who have examined themselves (1 Cor. 11:27), the same be used and eaten. The believers shall maintain such [practice] continually (as time and place permit) until Jesus Christ appears from heaven (1 Tim. 6:14).

Of this institution and ordinance of Christ, read: "And when they ate, Jesus took the bread, said thanks and broke it, and gave it to his disciples, and spoke: 'Take, eat, this is my body.' And he took the cup and said thanks, and gave it to them, and said: 'This is my blood of the New Testament, which shall be shed for many people for the forgiveness of sins. And I say to you, I shall from henceforth no longer drink from this fruit of the vine until the day when I shall drink it anew with you in my Father's kingdom." Matt. 26:25 [:26-29]; Mark 14:22; Luke 22:19.

How the apostles (following this) have used and maintained the same also in one form and shape, read: "I have received from the Lord that which I have given you. For the Lord Jesus in the night when he was betrayed, took the bread and gave thanks, and broke it, saying, 'take, eat, this is my body which is broken for you, this do in my remembrance.' Similarly, after supper he took the cup also, saying, 'This cup is the new testament in my blood. As often as you drink from this, you do it to my remembrance.' And as often as you eat of this bread and drink from this cup, so shall you proclaim the Lord's death until he comes. So whoever eats of this bread unworthily, or drinks from the cup of the Lord, is guilty of the body and blood of the Lord. For a person must examine himself, and in this way eat of this bread and drink from this cup. For whoever eats and drinks unworthily, eats and drinks judgment upon himself because he does not discern the body of the Lord." 1 Cor. 11:22 [:23-29]; Acts 2:42 and 20:7, 11.

How the bread and wine in the Lord's Supper are not in essence [*wesentlijke*] the body and blood of Christ, but signs of his fellowship with believers, read: 1 Cor. 10:4, 16; John 6:35, 63.

XXIII. [Footwashing]

Concerning the footwashing of believers, it is confessed that after our predecessor [*voorgangher*] Christ Jesus held the Lord's Supper with his apostles, and before his time of suffering, he used another ordinance [*ordinantie*] among his members and commanded them to maintain the same amongst each other. Girt about with a linen cloth, he stood up from the Lord's Supper (John 13:4), and took water in a basin and washed the feet of his disciples and dried them with the linen cloth. Thereafter he spoke to his disciples saying, "You call me master and lord, and you say it correctly, for so I am (John 13:13). If I, your master and lord, now have washed your feet, so you should also wash each others' feet. I have given you an example of what you should do, just as I have done to you." And further explaining this, "If you know this, blessed are you if you do it (John 13:17)." And one finds that among the apostles all such ordinances of Christ were thereafter maintained. Who also described this ordinance of Christ (as a ministry of the saints) (1 Tim. 5:10) as among the good works and for the improvement of the faith. For this reason shall all such ordinances of Christ be used and maintained by the believers (as successors and disciples of Christ) (Eph. 5:1; Heb. 6:12) and his apostles, as time and place allow. When believers receive visits by their companions in the faith, they shall, out of love, receive their companions into their houses with humble hearts (Phil. 1:12, 17; Matt. 10:40; 3 John 1:9), with a kiss of love and peace (Rom. 16:15; 2 Cor. 13:12; 1 Thess. 5:26; 1 Pet. 5:14), and as a service to the neighbour (following the humility of Christ), they shall wash the feet of the same (1 Tim. 5:10); hereby wholeheartedly remembering how the high, praiseworthy Son of God lowered and humbled himself, washing not only his apostles' feet, but much more, washing and purifying our soul and conscience with his valuable death and blood from the stain of eternal damnation (Rev. 1:5).

How Christ practiced this ordinance with his apostles and commanded them to observe it, read: John 13:4 to 17.

And thereby, how the same is furthered by the apostles among the good works and thereby to be practiced among believers, read: "And let no widow under sixty years of age be chosen and only if she has been the wife of one husband, and has a testimony of good works and has raised children and shown hospitality, and has washed the feet of the saints." 1 Tim. 5:9.

How God-fearing ancient fathers have used this ordinance toward their received guests, read: Gen. 18:4 and 19:2; and still Luke 7:38; John 11:2; Acts 16:33.

XXIIII. [Good Works]

Concerning good works, it is confessed that all believing, reborn children of God who receive the word of God (1 Thess. 2:13) and in whose heart it is inscribed by the Holy Spirit (2 Cor. 3:3), will necessarily (as signs and fruits of this) (Matt. 7:17) produce and show from their faith good works and virtues (2 Pet. 1:5). Observe the word of God (which is compared to leaven [Matt. 3:33], rain and snow [Isa. 55:10]), that nothing vain nor unfruitful remain hidden. It must (according to its character and nature) work and show its strength and properties through God's Spirit in the individual (1 Thess. 2:13; Rom. 13:12). Truly, where the kingdom of God is received in the heart through the clear light of God's word, there the deadly works of darkness (like the night before the clear sun light) must be removed, departed from, and disappear. And thus [we must] remove and take off the old man (Col. 3:9) with his evil works, and remain neither vain nor unfruitful (2 Pet. 1:8). [We must] adorn and clothe ourselves inwardly with the weapons of light (Rom. 13:12), and thus display divine virtues that arise out of faith (2 Pet. 1:5). And as obedient children of God in everyway express the nature of Christ (Phil. 2:5), not in human self-chosen holiness (Col. 2:18) nor to please any mortal humans (which is nothing but a useless and vain religion) (Matt. 15:9; Mark 7:7). For believers must live according to the word of the Lord and the blameless example of Christ and his apostles (Phil. 2:17), learning from Christ to be humble and modest in the heart (Matt. 11:29). And since avarice is a root of all evil (1 Tim. 6:10), which means to collect money and goods unjustly (Matt. 15:19); lay all such aside, and put on again the mercy of our heavenly Father, and thus display love in deed and truth with mercy and pleasure towards all people (Gal. 6:12). Similarly, pride must be seen as the beginning of all destruction (Tob. 4:10; Gen. 3:5); it originates from the heart (Matt. 15:19) and reveals itself in clothing (Sir. 19:25; 1 Pet. 3:3; 1 Tim. 2:9), housing, speaking, eating, and drinking. Lay aside everything and arm yourselves against these with the humility of Christ (Matt. 11:29; Titus 2:1; Gal. 5:19). For all vain pleasures of the world exist in drunkenness, feasting, unchastity and similar things. Inspect and avoid all of it, and be chaste and pure (2 Cor. 6:4), with humble fasts, prayers and supplications in the Spirit to God [so that you may have] the power and strength to keep wrestling (Col. 1:29). In this way, through patience in good works, seek eternal life (Rom. 2:7), endeavouring to become like Christ. In this way, believers (as a tree with its fruits) (Matt. 7:20) will be known and distinguished from all unbelievers (who walk on their own chosen paths). For believers thus endeavour to do their best in good works according to their calling (Titus 3:8, 14). By this they must not believe in any way to be earning salvation by their works (Eph. 2:8; 2 Tim. 1:9), or that God is somehow still in debt to them for these things. But all believers must regard themselves as not other than as unnecessary servants (Luke 17:10), who are able to do nothing good through their own strength (John 15:6; 2 Cor. 3:5, 6). From the beginning, middle and end, it is only God the Lord who works the good in them through his own Spirit (Phil. 2:13). On their own they are imprisoned in a body of sin and death (Rom. 7:25) which lusts against the Spirit (Gal. 5:17). [But] with the armour of God they struggle continually (2 Tim. 4:7) and will conquer by God's help (1 Cor. 15:57). Their walk is crippled and imperfect (Phil. 3:12), and therefore, they must pray daily for the forgiveness and remission of sins (Matt. 6:12; Eph. 4:32; Col. 1:13 [:13-14]) until the last enemy (which is death) is defeated by God's grace (1 Cor. 15:26). They thus seek to be saved through the undeserved grace of our Lord Jesus Christ (Rev. 15:2; Eph. 2:4; Titus 3:5).

Of the deadly works of darkness, which separates humanity from God, and which one must reject and remove through faith, read: "Take off the old man with his works, and put on the new." Col. 3:10.

Read further, of the 23 sins, which are worthy of eternal death. Rom. 1:29. Of the ten unjust works which shall not lead to God's kingdom, 1 Cor. 6:10; and the seventeen works of the flesh, which separate one from the kingdom of God, Gal. 5:19; Matt. 7:23.

Of the good and virtuous works, which believers should display from their faith as fruits of thankfulness, read: "Let your light so shine before people, that they shall see your good works." Matt. 5:16; 1 Pet. 2:12; Phil. 2:15.

"Praise and honour and the imperishable being of those who with patience in good works seek eternal life." Rom. 2:7; John 8:39; James 2:22; Gal. 5:6.

"As it befits women, who profess their righteousness in good works." 1 Tim. 2:10.

"That they do good and become rich in good works." 1 Tim. 6:16.

Of the nine blessed works, read: Matt. 5:1.

Of the six works of mercy, read: Matt. 25:35.

Of the nine fruits of the Spirit, read Gal. 5:22.

Of the seven main virtues, which one must display out of faith, and if one does not follow one becomes blind, read: 2 Pet. 1:6.

How one is not saved through any completed works, but only through the grace of God, read: "But we believe to be saved through the grace of the Lord Jesus Christ." Acts 15:11.

"Not on account of the works of righteousness which we have done, but according to his mercy, has he made us righteous." Titus 3:5; Eph. 2:4; 2 Tim. 1:9; Luke 17:10; Acts 4:12.

XXV. [Marriage]

Concerning marriage, it is confessed that it is an honourable ordinance [*ordinantie*] of God (Heb. 13:4). He originally established this estate with the two first humans who were created in the image of God (Gen. 1:28; Matt. 19:6), whom he blessed and brought together. Subsequently, this divine ordinance has fallen into great disorder due to the hardness of hearts and evil lusts of humans, so that men, through the lusts of the flesh, have married whom they will and have taken many women (Gen. 6:2). For many reasons, they have abandoned their wives through a letter of divorce and married others (Deut. 24:1). So it is that Christ, as a perfect law-giver (James 4:12), rejected and abolished the letter of divorce as a concession of Moses (Matt. 19:8), along with all abuses. And he pointed all his hearers and believers again to the first ordinance of his heavenly Father (made with Adam and Eve in Paradise) (Matt. 19:4; Gen. 2:24; Eph. 5:31), and he has reconfirmed marriage as [an act] between one man and one woman; [he has] tied the bond of marriage firmly so that it cannot break. A person cannot be separated and marry another for any reason (Matt. 19:9 and 5:32; 2 Cor. 7:10), apart from adultery and death. For this reason all believers (who commit themselves to marriage) shall follow this teaching of Christ and the given examples, to bind themselves in marriage only to one who is born from above (John 3:3; 1 John 5:4) into a similar faith (2 Pet. 1:1), renewed, and created according to the image of God (Eph. 4:24). All such persons, after they have received the consent of their parents (Eph. 6:1; Col. 3:20) and of the church, shall be brought together by a minister (Tob. 7:16) in the presence of the church with fervent prayers to God (Eph. 6:18). All such we regard to be married in the Lord (1 Cor. 7:39), of which God himself is the author and the one who brings [persons] together. All those who have not been reborn, who have not been sanctified through faith in Christ and marry, we also regard as being in an honourable state of marriage (Heb. 13:4; 1 Cor. 7:12)—but not in the Lord. In the same way Christ does not accept anyone as his bride and member of his body (Eph. 5:37) except those who have been united with him by faith (Gal. 3:26). In this way believers do not have the ability to remove themselves from Christ, for their bodies have been sanctified by God and given over as members of Christ and temples of the Holy Spirit (1 Cor. 6:15). Neither are they to bind themselves in marriage with those who have not been reborn, and in this way take on a strange yoke with unbelievers (2 Cor. 6:14) who are not regarded as brothers or sisters by the church, through the faith and Christian baptism in the fellowship (Acts 2:41, 42). Take note of baptism, which is the first Christian ordinance in the church, after which all other ordinances of God follow. Thus is the state of marriage advised through the Holy Spirit, so as to avoid adultery and all impurity (1 Cor. 7:2; 1 Thess. 4:4; Eph. 4:19 and 5:3). Anyone who has no need for this, and who can maintain himself pure and undefiled in a state of virginity in order to serve the Lord better and without hindrance (1 Cor. 7:35), is even more highly praised. Therefore the estate of marriage is a free concession for each one, and not a command (1 Cor. 7:6).

How God the Lord originally ordained the state of marriage, read: "And the Lord spoke, it is not good that the man be alone; I will make a help for him who will stand by him. And God the Lord made a woman from the rib which he took from the man, and brought her to him. Therefore shall one man leave his father and mother, and cling to his wife, and the two will be one flesh." Gen. 2:18, 22, 24.

How Christ rejected all abuses of marriage and renewed the ordinance of his Father, read: "'Have you not read, that he who made humans from the beginning, made them a man and woman?' And he spoke, 'therefore shall a man leave father and mother and cling to his wife, and they shall be two in one flesh, so then they are not now two, but one flesh. Therefore shall no one separate what God has brought together.'" Matt. 19:4 [:4-6], 8.

"Marriage is honorable for all, and the bed undefiled. For God shall judge the fornicators and adulterers." Heb. 13:4; 1 Cor. 7:2.

"A wife is bound to the state of marriage so long as the husband lives; but if her husband dies, she is free to marry whomever she wishes, only that it occur in the Lord." 1 Cor. 7:39; Gen. 1:26 and 24:4; Exod. 34:16; Num. 36:6; Deut. 7:3; Tob. 7:15.

The transgressors of this, and their punishment, read: Gen. 6:2 and 34:15; Num. 25:1; 2 Esd.13: 26, 27; 1 Kings 11:1 [:1-4].

XXVI. [Swearing of Oaths]

Concerning the swearing of oaths, it is confessed that the people of the Old Testament in different ways were allowed to swear by the name of the Lord (Deut. 6:13, 10:20), be it with their hands raised to heaven (Gen. 14:23), or laying them on someone's thigh (Gen. 24:9, 47:29). As a result there entered in diverse abuses (through human hypocrisy), so that people have sworn by heaven and earth (Matt. 23:15; Matt. 5:34), Jerusalem, their head, the temple and the gold of the temple, and the altar and sacrifices. Concerning this, the Lord Christ, who came from and was sent by God (John 8:42, 16:28) to re-establish justice and righteousness upon the earth (Jer. 23:5, 33:15), being the only law giver (James 4:12) has entirely abolished and forbidden all aforementioned swearing of oaths (whether they were done freely or hypocritically) (Matt. 5:34, 23:21; James 5:12; 2 Cor. 1:20). In its place he has commanded all his listeners and disciples to only say "yes" and "no" (according to the truth). The high apostles of Christ (as obedient sheep they hear their sole shepherd's voice) have also followed the teaching of Christ in this (James 5:12; 2 Cor. 1:20). For this reason all believers are responsible to follow obediently after this teaching of Christ and the example of his apostles, laying aside all lies (Eph. 4:25; Col. 3:9) and proceeding only with truth, and also to confirm all true things (be they toward the authorities or whoever it might be) only with a "yes," whatever is yes. And whatever is no, to testify only with "no," without adding anything further (Matt. 5:37). [Believers] are firmly to keep all such little words (which seem insignificant but are actually very significant] like a sworn oath (Ps. 15:4), thereby demonstrating that they are obedient disciples of Christ and his apostles.

Of the rejection and abolition of the old custom of oath swearing and how Christ has commanded in its place "yes" and "no," read: "'Furthermore, you have heard that it was spoken to the elders, you shall give no false oaths, but you shall keep your oath to God. But I say to you people, that you must not swear in any manner, neither by heaven, for it is the throne of God, nor by earth, for it is his footstool, nor by Jerusalem, for it is a city of a great King. Neither should you swear by your head, for you cannot make one hair black or white. But your words should be 'yes' [or] 'no.' And all that is done beyond this is evil.'" Matt. 5:33[:33-37] and 23:21.

"My brothers, above all things do not swear, neither by heaven, nor by earth, nor by any other oath. But your word shall be 'yes,' for what is yes, and 'no,' for what is no, so that you not fall into hypocrisy." James 5:12.

"Have I therefore lightly used this when I thought this? Or are my thoughts fleshly? No they are not. But for me yes is yes and no is no. For all promises of God are kept and are final." 2 Cor. 1:17, 20.

XXVII. [Relationship to the Civil Authorities and the Worldly Powers]

Concerning the office of the magistrate and worldly powers [*overheydt ende wereltlijcke macht*], it is confessed that the office of the magistrate is an ordinance and institution of God (Rom. 13:2; Wis. 6:4), who has willed and ordained all such authority over all lands (Sir. 17:14 [:17?]); so that through these authorities, lands and cities might be ruled in order to maintain peace and a good, civil life (Rom. 13:4) through good policing and laws (by punishing the evil and protecting the good) (1 Tim. 2:2). And without this authority of the government, the world (being over run with evil) (1 John 5:19) cannot survive. For this reason all believers are responsible (not only on account of the [fear of] punishment, but also for the sake of their conscience) (Rom. 13:5; Titus 3:1) to submit to this authority, and to be obedient as good subjects, with fear and respect. They are to pay willingly and without murmuring all of their human ordinances and laws (1 Pet. 2:13), be they tolls, tributes, or excises (Rom. 13:7; Matt. 17:24 and 22:21), and they are to pray with humble hearts for the life and well being of these authorities (1 Tim. 2:2), and thus with faithful hearts, seek the prosperity of the land and city (wherein they live) (Jer. 29:7; Bar. 1:11). Even if it should happen that on account of the word of God we must suffer persecution (Matt. 5:44), robbing of goods and death, yet one must not slander the same [authorities] (Titus 3:2) nor in any way oppose them with weapons and resistance (Matt. 5:39), but only commend them to the vengeance to God (Rom. 12:29; Heb. 10:30), and after this life expect the comfort of God. But if the magistrate through Christian fairness allows the faith to live free in all its parts, then to such is one so much more obliged with submissive obedience. But in so far as the magistrates abuse their God-given office (Rom. 13:1) (which extends only to the temporal ruling of the body, in physical things) by interfering with the office of Christ (which alone has the authority over the spirit [Heb. 12:9] and soul of people [Matt. 10:28; Luke 12:4]), and using human laws to press and force people to act against the word of God, then one must not follow them in these matters, but must be more obedient to God rather than to humans

(Acts 5:30, 4:19). Observe that Christ was installed as a head in his church by God his Father above all government and force (Eph. 1:21) and we have become obedient to this Father of spirits (Heb. 12:9; Matt. 17:5; 2 Pet. 1:19) (in all the things concerning faith). And since Christ's kingdom is spiritual and not of this world (John 18:36), so he has also dissuaded and forbidden all of his ministers and disciples from all worldly ruling and highness (Matt. 20:26; Mark 10:43; Luke 22:26) allowing the worldly office to be a part of the worldly regiment. He has commanded his church to fight only with spiritual weapons (which is God's word) (Eph. 6:17; 2 Cor. 10:4), seeing that neither Christ nor his apostles have prescribed any laws or rules for believers whereby they might rule the world. Nor have they pointed to the Jewish laws, much less to the Roman emperors' or heathen's laws, by which they might regulate themselves. But they have prescribed only good teaching for believers (Rom. 13:1; Titus 3:1; 1 Pet. 2:13)—how they should conduct themselves as obedient subjects under the ruling of the magistracy (in all Christian ability). [Christ] points them to his own example (Matt. 20:28; Mark 10:45); he who has eschewed all highness of this world (John 6:15) and shown himself only as a poor servant. Hence, his disciples must also refuse and not administer the office of government in all its parts, and in this way follow after the image of Christ and his apostles, among whom their church was not served by these mentioned offices, as is well known by all who understand. And just as all the righteous are not allowed, but forbidden, to slander anyone (Titus 3:2; Rom. 12:17; 1 Cor. 5:11, 12) nor to judge (Matt. 7:1), we also desire much less to despise the magistracy, nor to speak against it, but to regard the same as servants of God (Rom. 13:4) and to remember them to our best ability in our prayers (1 Tim. 2:2), that God will bless and save them.

How the government is from God, and to what end it is established, read: "For there is no authority except from God. The authority that is there, is ordained by God, so that whoever opposes the authority, opposes God's ordinance. And whoever opposes this, shall receive judgment upon themselves. For the ruler is not to be feared by those who do good but by those who do evil. Thus if you do not wish to fear the authority, do good, and so you will be praised by him. For he is

God's servant for your own good. But if you do evil, then fear, for he does not carry the sword in vain, for he is God's servant, and an avenger to punish those who do evil." Rom. 13:1; Sir.17:18.

"Jesus answered Pilate, 'You would have no authority over me, were it not given to you from above.'" John 19:11; Wis. 6:4; Dan. 2:21 and 4:24 and 5:21; Jer. 27:6.

How Christ has forbidden the magistrate's office among his disciples, read: "But he called and said to them: 'you know that among the heathen there are those who are regarded as lords, who have lordship over them and their princes have authority over them. But it shall not be so among you, for whoever will be the greatest among you, shall be your servant. And whoever among you will be the first or principal among you, this one shall be slave of all. For the Son of Man has not come to be served, but to serve, and give his life as a payment for many'." Mark 10:42 [:42-45]; Matt. 20:25; Luke 22:25.

"Jesus answered: 'My kingdom is not of this world. Were my kingdom of this world, then my servants would have fought for me, so that I would not have been delivered to the Jews. But now my kingdom is not from here.'" John 18:36 and 6:15; 2 Cor. 10:4; Eph. 6:13; Isa. 2:4; Mic. 4:3; Zech. 9:10; Ps. 76:4; Matt. 5:39.

Read further, not about laws by which believers can rule over unbelievers, but only how they must keep themselves obedient as the church of Christ under the government, read: "Each one is subject to the government and authority. There one must be subject, not only on account of punishment, but also on account of the conscience. Therefore, each one give what they owe: tributes to whom tributes are owed, tolls to whom tolls are owed, fear, to whom fear is owed." Rom. 13:5, 7.

"So give to the emperor what is owed the emperor, and God, what is owed to God." Matt. 22:21; Mark 12:18.

"Be submissive to all human ordinances, for the Lord's sake, whether it is the king as the head, or his governor [*stadholder*] as his representative sent by him to the punishment of wrongdoers and to the praise of the good." 1 Pet. 2:13.

"Admonish them to be submissive to the rulers and authorities and obedient to the government, to be prepared to do good works, slandering no one, not quarrelling, but to be friendly, to show meekness toward all people." Titus 3:1 [:1-2]; 1 Tim. 2:1; Jer. 29:7; Bar. 1:11.

XXVIII. [Church Discipline]

Concerning Christian discipline and the separation of offending members, it is confessed that a house or city cannot stand without having doors, gates and walls through which the evil people are expelled and averted, and the good and righteous ones can be taken in, preserved and protected. (For the preservation of his church) Christ has thus given [his followers] the keys of heaven (Matt. 18:18; Matt. 16:19; John 20:23; 2 Cor. 10:8, 13:10) (which are his word), so that they shall judge and punish according to the truth, and for the good, all who are considered among their fellowship, whose teaching and behaviour is offensive (that is, against any commands and ordinances of God given to his church). In this way the disobedient shall be separated from the fellowship (1 Cor. 5:3), so that the church will not be misled (through false teaching [Rom. 16:16] and impure action [1 Cor. 5:5]) and become participants in their sins (1 Tim. 5:22). [Through this] the righteous will also become fearful of doing such evil through these ones (Deut. 13:11; 1 Tim. 5:22). This punishment of the offending ones was commanded by God through Moses to be exercised according to the seriousness of their misdeed. Those, who through ignorance and weakness, and who otherwise transgressed in some small way against some commandments of the Lord (Lev. 5:17; Num. 15:27), could be reconciled with God through various sacrifices and the intercession of the priests. But the public and more serious transgressors of the law could not be reconciled through such sacrifice, but had to die without mercy according to the testimony of two or three witnesses (Heb. 10:28; Num. 15:30; Deut. 17:10). For this reason Christ has also taught in the New Testament to apply Christian punishment according to the seriousness of the misdeed; not to the destruction of the people, as was the punishment of Israel, which occurred with death (Num. 15:36), by which those who were punished were robbed of the chance to repent and amend their ways. But Christ, having come in order to preserve the soul of humans (Luke 9:56, 19:10), has established this punishment for the betterment of the sinners. And he willed that if anyone sees his brother sin (Matt. 18:15; 1 John 5:16) in such a way that it is recognizable that it is a sin, but not so great that it has given birth to death in him (James 1:15), so shall one speak to him (about this) (out of Christian love, as those who love his soul) (Sir. 17:12) with God's word (Sir. 19:16 [:16-17]; Lev. 19:17), and show and chastise him about his sins. If he gives attention to such Christian admonition, you have won your brother, and, out of love (1 Pet. 4:8) you shall keep silent about his sin (James 5:20). However, if he does not attend to his sin, one should take one or two others so that all things in this way may be understood (Matt. 18:16; Deut. 17:11). If he does not listen to these witnesses, then the matter must be brought before the church. If he does not listen to the church (1 Cor. 15:23 [5:2-3]; 2 Cor. 10:6), then he must be cut off by the church (of which all members are judges) (2 Cor. 2:7) from the brotherhood. For if anyone participates in the public works of the flesh (Gal. 5:19), whereby the church understands that he has separated himself from his God through these sins (Isa. 59:1) and transferred himself into the wrath of God, all such shall be cut off by the church from the brotherhood on account of his sins (2 Cor. 2:7) (without any of the aforementioned admonition and speaking to the transgressing sinner) (1 Cor. 5:3). [This shall take place] so that the sinner may again repent and amend his ways by God's grace (1 Cor. 5:4; 2 Cor. 10:8), having been separated from God by the flesh's evil works. Thus the church shall knowingly maintain no one in its fellowship who has been separated from God through their sins (Isa. 59:2; Jer. 2:16). But no one should be cut off from the fellowship (John 15:2, 6) except those who through their sins have previously separated themselves from God. Neither should anyone (2 Cor. 2:7; Phil. 1:12) be readmitted and given the word of life and peace (Ezek. 13:19, 10, 16) except if they previously have been received by God's grace through faith and true repentance; since only true fruits of repentance (Matt. 3:8; Luke 3:8) (that is, that one confess and leave his sins) [Prov. 28:13; Ps. 32:5; Sir. 35:3], ceasing from doing wrong, and seeking to replace the practiced evil with well-doing, according to one's ability) open the entrance into the kingdom of God (2 Pet. 1:11), which previously had been closed on account of sins. In this way the church of God with its [practice of] separation and restoration may follow and walk after the previous separation and inclusion by God in heaven according to his word (2 Cor. 2:12; Num. 12:15), which is proof and proclamation of what the church does. Since with God there is no consideration of persons (Rom. 2:11; Deut. 10:27, 2 Chron. 19:7), the church of God must use these keys of the divine word correctly and in punishment excuse no one, be they minister or brother, man or woman, small or great (Deut. 1:17). [All should be judged] according to the identical rule and measure of God's word, and according to the truth (John 17:17, 12:48). And as all disobedient sinners with the agreement of the church (1 Cor. 5:3; 2 Cor. 2:8) and from the brotherhood are cut off, without sorrow and sadness (1 Cor. 5:2) and are shown [the way of] repentance and improvement, so shall also all obedient, repentant sinners, through the elders of the church (1 Tim. 5:22) with the consent and agreement of the church (2 Cor. 2:9), be received again. And just as one is bound to rejoice over the finding of a lost sheep, penny or son (Luke 15:5, 32), so shall the believers with all the angels of God also rejoice (Luke 15:10) over the repentance and conversion of their erring brother or sister (James 5:20).

Of the small sins, be they through weakness or ignorance, how they were reconciled through the priest, with various sacrifices, read: Lev. 4:27 and chapter 5; Num. 5:6 and 15:22.

But the public transgressors of the law are judged to death on the basis of [literally, in the mouth of] two or three witnesses, read: Num. 15:30; Lev. 24:14; Deut. 17:11 and 19:15; Heb. 10:28.

Read here the reasons of the high priest Eli: "If anyone sins against a human, then the judge can mediate, but if anyone sins against the Lord, who can mediate?" 1 Sam. 2:25.

How Christ has commanded to punish the small transgressing sin between brother and brother, read: "If your brother sins against you, then go to him and chastise him between you and him alone. If he hears you, so have you won your brother. But if he does not listen, take further one or two with you, so that all matters may be understood by two or three witnesses. If he does not listen, then tell the church. If he does not listen to the church, then regard him as a heathen and publican.

Verily I say to you, what you shall bind on the earth shall be also bound in heaven. And what you loose on earth shall also be loosed in heaven." Matt. 18:15 [:15-18]; Luke 17:3; Gal. 6:1; James 5:19.

"If anyone sees his brother sin—a sin not unto death—he will pray and give him life, whose sin is not unto death." 1 John 5:16.

But public, offending members, Christ has commanded to cut off and cast away, without exercising admonishment, intercession or forgiveness. Read: Matt. 18:8; Mark 9:42.

Following the teaching of Christ, the apostles have therefore kept from eternal life all [doers of] public works of the flesh and judged them for death, and with the word and authority of the Lord Jesus Christ gave over the Corinthian prostitutes to Satan, without using the above-mentioned admonition for the same ones. 1 Cor. 5:3. Read further: 1 Tim. 1:20 and 5:20; 2 Cor. 13:2.

"There is a sin unto death, for this one I do not say that anyone should pray." 1 John 5:16; Num. 15:30; Heb. 10:28; 1 Cor. 5:12; 2 Cor. 13:2; Ps. 1:6; 2 Tim. 2:20; 1 Cor. 6:9; Gal. 5:21; Eph. 5:5.

XXIX. [Separation]

Concerning the withdrawal and inspection of the apostate and separated members, it is confessed that separation is commanded by God for the improvement of the sinner (2 Cor. 10:8 and 13:10; 1 Cor. 5:4 [:4-5]), and for maintaining the purity of the church. Thus God has also commanded and willed that one should withdraw and shun [*schouwen ende mijden*] those who have been separated (Titus 1:10; 2 Tim. 4:15) (so that they will feel compelled to improve themselves) (2 Thess. 3:14). Such withdrawal arises from the separation, and is a fruit and proof of the same, and without which the separation is vain and useless. For this reason, all such ordinances of God regarding the separated ones (2 Thess. 3:6) shall be kept and maintained by all believers. Withdrawal pertains to all spiritual fellowship, such as the Lord's Supper (Acts 20:7), the evangelical greeting (2 John 1:10), the kiss of peace (Rom. 16:15 [:15-16]; 1 Cor. 16:20), and the like. Similarly this withdrawal applies to all temporal and physical things, such as eating (1 Cor. 5:10 [:10-11]), drinking (John 4:9), buying and selling, daily living and conversation (1 Tim. 4:15; Titus 3:10) and with whatever is associated with these activities. Similarly, believers shall withdraw themselves from the separated ones, in all spiritual, evangelical matters, also in all physical and temporal things, according to God's word. As in the practice of separation, no persons might be exempted or spared (Rom. 2:11; Deut. 1:17), but must with the consent of all true members of the body be cut off (1 Cor. 5:3; 2 Cor. 2:8), hence, no one may be spared nor excluded in the withdrawal (existing in all spiritual and temporal matters), be they man or woman (Deut. 13:6; 2 Thess. 3:6), elder or child, or whatever blood relation there might be. Notice that nowhere does it say [in the Bible] (where God has given his church a general command or ordinance) that some members of the church have been exempt from such a commandment. On the contrary it appears in many places [of Scripture] that all the people (without exception) must regulate themselves according to one rule established by God (Eph. 4:4; Lev. 24:14; Phil. 2:16). For this reason, all ordinances of God shall be used and maintained by all members of the body of Christ in the fear of God in order to humble and improve sinners (2 Thess. 3:14), so that the one who is punished is received again by the church.

But as all divine commands must be measured with Christian courtesy and modesty (Lev. 2:13; Mark 9:48; Col. 4:4), the same must also have its place in this matter (the withdrawal). Therefore the believers must conduct themselves toward the separated ones with greater distinction and fairness than the scribes and Pharisees with the Sabbath, who appeared to prefer to allow people to perish than to help them on the Sabbath (Luke 13:12; John 5:10, 9:14; Matt. 12:1), believing that by doing so [i.e., helping others] they would break the Sabbath, even though they themselves had contravened the Sabbath in diverse lesser matters (in such cases). Similarly the righteous disciples of the law have not sinned nor broken the Sabbath (Matt. 12:5) when they did not do their own works but those commanded by God (John 7:23). Thus the believers have neither transgressed nor sinned, nor proceeded against the command of withdrawal when they perform not their own works but those commanded by God towards the separated ones, as when in need they serve the same with food and other things necessary for the body (Gal. 6:12; Luke 10:37) and with God's word for the soul (2 Thess. 3:15; Matt. 5:45). Therefore all believers are also responsible to show support for the separated ones (based on God's command) in [times of] water, fire and the like.[16] Therefore (with great carefulness) [they should] search for the lost and lead the straying back onto the right path (Luke 19:10, 15:5), correcting and instructing the same with God's word (James 5:19) where such Christian admonition must have its place according to the example of Christ (Eph. 4:29). But in all human works (1 Cor. 5:10), the believers shall withdraw themselves from the separated ones, with all diligence (2 Thess. 3:6; Gal. 2:12), for their betterment, and so that they might be united with the church again.

In order to understand this matter properly, it must be pointed out that the people of Israel (at the time of Christ) sat under the force and rule of the Romans and were not able to punish the transgressors of the law of Moses. This they did to those who departed from their fatherly law and had run to the heathens, Samaritans or publicans, separating and shunning them from their fellowship, read: "The same they regarded as impure and as a horror, just as they regarded the heathens and enemies, dismissing and withdrawing from their business and manners, and hindering in their profit." 3 Macc. 69 verses. Read further: John 18:31; John 4:9; Acts 10:28 and 11:3; Gal. 2:12.

This custom Christ and his apostles also applied to treating the disobedient of the church, in this way commanding and saying, "If he hears not the church, hold him as a heathen and publican." Matt. 18:17.

Such was also used and practiced by the apostles (following after the teaching of Christ), read: "I have written to you in the letter that you should not have anything to do with the unchaste, but I did not mean the unchaste of this world, or the greedy or the robbers or the servants of idols, since you would then have to leave the world. But now I have written to you not to have anything to do with these; namely, if anyone regards himself as a brother and yet is an adulterer or greedy, or servant of idols, or evil-speaker, or drunkard, or robber, one should not even eat with such a one." 1 Cor. 5:8.

Here the holy apostle has forbidden any kind of interaction or eating with the fallen brothers or sisters, by which he did not mean or forbid [interacting or eating with] the world, for with the same it is freely permitted; otherwise one would have to evacuate the world, since the entire world is given over to evil. All such must therefore be understood as daily routine—eating, buying and selling and similar such things—as necessary. [Rather] "shun a heretical person, once he has been admonished once or twice." Titus 3:10; 2 Tim. 2:20 and 4:15; 2 John 1:10.

"But if there is anyone who is not obedient to our words which are signed in a letter, have nothing to do with him, and let him be ashamed." 2 Thess. 3:14.

How this withdrawal must be practiced by all believers toward all those who have fallen, and who walk improperly, without regard for the person, read: "Now we command you dear brothers, in the name of the Lord Jesus Christ, that you withdraw from all brothers who walk improperly and not according to the tradition that he has received from us." 2 Thess. 3:6.

Understand this withdrawal according to the Scriptures: Gal. 2:12; 3 Macc. 69 verses and similar, according to an evangelical manner.

How the believers must seek the lost and not hold the separated ones as enemies, but admonish them as brothers, read: 2 Thess. 3:15; James 5:19; Luke 19:10 and 15 entirely.

XXX. [The Last Day and Return of Christ]

Concerning the Last Day and return of Christ from heaven, it is confessed that when the great God of heaven, in the beginning created heaven and earth out of nothing with all visible things (Gen. 1:2; Heb.11:3; 2 Macc. 7:28), he appointed a day and time (2 Pet. 3:10; Matt. 14:44) (which cannot be known by angels of God [Matt. 24:16; Mark 13:32], much less by any mortal humans. It shall overtake humanity like a snare of birds [Luke 21:34] or a thief in the night [Rev. 3:3; 2 Pet. 3:12; Mal. 4:1]) at which time the mighty God will destroy all the earthly, the visible regime and burn it with an eternal fire; but will exclude humans who have carried out the will of God and who will thus live into eternity (1 John 4:17). In the great, last day of the Lord, the Son of God, Christ Jesus, who in the presence of the apostles rose up from the earth to heaven (Acts 1:9)—the same shall come again from heaven, in the clouds of the heavens (Luke 21:27; Acts 1:11; Rev. 1:7). But he will not come in the same humbled, servant-like form like he first came into the world at Bethlehem (Luke 2:7; Phil. 2:7; Heb. 2:7, 9); but in his second coming he shall reveal himself in the clouds as a mighty King of all kings and Lord of all lords (Rev. 19:6, 17:14, 1:5; 1 Tim. 6:14), with the power and glory of his almighty Father, and all the angels of God with him (Matt. 25:31). And thus he will make an unspeakable sound and shout through the trumpet of God (1 Thess. 4:16), and the voice of the archangel. Hence, heaven and earth, all mountains and islands, will be moved, the sun and moon lose their brilliance (Matt. 24:29), the stars will fall from heaven, and all tribes of the earth will weep and cry for themselves (Rev. 1:7) out of fear and expectation of the things that shall occur (Luke 21:24). And all people will see the Son of Man come with great power and glory (Rev. 1:7).

Concerning this last day of the Lord, read: "And as he sat on the Mount of Olives, his disciples came to him alone and said, 'Tell us when shall this happen? And what shall be the signs of your coming and the end of the world?'" Matt. 24:3.

"The day of the Lord shall come like a thief in the night in which the heavens shall perish with a great sound, the elements shall melt from heat, and the earth with the works therein shall be burned." 2 Pet. 3:10; Sir. 16:18; Mal. 4:1.

"For you yourselves know certainly that the day of the Lord shall come like a thief in the night. For when they shall say, there is peace and no reason to be concerned, then shall destruction fall quickly upon them, just as the woe of childbirth comes over a pregnant woman." 1 Thess. 5:2.

"Heaven and earth shall perish, [but] my words shall not perish. For of this day and hour no one knows, nor the angels in heaven, but only my Father." Matt. 24:35; Mark 13:31; Ps. 102:27; Isa. 51:6.

Of Christ's coming from heaven, read: "You men of Galilee, why do you stand here and look up to heaven? This Jesus who was taken up into heaven shall come just as you have seen him ascend into heaven." Acts 1:11.

"For the Lord himself shall come down out of heaven with a shout and a voice of the archangel, and with the trumpet of God." 1 Thess. 3:26.

"See he comes with the clouds, and all eyes shall see him, [even] those who pierced him. And all the tribes of the earth shall cry for themselves." Rev. 1:7; Matt. 24:30; Luke 21:28. Read further: 1 Thess. 1:10; 2 Thess. 1:7; Dan. 7:13; Jude 1:14.

XXXI. [The Resurrection of the Dead and Eternal Judgment]

Concerning the resurrection of the dead and eternal judgment, it is believed and confessed that just as in the spring the sun, through its glorious shining and brilliance pulls both fragrant plants out of the earth as well as the thistles and thorns which are cast into the fire prepared for them (Matt. 5:45), so also shall (in this great last day and hour) Christ Jesus, the true Son of righteousness (Mal. 4:2; Wis. 5:6), through his glorious coming (1 Thess. 4:16; 1 Cor. 15:52) and appearance in the clouds of heaven, also pull all people, the evil and righteous, out of the earth and raise and resurrect them. This great God, through his mighty and commanding voice, through which he originally had spoken "Let it become heaven and earth (2 Esd. 6:38; Gen. 1:1)," has therefore been a perfect work, and all visible things have arisen out of the invisible (Heb. 11:3; 2 Macc. 7:28). This same God has created humans from the dust of the earth (Gen. 2:6; Acts 17:25) through his unchangeable power and almighty word (John 5:28; 1 Cor. 6:14; Rom. 6:5, 8:11). On the last day all humans, who have turned to dust and earth and who have been consumed by fire, birds and fish—these shall be called out of the dust (Ps. 90:3) and raised up and resurrected, everyone with his own body, flesh and bone with which they have served their Creator or the world (Job 19:16; Rom. 8:11; Isa. 26:19; 2 Cor. 5:10). Just as a woman who is giving birth (having come to her hour) is not able keep it in, but hastens in order to produce the fruit that is sowed within her (2 Esd. 4:42, 8:8; John 16:21), in that way shall it also be in this last hour: death, earth or hell and sea, will hasten to give up again the great number of the dead which are sowed in dust and ashes and have perished in them (Rev. 20:13; Ps. 90:3). These shall all again stand and rise up (John 5:28), with their own bodies (Job 19:26; Isa. 26:19; 1 Cor. 15:54), into imperishableness, which will be reunited with the soul or spirit (which through death was separated from the body [Heb. 4:12] and remained immortal [Matt. 10:28]), at which time the righteous shall be glorified, from the mortal and perishable to the immortal and imperishable (1 Cor. 15:53; Phil. 3:21), out of weakness and infirmity into strength and glory, being like the angels of God and the glorious body of Christ (Matt. 22:30; Phil. 3:21). In this way, those who are alive and remaining at the time of Christ's sudden return from heaven shall be changed and glorified after the likeness of Christ (1 Cor. 15:52; 1 Thess. 4:15).

Then shall the entire multitude of people (Matt. 25:31) be placed before the tribunal and judgment throne of Christ (2 Cor. 5:10; Rom. 14:10), and each in his own body shall receive according to the worth of his deeds. On this great and last judgment day, Christ Jesus, being set by God his Father as a judge over the living and dead (Acts 10:42; Acts 17:31), will require no testimony, but each heart, sense, mind, and conscience will be uncovered and made known as an open book before him (Rev. 20:12; Rev. 2:23). He shall then judge (without regard of any persons) (Eph. 6:9) the whole circle of the earth with justice (Acts 17:31; Ps. 7:11). And he shall, as the lord and great shepherd of the sheep (Heb. 13:20), separate the evil and good people, placing the righteous on his right and the unrighteous on his left hand (Matt. 25:33), and loudly declare over the same an eternal and irrevocable order (Heb. 6:5). To all believing reborn ones who in this life, through [Christ's] calling voice, have come to Christ and followed him (Matt. 11:29 and 19:28), he shall speak, "Come you blessed ones of my Father; possess the kingdom which is prepared for you from the beginning of the world (Matt. 25:34)." And to all the unbelievers, who in this life have neither willed nor sought after Christ and his word, and through unbelief have not yielded to him, he shall say: "Go you damned ones into the eternal fire that was prepared for the Devil and his angels (Matt. 25:41)."

How in the return of Christ the dead shall stand and rise up through Christ, read: "For the Lord himself shall with a shout and voice of the archangels, and with the trumpet of God come down from heaven and the dead in Christ shall rise up first." 1 Thess. 4:16.

"And be not amazed, for the hour comes in which all who are in the grave shall hear his voice and those who have done good there shall come forth into the resurrection of life; but those who have done evil, to the resurrection of the condemned." John 5:28.

I know that my redeemer lives and at the last he shall awaken me from the earth. And after my skin has been removed, in my flesh I shall see God. The same shall I see, and my eyes shall behold him." Job.19:25 [:25-27].

Read further: Isa. 26:19; Dan. 12:12; Matt. 22:31; Luke 20:35; John 6:40 and 11:25; 1 Cor. 15 entirely; Ps. 90:3.

How in the resurrection of the dead, the miserable bodies of humans shall be glorified, read: "In the resurrection they neither marry nor are given in marriage, but they are like the angels in heaven." Matt. 22:30.

"But our journey is in heaven, from where we expect the Saviour Jesus Christ our Lord, who shall purify our insignificant body; that it become like the body of his clarity, according to the working whereby he can subject all things to himself." Phil. 3:20 [:20-21]; 1 Cor. 15:42, 53.

And how the entire human race shall appear before the judgment throne of Christ to receive an eternal judgment, read: "For we must all be revealed before the judgment seat of Christ, so that each one may receive in his body according to what he has done, be it good or evil." 2 Cor. 5:10; Rom. 14:10.

"And I saw the dead both great and small standing in the presence of God, and the books were opened, and another book was opened in which the living and the dead were judged according to things that were written in the book, according to their works." Rev. 20:12; Dan. 7:13.

"And when the Son of Man shall come into his glory and all holy angels with him, then shall he sit on the throne of his majesty and all people shall be gathered before him and he shall separate them from

each other just as the shepherd separates the sheep from the goats."
Matt. 25:31 and 16:27 and 26:62; 2 Thess. 1:7.

XXXII. [Death, Hell and Damnation]

Concerning death, hell and the damnation of the unbelievers, it is
confessed that through the Devil's envy (Wis. 2:24) and the sin of our
first parents (Rom. 5:12; 1 Cor. 15:21; Gen. 3:6), death has come
into the world. The entire human race having thus fallen in sin, has
become subject to physical death, so that human beings are destined
to die once and thereafter [to experience] judgment (Heb. 9:28; Gen.
3:19). Observe that this perishable, sinful flesh and blood (1 Cor.
15:50) cannot possess the eternal, imperishable, but it must be renewed
and glorified by God through the death and resurrection. Just as when
a person falls into a deep sleep, and his heart, soul or spirit does not
sleep as completely as the body (Song of Sol. 5:2), so also the spirit or
soul of human beings does not die (Acts 7:59; Ps. 31:6) or pass away
with the body (Wis. 3:1), but is and remains an immortal spirit (Matt.
10:28). Seeing that in the scriptures the natural death is called a sleep
(1 Cor. 15:6; Matt. 9:24) and the resurrection of the dead an awakening
from this sleep of death (John 11:11; Dan. 12:13), and just as a sleeping
person can receive and use neither for his soul nor his body any good
gifts, much less any punishment, pain and torment until he has been
first awakened from his sleep (Gen. 40:5), in this way believers cannot
receive the perfect heavenly nature, nor the unbelievers the eternal
death or pain of hell, neither in the soul nor the body, until they have
been first awakened and raised up from this sleep of death through the
coming of Christ (1 Thess. 4:16; John 5:29). Until this last judgment
day the souls of the believers are in the hands of God (Wis. 3:1) under
the altar of Christ (Rev. 6:9), expecting to receive their reward in their
body and soul (2 Cor. 5:10; Matt. 10:28). In this way the souls of the
unbelievers are also preserved (2 Pet. 2, 4, 9), so that on the Day of
Judgment they will be punished in their soul and body.

In the Last Day of the Lord (2 Pet. 3:10), God who is righteous
shall take away all good gifts from this world, so that the sun, moon
and stars will lose their glimmer (Matt. 24:19; Mark 13:24) and all of

the world's light and glory will be changed into an eternal darkness (Matt. 8:12, 2:13; Jude 1:13); at which time the earth, waters and brooks shall be changed into burning pitch and sulphur, which shall burn from eternity to eternity (Isa. 34:9; 2 Pet. 3:12). And seeing this earth, which in many places in the Scriptures is named hell (Num. 16:32; Gen. 37:35; Ps. 16:10; Acts 2:27)—and nowhere does it mention another hell—is maintained as the same hell and place of damnation, in which exists a fiery pool and utmost darkness (Rev. 21:8), all unbelievers finally must suffer the burning hell and eternal damnation. Thus with all visible things, which in this life unbelievers preferred to serve (Wis. 11:17; James 5:3) more than eternal, invisible things (Heb. 12:16), shall they also be punished and tormented with the same. In this place of darkness and pools of fire all unbelievers, after the resurrection, when their soul is reunited with their own body (Matt. 10:28) by Christ (Matt. 25:42), then shall be fulfilled what is written of this last sad separation day: when one out of two in the field, on the bed and at the mill (Matt. 24:40 [:40-41]; Luke 17:34) will be taken and caught up to meet the Lord in the air (1 Thess. 4:17). But the others shall be left here and be cast into the aforementioned pool of darkness where they, with the Devil and his angels (Matt. 25:42; Judith 16:25; Mark 9:47; Isa. 66:24), will be tormented, and where they will burn and suffer eternally (Rev. 20:6) (which is the second death), abiding eternally robbed of and absent from all grace and mercy of God (Matt. 25:11).

Of the first or temporal death, which came through the first sin, read: "For you are dust and shall return again to dust." Gen. 3:19; Sir. 25:33 [?]

"And just as the human is made to die once." Heb. 9:28.

"For just as through one man death came." 1 Cor. 15:21; Rom. 5:12; Wis. 2:24.

Of hell and the place of the damned, read: "For it is the day of the wrath of the Lord, and the year of repayment in order to avenge Zion. Then shall their brooks become pitch, and their earth become sulphur; yes, their land shall become burning pitch which will not be extinguished neither day nor night, but there shall be an eternal smoke going up from them." Isa. 34:8; 2 Pet. 3:10; Sir. 16:18.

"And when Moses had spoken these words, then the earth split open under them and opened its mouth and swallowed them up with their tents and with all the people who were with Korah and with all their possessions, and took them alive down into hell, with all that they had." Num. 16:31 [:31-33].

Read further concerning Sodom and Gomorrah, how they were turned over and were damned and made into an example. And how the earth is called Hell: Gen. 19:24; Jude 1:7; Gen. 37:35 and 42:38 and 44:49; Acts 2:27, 31; Ps. 16:11.

"That they should know that anyone who will suffer through the same things." Wis. 11:17.

"Your gold and silver has rusted and their rust shall be a testimony to you and shall eat your flesh as a fire." James 5:3.

How the souls of unbelievers are kept by God until the last day of vengeance so that then after the resurrection they will be punished with their bodies, read: "For the judgment shall come after death, when we shall become living again; then shall the names of the righteous shine and the godless works shall be repaid according to the deed." 2 Esd. 14:35.

"See there comes a day which shall burn like an oven; then shall all arrogant, and violent and unrighteous perpetrators with the godless be like straw and the coming day will ignite them, says the Lord." Mal. 4:1.

"The Lord knows how to deliver the godly out of temptation, and to keep the evil and unrighteous until the day of judgment for punishment." 2 Pet. 2:9.

"These ones he has kept until the judgment of the great day, who are kept in a deep darkness into eternity." Jude 1:6, 3 [13]; Matt. 25:31; Rom. 14:10; 2 Cor. 5:10.

Read further of the fearful and insufferable pain of hell: Judith 16:25; Mark 9:46; Matt. 22:13 and 24:51 and 25:30, 42; Rev. 19:20 and 21:8.

XXXIII. [The Kingdom of Heaven and Eternal Life]

Concerning the kingdom of heaven and eternal life, it is confessed that just as there is a visible, perishable kingdom of this world (Matt. 4:8), which through the sins and evil of humanity is covered in darkness (John 5:19), where Satan and the spirit of evil (Eph. 2:2, 6:12) (which works among the children of disbelief) is the supreme prince of this darkness, who at the end, with all his servants, shall be moved to an eternal cry where he will mourn and perish (Matt. 24:29; 1 John 2:17: 2 Pet. 3:10); so also is there an eternal, immovable and invisible (Heb. 12:28; 2 Cor. 4:18) kingdom of heaven (Matt. 25:35), of which Christ Jesus is the king, prince, and lord (Matt. 25:34, 16:16; Rev. 19:16). Through him, all believers shall live eternally (Matt. 25:46; Ps. 125:1) with God in an eternally everlasting joy (Matt. 25:23). From the beginning of the world (2 Tim. 1:9) God has called the fallen human race by his grace and goodness to this glorious kingdom of heaven; first, through his servants, the prophets (Heb. 1:3), and thereafter through the Son himself who for a time left this his kingdom (John 16:28) and came preaching and inviting all people (Matt. 28:20; Isa. 45:22) to flee the shadow of this world and hasten to enter into this eternal rest (Heb. 4:11). For this reason the fat animals are slain and this glorious feast prepared (Matt. 22:4), so that humans do not need to make an excuse on account of their fields, beasts, and wives (Luke 14:18); for the way through the gate is open and well prepared (Heb. 10:20; John 10:9, 14:6; Rom.5:2). This glorious kingdom of heaven has been depicted and set forth to us as a city full of all goods (2 Esd. 7:6). The new Jerusalem, coming from heaven (Rev. 21:2, 21:10; Heb. 12:22) is well prepared by God as an adorned bride for her husband; where the streets are built of pure gold and the gates, and the walls of diverse pearls and precious stones are beautifully adorned. In this city is the purity and glory of the almighty God (Exod. 13:21), which neither Moses on Mount Zion nor any mortal human eyes has seen (Deut. 4:12; 1 Tim. 6:16; 1 John 4:12; John 1:18). Radiance and eternal light shall shine and illuminate this city forever (Rev. 21:23; Isa. 60:19; Rev. 22:5). Here shall all suffering and crying, cold, nakedness, hunger and thirst be changed into an eternal satisfying joy and comfort (Rev. 7:16). This glory and rejoicing is so great and unspeakably above all measure, that never has any eye seen nor ear heard, nor has anything entered the human heart, which God has not prepared for those who love him (1 Cor. 2:9; Isa. 54:17). And into this incomparable heavenly state—when the dead are resurrected—all believing and God-pleasing people shall have their souls reunited with their bodies, which through the death of the body were separated (Tob. 3:6), but protected in the hands of God until the end (Wis. 3:1). Thus, [all believing people] shall be taken out of this earthly darkness to meet the Lord in the air (1 Thess. 4:17). And just as a bride is received by her bridegroom (Isa. 61:10; Wis.15:7 [?]), so shall all true children of God be then received by Christ Jesus with body and soul (out of grace) (Matt. 25:23, 34; Col. 3:4) and be admitted into this glorious rejoicing, where, because they are like God in his unspeakable glory, they shall see and behold him with all the heavenly hosts (1 John 3:2, Isa. 33:17; Job 19:26). Then shall their clothes of mourning or mortal cloak of flesh be taken off (1 Cor. 15:53; 2 Esd. 2:45), and the immortal put on; they shall be clothed with white shining clothes (Rev. 3:5; Matt. 13:43) and with all of God's elect they shall be fed by the Son of God (whom they have confessed here in the world) (2 Esd. 2:47) with the hidden heavenly bread (Rev. 2:17), and they shall eat of the tree of life (Rev. 2:7) and drink from the fountain of living waters (Rev. 7:17) and in the likeness of angels (Matt. 22:30) they shall sing a new song (Rev. 14:3) with joyful tongues and mouths in a sound of rejoicing with unspeakable, glorious rejoicing (1 Pet. 1:8), to the honor of the Lamb their bridegroom (Isa. 23:18 [?]), which no one can take away from them (John 16:22). For they shall be kings[17] and priests of God[18] and live and reign with Christ from eternity to eternity. To God, full of grace and mercy and of all comfort, who has called us from the beginning to his heavenly kingdom and glory (1 Pet. 5:10), who has gifted us unworthy humans with his good Spirit (Ps. 51:13) and made us worthy so that we may come towards him (Can.1:3 [Song of Sol. 1:3-4?]; John 6:14); that we might pursue (Phil. 3:14) and run after this high prize (2 Cor. 9:14; Isa. 40:31) and receive and enjoy the same (by grace) through Jesus Christ into eternity [be praise] (2 Tim. 4:8). Amen.

Of the eternally everlasting kingdom of heaven, and its king, read: "For those of us who receive the unshakeable kingdom, let us have grace." Heb. 12:28.

"My kingdom is not of this world, for if my kingdom were of this world, then should my servants fight for me, so that I not be handed over to the Jews; but now my kingdom is not from here." John 18:36.

"Receive the praiseworthy gifts and be joyful, thanking him who has called you to his heavenly kingdom." 2 Esd. 2:37; Col. 1:12; Ps. 22:29.

Read further how this eternal king, Christ Jesus (in his return from heaven, after the dead are raised and the eternal judgment is held) shall receive all the members of his kingdom into his eternal glorious kingdom of heaven, where they shall behold God in inexpressible glory. "Then shall the king say to those who shall be at his right hand: 'Come here you blessed of my Father, possess the kingdom that is prepared for you from the beginning of the world.'" Matt. 25:34.

"But the righteous shall live eternally and the Lord is their reward and the Most High takes care of them. Therefore shall they receive a glorious kingdom and a beautiful crown from the hand of the Lord." Wis. 5:16 [:15-16]; 1 Pet. 5:4; 2 Tim. 4:8; 2 Esd. 2:43; Rev. 2:10; James 1:12.

"Thereafter we who are alive and remain shall together with them be caught up into the clouds to meet the Lord in the air and thus be with the Lord for all time. For this reason comfort each other with these words." 1 Thess. 4:17; 1 Cor. 2:9; 1 Pet. 1:8; John 16:22.

"My beloved, we are now God's children and it is still not yet revealed what we will be. But we know, when he is revealed, that we shall be like him, for we shall see him as he is." 1 John 3:2; Phil. 3:21.

"But when Christ (who is our life) is revealed, then shall you also be revealed with him in his glory." Col. 3:4.

"Your eyes shall see the King in his beauty. Then shall the land be prepared for you so that your heart shall be amazed." Isa. 33:17.

All who from sincere faith show the required spiritual virtue and persevere in the divine calling until the end: "If you do these things, then you shall not fall, and thus shall the entrance into the eternal kingdom of our Lord and Saviour Jesus Christ be abundantly prepared for you." 2 Pet. 1:10-11.

FINISHED

Since there was some empty space here, we have filled it
with some writings of our old teachers
to substantiate these articles.
Menno Simons in the Summary Book,[19] fol.123, Concerning the
eternal God and eternal divine nature.

This one, only, eternal, almighty, unknowable, invisible, unspeakable and indescribable God, we believe and confess with the Scriptures to be the eternal, incomprehensible Father, with his eternal, incomprehensible Son and with his eternal, incomprehensible Holy Spirit. The Father we believe and confess to be a true Father, the Son a true Son, and the Holy Spirit a true Holy Spirit, and that [they are] not fleshly and comprehensible, but spiritual and incomprehensible.

And further, fol.134.

Thus we believe and confess before God, before his angels, before all our brothers, and before the whole world, how these three names, their working and power, namely, Father, Son and Holy Spirit (which the fathers have named three persons, whereby they have meant the three true divine beings), are an incomprehensible, indescribable, almighty, holy, singular, eternal and glorious God. Just as John said: "there are three who give testimony in heaven: the Father, the Word, and the Holy Spirit, and these three are one." 1 John 5:7;[20] Matt. 3:16, and 28:19; Mark 1:10; Luke 3:22; John 14:16, and 15:26; 1 Cor. 12:6; 2 Cor. 13:13.

Dirck Philips in his *Handbook*, fol.4

The Father we confess to be the eternal God and heavenly Father, who is an independent being of all things (Eph. 3:14; 1 Cor. 8:5; Eph. 1:14), from which all that is has its being; a fountain of all good (Jer. 2:10; James 1:17), from which all that is good has its origin and beginning; yes, out of which his only born Son, Jesus Christ, was born divine and inexpressible from the beginning and from eternity (Mic. 5:1), and from which the Holy Spirit proceeds. Therefore he is a God and Father over all (Eph. 3:15)."

Concerning the eternal birth of the only Son of God. Menno Simons in the *Summary Book*, fol.123.

Since God is such a Spirit, as is written, so we believe and confess also of the divine procreation of the heavenly Father and of his procreated Son Christ Jesus. Brothers, understand my writing well, that he is as spiritual (1 Cor. 2:13) and incomprehensible as his Father himself who had procreated him (Isa. 53:11; Acts 2:32)—as like procreates like, undeniably (John 3:6). And this same one is an incomprehensible, inexpressible, spiritual, eternal, divine being, who was born, divine and incomprehensible, before all creatures, out of the Father (Col. 1:15; Mic. 5:1). We believe and confess that this one is Christ Jesus, the first born and only born Son of God, the first born before all creatures (John 1:18, 3:16).

Dirck Philips in his *Handbook*, fol.87.

Seeing that the stone is sheered from the mountain without hands (Dan. 2:45), signifying to us the wonderful, incomprehensible and inexpressible birth of the Son of God, Jesus Christ (Isa. 53:11; Acts 4:11; Prov. 8:22), which took place out of God his heavenly Father, before the beginning of all creatures (Col. 1:15), therefore, all creatures are unable to comprehend or express this. It is enough that we know without any doubt and firmly believe that Jesus Christ is born from

God as the Son of the living God (Matt. 16:16; Mic. 5:1), from the beginning until eternity. He has his genesis and origin from God, as the Scriptures richly testify in many places (John 3:6). Hence his genuine divinity is proven, and witnessed to enough, and also established. For it is an unquestionable word, yes the testimony of Jesus Christ himself, that he was born like from like. And therefore his Father and his only born Son Jesus Christ are one divine being, just as the great mountain and the stone, which is sheered from it without hands, are one substance.

Concerning the Holy Spirit, Menno Simons in the *Summary Book*, fol.133.

Concerning the Holy Spirit, we believe and confess [that there is] a true, real, or personal Holy Spirit (just as the Father named him), and in a Godly manner, is just as the Father is a true father, and the Son a true son. This Holy Spirit is incomprehensible, inexpressible and indescribable by all children of humanity, just as we have testified above concerning the Father and Son. He is divine, with his divine gifts, proceeding from the Father through the Son (John 15:16), although he always remains with God and in God, and in the being of the Father and Son is never separated. And that the Scriptures call us to confess him as a true, real, Holy Spirit; for he descended in the physical form of a dove upon Christ during his baptism (Matt. 3:16; Mark 1:16; Luke 3:22; John 2:32).

Dirck Philips in his *Handbook*, fol.6.

Concerning the Holy Spirit, we confess it to be an eternal and only Holy Spirit who is a spirit of both the Father and the Son, a spirit of truth, and of all heavenly wisdom, and of all divine understanding, a distributor of the faith and of all spiritual gifts, a comforter of consciences, through which all Christians pray to God, and call Abba, Father. 1 Cor. 12:2; John 14:28 and 16:7; Wis. 1:5; 1 Cor. 2:10; Rom. 12:3; 1 Cor. 2:4; John 15:26; Rom. 8:15.

Concerning the humbling and incarnation of the eternal Son of God, Menno Simons, *Against Johann a Lasco*, fol.24.

Even though the Father is unsuffering, immortal and immutable, the Son humbled himself, and became corporeal and immortal for us, according to the testimony of all Scriptures— Phil. 2:7; Heb. 2:7, 9; 1 Pet. 1:20; 2 Cor. 8:9; John 3:16—and very many similar places and chapters. Therefore he desired from his dear Father that he might again obtain his glory which he had lost when he became human (John 17:5). If he then had remained immutable in his divine form, and suffered the things that he had received from the earth (as you say), tell me, most beloved, what has he then lost, that he desires again to receive from his Father? Look correctly to the Scriptures, and pray that your eyes will be properly opened (through the Lord's grace, in order to behold the truth of Christ).

Dirck Philips in his *Handbook*, fol.73.

A Christian indeed understands from this that God's eternal word (John 1:1), God's own, only born (John 3:16; Rom. 8:32) and first born Son (Col. 1:15), yes God himself (John 1:14; Rom. 9:5; 1 John 5:20; John 20:28), has become human, and has taken off his divine form, abandoned his glory, and taken on a form of a human and servant. In sum: he who was God, has become man, and become the human who is God and man, and who is God and man, who died as a man, and he who died as a man, shall stand up from the dead as God (John 10:18).

And further, fol.92.

In this way has the only born Son of the living God—who before the beginning of the world was with God (John 17:5), who has become a mortal man, who was rich and has for our account become poor (2 Cor. 8:0 [:9]); who was in the form of God (Phil. 2:6)—appeared in human and servant form. The wisdom which was born before the beginning of all creatures (from God) (Prov. 8:12), has let himself be seen upon the earth (Bar. 3:38. [?]), and has lived among humans (John 1:14). The word that was in the beginning with God, and God was that word—he has become flesh (says John) and has dwelt among us, and we have seen his glory, as the glory of the only born one of the Father (John 1:1, 14).

FINISHED.

12

The Confession of Jan Cents (1630)

Introduction

By the early seventeenth century Mennonites of the North German and Dutch lowlands were seriously divided. Differences in theology, church polities, church practices, and culture assumptions led to numerous church conflicts and schisms. Such divisions served to weaken the Anabaptist movement with the result that Calvinism eventually superseded Anabaptism to be become the dominant Protestant reform group in the Netherlands. The divided nature of late sixteenth-century Anabaptism led virtually all the different Mennonite groups to consider ways in which they could be united.

Initial efforts were not very successful, but in the 1620s a group of High Germans, Frisians, and Flemish found a way to move forward. At the centre of the drive were Flemish leaders who formulated three questions as a way of encouraging their own congregations to consider closer ties with other groups. The questions were stated as follows: "(a) What are the basic marks of a Christian Church? (b) Are these distinctives only found in Flemish congregations? (c) Is making peace forbidden by the Scriptures?" (*Mennonite Encylopedia IV*, "Olijftacxken"). When the congregations failed to respond adequately to the questions, the leaders proceeded to address the questions themselves in the form of a confessional statement, the so-called Olive Branch Confession. In the fall of 1627, the Olive Branch was distributed to the congregations along with additional materials indicating a strong desire to be reconciled with the Frisians. On January 2, 1628, these leaders also called for a time of fasting and prayer, underscoring the seriousness of their intentions.

While some Frisians and Flemish did not welcome these initiatives, a group of United Frisians and High Germans, which had earlier left the Conciliated Brotherhood under Leenaert Clock, showed an interest in dialogue (see the introduction to the Concept of Cologne). A meeting was called at Amsterdam, October 3-5, 1630, at which time the United Frisians and High Germans presented a document of their own as a response to the Olive Branch Confession, the Confession of Jan Cents. The drafting of the confession was a team effort, but the primary author likely was Jan Cents. The results of the meeting were positive, and in the following years negotiations between the High Germans, Frisians, and Flemish continued until unity was finally achieved in 1639.

The confession reflects the concerns of a group wanting to hold to the doctrines and practices of the past. It preserves the Melchiorite doctrine of the incarnation, and retains fairly strict views regarding church discipline. Interesting to observe is that the confession does not have an explicit article on salvation. Scholars have noted that whereas in the first decades of the Anabaptist movement there was much attention given to soteriology, in subsequent decades Anabaptists such as Menno Simons became increasingly occupied with the nature of the church. Evidently, this characteristic trajectory of later Anabaptism, where soteriology was subsumed under ecclesiology, emerges here as well.

The importance of the Confession of Jans Cents transcends its initial purpose as a representative confession among the United Frisians and High Germans. It played a role in negotiations that eventually led to unity among the Frisians, Flemish and High Germans in 1639. It also found its way into the later Dutch confessional statements and was reprinted in van Braght's *Martyrs Mirror*. This translation by Walter Klaassen is based on the text found in *Vrede Handelighe*.

Bibliographical Sources

"Corte Confessie Ofte Belijdenisse des Gheloofs," in *Vrede Handelighe, Openbaer Gehouden tot Amsterdam den 3.4. en 5. October 1630* (Amsterdam: Jacob Aertsz. Colom, 1630); Karl Koop, *Anabaptist-Mennonite Confessions of Faith: The Development of a Tradition* (Kitchener: Pandora Press, 2004); Christian Neff and Nanne van der Zijpp, "Olijftacxken," *Mennonite Encylopedia IV*, 54-55.

The Confession of Jan Cents (1630)

Translated by Walter Klaassen

Introduction

Very dear and honoured friends, as the facts reveal, the peace negotiations between you, dear friends, and the churches with us have progressed so far that the representatives of your brotherhood here have attempted to answer and clarify our holy faith and the virtues and fruits which inseparably belong to it. This was not the only thing that gave us joy. But, following the teaching of Peter, you were willing and ready, dear friends, to give to everyone a reason for the faith that is in us. The following is the public, vocal declaration of our faith and our common life as Christians done before you, dear friends, and all the others there present through our common desire by our brother Jan Cents in your large warehouse. After questions posed by some had been answered by us some of your people requested that we also make our spoken confession available in writing so that everything could be more closely examined in the fear of the Lord, and then to send you in writing the fitting response. In order therefore that all is done openly we respond to your request, dear friends, and send you the following confession. It is our loving and friendly desire that you will read and consider it with god-fearing hearts. We hope that nothing will be found in it which would be enough to frustrate the desired peace.

A Short Confession or profession of faith and of the principal parts of Christian teaching, and how these are taught with the authority of Scripture by those who are called by the common name the United Frisians and High Germans.

[I. God]

We believe with our hearts and confess with our mouth that there is one (Rom. 10:9; Deut. 6:4; Isa. 45:5; Rom. 3:30) undivided, eternal (1 Cor. 8:4; Eph. 4:6; Gen. 21:33; Ps. 90:2; Isa. 40:28), inconceivable (1 Cor. 8:27; Ps. 145:3; 4; [2] Esd. 8:21), spiritual (James 4:24), being (Num. 1:20) who in the Holy Scriptures is called God and to whom alone is attributed omnipotence (Gen. 17:1; 2 Cor. 6:18), mercy (Exod. 34:6; Luke 6:36), righteousness (Ps. 11:7; Col. 3:24-25), perfection (Lev. 19:12; Matt. 5:48), wisdom (1 Tim. 1:12), all goodness (Ps. 103:8; Matt. 19:17), and omniscience (Ps. 139). He is called the fountain of life (Jer. 2:13) and the source of all good (James 1:17). He is the Creator of all things (Gen. 1:1; Exod. 20:11; Acts 4:24) and their sustainer (John 5:17; Heb. 1:3). In the Old Testament he is called by various names, the God of Abraham, Isaac and Jacob (Exod. 3:6; Matt. 2:32), God Shaddai, God Jehovah (Exod. 6:6 [:3]), the God of Israel (Exod. 5:1), I Am Who I Am, the Alpha and Omega (Rev. 1:8, 22:13) and other similar names. But in the New Testament he is known by three distinct names, God, Father, Son, and Holy Spirit (Matt. 28:19). We confess them to be distinguished as follows: that the Father (John 3:6; Rom. 8:3), in so far as he is Father, is other than the Son (John 16:28; Rom. 5:10), and the Son, insofar as he is the Son, is another from the Father and the Holy Spirit, and the Holy Spirit (John 14:16), insofar as he is the true Holy Spirit, is another from the Father and the Son. Although they are distinguished by name they are nevertheless one undivided God in their divine essence and attributes according to the witness of the apostle ([1] John 5:7): three witness in heaven, the Father, the Word, and the Holy Spirit, and these three are one.

[II. Creation]

This holy God through his great power and incomprehensible wisdom created heaven and earth and all visible and invisible things in five days (Gen. 1:6, 9, 13, 24; Jer. 32:147 [:17]; Acts 17:24) from nothing (Gen. 1:26). On the sixth day he prepared for man a body of the stuff of the earth (Gen. 2:7) and blew into his nose living breath. Thus he made him into a living soul or human being. He also elevated the man above all the creatures (Sir. 17:5) and gifted him with wisdom, understanding and reason (Gen. 1:28). He made him lord over all creatures. Above all he was created in the divine image in holiness and righteousness for immortality (Wis. 2:23). He placed him in the pleasure-garden Eden (Gen. 2:8) for eternal well-being. But he demanded of him a true, obedient heart (Gen. 2:9 [:17]), when he told them that they could eat from all the trees of the pleasure-garden except from the tree of knowledge of good and evil. They should not eat of it, for in the hour you eat of it you will die. From this we understand about human free will.

[III. The Fall]

We believe that the man and his wife were led into disobedience to their creator by the cunning of the serpent (Gen. 3:1) and the envy of the devil (Wis. 2:24). They and all their descendants (4[2] Esd. 7:48; Rom.5:12; 1 Cor. 15:21) fell into death and condemnation and so descended from being the most glorious to the most wretched creature.

When the Lord God saw the fall of his most glorious creature (Ps. 49:8; Rev. 5:3), and that his creature could not be redeemed by himself or anything creaturely, he revealed that he was a gracious and merciful God (Ps. 33:5; Matt. 19:17), and that his supreme and only goodness was expressed when he sought to reconcile human beings (Rom. 5:12) and all who fell with them with himself through sheer grace (Rom. 3:24) and without any merit on their part (2 Cor. 5:19).

Now since the righteousness of God required that the sin which was committed could not remain unpunished (Rev. 5:3), and since, as already said, no creature could accomplish it, God not only gave many promises to send his only beloved Son as a Saviour (Gen. 3:15, 12:36, 16:4, 18:49; Num. 24:19; Isa. 7:5, 9, 5:11, 10:53; Jer. 23:5, 6, 33:5; Dan. 7:13, 9:24; Mic. 5:1; Acts 2:24; Matt. 3:1) but also prefigured it with many images (Exod. 12:3, 25:17).

[IV. Free Will]

Both before and after the Fall the Lord gave free will to human beings (Deut. 30:15; Prov. 15:14) so that they could accept or reject the offered grace of God through faith in the promised Saviour. This can be seen not only in the sending of his prophets, apostles, and disciples (Matt. 28:18; Mark16:16; Acts 17:30) but also through the friendly urging of his beloved Son (Matt. 11:29, 22:9; 1 Tim. 1:15; Titus 2:11). This was fitting so that he could be a just judge and have proper reasons to punish his despisers with the pains of hell (2 Thess. 1:8; Acts 13:46; Rom. 2:5) and reward his obedient sheep with heavenly joy at the Last Day (Bar. 3:39; John 3:16, 36; 2 Thess.1:7; Heb. 6:10).

[V. The Incarnation]

Since the Lord is also a faithful God (1 John 5:20; Deut. 7:8) who does not repent of what he has promised, when the time was fulfilled (Gal. 4:4) he sent his only own and true Son into the world as a Saviour according to his heavenly, secret purpose.

There have been many long years of dispute about the human birth of our Saviour and it continues today. Nevertheless, we believe and confess that it was a supernatural birth which cannot be fathomed by human reason. We believe and confess on the strength of Scripture that the eternal Word was not merely spoken (John 1:1) but essential and self-revealing. Before the foundation of the world (John 17:5) this Word was with the Father in supernal clarity. He was before Abraham (John 8:58), in the beginning with God (John 1:1), and was God, whose origin was in the beginning (Mic. 5:1) and in eternity. Through him all things were created (John 1:3) and received their being. That same essential Word proceeded from the Father (John 10:28) in the fullness of time (Gal. 4:4) and came down from heaven into the lowest parts of the earth (Eph. 4:9). According to the prophecy of Isaiah (Esd. [Isa.] 7:14) he was conceived in the virginal body of Mary (Matt. 1:21)—who was betrothed to Joseph of the house of David but had no sexual relations with him (Luke 1:31)—through the power of the Most

High God and the overshadowing of the Holy Spirit. This happened in Nazareth so that he could be called Nazorean (Matt. 2:23). He did not take on flesh but became flesh (John 1:14), remaining what he was, namely God and God's Son, and becoming what he was not (Rom. 9:5), that is a man and a son of man (Ps. 2:7; Matt. 3:17). In this manner, therefore, we confess that the child which Mary bore and gave birth to in Bethlehem grew up (Luke 2:6, 40) and suffered on the cross (Matt. 27). He was a pilgrim among us (John 1:14), externally and internally, visible and invisible, the only, the fitting and true Son of God (Matt. 17:5) and the Saviour of us all.

[VI. Christ's Offices]

We also believe and confess that he has come to redeem us from the curse of the law (Gal. 3:13, 4:5). He was made subject to the law (Gen. 17:12; Gal. 4:4), circumcised on the eighth day (Luke 2:21), and given the name the angel spoke before his birth (Matt. 1:21), namely Jesus. The holy name was to reflect his holy task namely (Matt. 18:11; Luke 19:18), that he should save his people from their sins.

We further confess that he is our only true great prophet (Deut. 18:15), high priest (Ps. 110:4; Heb. 3:11), and spiritual king (Jer. 33:15; Matt. 21:5). By his prophetic office he proclaimed to us the great, secret, hidden counsel of God (Matt. 13:35) concerning the eternal peace with God (Luke 10:5) through the holy Gospel and everything we needed for the new life (John 3:3; Matt. 18:19). By his priestly office he not only offered a sacrifice on the wood of the cross for his faithful sheep (Eph. 5:2) which is of eternal worth (Heb. 10:12), but through his glorious resurrection he entered into the holy of holies, indeed, the most holy (Heb. 9:12), namely heaven itself, not through the blood of rams or calves, but through his own blood he obtained eternal redemption for all believers. He sits at the right hand of God (Col. 3:1; Rom. 8:34) his heavenly Father, where as High Priest he utters his holy prayers for the ignorance of his people (Heb. 5:2, 5) and obtains pardon for them. By his royal office he conquered death (2 Tim. 1:10), devil and hell and all our enemies (Heb. 2:14-15) as a victorious prince. He prepared a place for the citizens of his kingdom

(John 14:12) in which he reigns with the sceptre (Ps. 45:7 [6]) of his Word, protecting [reference indecipherable] those who trust in him, and helping them to prevail in the battle (2 Cor. 1:16) until they receive the eternal kingdom from his hand.

[VII. Concerning the Suffering and Death of our Lord Jesus Christ]

Since his kingdom was not of this world (John 18:36), he also did not enter upon it with physical weapons of iron or steel (Matt. 4:1; Luke 4:1; Mark 16:21) but through suffering and struggling in the flesh, preparing for him purification through temptation, distress and suffering, and treading the cursed death (Gal. 3:13; Deut. 21:13) on the cross under Pontius Pilate (I Tim. 6:13).

We believe and confess that the same Lord Jesus Christ, who was crucified near Jerusalem (Matt. 27; Luke 23) whose suffering spirit cried out on Mount Calvary (John 19:18) amidst the movement of heaven and earth and who there tasted death, was God's only (John 3:16) and true Son. We believe that we are reconciled with God (Rom. 8:22, 5:10) through the blood and death of his Son who accomplished the cleansing of our sins in himself (Heb. 1:3) As evidence that he was truly dead he was taken from the cross by Joseph of Arimathea, wound in a clean white garment, and laid in a newly hewn tomb which was sealed with a great stone and secured by watchmen (Matt. 27:56).

[VIII. Christ's Resurrection and Ascension]

But since it was impossible that he should be held by the bonds of death (Acts 2:24) and that the Holy One should see corruption (Ps. 16:11), we believe and confess also that on the third day, according to the prophets he was raised from the dead in the body through the glory of the Father (Rom. 6:4; Acts 13:34) accompanied by the movement of heaven and earth. He confirmed his resurrection through forty days with words, signs and miracles. He taught, comforted (Matt. 28:2; John 20:4; Luke 24:36) and admonished his disciples. Finally he was enfolded by a cloud on the Mount of Olives (Acts 1:12; Luke

24:30) and visibly ascended into heaven as the disciples watched. He entered the Holy of Holies as a true high priest (Heb. 9:12), mediator (1 John 2:1), and advocate (2 Tim. 2:5) between God and humanity, and took his seat at the right hand of the majesty on high (Heb. 12:9). There he appears constantly before the face of his Father to pray for his believers (Rom. 8:34).

[IX. The Sending of the Holy Spirit]

While he taught and comforted [his disciples] through his costly suffering (John 14:1, 15:26, 16:7) that their hearts should not be afraid after he ascended into heaven, he promised to send them another comforter, the Holy Spirit. Thus we also believe that our Lord and Saviour Jesus Christ (Matt. 21:3), eternally blessed, in this too, as the faithful God (Rom. 9:5; 1 John 5:20), was found trustworthy. Ten days after his ascension he sent the Holy Spirit visibly to and upon his apostles in Jerusalem (Acts 2:2). This same Holy Spirit is the wisdom, strength (Luke 1:31), and power of God, who proceeds from the Father through the Son (John 15) and, no less than the Father and the Son is the eternal undivided God (Acts 5:3). He is also the teacher (John 14:26) leader and guide of all who fear God and the comfort of longing souls, and who will in the end help them arrive at the spiritual Canaan.

[X. The Nature of the Church and its Leadership]

We further believe that the Lord God chose a penitent and believing people, in first place the holy angels in heaven, then the two holy persons in Paradise (Gen. 2:22), and finally from all the multitudes of the peoples of the earth (4 [2] Esd. 5: 27). They would not only be called a universal Christian church or gathering of God-fearing people; for the Lord Christ bought them with his costly blood (Acts 20:28), and washed and cleansed them with the water of the Holy Spirit (Eph. 5:26), in order that he could present them an honourable church without spot or wrinkle or the like. This same holy church is so precious to him (1 Cor. 6:20) that for the well-being and growth of his kingdom he would not leave it uncared for (Luke 10:1; Eph. 4:11; 1 Cor. 12:28).

Not only before but after his ascension he equipped her with faith, hope, and love and other ordinances and provided her especially with two special services, namely the service of the holy Word, and the care for the poor or the diaconate. He also appointed prophets, pastors, teachers, helpers, and rulers [*Regierders*] to care wisely for the churches of God with united counsel (Mark 16:16; Acts 6:3, 16:2), and sent them out. The apostles commanded their successors to choose men [to these offices] with fasting and prayer. They are first to be examined (1 Tim. 3:10) and only then allowed to serve. The believers are to honour, love, and obey these men (1 Thess. 5:13; Heb. 13:17; 1 Tim. 5:17, 18).

This community also bears the image of the true reality in heaven. Here on earth they use the preaching of the Word, baptism, the Lord's Supper and other Christian ordinances externally, and are inwardly in the Spirit, one true community (Acts 4:32; Heb. 12:22) here and also in heaven with God and all the Lord's saints. The true reality will be revealed on the Last Day.

Meanwhile those who unite in this community will obediently and with good will submit to the precepts, laws, and ordinances which the Lord Christ as head of his holy church (Eph. 5:23), and the only lawgiver of the New Testament (Matt. 28:20) has ordained for his church, and which we teach and is our polity in all human frailty. These are:

[XI. Baptism]

First, the baptism of penitent and believing adults (Acts 2: 38; Mark 16:15-16; 8:11) is an external, evangelical act (Acts 8:34, 37) in which a person who is truly sorry for sin, whose heart is clad with faith in Christ (Acts 10:43, 8:36; 1 Cor. 3:5) and so dies to and buries his past earthly life, and rises to a new penitent life (Rom. 6:4). This baptism is administered by an ordained and blameless servant with ordinary water (Matt. 3:10; 4; Acts 10) in the name of the Father, the Son, and the Holy Spirit (Matt. 28:19) for the forgiveness of all sin (Acts 2:38) and to lead that person to true repentance and Scriptural faith. A person once baptized, we do not baptize again (Eph. 4:5; Heb. 6:3).

[XII. The Holy Supper]

Second, the Holy Supper of the Lord is also called the Christian unity (Matt. 26:25; Luke 22:19). It is observed among believers only (Acts 2:46, 20:7) and not with consecrated but with ordinary bread and wine. It is done not merely as a memorial of the costly, holy, and bitter suffering and death and the glorious resurrection of our Lord and Saviour Jesus Christ. It is also the consoling fruit which is provided in it for all believers (Mark 14:22, 23; John 6:51; 1 Cor. 10:16, 17). In their strength believers are moved not only sincerely to sorrow over the bitter suffering and death of Jesus Christ which was necessary for redemption from their sins (1 Cor. 11:23, 24), but also to praise and bless the Lord for the benefits which flow from the Supper with inner spiritual thanksgiving. It also strengthens their Christian brotherly and spiritual unity with a holy God-pleasing life to the praise of the Lord.

[XIII. Footwashing]

Now follows the foot washing of the saints. When our fellow-believers come to visit us from foreign places, according to the occasion, we wash their feet according to the usage of the Old Testament and the example of Christ (Gen. 18:4; John 13:5; 1 Tim. 5:10). Thus we express our humility before God and our neighbours (Luke 22:25; Phil. 2:3) with a humble prayer that the Lord will strengthen us more and more in humility. May it please the Lord that as we have washed each others' feet, he will wash and cleanse our souls from all stain and uncleanness with his blood and the water of the Holy Spirit, so that we may appear clean and blameless through his Father.

XIV. Works of Love

The works of charity we divide into three parts: 1.The believer is obligated to bring his alms to the feet of the deacons as the Lord has blessed (Matt. 6:1; Luke 12:33, 16:9; Acts 6:13), in order that they may have means adequately to support poor believers. 2.Visiting the sick, the imprisoned, and the afflicted, to comfort, serve and care for them according to need (Matt. 25:35; Heb. 13:1, 2:3). If fellow believers are in difficult household and economic circumstances, to assist them with advice and support, in preference to strangers.

[XV. Marriage]

Marriage was well and firmly established in Paradise (Gen. 2:24). After that it fell into abuse through lust by the children of the first world (Gen. 6:1, 2) and also through the hardness of heart of the Jews (Deut. 24:1; Matt. 19:8). The great Lawgiver of the New Testament established the original order, Matt. 9:4. The apostle says in 1 Cor. 7 that the wife is bound to her husband as long as the husband lives. If he dies, she is free to marry whomever she desires. But it must be in the Lord. We understand this to mean that a believer has no liberty to enter marriage with an unbeliever. A believing woman, who with her husband is born of one heavenly Father from imperishable seed (1 Peter 1:23) and thus from a new, heavenly and spiritual generation (John 3:15), and who in baptism has offered her members to God and has submitted in obedience to Christ her head, cannot now take those members from Christ her head and enter into a yoke with one who has not been born again (Rom. 12:1; 1 Peter 1:22; Eph. 5:23).

[XVI. Secular Government]

We regard the office of secular government (Rom. 13: 2-3) to be an ordering of God for the protection of the godly and the punishment of the wicked. We are obligated to give honour, obedience, tax and tribute, and to pray for her (1 Peter 2:13; Acts 4:19; Matt. 22:17; Rom. 13:7; Titus 2:2; Jer. 29:7, 1 Cor. 12:28). We do not find, however, that Paul includes secular government in the offices of the church, nor that Christ taught this to his disciples nor that he called them to exercise it (Matt. 20:25; Luke 22:25). On the contrary, he urged them to follow the footsteps of his life bearing the cross without weapons (John 8:12, 10:27; Heb. 12:2; 1 Peter 2:21). He forbade them vengeance, and not only with weapons, but also not to return insult with insult (Rom. 12:19). Instead he bade them pray for their enemies, do good to those who do evil to us and to many who cling to the office of government (Matt. 5:44). For this reason we quietly serve in the offices of our Christian calling.

[XVII. Swearing of Oaths]

The swearing of oaths was permitted in the Old Testament (Deut. 6:13, 10:20). Because much abuse had wormed its way in, Christ in Matt. 5 and James (Matt. 5:37; James 5:12) forbade swearing without any distinctions. That is why no Christian is permitted to swear the oath [*eedt van Calumnia te doen*].

[XVIII. Church Discipline]

Even as in a good republic laws will be of no effect without sanctions, so the Lord did not forget to add penalties to his laws. For Paul said that he who sins is punished in public so that others may fear (1 Tim. 5:20). Also Christ taught in Matthew 18 to punish sinners and Paul teaches that the leaven has to be swept out, and to put away from among us those who are evil (1 Cor. 5:6; Deut. 13:5; 1 Cor. 5:12). We understand this to refer to the Christian ban which was established to shame and convert sinners, and to keep the church pure (2 Thess. 3:14), so that even a little leaven will not spoil the whole lump of dough (Gal. 5:9). Other passages are Matthew 16:19: "I will give you the keys to the kingdom of heaven," and Matthew 18:18: "Whatever you bind on earth will be bound in heaven, and what you loose on earth shall also be loosed in heaven." This punishment is used with those who have received the light and the wholesome teaching of Christ, but then fall away into false teaching and heresy (Titus 3:10). If they persist in their error after they have been spoken to once or twice, they are to be excluded by the Christian ban and shunned. The ban is also used with those who wander into gross fleshly behaviour (Gal. 5:21; Eph. 5:5; 1 Cor. 5:3; 1 Cor. 6:9). This must be substantiated by the persons concerned themselves and by reliable witnesses without which the ban of exclusion may not be used.

Thirdly, we also regard marriage outside the faith as a sin (Deut. 7:3; Exod. 25:32). It conflicts with the prohibition of the Lord and is variously condemned by the Lord and his prophets with deeds and words (Josh. 23:12; Gen. 7:11; Neh. 13:25). Since it is a sin flowing from fleshly, sensual life or from want of trust in God that he would not provide him with a virtuous spouse, and in addition is done deliberately, such a one is not included in Galatians 6:1: "If anyone is overtaken by a transgression, restore such a one in a spirit of gentleness." Rather he is to be included under Numbers 15 where the Lord says: " The soul that sins with deliberate audacity shall be cut off from among the people." Many godly persons gathered at different times have also understood that marriage outside the faith to unrepentant unbelievers is to be punished with exclusion from the church so that they may repent.

Not all sins are equally grievous and do not immediately deserve exclusion even without previous admonition. Here the reproof between brother and brother follows the rule of Matthew 18: [15]. And if someone is overtaken with a transgression the rule to be followed is Galatians 6:1.

[XIX. Concerning Shunning]

We also understand that there can be no exclusion where no withdrawal has taken place. We believe that we are obligated to admonish any who are banned (2 Thess. 3:15) so that through honest repentance there may be reconciliation with the church. If with a willing spirit he is ready to be reconciled the anointing or reinstatement should be done quickly (2 Cor. 2:8), and not to wait for those who have married outside until they bring the married spouse with them. But if the friendly admonition is carelessly rejected because of godless, apostate, offensive, contagious, scandalous behaviour, and the sinner himself grows more and more rigid in his evil life, we believe that persons so excluded or punished with the ban should be avoided and shunned immediately, without even the forementioned admonition (1 Cor. 5:5; 2 Tim. 2:16-18; 2 Thess. 3:13; Titus 3:10). This includes the ordinary things freely done in the world such as eating and drinking, buying and selling and other inessential matters, but that it happens with such care, moderation and modesty that God's Word everywhere remains primary and the higher laws and commandments of the Lord by which the believer and the banned are united are not broken, but that in all things needful, words, promises, love, charity, mercy, righteousness and Christian moderation be observed (2 Thess. 3:15; Luke 6:36; 2 Pet. 1:6).

If someone should understand the words about shunning more important and someone else less important according to 1 Corinthians 5, but both are God-fearing in their living, should they not bear with each other in love without quarrelling or disputing until they find further light on the matter?

[XX. Concerning the Forgiveness of Sins]

Whoever, in human weakness, seeks to live out this commandment along with the principal and other commandments, teachings, and ordinances of the Lord expressly stated in his Word and so to live out his pilgrimage on earth, such a person, we believe, at the departure from this earth, will feel, not only a certain witness of his conscience and have a joyful hope, but will find, at the resurrection of the dead, that all his sins will be forgiven through holy merits and the comforting intercession of Christ (Luke 24:46; Col. 1:14; Acts 13:38; 1 Tim. 2:5; 1 John 2:1; Rom. 8:38).

[XXI. Concerning the Last Things]

Finally, we believe that our Saviour Jesus Christ (Matt. 1:21; Acts 4:12; 1 Tim. 4:15), blessed for ever, will return visibly in the clouds (Acts 1:11) as before he ascended (Rev. 1:7; Acts 1:11; Matt. 24:30; 2 Thess. 1:7). It will be a coming not in humility, lowliness, and servanthood as in his holy incarnation he appeared in the world, but will be magnificent with glorious power and all his angels (Matt. 25:31, 16:27), not to call sinners to repentance but to exercise a perfectly just judgment (Acts 17:31; Jude 14; Dan. 7:9,13). To accomplish this not only will he sit upon the throne of his glory (Matt. 25:31), but as the earthly sun in the spring brings forth from the ground not only flowers, herbs, and good fruit, but also nettles, thistles and thorns, so the true sun of righteousness, Jesus Christ (Mal. 4:2), blessed for ever, will draw out of the earth and resurrect with the blowing of the trumpet (1 Thess. 4:16; Matt. 24:31; John 5:29; Dan. 12:2; 1 Cor. 15:42) the enormous number of the dead who have lived and died from the beginning of the world to this day. They sowed their perishable bodies in the earth like the fruit in the womb (4 [2]Esd. 7:42). The sea, hell, and death will give up their dead (Rev. 20:13). They will be covered again with their own skin and see God with their own eyes (Job 19:26; Rev. 1:7; Rom. 2:6). They will be clothed with their own body in which they here served the Lord or despised him (2 Cor. 5:10; Matt. 16:27). After that, those who are still alive will be changed in one moment into immortality (1 Cor. 15:51). Finally the whole mass of humanity will be gathered before the throne of God (Matt. 25:32). There the books of conscience as well as the other book, the book of life, will be opened (Rev. 20:12), and the dead will be judged according to what is written in the books, and all will receive in their own bodies (John 5:29; 2 Cor. 5:10) according to what they have done here, good or evil. The Lord, the righteous judge will separate the believing and the godless as a shepherd separates the sheep from the goats (Matt. 25:32; Ezek. 34:17). He will place the believers as his obedient sheep on his right hand and the unbelievers as the malicious, obstreperous, stinking goats at his left (Matt. 25:33). Then he will look at his lambs with loving eyes and bless them with his honeyed voice, Matthew 25: "Come you blessed of my Father. Receive the kingdom prepared for you from the beginning (Matt. 25:34)." But to the goats he will turn his wrathful countenance flashing as the lightening, and speak to them in a voice of thunder: "Depart from me, you cursed into the eternal fire prepared for the devil and his angels" (4 [2] Esd. 16:10; 2 Thess. 1:8; Luke 17:24; Matt. 25:41).

We believe and confess that the heavens will pass away with a great noise, the sun be darkened, the moon turn to blood, and the stars fall from heaven, and the earth and everything in it will be burned with fire (2 Peter 3:10; Rev. 6:12). Then will the inexorable sentence of the most high king be executed. All the ungodly, as sheep for the slaughter (Ps. 49:15) will be driven into hell and thrown into the great abyss, where there will be no shortage of fuel (Isa. 30:33). There they will lie, not on beds of down, but on biting maggots, and covered with gnawing worms (Isa. 14:11). They will be tortured with flames of fire where their worm does not die and their fire is not quenched. The suffering of their torment will rise like the smoke from a fiery furnace and will last for ever and ever (2 Thess. 1:9; Mark 9:47 [48]; Isa. 66:24; Rev. 9:2; 14:5). On the other hand, we confess that the blessed of God will be lifted up into the clouds to meet the Lord in the air (1 Thess. 4:17) and will then be led into the presence of God, in heaven, before the throne of God by the Lord Christ, their spiritual bridegroom (Matt. 25:6). Then he will turn the kingdom and all power over to the Father so that God may be all in all (1 Cor. 15:28). Those blessed of God will be changed from one glory to another through the glory of God (2 Cor. 3:18; Phil. 3:21). Their tears will be dried, the crown of life, of glory, and of joy will be placed on their heads, palm branches of honour given into their hands, and clothed with the white garment of righteous saints (Isa. 25:8; Rev. 7:17; James 1:12; 2 Tim. 4:8; 4 [2] Esd. 2:43, 46; Rev. 7:9, 19:8). They will be united with all the saints of God, and led to the fountain of living waters. They will be satisfied with eternal comfort and led to pasture on the spiritual Mount Zion (Matt. 8:11; Rev. 7:17; Isa. 25:8; Matt. 4:2; Rev. 14:1,4). They will follow the sweet Lamb Jesus Christ, who bought them with his blood and death, on the heavenly pleasure-grounds through contemplation of the vision of the holy God on his incomprehensible throne. They will see the heavens in their beauty and the angels in their joy. God's blessed ones will overflow with heavenly joy. With the tongues of angels and heavenly voices they will begin to sing the new song with all the saints of God, and give to the One who sits on the throne and to the Lamb praise and honour and glory and blessing for ever and ever. Amen (4 [2] Esd. 8:21; Baruch 3:24; Rev. 14:3, 7:9).

[Conclusion]

Worthy and beloved friends, this is a brief confession of our most holy and Christian faith, along with the principal virtues which we believe belong to faith. We fervently hope in God the Lord that with this faith, which in weakness we seek to live to the end of our lives, we will have a favourable and tranquil departure from this world and, at the last day in the resurrection of the dead, to find our way to a gracious God and the priceless comfort of eternal life. We therefore, in friendship and love, desire our dear friends to examine in the fear of the Lord what we have presented and see whether it is sufficient, so that the desired peace may be planned to the honour of God, the establishing of his churches, and the comfort of our souls. Or perhaps they will point out to us any weighty reasons which would be sufficient to prevent such peace. We hope they will examine such with God-fearing hearts and to confirm what is best. We had been inclined to present our confession in a different manner and style, although identical in content and foundation, and at some greater length. But some of our number considered that the form we used was the most suitable. We hope that your people will take note of the sense, understanding, and basis of our confession. We persist therefore in our expressed desire that our beloved friends will respond to our confession with their considered judgment in writing so that we may know what to report to our congregations. Trusting that this is acceptable, we wish you, dear friends, as well as ourselves, everything that contributes to the supreme comfort of our souls for eternal life through our Lord Jesus Christ. Amen.

Done by us the undersigned servants, teachers, and elders of the United Frisian and High German churches for ourselves as well as in the name of our fellow-brothers and servants, together with our countrymen who gathered with us here in Amsterdam in this matter. 7 October, 1630, new style.

Jan Cents	Tielman Tielen
Cornelis Ballinghs	Gerbrant Pauwels
Pieter van de Venne	Doye Frericks
Reynck Pieters	Feyke Goyes
Jan Erricks	Rennert Syderdts
Joost Jelys	Pieter Everts
Arent Syverts	Wilhelm Ley van Bevehen

13

Dordrecht Confession (1632)

Introduction

Following the church schisms of the sixteenth century, Flemish Anabaptists had been successful at initiating meetings to work out differences with the Frisians and High Germans, but they had not fully reconciled their own internal conflicts (See the introduction to the Confession of Jan Cents). As far back as 1586, in Franeker, Friesland, an elder of the Flemish congregation, Thomas Byntgens had purchased a house in a questionable manner. An ensuing dispute over this matter was mediated by the congregations of Amsterdam, Haarlem, and Hoorn, but to no avail. Eventually most of the Flemish churches were drawn into the conflict and were divided into two camps: the housebuyers who supported Byntgens and the contra-housebuyers who were opposed to Byntgens. On the surface, the initial incident was trivial; yet the quarrel evolved into a serious dispute because it was linked to two different understandings regarding the nature of the church and the role of church discipline and the ban. By the end of the 1520s, however, the Flemish churches were willing to move beyond their differences and find a way to be reconciled with one another.

Under the leadership of Adriaan Cornelis, an initial attempt to meet in the city of Dordrecht failed due to resistance from local town officials as well as a small but vocal group of Flemish leaders who were opposed to unity discussions. Eventually a meeting on April 21, 1632 took place, and a "Confession and Peace Agreement" was adopted. The confession came to be known as the Dordrecht Confession. Most of the 51 ministers who signed the confession were Flemish, but some were also Frisian and High German. Like the Confession of Jan Cents, the Dordrecht Confession laid the foundations for conversations between the Flemish, Frisians, and High Germans that eventually led to a formal union at Amsterdam in 1639.

The formal union between the three groups was significant since they had been separated for over a half a century. Unfortunately the Waterlanders were not able to participate in the celebrations at Amsterdam, and further attempts by them to unite with the other groups failed. In 1647, the Waterlanders proposed a merger, but it was rejected. The Flemish, Frisians, and High Germans were anxious that the Waterlanders were not taking doctrine and the authority of the confessions seriously enough. They were concerned that the Waterlanders were not strict enough in matters of church discipline, and that their theology was too spiritualistic.

Eventually these issues became a concern of virtually every Mennonite group in the Netherlands, including the Waterlanders. In the 1650s and 1660s Mennonites would become embroiled in a much larger dispute known as the War of the Lambs that would divide Zonists and Lambists, confessionalists and anti-confessionalists. Unfortunately, the confessions of faith, which were initially intended as instruments of unity, could also become divisive instruments of disunity.

The Dordrecht Confession was primarily an internal document of the Flemish, but like the Jan Cents Confession it was reprinted in later Dutch collections and in the *Martyrs Mirror*. Soon it also became significant for groups outside of the Netherlands. The Swiss Brethren adopted the confession in 1660, and it was brought to the new world and used by Mennonites of Swiss/South German descent. In the 20th century Mennonite missionaries carried the confession abroad, and also used it among immigrant groups within North America. It has been reprinted numerous times in at least five different languages.

Like the Waterlander and Jan Cents confessions, the Dordrecht statement supports church discipline, but gives primary importance to the marriage relationship and its vows of commitment. The Flemish speak well of the ruling, secular authorities, yet maintain a strong peace position. Speaking out of a tradition that experienced significant persecution and loss, the Flemish insist that it is better to flee from one place to another and suffer material loss than bring harm to another (article XIV).

This translation by Irvin B. Horst, is based on the 1633 edition entitled "Confessie Ende Vredehandelinge." Horst's translation first appeared in his *Mennonite Confession of Faith*, published by the Lancaster Mennonite Historical Society. The translation in this volume is virtually identical.

Bibliographical Sources

Hans-Jürgen Goertz, "Zwischen Zwietracht und Eintracht: Zur Zweideutigkeit Täuferischer und Mennonitischer Bekenntnisse," *Mennonitische Geschichtsblätter* 43/44 (1986-87): 16-48; Irvin B. Horst, "The Dordrecht Confession of Faith: 350 Years," *Pennsylvania Mennonite Heritage* 5.3 (July 1982), 2-8; Irvin B. Horst, trans. and ed., *Mennonite Confession of Faith* (Lancaster: Lancaster Mennonite Historical Society, 1988); Karl Koop, *Anabaptist-Mennonite Confessions of Faith: The Development of a Tradition* (Kitchener: Pandora Press, 2004); Christian Neff and Nanne van der Zijpp, "Flemish Mennonites," *Mennonite Encyclopedia* II, 337-340.

[Dordrecht Confession (1632)]

Translated by Irvin B. Horst

Confession and Peace Agreement

Reached at Dordrecht, Anno 1632, on the 21st of April
between the Mennonites [*Doopsgezinden*] called the
Flemish: in which everyone can see and perceive how and
on what this peace has been made and established.

Matthew 5:9

Blessed are the peacemakers: for they shall be called the
children of God.

Hebrews 12:14

Follow peace with all men, and holiness, without which no
man shall see the Lord.

I Corinthians 7:15

God hath called us to peace.

HAARLEM

Printed by Hans Passchiers van Wesbusch, Printer
at the Marcktveldt in den beslagen Bybel, 1633.

Preface to the Peace Agreement Reached Among the Mennonites Called the Flemish on April 21, 1632, at Dordrecht

Mindful and peace-loving reader, seeker after happiness and truth, we hear daily of some persons who are not favorable to our peace agreement. Failing to comply with the nature of love, which sees the best in everything, they do not speak well of it. Thereby they cause innocent and unlearned persons—who regrettably at times are more impressed by men of today than by the teaching and life of our Saviour Jesus Christ and his beloved apostles—to shy off and to turn away from it. These opponents not only reject us but also the peace so highly commended by the Son of God and his apostles. They do not obey, it seems, the exhortation of Christ: "Blessed are the peacemakers: for they shall be called the children of God," Matt. 5:9. "Follow peace with all men, and holiness, without which no man shall see the Lord," Heb. 12:14. "Have peace one with another," Mark 9:50. "On earth peace," Luke 2:14. "Peace I leave with you, my peace I give unto you," John 14:27. "How beautiful are the feet of them that preach the gospel of peace, and bring glad tidings of good things," Rom. 10:15 and Isa. 52:7. "Behold, how good and how pleasant it is for brethren to dwell together in unity! It is like the precious ointment upon the beard, even Aaron's beard: that went down to the skirts of his garments; as the dew of Herman, and as the dew that descended upon the mountains of Zion: for there the Lord commanded the blessing, even life for evermore," Rom. 12:18. "If it be possible, as much as lieth in you, live peaceably with all men," Rom. 12:17. "For the kingdom of God is not meat and drink, but righteousness and peace, and joy in the Holy Ghost," Rom. 14:9. "Let us therefore follow after the things which make for peace, and things wherewith one may edify another." "God hath called us to peace," 1 Cor. 13:11. "Finally, brethren, farewell. Be perfect, be of good comfort, be of one mind, live in peace; and the God of love and peace shall be with you.

Taking these and other Scriptures for our learning to heart and considering them in the fear of God, we found that we had strayed from them and, in so doing, had left the way of peace. Like David in Ps. 119:59 we thought about our ways and found it high time to return to the instruction of the Lord, to humble ourselves before God and our brethren, and to say with Jeremiah in Lam. 3:42: "We have transgressed and have rebelled: thou hast not pardoned." With our mind kindled by this and opening our hearts with Lydia, Acts 16:14, we sensed that the time had come to re-establish the broken peace. We desired to live and walk again in peace and love with each other, with the scattered sheep—of whom we were not the least—who are one with us in faith, doctrine, and practice and in this way magnify God's great and holy name. We undertook this then for the upbuilding and betterment of our own ways, for the edification of our fellowmen, and finally for the common salvation of our souls. We trust that the merciful God—who is a God of peace rather than of wrangling and discord— will give his gracious blessing through his blessed Son, our Saviour and Lord. Apart from him we can do nothing, John 15:5. Amen.

For the reason mentioned at the beginning of this preface, we could not neglect to inform all true lovers of peace and at the same time to make public in what capacity and upon what articles of faith the peace is again built and established—at Dordrecht, on April 21, 1632, the peace was renewed and took place by a mutual, complete forgiving of, freeing from, and acquittal of all previous faults and mistakes, wrong actions, and restrictions—that no one from now on through ignorance should speak unjustly about something of which he is not informed. Use what follows for your profit.y a Lover of Peace.

[Introduction]

Brethren, we along with our elders and ministers (unworthy as we are) of the united church of God here at Dordrecht; also, we, the undersigned elders, ministers, and brethren—who as co-workers were invited, delegated, and came, each for himself and for his church—are gathered in the Lord's name in the church at this place and are one with it: wish heavenly wisdom, divine enlightenment from the almighty, eternal, and incomprehensible God for all churches, coworkers, brethren, and partakers of our common Christian faith in all towns and places where this—our brotherly union, appeasement, and agreement—will be presented and read. May this divine wisdom enable you to test, discern, and pursue what is necessary for our common peace and mutual improvement. Such peace is pleasing to God, agreeable to men, and enables us to walk as becomes our calling. In order that we and you with us after this life, along with all God's chosen, holy, and beloved saints, may be eternally saved through our Lord Jesus Christ. To this end may the kind and faithful God help us and grant his gracious blessing to make you and us worthy and acceptable. Amen.

Further, this must be mentioned: it is public knowledge for quite some time in many or at least some place that for various reasons an unhappy contention leading to confusion—yes, even separation and schism—rose and continued among fellow believers of the same persuasion and brotherhood of faith. Not the least among these contentions was the division of the House-Buyers which continued for many years. As a result of this and all that developed from it, God's worthy name was slandered and disgraced, and the church became an object of reproach and contempt. Along with this there was much giving and taking of offense as well as provocation and insult, especially in the church at Franeker but also elsewhere. One might well lament such matters with regret and remorse and wish they had never happened. Mistakes are usually better seen and discerned afterwards than before as is the case with these contentions. The more one considers them, especially with an impartial mind, the stronger one is convinced that the cause as well as the unfortunate results cannot entirely be laid at the feet of one side. Both sides have been greatly at fault; both have been overzealous and immoderate in the use of discipline, of rejection and separation from each other.

Both sides lacked a recognition of love as the principal garb and characteristic of the true followers of Christ. Love is the sum of the great commandments, the fulfillment of the law (John 13:35; Col. 3:14). Love is indeed the bond of perfection; it binds believers in a harmonious relationship with the Lord; it binds believers as one heart and soul to each other in peace and unity. As members of one body they are closely related to each other at all times and in every way: to bear and forgive the shortcomings of each other (Luke 6:36), to cover the failures of neighbors. They deal gently with each other, showing compassion and mercy; they do not increase the hurt of the injured nor oppress or reject the weak (2 Cor. 5:11; Ezek. 34:4). Instead each esteems the other person more than himself (Phil. 2:3), and in this way the weaker members receive attention and respect (1 Cor. 12:23). Indeed, love was too much lacking on the part of both sides and much unhappiness, strife, and contention were the result.

If this bond of love becomes weak and cold—or actually broken by many—the enemy sows tares [seeds] in the hearts of many dozing members (Matt. 13:25) which take root in bitterness (Heb. 12:15). All kinds of confusion and error result and bear fruit such as envy, discord, backbiting, hate, and strife. As a tiny spark, if it is fanned and not extinguished in time, can cause great destruction so it has gone in this matter. Also, one may truthfully say that not the House-Buyers only, nor only the results of this affair and all that was attached to it, but much rather the sins of both sides should be acknowledged as contributing to the cause of the contention.

All of this we here at Dordrecht as well as brethren at many other places have taken to heart and given thought and considered. In this we profit from the many excellent examples in Scripture, how the patriarchs and prophets, along with the apostles as shepherds, fathers, and leaders in the church, truly sought the unity of fellow believers. Their instruction is given to us as pointers so that we can see as in a mirror how we ought to act and treat each other in matters of contention and disagreement. We see in this mirror their endeavors to meet each other with respect. These fathers and leaders have highly recommended all Christian believers to follow them in such matters as they followed the great Shepherd (Heb. 13:20). With these examples before us to follow, quarreling, wrangling, backbiting, and destruction ought finally to cease. We should now accept each other in loving kindness and in trust. Yes, meet each other in love and peace (Ps. 85:11). As much as possible should be done to seek the lost (Matt. 18:12), to bring together those scattered and gone astray, to bind up the wounded (Ezek. 34:16), to repair the breaches (Isa. 58:12), to level the hills and remove the rocks of offense, to repair the roads and make a straight path so that on it the wayfaring man shall not err (Isa. 57:12). Always on every occasion we must seek what is pleasing to God, what is necessary for the welfare of the church, as well as what makes for peace and healing among each other.

We of both sides have earnestly prayed to God and constantly labored that what happened and continues to happen in the dispute over the House-Buyers be brought to an end: that following the example of the patriarchs, according to the teaching of Scripture, we might again meet each other in love, reconciliation, and unity. Finally, by the grace of God and with his help it was possible that we together in mutual agreement, representing both sides, the one as well as the other from many different places, were called by letter to come to Dordrecht.

And so both sides assembled here in the Lord's name (unworthy as we were) in love and friendship. Insofar as it was fitting, we have spoken about and discussed these matters in the fear of the Lord. After this we turned to prayer and supplication, for which the Lord had prepared our hearts so that we were inclined towards each other. For this be the praise and thanksgiving only to him. Unshackled, free, and unbound as we had now been made (Isa. 58:6), with sincere confession of guilt in regard to the matter mentioned above, we also set free and unbound all those whom we and our former leaders, together with their congregations, had bound, banned, or burdened in any way.

And moreover, in sincere repentance and contrition we begged each other for forgiveness; thereafter we forgave each other and acquitted each other of everything which had been done by us or our former leaders or the congregations involved, specifically or in a general way in regard to the matter of the House-buying at Franeker. This included everything connected with it whether words, acts, books, letters, or any form of mistreatment or indebtedness—nothing excepted—wherever up until now we together as a group or separately as individuals of either side had grieved, hurt, or offended others.

In regard to this matter we have also at the same time together in sincere and earnest confession prayed and implored our merciful God and heavenly Father in the name of his dear Son, our Lord Jesus Christ, for complete forgiveness of everything done until now in this matter by us and our brethren on both sides (Matt. 6:12; Prov. 28:9). We desired complete forgiveness for everything we have in any way done against God in his majesty or against each other or any other person.

In evidence and confirmation of this complete agreement, reconciliation, and unity, we have received each other with the hand and with the brotherly kiss of peace. Each accepted the other in the name of the Lord as is becoming for those who are bound to each other in one fellowship with him.

In this union we have accepted and included all fellow members, present and absent, both as a group and as individuals, those residing here as elsewhere, those invited as well as all others—excluding none. Just as we included those who were with us, the invited and their proxies, and who stand with us united in goodwill, doctrine, and practice, we have not overlooked those who hereafter wish to follow our example and thus live to the honour of God and for the building up, edification, and improvement of the church so that together we might with heart and soul live and walk peaceably (Acts 4:12). Such a walk becomes our calling and is in keeping with our common Christian faith, the principal articles of which are briefly drawn up—from the Word of God—and here added.

The Principal Articles of Our Common Christian Faith as Taught and Practiced by Our Church

[I. God and Creation]

Scripture testifies that without faith it is impossible to please God, for everyone who comes to him must believe that he is and that he rewards those who seek him. Therefore, we confess with the mouth and believe with the heart—in company with all devout men and women and in keeping with Scripture—in one eternal, almighty, and incomprehensible God: the Father, Son, and Holy Spirit. There is only one God—none other before him and none other after him—for from, by, and in him are all things. All praise and honour be to him forever. Amen. Heb. 11:6; Deut. 6:4; Gen. 17:1; Isa. 46:8 [45:9]; [1] John 5:7; Rom. 11:36.

We believe and confess that this one God is the creator of all things, visible and invisible. During six days he created the heaven and earth, the sea, and everything in them. We also believe that he continues to rule and maintain his creation by his wisdom and by the power of his word. 1 Cor. 12:6; Gen. 1; Acts 14:14 [:15].

And when he had completed his work in keeping with his good pleasure and had ordered it as perfect and right, each part in keeping with its nature and being, he also created the first man, Adam, the father of us all. He gave him a body made from a lump of clay and breathed into his nostrils the breath of life. Thus Adam became a living soul from God, created in his own image and likeness in true righteousness and holiness unto eternal life. God regarded him as above all other creatures and adorned him with many great and glorious gifts. He placed him in the delightful garden, or Paradise, and gave him a command and a prohibition. After this he took a rib from Adam, made a woman of it, brought her to him, and gave her to him as a helper, companion, and wife. Accordingly, God caused that from this first man, Adam, all men living on the entire earth have generated and descended. Gen. 1:27; 2:7; 5:1; 2:18; 2:17; 2:22; Acts 17:26.

[II. The Fall of Man]

We believe and confess, according to Scripture, that our first parents, Adam and Eve, did not continue long in the happy state in which they had been created. They became disobedient and broke God's high command, for they were seduced and misled by the snake and the malice of the devil. In this way sin entered the world, and death by sin has passed upon all men, for all have sinned and incurred the wrath of God and fallen under his condemnation. Therefore, Adam and Eve were driven by God from Paradise or the delightful garden to cultivate the earth, in sorrow to provide for themselves, and to eat their bread in the sweat of their faces—until they returned to the earth from which they came. We believe that through this one sin they fell so deeply, became estranged and separated from God, that neither they themselves, nor any of their posterity, nor angels, nor an other creature in heaven or earth could help them, redeem them, or reconcile them to God.

They would have been eternally lost had not God in compassion for his creatures intervened in his love and mercy. Gen. 3:6; 4 Esd. 3:7; Rom. 5:12, 18; Gen. 3:23; Ps. 49:8 [:7]; Rev. 5 [:1-5]; John 3:16.

[III. The Restoration of Man]

We believe and confess that God—notwithstanding the fall of the first man and his descendants, their sin and wrongdoing, and their helplessness to save themselves—did not abandon men and women to be cast off entirely nor to be eternally lost. No, God called them back to himself again; he comforted them and showed them that there was yet a means of reconciliation. This was the unspotted Lamb, the Son of God, who was prepared for this purpose before the foundation of the world. While our first parents were still in Paradise, he was promised for consolation, redemption, and salvation to man and his posterity. In truth, he was granted to them by faith from that time on so that all of the devout patriarchs, to whom this promise was often renewed, have longed for, desired, and seen by faith its fulfillment. They know that his coming would save and free men and women from their sins, guilt, and unrighteousness and restore them again to God's favour. John 1:29; 1 Pet. 1:19 [:19-20]; Gen. 3:15; 1 John 3:8 [:5]; 2:1; Heb. 11:13, 39; Gal. 4:4.

[IV. The Coming of Christ]

We also believe and confess that when the time of the promise came and was fulfilled—the time so much longed for and awaited by all the devout patriarchs—then the promised Messiah, Redeemer, and Saviour, going out from God, was sent into the world. This was in keeping with the prediction of the prophets and the witness of the Gospel writers. Yes, came in the flesh and revealed himself: the Work itself became flesh and man. He was conceived in the virgin Mary (who was engaged to Joseph of the house of David); and when she gave birth to him as her first born at Bethlehem, she wrapped him in swaddling clothes and laid him in a manger. John 4:25; 16:28; 1 Tim. 3:15 [:16]; John 1:14; Matt. 1:22; Luke 2:7, 21.

We believe and confess that he is the same one whose origin is from of old, from the days of eternity; his years have no beginning, his life, no end. Of him it is testified that he is the Alpha and the Omega, who is, was, and is to come. He is the one who was forseen, promised, sent, and came into the world; he is God's own, first, and only Son. He was before John the Baptist, before Abraham, before the world; yes, he was David's Lord and the God of all the world, He is the first-born of all creatures who was sent into the world and yielded up the body prepared for him as an offering and sacrifice whose fragrance was pleasing to God. This was for the solace, redemption, and salvation of all men and women, for the whole human race. Mic. 5:1 [:2]; Heb. 7:3; Rev. 1:18 [:8]; Rev. 1: 18; John 3:16; Heb. 1:6 [:16]; Rom. 8:32; John 1:30; Matt. 22:41 [:43]; Col. 1:15; Heb. 10:5.

But as to how and in what manner this body was prepared, how the Word became flesh, and he himself man, we are content with the explanation given by the faithful Gospel writers. Therefore, we confess with all the saints that he is the Son of the living God. In him is all our hope, comfort, redemption, and salvation, and we should not seek the same in any other. Luke 1:30-31; John 20:30-31 [:31]; Matt. 16:16.

Further, we believe and confess with Scripture that, when he had finished the work for which he had been sent into the world, he was—in keeping with the providence of God—delivered into the hands of evil men; that he suffered under the magistrate Pontius Pilate; that he was crucified, died, and was buried. On the third day he rose from the dead and ascended to heaven and took his seat at the right hand of the throne of Majesty in the heavens. From that place he shall come again to judge the living and the dead. Luke 22:53; 23:1; 24:5-6; 24:50.

The Son of God also died, tasted death, and shed his precious blood for all men; in this way he bruised the serpent's head, destroyed the works of the devil, cancelled the bond which pledged us to the decrees of the law, and achieved the forgiveness of sins for the entire human family. Thus he effected salvation for all, from the time of Adam to the end of the world, who believe in and obey him. Gen. 3:15; 1 John 3:8; Col. 2:14; Rom. 5:18.

[V. The Law of Christ]

We also believe and confess that before his ascension Christ set up and instituted his new covenant. And because it was to remain an eternal covenant—which he confirmed and sealed with his own precious blood—he highly charged and commissioned that it not be altered, neither by angels nor men, nor be added to nor diminished. And since it contained the whole counsel and will of his heavenly Father as far as is necessary for salvation, he has caused it to be published by his dear apostles, messengers, and servants, whom he has called and chosen for that purpose. He sent them to every part of the world to preach in his name to all nations, people, and tongues, proclaiming repentance and forgiveness of sins. Accordingly, he has declared in his covenant that all men without distinction as his children and lawful heirs, insofar as they follow and live up to its precepts by faith, are not excluded from this glorious inheritance of salvation. Excepted are the unbelieving and disobedient, the obstinate and unrepentant, who despise such salvation by their sinful actions and thus make themselves unworthy of eternal life. Jer. 31:31; Heb. 9:15-17; Matt. 26:27 [:28]; Gal. 1:8 [:18]; 1 Tim. 6:3; John 15:15; Matt. 28:19; Mark 16:13 [:15]; Luke 24:45-46 [:46-47]; Rom. 8:17; Acts 13:46.

[VI. Repentance and Amendment of Life]

We believe and confess, since man is by nature inclined to do evil from his youth and is prone to sin and wickedness, that, therefore, the first lesson of the new covenant of the Son of God is repentance and amendment of life. Men and women with ears to hear and minds to understand should show the fruits of repentance and amend their lives. It means to believe the Gospel, to depart from evil and do good, to cease to be unjust, and to reject sin. In short, it implies a discarding of the old nature with its deeds and putting on the new nature, which is created after God in righteousness and true holiness. For neither baptism, nor the Lord's Supper, nor church membership, nor any other outward ceremony can without faith, the new birth, and the amendment of life make it possible for us to please God and to receive the solace and promise of salvation. With sincere hearts and completely by faith we must come to God and believe in Jesus Christ as Scripture speaks and testifies of him. By this faith we receive forgiveness of sins, are justified and sanctified, and are made children of God—yes, partakers of his image, nature, and being: born again from above by the incorruptible seed. Gen. 8:21; Mark 1:15; Ezek. 12:1; Mark 1:15; Col. 3:9-10; Eph. 4:21-22 [:21-24]; Heb. 10:21-22; John 7:38.

[VII. Baptism]

With regard to baptism we believe and confess that all penitent believers who by faith, the new birth, and the renewing of the Holy Ghost are made one with God, their names written in heaven—upon a scriptural confession of faith and amendment of life—ought to be baptized with water in the name of the Father, the Son, and the Holy Spirit. This is in keeping with the doctrine and command of Christ and the practice of his apostles: for the burial of their sins and in order to become incorporated into the fellowship of the saints. In consequence of this they must learn to keep all that the Son of God taught and commanded his followers. Acts 2:38; Matt. 28:19 [:19-20]; Matt. 28:20; Rom. 6:4; Mark 16:15 [:16]; Matt. 3:15; Acts 2:28 [:38], 8:11 [12], 9:18; 10:47, 16:33; Col. 2:11-12.

[VIII. The Church of Christ]

We also believe and confess a visible Church of God—namely, of those who, as explained above, truly repent, believe rightly, and have received true baptism. They are united with God in heaven and incorporated into the fellowship of the saints on earth. These persons we hold to be the chosen race, the royal priesthood, the holy people, who have the witness that they are the spouse and bride of Christ. Indeed, they are children and heirs of eternal life, a tent, a tabernacle, and house of God in the Spirit, built upon the foundation of the apostles and the prophets—Christ being the chief cornerstone. This church of the living God he bought and redeemed with his own precious blood. According to his promise, he will always stand by this church: to comfort and protect even to the end of the world. He will dwell and walk with her and keep her so that neither floods, nor tempests, nor even the gates of hell shall ever move or conquer her. This church is to be known by her Scriptural faith, doctrine, love, and godly life; also by a fruitful living up to, use, and observance of the ordinances of Christ which he so highly commended and enjoined upon his followers. 1 Cor. 12 [:13]; 1 Pet. 2:9; John 3:29; Rev. 19:7; Titus 3:6-7; Eph. 2:19-21; Matt. 16:18; 1 Pet. 1:18-19; Matt. 28:20; 2 Cor. 6:16; Matt. 7:25; 16:18.

[IX The Choosing and Ministry of the Teachers, Deacons, and Deaconesses in the Church]

With regard to offices and election in the church, we believe and confess—since the church can neither exist and grow nor continue as a structure without offices and ordination—the Lord Christ himself as a father in his own house has instituted offices and ordinations and regulated how each should walk in this respect in keeping with his own work and calling and do that which is right and necessary. For Christ himself as the faithful, chief shepherd and bishop of our souls was sent and came into the world, not to wound or to break or to destroy the soul of men but to heal and cure, to seek the lost, to break down the barrier and dividing wall, to make one out of two, and thus to gather Jews, Gentiles, and people of all nations into one fold—that is, one fellowship in his name. For this he gave his life so that none should go astray; thus he made a way for their salvation by redeeming and releasing them when there was no one to help or assist. Eph. 4:10-12; 1 Pet. 2:29 [:25]; Matt. 12:19 [:20], 18:11; Eph. 2:13 [:14]; Gal. 3:28; John 10:9; 11:15; Ps. 49:8 [:7].

We also believe that before his departure Christ provided for his church faithful ministers, apostles, evangelists, pastors, and teachers—whom he had chosen by the Holy Spirit with prayer and supplication—to feed his flock, to govern the church, to watch over and nurture her, and in every way care for her—yes, to do in all things as he had done before them by way of example and precept. Eph. 4:11; Luke 10:1; 6:12-13; John 2:15; Matt. 28:20.

Also, that the apostles likewise, as faithful followers of Christ and leaders in the church, were diligent with prayer and supplication to God to provide from among the brethren: bishops, pastors, and leaders for all the cities and places where churches existed; to ordain such persons who took heed to themselves, to the doctrine, to the church and who were sound in the faith, godly in life and conduct with a good reputation within as well as without the church. That so they might be an example, light, and pattern in all godliness and good works; that they might worthily administer the ordinances of baptism and the Lord's Supper. And that they might appoint in all places faithful men as elders capable of teaching others, ordaining them by the laying on of the hands in the name of the Lord to enable them to minister to the church according to their ability that as faithful servants they might invest their Lord's talent, gain by it, and consequently save both themselves and those who hear them. 1 Tim. 3:1; Acts 1:23-24; Titus 1:5; 1 Tim. 4:16; Titus 2:1-2; 1 Tim. 3:7; 2 Tim. 2:2; 1 Tim. 4:14; I Tim. 5:2; Luke 19:13.

And that they also should diligently see to it, each where he has oversight, to provide in all places deacons to look after and minister to the poor that they might receive gifts and alms and in turn faithfully distribute them, with all honesty as is becoming, to the saints in need. Acts 6:3-6.

Also, that honourable, older widows should be chosen and ordained as deaconesses for the purpose of assisting the deacons to visit, comfort, and provide for the poor, infirm, ill, and distressed. Also, they should visit widows and orphans in order to comfort and care for them; further, to help look after the necessities of the church according to the best of their ability. 1 Tim. 5:9; Rom. 16:1; James 1:27.

What further concerns the deacons, that they, especially those gifted and chosen from the church for this purpose and ordained—to help lighten the work of the bishops—may also admonish and assist in work and doctrine in order to serve one another in love with the gift they have received from the Lord. So that through the mutual service and assistance of every member, according to his ability, the body of

Christ may be improved and the Lord' vineyard and church may increase in growth while keeping the structure properly in order.

[X. The Lord's Supper]

We also believe in and observe a breaking of bread or Lord's Supper such as the Lord Christ Jesus instituted with bread and wine before his suffering. He ate it with his apostles and commanded it to be done in remembrance of himself. Accordingly, his apostles also taught and observed it in the churches and commanded the believer to do it in memory of the Lord's death and suffering, that his body was broken and his precious blood shed for us and for all mankind. Remembering also its effect—namely, the redemption and salvation he accomplished—which showed us sinful men such a love whereby we are highly admonished to love and forgive each other and our neighbor as he has done unto us. Also, to keep in mind and to practice the unity and fellowship we have with God and each other, a unity represented and signified in the breaking of the bread. Matt. 26:25; Mark 14:22; Acts 2:42; 1 Cor. 10:6 [:16], 11:22 [:23]; Acts 2:46.

[XI. Footwashing]

We also confess a washing of the saints' feet just as the Lord Christ instituted and commanded but also exemplified by washing his apostles' feet himself even though he was their Lord and Master. This was an example that they should wash each other's feet. They followed this example and taught the believers to observe it as a sign of true humility; also as a special sign of the true washing by which we are washed in his precious blood and our souls are cleansed. John 13:4-17; 1 Tim. 5:10; Gen. 18:4; 19:2.

[XII. The State of Marriage]

We believe and confess that in the church of God there is an honourable state of marriage between two free and believing persons in keeping with and as God originally ordained in Paradise and established himself, between Adam and Eve. And likewise the Lord Christ approved it and removed all the abuses which had gradually crept in by restoring it to its first order. The apostle Paul also taught and permitted marriage in the church leaving it to everyone's free choice to marry in the Lord in keeping with the original plan. By the phrase "in the Lord" we think it ought to be understood that, as the patriarchs were to marry among their own relatives or kindred, no other liberty is granted to the believers of the new covenant. They are to marry among the chosen generation and the spiritual kindred of Christ (and none other), those who have been united to the church as one heart and soul, having received baptism and standing in the same fellowship, faith, doctrine, and walk before they are united in marriage. Such are then joined together in his church, according to the original ordinance of God. This is called "marrying in the Lord." Gen. 1:26 [:27]; Gen. 2:22 [:18-24]; Matt. 19:4 [:4-6]; 1 Cor. 7; 1 Cor. 9:5; Gen. 24; Gen. 28; 1 Cor. 7:39.

[XIII. The Office of Civil Government]

We also believe and confess that God instituted civil government for the punishment of evil and the protection of the good as well as to govern the world and to provide good regulations and policies in cities and countries. Therefore, we may not resist, despise, or condemn the state. We should recognize it as a minister of God. Further, we ought to honour and obey it and be ready to perform good works in its behalf insofar as it is not in conflict with God's law and commandment. Also, we should be faithful in the payment of taxes and excises, giving what is due to the state as the Son of God taught, practiced, and commanded his disciples to do. Besides, we should constantly and earnestly pray for the state and the welfare of the country that under its protection we may lead a quiet and peaceful life in all godliness and honesty. And further, that the Lord may be pleased to reward them here and in eternity for all of the privileges and benefits as well as the liberty we enjoy here under their laudable rule. Rom. 13:1-7; Titus 3:1; 1 Pet. 2:17; Matt. 17:27, 22:21 [:17-21]; 1 Tim. 2:1-2.

[XIV. Defense by Force]

With regard to revenge and resistance to enemies with the sword, we believe and confess that our Lord Christ as well as his disciples and followers have forbidden and taught against all revenge. We have been commanded to recompense no man with evil for evil, not to return curse for cursing, but to put the sword into its sheath or in the words of the prophet beat the swords into plowshares. From this we understand that following the example, life, and doctrine of Christ, we may not cause offense or suffering but should instead seek to promote the welfare and happiness of others. If necessary for the Lord's sake, we should flee from one city or country to another; we should suffer the loss of goods rather than bring harm to another. If we are slapped, we should turn the other cheek rather than take revenge or strike back. In addition, we should pray for our enemies and, if they are hungry or thirsty, feed and refresh them and thus assure them of our good will and desire to overcome evil with good. In short, we ought to do good, commending ourselves to every man's and woman's conscience, and, according to the law of Christ, do unto others as we should wish them to do unto us. Matt. 5:39, 44; Rom. 12:14; 1 Pet. 3:9; Isa. 2:4; Mic. 4:3; Zech. 9:8-9; Matt. 5:39; Rom. 12:20 [:19-21]; 2 Cor. 4:2; Matt. 7:12.

[XV. The Swearing of Oaths]

Concerning the swearing of oaths, we believe and confess that our Lord Christ forbade it and taught his followers that they should not swear at all. Rather, they should let their yes be yes and no, no. From this we understand that all oaths, great or small, are prohibited. Instead, all our promises, commitments, and contracts, yes, also our statements and bearing of witness, ought to be confirmed only with our word— yes in what is yes, no in what is no—provided that at all times we keep our word and live faithfully as if we had confirmed and established it with an oath. And if we do this, we have confidence that no man, not even the magistrate, will have just reason to lay a heavier burden on our mind and conscience. Matt. 5:34-35; James 5:12; 2 Cor. 1:17 [:17-18].

[XVI. Excommunication or Separation from the Church]

We also believe and confess a ban, separation, and Christian punishment in the church for amendment and not for destruction, whereby the pure may be distinguished from the impure. In other words, if anyone, after he is enlightened, has attained knowledge of the truth, and has been received into the fellowship of the saints and afterward either willfully or out of presumption against God or otherwise falls back into the unfruitful works of darkness by which he is separated from God—so that the kingdom of God is denied him—that such a person, after the matter is made public and sufficiently known in the church, may not remain in the congregation of the righteous. As an offensive member and public sinner he ought to be set aside, punished before all, and purged as bad leaven: this for his amendment and as an example and warning to others; also that the church may be kept pure and free of scandals so that the name of the Lord be not dishonoured and the church be not an offense to those who are without. Finally, a sinner should not be condemned along with the world but that he may be convinced in his heart and mind and again brought to contrition, repentance, and amendment of life. Isa. 59:2; 1 Cor. 5:5 [:5-6]; 1 Cor. 5:12; 1 Tim. 5:20; 1 Cor. 5:6; 2 Cor. 10:8; 2 Cor. 13:10.

Concerning brotherly reproof and exhortation and also the instruction of those who err, it is necessary to use all diligence and care in watching over them and admonishing them with all meekness with a view to their correction and amendment; and in case any should remain obstinate and unconverted, to reprove them as seems fit. In short, the church ought to put away from their company those who are evil—whether in doctrine or in life—but no other. James 5:19 [:19-20]; Titus 3:10; 1 Cor. 5:12.

[XVII. The Shunning of the Excommunicated]

With regard to the withdrawal from or shunning of the separated, we believe and confess that, when someone has so far fallen away either by his wicked life or false doctrine so that he is estranged from God and as a consequence justly separated from and punished by the church, such as person must be shunned according to the doctrine of Christ and his apostles and avoided without partiality by all members of the church (especially by those to whom it is known). In eating and drinking and other similar fellowship such a person should be shunned and avoided so that one is not involved with his way of life or a partaker of his sins. This should be done so that the sinner may be ashamed, struck in his heart and conscience, and thus be induced to an amendment of his ways. Such a shunning, we believe, ought to be used in Christian moderation so that it may have the effect not of destroying but of healing the sinner. If he is in need, hungry, thirsty, naked, ill, or in any form of want, then we ought—according to the love and teaching of Christ and his apostles—to help and give him assistance. Otherwise, the shunning leads to ruin instead of correction or amendment. Such persons should not be considered enemies but should be admonished as brethren. Again, the purpose is to bring them to acknowledgement, contrition, and repentance of their sins in order that they may be reconciled to God and again received into the church. In this way love can have its way with them as is becoming. 1 Cor. 5:9-11; 2 Thess. 3:14; Titus 3:10; 2 Thess. 3:14.

[XVIII. The Resurrection of the Dead and the Last Judgment]

As to the resurrection of the dead we believe and confess in keeping with Scripture that all who have died and fallen asleep shall be awakened, made alive, and raised up on the last day by the incomprehensible power of God. These together with those who are then alive shall be changed at the sound of the last trumpet and appear before the judgment seat of Christ. There the good shall be parted from the evil so that everyone may receive in his own body according to his deeds whether they be good or evil. The good or the devout shall be taken up with Christ as the blessed, enter into life eternal, and receive that joy which no eye has seen nor ear heard to reign and triumph with Christ forever. On the other hand, the wicked or the ungodly shall be driven away as accursed and thrown into great darkness, into the eternal pains of hell, where in the words of Scripture the worm dieth not and the fire is not quenched. There they shall never have any hope, comfort, or redemption. May the Lord by his mercy make all of us fit and worthy that no such thing befall any of us but that we may take heed to ourselves and be diligent so that at that time we may be found before him in peace, without spot, and blameless. Amen. Matt. 22:30-31; Dan. 12:12; Job 19:26-27; Matt. 25:31; John 5:28; 2 Cor. 5:10; 1 Cor. 15; Rev. 12:4 [:11]; 1 Thess. 4:13; 1 Cor. 2:9 [15:51]; Mark 9:44; Rev. 14:11.

These now, as briefly stated above, are the principal articles of our common Christian faith as in our church and among our people are taught and practiced. They are, according to our judgment, the only true Christian faith, which the apostles in their time believed and taught. Yes, they testified to this faith with their lives and confirmed it with their death; some of them sealed it with their blood. With them and all godly men and women we seek in our weakness to abide by the same in life and death that by the grace of the Lord with them we may obtain salvation.

It was decided that two exact copies, signed by us as principals of the meeting, should be kept as a matter of record—one to be retained here at Dordrecht and the other, at Amsterdam. Also, that all elders now present at this meeting should receive a copy to show at home. Furthermore, that each elder obtain a copy for the congregations he serves.

So, beloved fellow workers, brothers and sisters, and all companions in Christ, we trust that with this short, written explanation our efforts and work in this matter, carried out in love, will be understood. To this end we humbly pray and sincerely request that you will accept this from us (unworthy as we are) for the good, and will follow the same in love, and that you willingly and in good faith will let it serve you together for your deepest peace and betterment. So that in this way also, the God of peace will dwell in and abide with you and us together, according to his promise; and that the good work begun may continue to bring honour and glory to the Lord, that it may serve for the growth and upbuilding of his church. To this end and further in everything that is necessary and pleasing to him, the good and merciful God will help us and you, granting his gracious blessing and strengthening and approving our efforts that we together may be made worthy and able. Amen.

We request, pray, and desire in all friendliness that everyone, and in particular those who receive our above-mentioned statement in their hands or obtain knowledge about it by way of seeing, hearing, or reading—and find they cannot accept, approve, or see through it in all its parts—that in such cases you still will always speak well of it to others. One should recall that it has been written: he who speaks well of a matter (and explains all with a good interpretation) such a one in turn is well spoken of. To recall also that Gods' Son has charged and commanded: whatsoever ye would that men should do to you, do ye even so to them.

As notice, witness, and full confirmation of what was transacted and done here by the congregation and our countrymen together as stated above: Thus we the undersigned elders, minister [*dienaren*], and brethren as such and in the name of and in behalf of the request of this, our as now united congregation at this place, as also for ourselves and in behalf of each congregation, the same as our public and general Brotherly Union, Pacification, and Agreement, have endorsed and undersigned. Use it for your benefit. And hereby we commend you to God Almighty in his gracious keeping unto salvation. Sincere greetings with the everlasting peace of the Lord from all of us and from the congregation here. Amen.

Transacted and concluded in our united congregation in the town of Dordrecht, April 21st, Anno 1632. New Style. Farewell.

And was undersigned by

Dordrecht Isack de Coningh, and in behalf of our ministers, Ian Jacobs.

Middleburg
    Bastiaen Willemsen
    Ian Winckelmans

Vlissingen
    Oillaert Willeborts
    By Iacob Pennen
    Lieven Marijness

Amsterdam
 Tobias Govertsz
 Pieter Iansen Moijer
 Abraham Dirckxsz

Bommel
 Willem Iansen van Exselt
 Ghisiert Spiering

Dordrecht
 By me, Hans Cobrijssen
 By me, Iacuis Terwen
 Claes Dircksen
 Mels Ghijsbaerts
 Aeriaen Cornelissoon

Crefeld, ditto
 Herman op den Graff
 Weylm Kreynen

Haarlem
 Dirck Wouters Kolenkamp
 Pieter Ioosten

Schiedam
 Cornelis Bom
 Lambrecht Paeldinck

Blokzijl
 Claes Claessen
 Pieter Peters

Haarlem
 Ian Doom
 Pieter Grijspeer

Rotterdam
 Balten Centen Schoenmaker
 Michiel Michielsz

From the Upper Country
 Peeter van Borsel
 Antonij Hansz

Zeeland
 Cornelis de Mior
 Isaac Claessen

Rotterdam
 Israel van Halmael
 Heyndrick Dircksz. Apeldoren
 Andies Lucken, de Jonghe

Leyden
 Mr. Christaen de Coninck
 Ian Weyns

Zierkzee
 Antheunis Cornelisz
 Pieter Iansen Timmerman

Utrecht

    Herman Segerts

    Ian Hendricksen Hoochvelt

    Daniel Lhorens

Amsterdam

    David ter Haer

    Pieter Iansen van Singel

Gorinchem

    Iacob van der

        Heyde Sebrechts

    Ian Iansz. vande Cruysen

Arnhem

    Cornelijes Iansen

    Derojck Rendersen

Utrecht

    Abraham Spronck

    Willem van Broeckhuysen

14

Prussian Confession (1660)
Confession or Brief, Simple Confession of Faith

Introduction

Many Anabaptists who experienced persecution in the Netherlands fled to cities along the North and Baltic Seas. Sailing on Dutch merchant ships Anabaptists reached the city of Danzig, probably by 1534, and soon found refuge in towns and settlements in the Vistula Delta region. In Polish Prussia (West Prussia) Protestant reforming movements were at first violently suppressed, but by the 1540s Protestants were tolerated, and after 1547, Anabaptists from Holland were invited to settle in the region with the view to developing the agricultural economy. Mennonite villages soon emerged and churches were established under the leadership of well known Anabaptist leaders such as Menno Simons and Dirk Philips.

From the seventeenth century onward, Mennonites living in Polish and Prussian territories adopted numerous confessional statements. The "Confession or Brief, Simple Confession of Faith" was likely the first Anabaptist confession in the region, and some scholars have considered it to be the most dominant among Mennonites of Prussia and Russia. Indeed, Mennonites reprinted the confession at least five times in Prussia (1751, 1756, 1781, 1797, 1854), three times in Russia (1853, 1873, 1912), and it was reprinted at least twice in the United States (1878, n.d.).

Unfortunately, many of the facts surrounding the confession of faith are vague, and little is known regarding who originally drafted the confession, and what the circumstances might have been that led to its formulation and adoption. That the oldest extant editions of the

311

confession are in the German language is also puzzling since the religious language of Mennonites during this time was mainly Dutch, with the language shift to High German taking place sometime in the eighteenth century. If the confession was not an internal document to be used by early German-speaking congregations in rural areas where the shift from Dutch to the High German language occurred first, it might have been a document for external use intended for German authorities who may have been asking about Mennonite beliefs. In the Vistula Delta region Mennonites were never fully tolerated like the Lutherans or the Reformed, and popular antagonisms were often directed against Mennonites for both religious and economic reasons.

The printed title of the confession suggests that it was a statement representing the views of Flemish, Frisian, and High German Mennonites in Prussia. According to Robert Friedmann, however, there was no such union in Prussia; there were, rather, two distinct groups, a conservative Flemish branch and a liberal Frisian group. The Flemish had a distinct confessional tradition, so this particular document may have been primarily Frisian. W. Mannhardt has observed that Frisian congregations were still using the confession in the nineteenth century.

According to W. Mannhardt and Christian Neff, the confession was a translation of an older Dutch confessional document, but they do not indicate whether the document originated in the Netherlands or in Prussia. Unfortunately, no Dutch edition has ever been found, although it is plausible that the origin of the confession was the Netherlands. In 1639 the Flemish, Frisians, and High Germans were united in the Netherlands, and in 1665 and 1666 their confessions were published in two separate collections. Earlier, in 1660 and 1661, representatives from the three groups considered adopting a common confessional statement, but whether a draft was ever produced has yet to be verified. Christian Neff, following Herman Schijn, also mentions the adoption of a united confessional statement in Utrecht in 1664, but here too, a linkage to a German Prussian Confession has not been made. It is possible that a draft of a united confession was in circulation among the Flemish, Frisians, and High Germans in the Netherlands, perhaps in the late 1650s, which Prussian Mennonites then adopted.

This translation by John Rempel and Karl Koop is based on the Prussian printed edition of 1660 entitled *Confession oder Kurtze und einfältige Glaubens-Bekentnis* as well as a handwritten copy dated in the same year. Some comparison was also made to Peter Klassen's translation that is located in the Loewen volume.

Bibliographical Sources

"Confession oder Kurtze einfeltige Glaubens Bekantnis derer so man Menonisten nenet in Preüssen" (Im Jahr des Herren Anno M.DC.LX., handwritten manuscript); *Confession oder Kurtze und einfältige Glaubens-Bekentnis derer/ so man nenne, Die vereinigte Flämische/Friesische und Hochdeutsche Tauffs=gesinnete, oder Mennonisten in Preussen* (Ausgegeben vonb denen obigen Gemeinen daselbsten, 1660*)*; Howard John Loewen, *One Lord, One Church, One Hope, And One God: Mennonite Confessions of Faith* (Elkhart, IN: Institute of Mennonite Studies, 1985), 113-126; W. Mannhardt, *Die Wehrfreiheit der Altpreussischen Mennoniten: Eine geschichtliche Erörterung* (Marienburg: Altpreussische Mennonitengemeinden, 1863); Christian Neff, "Bekenntnisse des Glaubens," *Mennonitisches Lexikon I,* 157-161; Christian Neff, J. C. Wenger, Harold S. Bender, "Confessions of Faith," *Mennonite Encyclopedia I,* 679-686; Horst Penner, "West Prussia," *Mennonite Encyclopedia IV,* 920-926; Nanne van der Zijpp, "The Confessions of Faith of the Dutch Mennonites," *Mennonite Quarterly Review* 29.3 (July 1955): 171-87.

[Prussian Confession (1660)]

Confession or Brief, Simple Confession of Faith of those who in Prussia are called Mennonites In the year of our Lord 1660

Translated by John Rempel and Karl Koop

I. Concerning God the Father

We believe from our hearts and confess on behalf of all[1] with our mouth (Rom. 10:10), according to the content of Holy Scripture, the Word of God, that there is one God (Deut. 6:4; Isa. 45:21-22) who is eternal (Ps. 90:2; Isa. 40:28), all-powerful (Gen. 17:1, 35:11), holy (Lev. 19:2; Isa. 6:3), just (Ps. 11:8; Jer. 11:20), true (Num. 23:20; 1 John 5:20), all-knowing (Ps. 139:1,4; Heb. 4:11), gracious (Exod. 22:27, 34:6), merciful (Ps. 103:8; Luke 8:36), alone good (Matt. 19:17; Ps. 36:5), perfect (Matt. 5:48), invisible and incomprehensible (Exod. 33:20; John 1:18; Col. 1:15), alone wise (1 Tim. 1:17; Rom. 16:26), the fountain of life (Jer. 2:10), and creator of heaven and earth (Gen. 1; Rom. 11:36) and of all things visible and invisible (Heb. 11:32; 2 Cor. 4:18). He sustains all things through the word of his power (Heb. 1:3; 2 Pet. 3:5) and works all things in all (1 Cor. 12:8). Heaven is his throne and the earth his footstool (Isa. 66:1; Acts 7:49). Great is his wisdom and mighty are his deeds (Jer. 32:19). He is lord of lords, and king of kings (Dan. 2:4; Ps. 95:3). His name is Lord Sabaoth (Isa. 47:4, 51:15). All lands are full of his honour and sincerity (Ps. 8:2; 113:4; Isa. 6:2); for everything is in his hands (Ps. 95:4). To him alone be laud, praise, honour, and glory for ever and ever, Amen (1 Tim. 1:17; Rev. 7:12).

II. Concerning Christ the Son of God

We believe in Jesus Christ who is our Lord and Saviour, redeemer and giver of salvation, who was begotten from eternity in an incomprehensible manner (Ps. 2:7; Heb. 7:3; Luke 1:30). He is the eternal living Son of God (Mic. 5:2); the one, who we see and read about in the Holy Scriptures, who the Father himself identified as his beloved Son (Matt. 8:12 [3:17]; Ps. 2:7). He was also recognized in this way by the beloved apostles and other righteous men of God, such as the apostle Peter (Matt. 16:16), Nathanial (John 1:49), John the Baptist (John 1:34), Thomas (John 20:28), Mary the sister of Lazarus, and others (John 11:27).

He was sent into the world (John 3:16) from the Father so that he might fulfill the plan that was laid at the foundation of the world (1 Pet. 1:20), namely, to save us from the eternal curse (2 Cor. 5:21; Gal. 3:13; Rom. 8:3). Through the wondrous work and power of the Holy Spirit, the Father sent his eternal Son from heaven (Isa. 9:5; John 17:3, 3:16), who, in the body of a blessed and holy virgin with the name Mary, became flesh and human (Matt. 1:21; Luke 1:35). He suffered for us under Pontius Pilate; he was crucified, he died and was buried for our sins as the four evangelists report (Matt. 27:31; Mark 15:25; Luke 23:32; John 19:18). He descended into hell in order to redeem us, and for our justification (Rom. 4:25), he rose again from the dead on the third day (Acts 2:24; Eph. 4:8-10). He ascended into heaven (Luke 24:15 [:51]; John 20:17) and sits at the right hand of the almighty Father (Mark 16:19; Eph. 1:20) from where he will come again to judge the living and the dead (Matt. 25:31; Acts 10:42, 17:31).

III. Concerning the Holy Spirit

We believe in the Holy Spirit (Matt. 3:16, 28:19; Ps. 51:13), who proceeds from the Father and the Son (John 14:6, 15:26), through whom the Father and Son work (Ps. 33:6; John 16:14; Job 33:4); that is, he is included in the divine being with the Father and the Son, which we can see in the history of creation (Gen. 1). For this reason we recognize them (John 10:30) to be one in will, action, sovereignty, rule, and accomplishment (John 14:11). This divine being has been revealed as Father, Son, and Holy Spirit (Matt. 3:16-17), as one true God (1 John 5:8).

We also believe in a common, holy, Christian church, the communion of saints (Matt. 16:13; Eph. 5:17 [sic]), the forgiveness of sins (Luke 24:47; 2 Cor. 5:19; Col. 1:14), the resurrection of the flesh, both the righteous and the unrighteous, who will all be placed before the judgment seat of Christ. Everyone there will be judged according to their works, whether good or evil (Matt. 25:32; John 5:29), thereafter comes eternal life (John 6:40; Rom. 2:6-8).

IV. Concerning the Church of God

Concerning the church of God and the communion of saints, we believe and confess that there is one church of God, which he has gained through his blood (Acts 20:28) and washed from sin through his own blood (Rev. 1:5; Eph. 5:26, 27). He gave himself for it in order to sanctify it and purify it through the washing of water by the word (Titus 3:5; Eph. 5:26) so as to present it to himself in splendour, namely, a church that is sincere [*die herzlich sey*] that has no spot or wrinkle at all, that is holy and blameless (Col. 1:22; 1 Pet. 1:15; Luke 1:75; Eph. 5: 27).

We believe that this church is made up of a large number of people around the earth who have separated themselves from the sinful world (Rom. 6:17; 2 Cor. 6:17; 1 Pet. 4:4; Rev. 18:4) through faith in Jesus Christ and obedience to the holy Gospel. They have communion through the Holy Spirit with God the Father, with Christ their head (1 John 1:3), with the multitude of many thousand holy angels in heaven, and with all who believe in Christ here on earth. And even though this church is scattered in various places of this world, still they are members of and constitute a single body in Christ (Rom. 12:4; 1 Pet. 1:1; Acts 8:1). He is their head and foundation, their shepherd (Eph. 4:15, 5:23; Col. 1:18; 1 Cor. 3:11; John 10:12), their Lord (Eph. 6:8-9; 1 Cor. 8:6) and king (John 18:37; Zach. 9:9; Matt. 21:5; John 12:15); they let themselves be ruled and guided by him.

The signs of the true church are the right fruit of conversion (Matt. 3:8; Luke 24:47; Acts 20: 21), the dread and avoidance of sins, life in all goodness, righteousness, and truth, according to the teaching of Christ and his apostles, true faith (Eph. 5:9; Matt. 5:16) in Jesus Christ through obedience to the divine Word (Col. 1:23; John 15:4-7), the use of his holy ordinances, baptism and the Lord's Supper (Matt. 3:15; Luke 22:19), and in the freely offered confession of God and Jesus Christ for the people (1 Pet. 3:15; Rom. 10:9), in fiery fraternal love toward one another (1 Pet. 4:8; 2 Pet. 1:7). [The church is called] to preserve the unity of the Spirit through the bond of peace (Eph. 4:3; Phil. 2:2); through taking up the cross and truly following Christ (Matt. 16:23 [:24]; Mark 8:34; Luke 9:28 [:23]).

Now these are the true signs of the church of God, whose members give evidence in godly and Christian virtue (Gal. 5:22-24; Eph. 5:9; 2 Pet. 1:5, 11; Rom. 8:14-16); who have been purified through Christ and are born again true members of the body of Christ and co-heirs of eternal life (Titus 8 [3]:5-7).

V. Concerning the Office of Teacher

We believe and confess according to the practice of Christ and his apostles that God has given his church the authority to elect teachers and servants (Titus 1:5), so that the saints may be prepared by means of the work of the [teaching] office, through which the body of Christ may be built up (Eph. 4:11-12). The election of such an office and service takes place when the servants and the church together earnestly call on the name of God, according to the example of the apostle Peter.

When the disciples of Jesus Christ put into place two leaders, Joseph, named Barsabbas, who was also called Just, Matthias prayed and said, "Lord, the one who knows every heart, between these two, show us whom you have elected, so that one may receive this responsibility and apostolic office [*Apostel-Ampt*] from which Judas turned away and went to his own place." And they cast lots and the lot fell on Matthew, and he was added to the eleven apostles (Acts 1:15 [:23-26]).

Now when the church requires such persons to be servants of the Word, they together pray earnestly to God—for this matter is beyond their own power (Matt. 9:38; Luke 10:2; James 5:16). And they humbly pray to God, that he, who knows every heart, will show through a united voice, whom he has chosen for such a service and office, knowing with complete confidence that Christ has himself promised that whatever we ask of the Father in his name, it will be given to us (Matt. 18:19; John 15:16). When he is in the midst of the believers who are gathered in his name, he already knows their desires before they ask (Matt. 6:8). He governs the humble through his Spirit, so that they will come to know whom he has chosen for his common purpose and service. Then will come to pass what God promised through the prophet Jeremiah with these words, "I want to give you shepherds according to my heart, who will feed you with wisdom and understanding" (Jer. 3:15).

After the election has taken place, a number of characteristics are to be expected from the one who has been elected. He must be blameless, a husband of one wife, sober, moderate, moral, hospitable, and able to instruct. He should not be a heavy wine-drinker, not boastful, not abrasive but gentle, not quarrelsome, not stingy. He should rule his house well, and have obedient and respectable children (1 Tim. 3:1-7; Titus 1:6-8, 2:7). He must hold fast to the Word which is dependable, and be able to teach so that he can powerfully admonish on the basis of saving doctrine and discipline those who oppose (Acts 20:28; 2 Cor. 1:21). He must be an example to the flock, and must feed the flock of Christ. This he must do willingly, not out of compulsion nor for the sake of dishonourable reasons, but rather from the heart, not as someone who rules over the people, but as an example to the flock. Then, when the chief shepherd appears, he will also receive the eternal crown of honour (1 Pet. 5:3-4).

VI. Concerning the Office of the Deacon

We read in the Acts of the Apostles: "In those days when the disciples increased in number, there was a complaint among the Greeks against the Hebrews because their widows were being overlooked in the daily distribution of food. Then the Twelve called the disciples together and said, 'It is not fitting that we neglect [the ministry of] the Word of

God and serve at tables for the sake of our beloved brothers and sisters. [Therefore,] search among yourselves and find seven men, who have a good reputation and are full of the Holy Spirit and of wisdom, who we can then choose for this pressing need. We, however, wish to devote ourselves to prayer and the service of the Word.' This discussion pleased the entire congregation and they elected Stephen, a man full of faith and the Holy Spirit, and besides him, others were also ordained for serving the poor" (Acts 6:1-6).

In this way, the church of God should follow the example of the holy Apostles, when they have a need to find men who will serve the poor. First they should turn to God in devout prayer, and after such prayer they should choose men who have a good reputation (1 Tim. 3:8-10) through whom the poor may, with loving hearts, be served the shared gifts and be taken care of in their time of need. For this purpose the members of Christ are also bound (Matt. 6:3; Eph. 4:28) to eat their own bread without depriving others, whether they have much or little. They help others honestly so that the needs of the poor may be taken care of, and so that the right hand is unaware of what the left hand is doing (Matt. 26:10; Mark 14:7). For Christ says, "The poor you will always have with you, and if you wish you can do good to them." Therefore they must follow the teaching of the Apostle Paul. If one holds an office, let him be true to it. If anyone teaches, let him apply himself to teaching. If one admonishes, let him apply himself to admonishing. If one shares, let him do so with simplicity. If one administers, he should do so conscientiously. If someone practices mercy, he should do it with joy; for love exists without hypocrisy (Rom. 12:7-9).

VII. Concerning Christian Baptism

Baptism is an outward, visible ordinance commanded by Christ himself for incorporation into his church. This practice consists in the following: that all those who hear the teaching of the holy Gospel and believe it, and with a penitent heart gladly receive it, must be baptized with water into a blessed life (Matt. 3:6), according to the command of Christ. For he says, "All power in heaven and earth is given to me; therefore, go and teach all peoples and baptize them in the name of the Father, the Son, and the Holy Spirit (Matt. 28:18 [:19]). Go into all the world and preach the Gospel to all creatures. Whoever believes and is baptized will be saved; whoever does not believe will be condemned" (Mark 16:15 [:16]).

The holy apostles have diligently heeded this commandment. [By] teaching and preaching they vigorously pursued faith in Jesus Christ; through them many became believing and let themselves be baptized, both men and women (Acts 8:13, 16, 38; 9:18; 10:48; 16:15, 33; 18:8; 19:5), as it occurred on the holy feast of Pentecost in Jerusalem. There the apostle Peter said to the Jews, "Now may the whole house of Israel know for certain that God has made this Jesus whom you crucified to be Lord and Christ." When they heard that their hearts were pierced. And they said to Peter and the other apostles, "Men and dear brothers, what shall we do?" Peter spoke to them, "Let everyone repent and be baptized in the name of Jesus Christ for the forgiveness of sins and you will receive the gift of the Holy Spirit for the promise is to you and your children and to all who are far away, whom the Lord will call together." Now those who gladly received his address were baptized and three thousand souls were added [to the church] that same day (Acts 2:36-40 [:41]).

In addition, those children who were still far away yet can understand the teaching of the holy Gospel that has come to their ears, and gladly receive it with penitent hearts and believe, they are fit to receive baptism. For the apostle Paul says, "Faith comes from the sermon but the sermon comes through the Word of God" (Rom. 10:17). The gain that comes to the truly believing from God's ways, applied to them through baptism, is not the putting away of the uncleanness of the flesh, but the washing of the inner sinful impurity of souls through the shed blood of Christ (1 Pet. 1:21; Acts 2:38, 22:16). Through it we have acquired the forgiveness of sins, through Christ's blood as the covenant with God of a good conscience through the resurrection of Jesus Christ. Thus believers can comfort themselves with the comforting promise of eternal blessedness (1 John 1:7; Rev. 1:5; Heb. 9:14; Acts 20:28). The duty to which the baptized commit and bind themselves in baptism is that through baptism into the death of Christ they let their sins be buried. [This is] according to the teaching of the apostle Paul, who says, "What then shall we say? Should we persist in sin in order that grace is made mightier? Far be it! How could we still want to live in sin when we have died to it? Don't you know that all of us who are baptized in Christ Jesus are baptized in his death. Thus we are buried with him through baptism into death, so that just as Christ was awakened from the dead through the glory of the Father, so also should we walk in a new life (Rom. 6:1-4). We put on Christ in baptism, as the apostle says, "As many of you as have been baptized have put on Christ" (Gal. 3:27). So then, everyone – according to the gift he has received – must maintain and improve that same body with earnest diligence in temporal and eternal matters. [The goal is to become] true members of God's household, fellow citizens of the spiritual Jerusalem (Eph. 2:12) and its legal citizens, to be obedient according to the teaching of Christ, their most exalted king and head, to all his commandments, being subject and obedient. For [Christ] says, "Teach them to keep everything I have commanded you" (Matt. 28:20).

VIII. Concerning the Lord's Supper

We understand [the Supper to be] an outward, visible evangelical act, according to Christ's commandment and the apostles' practice unto a holy life. Bread and wine are taken according to the example of Christ (Matt. 26:26; Mark 14:24). The bread is broken, and beside it the wine shared and given to those who are believers who are baptized upon their faith, according to Christ's ordinance (Mark 16:16; Acts 2:42). The bread is eaten by them and the wine is drunk. Christ's bitter suffering and death is thereby proclaimed, according to Paul who says, "I received it from the Lord, which I gave you. For the Lord Jesus, in the night that he was betrayed, he took bread, gave thanks and broke it and said, 'Take eat, this is my body, which will be broken for you. Do this in remembrance of me.'

In like manner he took the cup after the supper, and said, 'This cup is the new testament in my blood. Do this as often as you drink it in remembrance of me. For as often as you eat of this bread and drink from this cup, you should proclaim the Lord's death until he comes'"

(1 Cor. 11:23-26). In this outward Supper [the fact] is set before us and signified that Christ's holy body was offered on the trunk of the cross and his precious, worthy blood shed for the forgiveness of sins. Gloriously, in his heavenly being, he is our souls' life-giving bread, food, and drink (John 6:51) and unites himself in the holding of his spiritual Supper with all truly believing souls, according to his address, "Behold, I stand at the door and knock. If anyone hears my voice and opens the door, I will come in to him and hold the Lord's Supper with him and he with me" (Rev. 3:20). Furthermore, he teaches us to rise to heaven in our spirits and our hearts' thoughts, [and] through holy prayers to acquire the truly designated treasure (Col. 3:1).

[The Lord's Supper] exhorts us to thankfulness for God's great acts of kindness which he showed us through Christ in love (John. 3:16). [The Supper] unites us in peace, love, oneness of spirit, and true Christian communion among ourselves (Eph. 4:1). As the apostle says, "The blessed cup which we bless, is it not a communion of the blood of Christ? And the bread that we break, is it not the communion of the body of Christ? For as the bread is, so are we [who are] many one body, since we all partake of one bread" (1 Cor. 10:16-17).

IX. Concerning the Footwashing of the Lord

We confess that footwashing among the believers is an ordinance of Christ, which he demonstrated among his disciples as an example that is to be followed. He has exhorted believers with these words: "Do you know what I have done to you? You call me Master and Lord, and you are right for that is who I am. Since now, as Lord and Master, I have washed your feet, so you also are to wash each other's feet. I have set an example for you so that you may do as I have done unto you. If you know this, blessed are you who do it" (John 13:12-15, 17). The reason the Lord Jesus commanded [the practice of] footwashing is to lead us toward a true humble mind, [thus reminding us] that through grace by the blood of Christ we have been washed of our sins, and that by his example of profound humility we also are to be truly meek and humble toward each other. We are to demonstrate such work of love and humility to those we receive and host in our homes in the same way that the Apostle Paul introduced footwashing as one of the works of virtue (1 Tim. 5:10).

X. Concerning Holy Matrimony

We confess that this is an ordinance of God, which God himself instituted in Paradise and established for our first parents, Adam and Eve, a man and a woman, created in the image of God, while they were yet in [a state of] grace before God. He blessed them so that they might multiply and fill the earth (Gen. 1:28). In this ordinance fornication and impurity shall be avoided, and no abuse is to take place (1 Cor. 7: 2).

In such an ordinance, which the Lord Christ also upheld (Matt. 19:4; Mark 10:6), true believers belong together, except those too closely related by blood (Lev. 20:19). Such people, after prayer may be married and in a Christian manner live together until the end; that is, each man has his one wife, and each woman has her one husband. Through marriage, husband and wife are tied together and obligated toward one another so that under no circumstances and for no reasons are they to be separated from each other, except in the case of fornication and adultery, as we read from Matthew the evangelist where the Pharisees and Sadducees came to Jesus to tempt him and said, "Is it lawful for a man to divorce his wife for any reason?" He, however, answered them and said, "Have you not read that he who in the beginning created humans created them so that there would be one man and one woman. For this reason a man will leave his father and mother and join himself with his wife, and the two will become one flesh. Thus they are not two but have become one flesh. What God has joined together, let no one separate." Then they spoke again, "Why then did Moses command us to give a certificate of dismissal and to divorce her?" He spoke to them, "Moses allowed you to be divorced from your wives because of the hardness of your hearts, but at the beginning it was not so. But I say to you, whoever divorces his wife, except in the case of fornication, and marries another commits adultery, and whoever marries the one who has been separated, also commits adultery" (Matt. 5:32, 19:3-9; Deut. 24:1).

From this it is clearly seen and understood that the marriage bond is firm and indissoluble which can neither be broken nor separated unless, as noted earlier, in the case of fornication as the Lord Christ has spoken. In the church of God a brother may take as his wife a sister in the faith (2 Cor. 6:15; Deut. 7:3) and the sister has the freedom to accept or reject his [offer]. For the apostle says, "A wife is bound to the law as long as her husband is living. But if her husband dies, she is free to marry as she wishes, but only if it is in the Lord" (1 Cor. 7:39); that is, that [the marriage] takes place according to the Lord's orderly will and good pleasure.

XI. Concerning the Office of Government

We confess that God, who is king of all kings and lord of all lords (Ps. 95:3; Col. 2:10; 1 Tim. 6:15; Rev. 17:14) has established kings and government in all lands (1 Sam. 16:1; Dan. 2:21, 4:23; Joshua 1:2; Judges 6:14; 1Sam. 9:17; 2 Sam. 8:15) for [our] welfare and common good. [We are to lead] a good, honourable civic life, for there is no government without it being of God. Where there is government it is ordained of God; whoever opposes government strives against God's order. Those who strive against [it] will bring judgment upon themselves. Not those who do good works but those who do evil should fear the authorities (Rom. 13:1-3; Dan. 2:37-38).

Therefore everyone is called to be subordinate to the authority of government, for it is God's servant, an avenger to punish the evildoer. It does not bear the sword in vain. It is there to protect the righteous and punish the evil. Therefore, all believers, yes, all people are indebted, and according to God's Word obligated and duty bound by God's Word to fear and honour their esteemed government, to render obedience in all matters that are not contrary to the Word of God (Acts 4:19). In consideration [of the fact] that we must be subject to human authorities for the Lord's will, we give them taxes, tolls, and assessments. According to the teaching of the apostle Peter, we are to be submissive, when he says, "Be submissive to all human authority for the Lord's will, whether they be kings, governors, or councilors as [God's] envoys for vengeance against evildoers and in praise of the righteous (1 Pet. 2:13-14). We also have the duty to pray for them. According to the command of the apostle Paul, as he says, "I admonish you to make petitions, prayers, intercessions, and thanksgivings for all matters and all people, for kings and for all government so that we might lead a calm and quiet life in all godliness and dignity" (1 Tim. 2:1-2). May the Most High give them wisdom and understanding (Dan. 2:21) to rule their territories, their cities and subjects in peace, so that in the end they might receive the reward of eternal blessedness. To God, the eternal king, the immortal and invisible, who alone is wise, be honour and praise in eternity, Amen (1 Tim. 1:17)!

XII. Concerning the Swearing of Oaths

We understand and confess concerning the matter of truth that the fathers of the Old Testament were permitted to perform an oath in God's name (Deut. 6:13, 10:20). But we are obligated and bound to the laws of the Lord Jesus through a voice from heaven, the Son of the living God, the king, founder, and the one who instituted the New Testament (1 Tim. 6:15; Matt. 3:17). He has forbidden oath-swearing of every kind to believers with these words: "You have heard that it was said to the ancients, 'You shall not swear any false oath and you shall keep your oath before God.' But I say to you, do not swear concerning any matter, neither by heaven for it is God's chair, not by earth for it is his footstool, nor by Jerusalem for it is the city of a great king. You shall not swear by your head, for you are not able to make a single hair white or black. Rather, let your speech be, 'Yes, yes' 'No, no'" (Matt. 5:33-37). Whatever goes beyond that comes from evil. Therefore, we must not let ourselves be moved to more [than] a 'Yes' that [really] is a yes, a 'No' that [really] is a no. [We must] speak with complete truth; rather, our 'Yes' and 'No' must consist of the same perfect truth as the highest oath. Similarly, the apostle James admonishes with these words: "But in all cases, my brothers, do not swear, neither by heaven nor by earth nor by any other oath. [Keep] your word: a 'Yes' that is yes and a 'No' that is no – so that you do not fall into hypocrisy (James 5:12). From this it may be clearly enough noted that swearing, or taking an oath, is not permitted in the New Testament, but forbidden. Our words must be sincere; truth must be spoken from the heart (Ps. 15:2). We must not use 'Yes' and 'No' in light-hearted falsity (2 Cor. 1:17).

XIII. Concerning Revenge

From the words of the Lord Christ, who says, "You have heard that it was said, an eye for an eye and a tooth for a tooth. But I say to you that you are not to resist evil. Love your enemies, bless those who curse you, do good to those who hate you, pray for those who offend and persecute you, so that you may be children of your father in heaven. For he allows the sun to rise over those who are evil and those who are good, and allows rain to fall on the righteous and the unrighteous" (Matt. 5:38-45). We understand that one cannot practice revenge against one's enemy, which also the apostle Paul confirmed: "Do not avenge yourselves, my beloved, rather leave room for the wrath of God (Rom. 12:19-21). For it is written, 'Vengeance is mine, I will repay,' says the Lord (Deut. 32:35). So if your enemy is hungry, feed him; if he is thirsty, give him something to drink. If you do this, you will heap burning coals on his head (Prov. 25:21). Do not be overcome by evil, but overcome evil with good. The Apostle Peter also says, "It is [a sign of] grace when, for conscience sake before God, someone tolerates evil and suffers unjustly; for what credit is that when you suffer as a result of misdeeds. However, if you suffer and endure because of good works, you have God's approval. For this reason you have been called as Christ also suffered for us and has left us an example that we are to follow in his footsteps. He did not sin neither was deceit found in his mouth. He did not disgrace, even though he was disgraced; he did not threaten, even though he suffered. He left it to the one who rules justly (1 Pet. 2:19-24; Matt. 27; Isa. 53:9; John 8:50).

XIV. Concerning the Christian Ban In the Congregation

We understand and confess a practice of separation [*Absonderung*] in cases where members who through public sinfulness exhibit a disgraceful life. The practice of separation is meant for their betterment, not for their condemnation so that their spirit may be redeemed on the Day of the Lord (1 Cor. 5:5). For the Lord Jesus teaches as follows: If a brother sins against you, go to him and admonish him, between you and him alone. If he listens to you, you have won your brother. If he does not listen to you, then take one or two with you so that all matters can be based on two or three witnesses. If he does not listen, then inform the congregation. If he does not listen to the congregation, then regard him as a heathen and a tax collector (Matt. 18:19 [:15-17]; Lev. 19:17). These who remain obstinate in their sins and separate themselves from God (Isa. 59:2) no longer belong in the fellowship of Jesus Christ. Instead of being tolerated, they must be punished for the sake of all, so that others will be instilled by fear (1 Tim. 5:20). For the Apostle says, "Cast out from yourselves those who are evil (1 Cor. 5:13). Do you not know that a little sour dough spoils the entire dough? Therefore, sweep out the old sour dough, so that you can remain new dough and unspoiled" (1 Cor. 5:6-7). For what do believers have in common with unbelievers (2 Cor. 6:15)?

Concerning the removal of the unrepentant, we understanding the teachings of the apostle Paul to be applicable, through which the sinner is brought to shame (2 Thess. 3:14), is led to reconsider [his life], and is converted. For whoever allows himself to be called a brother, yet is an adulterer, is greedy, is an idolater, or scoffer, or drunkard, or robber—with such a person one should not eat" (1 Cor. 5:11). Again Paul says, "We command you, dear brothers, in the name of Jesus Christ that you separate yourselves from all brothers who lead a disorderly life, who cause destruction and discord in opposition to the teachings of Christ, and who stray from the same. These [persons] do not serve the Lord Jesus Christ, but rather their own appetites" [*sondern ihrem Bauche*] (2 Thess. 3:6; Rom. 16:17-18). Similarly, [one should] avoid a heretical person who has been admonished once or repeatedly (Titus 3:10). However, do not regard him as an enemy but admonish him as a brother (2 Thess. 3:15), in love, with helpful compassion, Christian humility, and justice (Eph. 4:31; Col. 3:13)—virtues that a Christian should demonstrate toward all people, even toward his enemies.

Concerning the reception of the repentant into the church of Christ, we understand that one must be willing and prepared at all times to accept the separated sinner into the fellowship of the believers, and forgive his previous mistakes when he has truly shown repentance and sorrow for his sins. In such a case, the apostle Paul says to the Corinthians, "It is enough that such a one who has been punished by many, should henceforth be forgiven and comforted—even more so, so that he does not sink into great sorrow. Therefore, I implore you that you show him love. For this reason I have written to you, so that I can recognize whether you are prepared to be obedient in all things. Whomever you forgive, I forgive also" (2 Cor. 2:6-10). So much concerning the Christian ban and the separation of the unrepentant, as well as the reception of the one who has truly repented.

XV. Concerning the Return of Christ, the Resurrection of the Dead, and the Last Judgment

We believe and confess that the Lord Jesus Christ is our one prophet (Luke 7:16; John 6:14; Luke 24:18 [:18-19]), priest (Heb. 3:1, 6:20, 9:11), and king (Ps. 2:6; Rev. 17:14; 1 Tim. 6:15; Matt. 25:34). Just as he visibly ascended to heaven (Acts 1:11), he will return again in the clouds of heaven with great power and glory (Matt. 24:30). With a war cry and voice of the archangel and with the trumpet of God the Lord himself will descend from heaven, and the dead in Christ will be resurrected first.

After that, we who are living and remaining will be caught up in the clouds together with the others in a twinkling of an eye to meet the Lord in the air, and so will we forever be with the Lord (1 Thess. 4:16-17). For the trumpet shall sound and the dead shall rise incorruptible with their own bodies (1 Cor. 15:52), through which they have done good or bad; some to eternal life and some to eternal condemnation and shame (Dan. 12:12). For the Lord Christ says, "The hour will come and it is already here, when all those who are in the graves will hear his voice, and those who have done good will go forth to the resurrection of life; those who have done evil, however, will go forth to the resurrection of judgment" (John 5:28-29). In what form the dead will arise, the apostle Paul tells us with many glorious proofs when he says, "It will be sown corruptible, and will arise incorruptible; it will be sown in dishonour, and will arise in glory; it will be sown in weakness, and will arise in power; it will be sown a natural body, and will arise in a spiritual body" (1 Cor. 15:42-44).

For we must all be presented before the judgment seat of Christ, and each one will give an account before God on his own behalf, so that each will receive according to the deeds done during his life, whether good or bad" (Rom. 14:10; 2 Cor. 5:10; Rev. 22:12). For the Lord will come in his glory, and all the holy angels with him, and he will sit on the throne of glory and all the nations will gather before him. He will separate them like a shepherd separates the sheep from the goats. The sheep he will place to his right and the goats to his left. Then the king will say to those on his right, "Come here, you who are blessed by my Father; inherit the kingdom that has been prepared for you from the beginning of the world (Matt. 25:31). These will go to eternal life (Matt. 25: 47), who on this earth through their faith have exemplified justice, love, and mercy (Isa. 58:7; Sir. 7: 36, 39). They will be with the Lord forever (1 Thess. 4:17) in whose presence there is fullness of joy and pleasure always (Ps. 16:11); where there is neither sorrow nor temptation. Instead they will be glad with unspeakable and glorious joy—in eternal heavenly glory among many thousands of holy angels (Rev. 21:24, 22:5; 1 Pet. 1:4-9) and in company with Abraham, Isaac and Jacob; indeed with all the saints and the elect, always and forever (Matt. 8:11; Luke 13:28). For this reason the apostle says to the believers, "Comfort yourselves with these words (1 Thess. 4:18) and watch, for you know that the Day of the Lord will come as a thief in the night" (1 Thess. 5:2; 2 Pet. 3:10; Rev. 3:3, 16:15). Then he will say to those on the left, "Depart from me, you who are cursed, into the fire that has been prepared for the devil and his angels" (Matt. 25:41). These are the unjust, the unbelievers who did not recognize God, who were not obedient to the Gospel of our Lord Jesus Christ (2 Thess. 1:8), and who also did not practice any works of love and mercy. These will go to eternal pain and suffering, to eternal damnation from the face of the Lord and from his glorious power (Matt. 25:42-46). When he will come and appear gloriously they will experience no grace, [but] wrath, sorrow, and fear. All people, who have done evil, will likewise experience this (Rom. 2:8-9). There will be wailing and gnashing of teeth. Their worm will not die, and their fire will not be put out (Matt. 25:30; Mark 9:45). Their portion will be the lake that burns with fire and brimstone, and they will be tormented day and night, forever and ever (Rev. 20:15, 21:8).

May God, who is full of grace and mercy, through Jesus Christ his beloved Son and through the power of the Holy Spirit, graciously protect us all from the terrible punishment of the godless. May he grant us his grace that we here on earth may live holy lives, die in blessedness and joyously rise from the dead unto eternal life and most desired blessedness. Amen! Amen!

Appendix

The Nicene Creed [381]

We believe in one God,
the Father, Almighty,
maker of heaven and earth,
of all that is,
seen and unseen.

We believe in one Lord, Jesus Christ,
the only Son of God,
eternally begotten of the Father,
God from God, Light from Light,
True God from true God,
begotten, not made,
of one Being with the Father;
through him all things were made.
For us and for our salvation
he came down from heaven,
was incarnate of the Holy Spirit and the Virgin Mary
and became truly human.
For our sake he was crucified under Pontius Pilate;
he suffered death and was buried.
On the third day he rose again
in accordance with the Scriptures;
he ascended into heaven
and is seated at the right hand of the Father.
He will come again in glory to judge the living and the dead,
and his kingdom will have no end.

We believe in the Holy Spirit, the Lord, the giver of life,
who proceeds from the Father and the Son,
who with the Father and the Son is worshiped and glorified,
who has spoken through the prophets.
We believe in one holy catholic and apostolic Church.
We acknowledge one baptism for the forgiveness of sins.
We look for the resurrection of the dead,
and the life of the world to come, Amen.

The Apostles' Creed [ca. 700]

I Believe in God the Father Almighty, Maker of heaven and earth

And in Jesus Christ his only Son our Lord; who was conceived by the Holy Ghost, born of the Virgin Mary, suffered under Pontius Pilate, was crucified, dead, and buried; he descended into hell; the third day he rose again from the dead; he ascended into heaven, and sitteth on the right hand of God the Father Almighty; from thence he shall come to judge the quick and the dead.

I believe in the Holy Ghost; the holy catholic church; the communion of saints; the forgiveness of sins; the resurrection of the body; and the life everlasting. Amen.

"The Nicene Creed" and "The Apostles' Creed" are reprinted by permission of the Office of the General Assembly, Presbyterian Church (U.S.A.) from *Book of Confessions* (Louisville KY, 1996).

Notes

Introduction

[1] This introduction draws directly from several chapters of the book *Anabaptist-Mennonite Confessions of Faith: The Development of a Tradition*, by Karl Koop (Kitchener: Pandora Press, 2004).

[2] See John Howard Yoder, trans. and ed., *The Legacy of Michael Sattler* (Scottdale, PA: Herald Press, 1973), 34-43. The English translation also appears in this volume.

[3] See J.F.G. Goeters, "Das älteste rheinische Täuferbekenntnis," in Cornelius J Dyck, ed., *A Legacy of Faith* (Newton, KS: Faith and Life Press, 1962), 197-212. The English translation also appears in this volume.

[4] *De Algemeene Belydenissen der Vereeinighde Vlaemsche, Vriesche, en Hooghdutysche Doopsgesinde Gemeynte Gods* (Amsterdam: Pieter Arentsz.,1665); *Handelinge Der Ver-eenighde Vlaemse, en Duytse Doops-gesinde Gemeynten, Gehouden Tot Haerlem, Anno 1649 in Junio Met De Dry Confessien aldaer geapprobeert or aengenomen* (Vlissinghe, Gelyen Jansz., 1666.)

[5] Michael D. Driedger, *Obedient Heretics: Mennonite Identities in Lutheran Hamburg and Altona during the Confessional Age* (Burlington, VT: Ashgate, 2002), 51.

[6] See Christian Neff, J.C. Wenger, Harold S. Bender, "Confessions of Faith," in *Mennonite Encyclopedia* I, 679-86; Dirk Visser, *A Checklist of Dutch Mennonite Confessions of Faith to 1800* 6/7 (Amsterdam: Documenta Anabaptistica Neerlandica, 1974-1975).

[7] Cornelius J. Dyck, "Foreword," in Howard John Loewen, *One Lord, One Church, One Hope, and One God: Mennonite Confessions of Faith in North America* (Elkhart, IN: Institute of Mennonite Studies, 1985), 17.

[8] Christian Neff, "Bekenntnisse des Glaubens," *Mennonitisches Lexikon* I, 157-161.

[9] Emil Händiges, *Die Lehre der Mennoniten in Geschichte und Gegenwart nach den Quellen dargestellt nebst einem Überblick über die heutige Verbreitung und Organisation der mennonistischen Gemeindschaft* (Ludwigshafen am Rhein: Kommissionsverlag der Konferenz der süddeutschen Mennoniten, e.V., 1921).

[10] Nanne van der Zijpp, "The Confessions of Faith of the Dutch Mennonites," *Mennonite Quarterly Review* 29.3 (July 1955): 186; Wilhelmus J. Kühler, *Geschiedenis van der Doopsgezinden in Nederland*, Tweede Deel, 1600-1735, Erste Helft (Haarlem: H. D. Tyeenk Willink and Zoon N. V., 1940); Hendrick W. Meihuizen, "Spiritualistic Tendencies and Movements among the Dutch Mennonites of the Sixteenth and Seventeen Centuries," *Mennonite Quarterly Review* 27.3 (October 1953): 259-304.

[11] Van der Zijpp, "The Confessions of Faith of the Dutch Mennonites," 177.

[12] Neff, Wenger, Bender, "Confessions of Faith," 679-86.

[13] Cornelius J. Dyck, "The First Waterlander Confession of Faith," *Mennonite Quarterly Review* 36.1 (January 1962): 5-13; "The Middelburg Confession of Hans de Ries, 1578," *Mennonite Quarterly Review* 36.2 (April 1962): 147-154, 161; "A Short Confession of Faith by Hans De Ries," *Mennonite Quarterly Review* 38.1 (January 1964): 5-19; "Hans de Ries, Theologian and Churchman: A Study in Second Generation Dutch Anabaptism" (Ph.D. dissertation, University of Chicago, 1962), 308-313.

[14] See Dyck in Loewen, *One Lord*, 16; Dyck, "A Short Confession of Faith," 5.

[15] See Sjouke Voolstra, "Mennonite Faith in the Netherlands: A Mirror of Assimilation," *Conrad Grebel Review* 9 (Fall 1991): 277-292.

[16] Initially the "Anabaptist Vision" was a presidential address for the American Society of Church History, delivered on December 28, 1943. It is found in numerous publications. See, for instance, Harold S. Bender, "The Anabaptist Vision," *Church History* 13.1 (March 1944): 3-24; "The Anabaptist Vision," *Mennonite Quarterly Review* 18.2 (April 1944): 67-88; "The Anabaptist Vision," in Guy F. Herschberger, ed., *The Recovery of the Anabaptist Vision: A Sixtieth Anniversary Tribute to Harold S. Bender* (Scottdale: Herald Press, 1957), 29-54. The "Anabaptist Vision" became the "consensus" view, but as Arnold Snyder has pointed out, it did not go completely unchallenged even in its "heyday." See C. Arnold Snyder, *Anabaptist History and Theology: An Introduction* (Kitchener: Pandora Press, 1995), 401ff.

[17] Bender, "The Anabaptist Vision," in Herschberger, ed., *The Recovery of the Anabaptist Vision*, 37.

[18] Ibid., 35-36.

[19] Ibid.42.

[20] A. James Reimer, *Mennonites and Classical Theology: Dogmatic Foundations for Christian Ethics* (Kitchener, ON: Pandora Press, 2001), 164-65.

[21] Ibid.

[22] The programatic essay for this thesis came from James Stayer, Werner O. Packull, Klaus Deppermann, "From Monogenesis to Polygenesis: the Historical Discussion of Anabaptist Origins," *Mennonite Quarterly Review* 43.2 (April 1975): 83-121.

[23] The following articles, for instance, take up this issue: James C. Juhnke, "Mennonite History and Self-Understanding: North American Mennonitism as a Bipolar Mosaic," 83-99; Rodney J. Sawatsky, "Beyond the Social History of the

Mennonites: A response to James C. Juhnke," 101-108; James Stayer, "The Early Demise of a Normative Vision of Anabaptism," 109-116 in Calvin Wall Redekop and Samuel J. Steiner, eds., *Mennonite Identity: Historical and Contemporary Perspectives* (Lanham, New York, London: University Press of America, 1988); Mary S. Sprunger, "The Anabaptist Vision: Reflections from Dutch-Russian Mennonitism," *Conrad Grebel Review* 12 (Fall 1994): 299-307.

²⁴ Hans-Jürgen Goertz may be the notable exception. See his "Zwischen Zwietracht and Eintracht: Zur Zweideutigkeit Täuferischer und Mennonitischer Bekenntnisse," *Mennonitische Geschichtsblätter* 43/44 (1986-87): 16-48," and also "Kleruskritik, Kirchenzucht und Sozialdisziplinierung in den täuferischen Bewegungen der Frühen Neuzeit," in Heinz Schilling, ed., *Kirchenzucht und Sozialdisziplinierung im frühneuzeitlichen Europa*, Zeitschrift Für Historische Forschung (Berlin: Duncker & Humblot, 1994), 183-98.

²⁵ Loewen, *One Lord*, 48.

²⁶ Karl Koop, *Anabaptist-Mennonite Confessions of Faith: The Development of a Tradition* (Kitchener, ON: Pandora Press, 2004).

²⁷ Benjamin J. Kaplan, "Confessionalism and Popular Piety in the Netherlands," *Fides et Historia* 27.2 (Summer 1995), 45.

²⁸ Heinz Schilling, "Confessional Europe," in *Handbook of European History 1400-1600: Late Middle Ages, Renaissance, and Reformation*, vol. 2, ed. Thomas A. Brady Jr. et al (Leiden: E.J. Brill, 1995), 645.

²⁹ van der Zijpp, "The Confessions of Faith of the Dutch Mennonites," 175-76; Dyck, "Hans de Ries, Theologian and Churchman," 182-83.

³⁰ C. Arnold Snyder, "The Influence of the Schleitheim Articles on the Anabaptist Movement: An Historical Evaluation," *Mennonite Quarterly Review* 63.4 (October 1989): 344-45.

³¹ Piet Visser, *Broeders in de geest: De doopsgezinde bijdragen van Dierick en Jan Philipsz. Schabaelje tot de nederlandse stichtelijkde literatuur in de zeventiende eeuw*, I (Deventer: Sub Rosa, 1988), 112.

³² See, for instance, Letter of Hans de Ries to Elias Tookey, December 3, 1626, quotd in Dyck, "The First Waterlandian Confession of Faith," 6; Rynier Wybrandtsz, Pieter Andriessen en Cornelius Claassen, *Apologia ofte Verantwoordinghe tegen Nittert Obbesz, 1626* quoted in Dyck, "Hans de Ries: Theologian and Churchman," 180-81.

³³ Driedger, *Obedient Heretics*, 55.

³⁴ Thieleman Janz. van Braght, *The Bloody Theater or Martyrs Mirror*, 5th ed., trans. Joseph F. Sohm (Scottdale, PA: Herald Press, 1950).

³⁵ For a history of the Anabaptist-Mennonite martyr tradition see Brad Gregory, *Salvation at Stake: Christian Martyrdom in Early Modern Europe* (Cambridge: Harvard University Press, 1999), 197-249.

³⁶ Driedger, *Obedient Heretics*, 56.

[37] Scholars have paid little attention to the textual transmission of Anabaptist confessions of faith, although some observations regarding the Dordrecht confession have been made. See, for instance, Hanspeter Jecker, "Glaubensbekenntnis und Katechismus in Rahmen von Geschichte und Theologie der Schweizer Mennoniten, I and II," Unpublished Manuscripts, Associated Mennonite Biblical Seminaries, 1987-88; Irvin B. Horst, *Mennonite Confession of Faith* (Lancaster, PA: Lancaster Mennonite Historical Society, 1988), 14; Leonard Gross, "The Swiss Brethren and the Dutch Mennonites: A Particular Study in Contrasts," *Mennonite Historical Bulletin* 53:1 (January 1993): 2.

[38] Bender, "The Anabaptist Vision," 37. See also 41.

[39] Kenneth Ronald Davis, *Anabaptism and Asceticism: A Study in Intellectual Origins* (Scottdale, PA: Herald Press, 1974), 296.

[40] C. Arnold Snyder, "Spiritual Empowerment Toward Discipleship," in Dale Schrag and James C. Juhnke, eds., *Anabaptist Visions for the new Millennium: A Search for Identity* (Kitchener, ON: Pandora Press, 2000), 27.

[41] C. Arnold Snyder, *Following in the Footsteps of Christ: The Anabaptist Tradition* (Maryknoll, NY: Orbis Books, 2004), 27-28.

1 Congregational Order (1527?)

[1] The document has no title; the title indicated here reflects the label given at the State Archive of Bern. See Yoder, *The Legacy of Michael Sattler*, 53, n. 99.

3 A Confession of Faith by Jörg Maler (1554)

[1] [marginal note] Such a gathering does not consist in many persons, Matt. 18 [:20].

[2] [marginal note] No human, only God alone can judge one's secrets.

[3] [marginal note] It would be better not to sin, for we cannot raise ourselves up.

[4] [marginal note] Outside of the new birth and renewal of the Holy Spirit no one can eat or drink of Christ.

[5] [marginal note] In the discipleship of Christ one eats of this food (through faith); for this food is useless to him who is still dead in sin and of the old dough. Such a one eats judgment upon himself, 1 Cor. 11 [:29].

4 Swiss Brethren Confession of Hesse (1578)

[1] On the envelope or paper in which the Confession was preserved is a reference to 2 Cor. 13:5-6: "Examine yourself, to see whether you are holding to the faith. Do you realize that Jesus Christ is in you? Test yourselves -- unless you fail to meet the test. I hope you will find that we have not failed."

[2] The word is "selig," and literally means blessed; it could also be translated as justified. This introductory section is set to rhyme, hence difficult to translate.

[3] "erkennen" could be translated as understanding.

[4] The Zurich Bible of 1531 uses the word *Schadai*.

[5] Literally a righteous plant.

[6] Note that the words triumphant and victorious were left out by the Anabaptists in this rendering.

[7] The Confession treats Pontius and Pilate as if they were two persons.

[8] The word is "treibt," literally meaning driven by the Spirit.

[9] "*Von der buss*" could be translated also as penitence, although Anabaptists rejected the Catholic sacrament of penance.

[10] It is unclear how the Swiss Brethren put these verses into practice.

[11] That means they held to the traditional view that they should not charge interest for loans.

[12] The meaning of the original "*wo ir nit den ban aus euch vertilket*" is not clear. Presumably it meant they wanted to use the ban to rid the community of idolatry.

5 Kempen Confession

[1] It is not evident who this person is.

[2] It is unclear to whom the initials in this section refer.

6 Wismar Articles

[1] It is difficult to ascertain if a "sick conscience" refers here to a psychiatric problem.

7 Concept of Cologne

[1] "Overlandtsche," that is, "Oberdeutsche."

[2] "Ende nadien wy niet en hebben gevonden eenigh verschil ofte Goddelicke oorsaeck onsen vrede te beletten."

[3] "hant ende mont gegeven" – literally: "giving hand and mouth."

[4] This is a reference to Phil. 3:15.

[5] According to Christoph Hege, this should read Lambesheim (Palatinate). See *Die Täufer in der Kurpfalz: ein Beitrag zur badisch-pfälzischen Reformationsgeschichte* (Frankfurt am Main: Hermann Minjon, 1908), 152.

8 Waterlander Confession (1577)

[1] The meaning of this parenthetical reference is obscure. It is possible that the writers had in mind the eternal state of the patriarchs who lived before the incarnation

[2] The statement "in times of need" refers to the need for ministers and church workers, not to particular emergencies.

[3] The reference is undoubtedly to the "following" articles of faith, affirming the importance of the doctrines discussed, for the salvation of all who believed. It is an incomplete sentence in the original.

[4] While most Anabaptists-Mennonites based the practice of footwashing strictly upon the example of Jesus (John 13), and the words of Paul (1 Tim. 5), the Dutch Mennonites also emphasized the Old Testament pattern of footwashing as a sign of hospitality (Gen. 18:4, 19:2, 1 Sam. 25:40 et al). The reference to Timothy 8 may have been intended to be 1 Tim. 5:10.

10 The Thirteen Articles (1626)

[1] "Tweederleye" may also be translated "two kinds" of Word of God, but "two-fold" is nearer the intent of the writers here and in other documents of the time. See, for example, Hans de Ries, Ontdeckinge der dwalingen (Hoorn: J. J. van Rijn, 1627), 336 pp.

11 Thirty-Three Articles (1617)

[1] Such as Twisck's own *Chronijck vanden onderganc der tijrannen ofte Jaerlycklche Geschiedenissen in Werltlycke ende Kercklijke saecken* (Hoorn, 1620).

[2] "Driven" in translated from "*ghedreven*." By the time of the composition of this confession, the epithet "*gheest-ghedreven*" had come to refer to those Mennonites, who emphasized the continuing inspiration of the Spirit, and who were sometimes seen by their co-religionists as fanatics.

[3] This unusual Roman numeral style, which is evident throughout the translation, follows that of the 1617 printed edition.

[4] Twisck is stretching 1 John 5:7-8, which actually reads: "And the Spirit is the one that testifies, for the Spirit is the truth. There are three that testify: the Spirit and the water and the blood, and these three agree." (NRSV)

[5] That is, having come to the age of understanding.

[6] This section is intended to oppose the Reformed position on double predestination which stipulated that from eternity God had elected some to salvation and the majority of humanity to damnation, a theological position which was causing considerable controversy within the Reformed camp itself in the Dutch Republic thanks to the ideas of Jacobus Arminius.

[7] That is the Catholic reliance on scripture and tradition, the latter consisting of interpretations by church fathers, papal decrees and church councils.

[8] It seems that Twisck's target here is the teaching of Hendrik Niclaes, who believed that Jesus did not become divine until after his death and that the members of Niclaes' Family of Love sect can be similarly divinized, or "godded with god." See Alastair Hamilton, *The Family of Love* (Greenwood, S.C., 1981).

[9] John 1:16; that is, that Jesus has participated fully in the human state without receiving any sinful inheritance.

[10] Acts 10:41. The symbol for this reference is missing from the text.

[11] The concept of the three ages, of Abraham, Moses and Christ, was a popular one among the Anabaptists. See Walter Klaassen, *Living at the End of the Ages:*

Apocalyptic Expectation in the Radical Reformation (Lanham: University Press of America, 1992).

[12] In Margin: Understand each time for a great year with so many years as there are days in a half year, making about 1274 years. Read similar year days: Num. 14:34; Ezek. 4:5.

[13] On the controversial issue of Anabaptist community of goods, see James M. Stayer, *The German Peasants' War and Anabaptist Community of Goods* (Montreal and Kingston: McGill-Queen's University Press, 1991). It is somewhat surprising, given that the unsavory reputation of the Münsterite practice of community of goods had clung to all later Mennonites, that Twisck does not further qualify his affirmation of the practice.

[14] Meaning is unclear.

[15] The question of whether miracles were still to be expected was a major one for all Reformers who sought ways to counteract the appeal of Catholic miracles. Prior to the Münsterite fiasco, many Anabaptists gave great credence to special revelation and miraculous signs; thereafter, only a few did. For Twisck's opinion, see his *Comeet-Boecxken. Zijnde Een corte Chronijcsche beschrijvinge van alle de grouwelijcke ende schrickelijcke Cometen/ die haer aen den Heme vertoont hebben...tot Beteringhe van alle Menschen by een vergadert* (Hoorn, 1624); and *Ontdeckinghe des Pausdoms/ Vervatende een verclaringhe vande voornaemste plaetsen der H. Schrift/ de welcke op den Paus ende sijnen Aenhangh staen/ waer in bethoont wordt/ dat hy met de sijne is den Antichrist/ valsche Propheten/ Secten ende Comers/ daer in de Schrift deurgaens van gesproken wordt* (Hoorn, 1624). For a brief discussion see also Gary K. Waite, "Anabaptist Anticlericalism and the Laicization of Sainthood: Anabaptist Saints and Sanctity in the Netherlands," in *Confessional Sanctity (c.1550 - c.1800)*, eds. Juergen Beyer *et al.* (Mainz: Philipp von Zabern), or "Demonic affliction or divine chastisement? Conceptions of illness and healing amongst Spiritualists and Mennonites in Holland, c.1530-c.1630," in *Illness and Healing Alternatives in Western Europe*, eds. Marijke Gijswijt-Hofstra, Hilary Marland and Hans de Waard (London and New York, 1997), 59-79.

[16] Twisck appears to be opposing the strict forms of shunning practiced by some of his co-religionists.

[17] Biblical reference missing.

[18] Biblical reference missing.

[19] Presumably his *Fundament*.

[20] 1 John 5:7 actually reads: "There are three that testify: the Spirit and the water and the blood, and these three agree." NRSV.

14 Prussian Confession (1660)

[1] A reference, perhaps, to the Frisians, Flemish and High German Mennonites, or to the Mennonites of Prussia.

Scripture Index